OAKTON COMMUNITY COLLEGE

DES PLAINES, ILLINOIS   60016

PROBLEM SOLVING
AND
INTELLIGENCE

PROBLEM SOLVING
AND
INTELLIGENCE

HELGA A. H. ROWE
Australian Council for Educational Research

 LAWRENCE ERLBAUM ASSOCIATES, PUBLISHERS
1985 Hillsdale, New Jersey   London

Lawrence Erlbaum Associates, Inc., Publishers
365 Broadway
Hillsdale, New Jersey 07642

Library of Congress Cataloging in Publication Data

Rowe, Helga A. H.
    Problem solving and intelligence.

    Based on the author's thesis (doctoral) presented
under the title: Problem solving.
    Bibliography: p.
    Includes indexes.
    1. Intellect. 2. Intelligence levels. 3. Problem
solving. 4. Cognitive styles. 5. Human information
processing. I. Rowe, Helga A. H. Problem solving.
II. Title.
BF431.R725 1985   153.4'3   84-18855
ISBN 0-89859-347-6

Printed in the United States of America
10 9 8 7 6 5 4 3 2 1

Contents

PART IV: CONCLUSIONS

Preface

Problem Solving and Intelligence is the result of the author's efforts to understand the nature of human intelligence and the differences in the cognitive functioning of individuals which we observe again and again.

The book contains two types of material. First, it presents an overview of major contributions to the conceptualization and investigation of problem solving and intelligence, which was derived from the extensive, largely non-cumulative literature. Second, it reports a comprehensive, empirical study of the manifestation of intelligence in problem solving.

The subject matter is at the interface of three traditional areas of psychological inquiry; namely, the study of cognitive processes, individual differences, and the characteristics of the stimulus. What is innovative is that intellectual performance is investigated in relation to the simultaneous operation of variables from these dimensions.

The major issues addressed are the discovery and description of psychological functions which vary according to the task in hand, and contribute to individual differences in achievement; and the identification of the implications which a better understanding of the cognitive processes involved in intellectual performance will have for the development of more theoretically based, and hence more informative, measures of intelligence.

The general approach of this book is behavioral. It leans heavily on information processing aspects of human problem solving strategies. However, the book is also about psychometrics, for two reasons. First, much of its content was conceived by insights gained both from traditional psychometric approaches, and from dissatisfaction resulting from them. Second, and in a more direct sense, factor analytic and other traditionally psychometric procedures are utilized to summarize the data collected in the empirical study, and to test the coherence of the body of findings resulting from the study.

Large parts of the manuscript originated from the author's doctoral dissertation entitled *Problem Solving: A Study of the Joint Effects of Psychological Processes, Task Characteristics, and Individual Differences,* which was submitted early in 1980. The book differs from the dissertation in that it has extended the framework of the latter by relating problem solving to the broader concept of intelligence.

When this investigation was begun, nearly ten years ago, the literature contained only a small number of studies concerned with the *processes* of problem solving performance. For the past five years, and particularly at the present time, this field of cognitive research has been going through a period of rapid and fascinating expansion. In the preparation of this book for publication, an effort has been made to be as up-to-date as possible. The success of this endeavor may have been limited, however, as a result of the relative remoteness of the island on which the author lives, where the literature from other countries tends to be received only six to nine months after its publication.

This book is intended, primarily, as a contribution to the understanding and investigation of the nature of intelligent behavior. It is also an introduction to the intending specialist, both in research and in the field, in intelligence and problem solving. It may thus be found useful as a textbook for students in university departments of psychology and education, and in colleges of advanced education. I have tried to write clearly enough to be understood by advanced undergraduate students. For this reason, theoretical concepts and statistical procedures are explained, and many basic references are provided. This book contains a large number of citations and quotations from the work of other authors. These are included to provide the reader with a more direct appreciation of the diversity of flavors of the research literature.

However, I have kept in mind the interests and needs of a group of individuals not interested in specialization. This group consists of three distinct subgroups: one, the users of traditional intelligence and achievement tests; two, those who believe that intelligence is an outdated concept; and three, the general reader who is interested in problem solving and intelligence. For members of these subgroups, the book suggests a fresh look at intelligent behavior, and, hopefully, a more up-to-date and valid impression of this extensive branch of psychological knowledge and endeavor.

Many persons have contributed indirectly or directly to this book. My father allowed me to complete an academically oriented secondary education even though I was a girl. Professor D. McElwain, of the University of Queensland, accepted me as an adult, part–time student at a time when this was unusual. To him and to Dr. Ray Pike, I owe my interest in research methodology, psychometrics and multivariate statistics.

To the Australian Council for Educational Research, especially to its Director, Dr. J. P. Keeves, I express my gratitude for supporting me during the empirical study of this project.

I should like to thank all those colleagues who acted as subjects in the pilot study, and the students who provided the data for the empirical study reported in this book.

I am deeply indebted to Professor A. J. Wearing, of the University of Melbourne, the supervisor of my doctoral dissertation, not only for his guidance and intellectual stimulation, but also for his patience and encouragement, especially during times when traumatic external circumstances threatened the completion of the dissertation.

I should like to thank Professor Robert J. Sternberg, of Yale University, one of my examiners, for encouraging the publication of this volume. His comments on my dissertation were invaluable when it came to the writing of the book.

Above all, my gratitude goes to my husband, who contributed to the writing of this book at so many levels. He taught me English and made it possible for me to obtain a tertiary education. He helps me to find time for my research, typed much of the final manuscript of this book, and in addition provides me with continuing love and understanding.

His generosity, and that of our children, made this work possible. I therefore dedicate this book to my husband, Harold, and to our children, Michael, Nicholas, Ursula, Lucian, and Justin.

Helga A. H. Rowe

PROBLEM SOLVING
AND
INTELLIGENCE

FRAME OF REFERENCE

1 Preliminary Considerations

PROBLEM SOLVING AND INTELLIGENCE

The ability to solve problems is a central prerequisite for human survival, but the mechanics of the process itself remain a puzzle. Intelligence is generally regarded as a basic attribute of human beings, yet its meaning continues to be a matter of uncertainty and dispute.

Problem solving and intelligence are broad and indefinite terms which refer to complex cognitive processes rather than to behaviors which can be observed and measured as single units. Both have led to important and influential psychological research. They have certainly been key concepts in educational theory and practice, and in other fields of applied psychology.

The idea, reflected by the title of this book, that problem solving and intelligence should be investigated in combination seemed an obvious one. Whether used by professionals or by lay persons, both concepts imply a considerable amount of behavioral consistency, which tends to be applicable across situations.

Both the analysis of problem solving performance and the psychometric, particularly factor analytic, analysis of intelligence (i.e., test performance), claim to be able to detect similarities and differences in the cognitive functioning of individuals and groups. An obvious project, therefore, is to attempt to find out how problem solving and intelligence can be related to each other.

Psychometricians assume that a strong, reproducible factor of intelligence, for example of the type of Spearman's "g", corresponds to an ability or capacity of testees to solve problems, and to carry out certain types of activities. These activities are assumed to be analogous in some important ways. A first step to further investigate the nature of intelligence—or for that matter any specific abilities—is therefore, to collect information which might provide access to details of the processes which underlie the performance of individuals as they are attempting to solve typical items of tests which are commonly used for the assessment of this capacity generally referred to as intelligence.

Traditionally, the two concepts have been conceived as describing separate but intersecting branches of cognition. The area of intersection, that is, the overlap between the concepts, is reflected in such statements as "intelligence influences problem solving ability," and conversely, "problem solving requires and reflects intelligence." The ability to solve problems has, historically, been one of the criteria for the assessment of intelligence (Wechsler, 1958). This area of intersection provides the setting for the content of this book.

Problem solving can be defined broadly as the meeting of challenges. More specifically, the definition proposed in the Oxford English Dictionary notes that the problem solver, "is challenged to accomplish a specified result, often under prescribed conditions" (Fowler & Fowler, 1978, 883). In common usage, the word intelligence refers essentially to the processes involved in meeting challenges deriving from sources both internal and external to the organism. No matter what type of problem provides the challenge, it is generally accepted that intelligence influences problem solving performance, and that it manifests itself in the process of problem solving.

However, the assumption that the processes of intelligence are closely related to those of problem solving does not ignore the possibility that the former might encompass a great deal more than problem solving. It is necessary, therefore, to state briefly why the decision was made to conduct an empirical study of problem solving, rather than of some other aspect of intelligence.

As the beginning chapters of this book will show, the term intelligence is highly diversified and "slippery" (Armer, 1963). The term problem solving is still broad, but it serves to reduce the vast pervasiveness of intelligence to an area which is relatively more demarcated. However, as will be seen in Chapter 3, the degree of demarcation which is imposed on the problem solving activity by the task or experimental requirements may vary considerably. The design of the experiments and the findings depend not only on the kind of problem, the environmental conditions, and the characteristics of the subject; like all research, they are strongly influenced by the theoretical assumptions and orientation of the investigator.

The systematic study of problem solving began early this century, but the scientific study of intelligence was initiated only just over a decade ago. Intelligence has undergone development from a philosophical concept—an intervening variable—to being viewed as a process variable.

A wide gap exists between those who look at cognitive processes as a potential guide to understanding individual differences in responses to problem situations, and those who are concerned with normative aspects of the performance on cognitive tasks. This gap is not unlike the one which existed between the traditional perception theorists and the neo-cognitive psychologists of the 1940s and 1950s. The latter were concerned with variables that generate individual differences when they investigated how it is that different persons perceive, learn, and remember the same stimulus sets differently. In contrast, the classicists' approaches were normative and involved always some variant of the question, "How is it that people perceive their environment in such a way that they can act adaptively and survive?"

The measurement of intelligence is regarded by many as one of the great achievements of psychology. While fragmented attempts have been made to define what is being measured, most of the measurement has been based on the outcome of performance which requires intelligence, supported by a tacit understanding of what intelligence is. Differential psychology from Binet, through traditional test theory, up to recent developments in latent trait approaches (Fischer, 1974; Rasch, 1960, 1980; Wright & Stone, 1979) has been influenced strongly by E. L. Thorndike's (1914) postulate, that, "if a thing exists, it exists in some amount, and . . . it can be measured." (p. 141)

Until recently there has been a lack of consistent research effort aimed at finding process–related definitions of intelligence, i.e., to investigate intelligence within a cognitive-theoretical rather than within a psychometric framework.

A major problem faced by authors in any field of cognitive psychology is that the literature has become exceedingly large and " . . . seems fractured and chaotic. Apparently important issues go completely unresearched; seemingly trivial issues fill chapters. Negative evidence is given heavy weight in one case and lightly dismissed elsewhere" (Lachman, Lachman, & Butterfield, 1979, p. xi).

How then, might one deal with this kind of fragmentation and diversity? One approach might have been to attempt to reconcile existing differences. To this author it would seem naive to believe that one could accomplish this, and bridge these differences. Instead, the approach taken in this book is to gain an understanding of the impact of research in both areas, and to identify major trends and their current status in contemporary cognitive psychology.

The second aim of the book was to go beyond reviewing the literature, and to demonstrate in an empirical study an alternative methodology for studying problem solving, and thus to contribute to a better understanding of the nature of intelligence. Within a framework built against the background of the present state of the literature in the areas of intelligence (including that dealing with individual differences) and problem solving, this work is aimed at the scientific understanding of intelligence. The description of the structure of the processes of the intellectual performance itself, and the specification of person, task and functioning (behavior) variables which control the manifestation of behavior are seen as major requirements: "The task of assessing intelligence, construed as a scientific endeavor, requires the devising of measures that specify the important parameters of cognitive structure for particular individuals" (Bouchard, 1968, p. 29).

Perhaps one of the most obtrusive questions is why some persons can solve certain problems, whereas others are unable to do so. The search for explanations of variations in problem solving ability amongst people dates back to early civilization, and has remained an area of inquiry of prime psychological and educational concern. Since Binet (1905), the measurement of intelligence has been based on observed differences in individuals' performances on a variety of problem solving tasks. The general rationale for these collections of tasks, i.e., intelligence tests, is based on the sometimes implicit assumption that the intelligent person has accumulated a considerable amount of knowledge, and is able to solve problems.

Difficulties facing the designers of traditional intelligence tests have increased in recent times as a result of the problem of the sampling of items which are representative of the already vast and now exponentially increasing body of knowledge to which an individual may have been exposed. Some information scientists have estimated that the extent of knowledge may be increasing at a rate of between 8% and 15% per annum (Garfield, 1977b).

The reduction in validity of traditional intelligence tests which has resulted from the recent growth in the rate of information accumulation, combined with changes in social attitudes, the public questioning of issues concerned with the validity and legitimacy of measures of human abilities (e.g., Block & Dworkin, 1976; Cole, 1972; Darlington, 1971; Fincher, 1976; Fine, 1975; Horn, 1976; Houts, 1977; Humphreys, 1973; Jensen, 1969, 1973a,b; Kamin, 1974; Loehlin, Lindzey & Spuhler, 1975; Scarr-Salapatec, 1971; Schmidt & Hunter, 1974; Thorndike, 1971), and changes in educational philosophy and practice (e.g., Bloom, 1964, 1971; Cronbach & Snow, 1977; Elam, 1964; Gagné, 1965) have led to the need for a better understanding of the concept of intelligence than appears to have been required in the past.

From its beginnings the intelligence test was designed specifically to serve in the selection of people, and in the prediction of academic achievement. Educational decisions tended to be made on the basis of estimates of intellectual potential, provided by the scores on these traditional standardized tests of general ability. In contrast to this, more recent developments emphasize the malleability and adaptive functional development of cognitive skills, and it has been suggested that "the most significant use of measures of intelligence and aptitude should not be primarily for the purposes of prediction, but for indicating how intellectual performance can be improved" (Glaser, Pellegrino, & Lesgold, 1977, p. 508).

This approach to the purposes of measures of intelligence states explicitly that assessments of intelligence should estimate current status, rather than predict future performance. For measures of intelligence to be useful, it is thus not necessary that they carry direct implications about future potential, but rather that they identify characteristics in the testees' performance which might be manipulated and developed by means of learning experiences that match the specific needs of the individual.

Traditional intelligence tests have been useful in the context for which they were designed. Even if it were possible to produce updated versions of such tests, using the knowledge available to individuals or particular groups at the present time, this type of test is unlikely to contribute to the aim of improving intellectual performance because it does not provide any interpretation of general ability or aptitudes in terms of the variables that enhance or impede cognitive performance.

Focusing on the products, mainly the success/failure aspect of problem solving, has tended to block access to information about the way in which factors within the task and the performance itself may have contributed to the outcome of problem solving. The time taken to solve a task, the correctness, even the "elegance" of the solution, have traditionally served to evaluate performance. This approach has obvious limitations when the aim is to describe the processes underlying the performance of an individual, and to intervene in order to change performance by increasing the problem solving ability or efficiency.

In order to achieve this aim, it is necessary to analyze the performance itself with a view to identifying the components of performance which might generate the individual differences. The fact that many of the often unpretentious tasks included in individual and group intelligence tests discriminate so effectively between people would suggest that studies of the processes involved in carrying out the task are certainly warranted.

Though largely disregarded in traditional mental measurement, the structure and dynamics of the process of human intellectual functioning, particularly in problem solving, have been of interest to experimental psychologists at least since Helmholtz (1894). It is difficult to summarize the literature briefly because research has tended to be diverse and non-cumulative. Major trends and their theoretical contributions are reviewed and discussed in Chapters 2 and 3. The present discussion will, therefore, be limited to the clarification of a small number of issues, so that the general framework and scope of the present study become clear.

The systematic methods of investigation in early experimental psychology grew out of the work of physicists (e.g., Fechner, 1860, 1877) and physiologists (e.g., Bain, 1855; Gall, 1809; Helmholtz, 1856; Müller, 1838), who had come to recognize that the results which were obtained in experiments were strongly influenced by the human observer. This may explain the preoccupation of Wundt and his followers with sensory perception.

Initially a physician, Wundt studied with Müller, and, after himself becoming a physiologist, worked for many years in Helmholtz's Institute of Physiology at the University of Heidelberg prior to his appointment as Professor of Philosophy at Leipzig, where he founded his psychological laboratory in 1879. The *Grundzüge der Physiologischen Psychologie* (Wundt, 1873) remained an influential textbook well into the present century (West, 1964).

In the manner of the physicist, Wundt and his colleagues were concerned chiefly with analyses of the stimulus itself. The intensity and other aspects of stimuli met in such areas as vision, hearing, touch, taste, smell, and movement were investigated. As physiologists, the early psychologists were interested in the modes of reaction of the sense organs, and in their relationship to the central nervous system. For example, the studies of vision, the sense studied most frequently by early psychologists, were concerned with the rays of light, etc., but also with the reactivity of the eye itself and with its connections with the central nervous system. Problem solving was not a suitable phenomenon for investigation because it lacked the physical stimulus which was presumably required to elicit sensory reactions. Wundt expected psychology to be an experimental science, the subject matter of which was restricted to "immediate experience," in other words, sensation.

> He [Wundt] had much in common with the English associationists and particularly J. S. Mill: the mind is depicted as describable in terms of elements like those of sensation. The elements may themselves have attributes and are connected by association. (Flügel, 1933, revised by West, 1964, p. 151)

More recently the aims of Wundt and his followers were summarized as follows: "The task of the psychologist was to analyze these conscious processes into elements to discover by what means the elements were connected" (Radford & Burton, 1974, p. 40).

Behaviorism and Gestalt psychology emerged at about the same time, and although in different ways, both might be understood as reactions against Wundt's narrow focus on the *elements* of sensory experience. Both behaviorists and Gestalt psychologists sought to explain psychological *processes* rather than to identify more or less fixed elements of behavior. Problem solving processes and intelligent behavior were of concern to both.

As is discussed in greater detail in Chapter 3, the early Gestalt psychologists (Koffka, 1935; Köhler, 1925; Wertheimer, 1923) focused on "mental states" and "consciousness," and were concerned with such processes as "insight," "understanding," and "incubation," but did not define them operationally. They postulated internal mechanisms, "organization," not static elements, to correspond to psychological functioning. It was assumed that all organisms possess an innate tendency to organize the input received from the environment. Again reminiscent of the approach of physics, this organization was often represented in terms of fields. Perceptual reorganization, for example, tended to be thought of in terms of a change of organization of an electrical field in which an alteration of any one element would be expected to result in a reorganization of the field as a whole. The organism was seen as active and able to react.

Retaining certain associationist aspects of Wundtian psychology, but rejecting the method of introspection, the behaviorists (e.g., Watson, 1913, 1924; Skinner, 1938, 1953, 1957, 1958) extended the area of investigation to processes which neither Wundt and his colleagues nor the Gestalt psychologists had been able to investigate. In contrast to Gestalt psychology, the behaviorists rejected postulations of any built in organizing mechanisms, but regarded the organism as a passive receiver of stimulation; in other words, reacting only to input from the environment.

Gestaltists and behaviorists attempted to explain the processes underlying problem solving. Although their theoretical assumptions and methods of observation differed, both sought isomorphic identification of mental structures of physiological mechanisms corresponding to psychological processes. The behaviorists attempted to monitor these processes by means of strategically placed electrodes which—apart from being aimed at providing supplementary information in the experimental situation—were expected to detect small-scale physiologically determined activations which might accompany unobservable behaviors.

For the behaviorists, mental structures were inadmissible. They main-

tained that problem solving, like other behaviors, is learned through operant conditioning, i.e., selective reinforcement, and that individual
differences in performance are therefore a byproduct of environmental
control. While it cannot be denied that selective reinforcement may play
some part in the structure of problem solving processes, it does not explain the process fully. In the debate concerning the mechanisms of language acquisition, Chomsky (1959) criticized Skinner's *Verbal Learning*
(Skinner, 1957) by arguing that in addition to the operation of reinforcement and imitation processes the child has: "The remarkable capacity . . .
to generalize, hypothesize, and 'process information' in a variety of very
special and apparently highly complex ways which we cannot yet describe or begin to understand . . . and which may be largely innate."
(p. 52)

The innate system, postulated by Chomsky as a language acquisition
device (LAD), is not to be understood as an actual organ but as a hypothetical construct referring to a set of yet unexplained complex mechanisms which enable the child to process language. Proposing a system
more similar to the innate "organization" postulated by the Gestaltists
than to the search for the elements of behavior as exemplified by Wundt
and the early associationists, Chomsky was thus prepared to move beyond the total dependence on observable data as exhibited by the behaviorists in their extreme objectivism.

Chomsky's theory (Chomsky 1965, 1967) represented a definite return
to a position which allows for the existence of some fixed innate structures and which tolerates the possibility that human behavior may not be
completely malleable. Allowance may have to be made for the possible
operation of innate mechanisms analogous to those proposed by Chomsky's theory of language acquisition during the problem solving process.

The increasing interest in internal processes is perhaps best reflected in
the recent growth in emphasis and status of information processing psychology. This approach shows considerable concern with the manner in
which information is processed. Problem solving and other cognitive
processes are typically viewed as a series of operations which it is assumed can be made overt by means of verbal reports, or might be characterized in a computer program. The general availability of digital
computers constituted one of the most significant influences on research
in cognitive psychology. Analogies were drawn between the operation of
digital computers and human problem solving (e.g. Feigenbaum & Feldman, 1963; Feigenbaum, 1962; Hunt, 1968, 1971; Uhr, 1966). When the
differences between biological systems and digital computers (von
Neumann, 1958) became accepted, information processing and artificial
intelligence oriented research workers developed computer programs
modelling the solving of specific tasks in terms of sequences of informa-

tion processing operations (Greeno, 1977; Newell, Shaw, & Simon, 1958; Simon, 1969).

Information processing psychologists are particularly concerned with the form in which information might be stated and transmitted (e.g., Anderson, 1976; Chomsky, 1965; Greeno, 1973; Miller, Galanter, & Pribram, 1960), and with variables which might place constraints on the information process (e.g., Broadbent, 1958, 1964; Miller, 1956; Newell, Shaw, & Simon, 1962; Newell & Simon, 1972). As a research paradigm information processing makes use of process tracing, usually, the mapping of task requirements which might determine the problem solving strategies of individuals. While the aim of this research has been to find general laws for problem solving processes as functions of types and specific characteristics of the task (Newell & Simon, 1972), its results have tended to be restricted to the development of task specific models:

> Work in artificial intelligence has as its goal the construction of programs which when run on a computer will exhibit intelligent behavior of the same generality and power as that exhibited by human beings. During the past two decades many systems have been built that are capable of doing a single task in a well-defined and limited environment. Some of these systems are quite powerful; the tasks that they are capable of performing are difficult ones by human standards. However, none of these powerful systems is general. The capabilities that each possesses cannot be exploited in tasks different from the one for which it was designed. Furthermore, the designers of each of these systems have placed rather severe restrictions on the complexity of the environment with which their systems are capable of interacting. (McDermott, 1978, p. 459)

The contribution of research conducted within the theoretical framework of information processing and artificial intelligence is discussed more generally in Chapter 3.

"Experimental psychology at first restricted psychology primarily to the study of the generalized human mind" (Hilgard, 1980, p. 2). Differences between individual subjects were part of experimental error. Associationist, Gestalt, and behaviorist approaches to the study of cognitive processes largely ignored individual differences. Newell and Simon (1972) and others (e.g., De Groot, 1965; Rumelhart & Norman, 1975), investigating information processing, though generally concerned with the identification of processes used by particular individuals, have attempted to identify processes which might account for the performance by groups of individuals on particular tasks. In the latter case processes or rules of behavior are postulated and predictions of their occurrence are compared with averaged performance data obtained from the groups. While attempting to generalize beyond the single case, this approach ignores individual differences in relation to the subjects, the tasks, and the combination of both of these. The only group concerned with individual differences per se have been the psychometricians.

Psychometric research did not aim to describe intelligence test performance in terms of the psychological processes which might underly or contribute to intelligence test performance. In contrast to this, experimental and information processing psychology set out to develop models and theories aimed at providing an understanding of problem solving performance, but tended to disregard individual differences. The situation was summarized aptly by Whitely (1977):

> The different approaches of experimental psychology and psychometrics have resulted in practically important measures of intelligence which are not understood, in addition to cognitive theories which have no practical implications for measuring individual differences. (p. 465)

As a result of Cronbach's repeated call for a bridging of the gap between these "two disciplines" of psychology (Cronbach, 1957b, 1975; Messick, 1972), a number of low, but positive correlations were obtained in studies which related intelligence test performance to certain experimentally derived scores of theoretical variables (e.g., Allison, 1960; Dunham, Guilford, & Hoepfner, 1968). While these findings may be suggestive of the possibility of at least some common variance between psychometric tests and the experimental measures used, they did not contribute to an understanding of the performance itself. Carroll's (1974) suggestion to investigate "Psychometric Tests as Cognitive Tasks" complements the former approach. Carroll hypothesized that obtained correlations between intelligence test scores and experimental tasks might be explained on the basis of shared elements in the information processing domain.

Carroll (1974) suggested that investigations of the information processing requirements of intelligence test items may lead to a better understanding of the structural models developed by psychometricians. He (Carroll, 1976) started to describe the information processing requirements of each of the tests contained in the *Kit of Reference Tests for Cognitive Factors* (French, Ekstrom, & Price, 1963).

The influential studies of Hunt, Frost, and Lunneborg (1973), Hunt, Lunneborg, and Lewis (1975), and Lunneborg (1974, 1977) found scores on verbal intelligence tests to be significantly related to such aspects of information processing as speed of scanning data in short-term memory, speed of transforming sensory input into concepts, retention of order information, and the resistance of information stored in memory to interference.

Sternberg's (1977a,b, 1981a) monumental componential analysis of human abilities, in which he provides a sophisticated analysis of analogical reasoning with internal and external validation, demonstrates the possibilities of the suggested approach. Based originally on the work by Donders (1868), latencies are used to ascertain the duration of unobservable mental processes by subtracting reaction times for the initiation of earlier stages from those of later stages of tasks or subtasks. On the basis of this methodology extremely intricate techniques for the estimation of process components have been developed. Sternberg's work, which is discussed in more detail in later chapters, has made a substantial contribution to the linking of the experimental and the psychometric approaches in the investigation and modelling of intelligent behaviour.

Pellegrino and Glaser (1979) have recommended a welding together of the correlational and the components approaches and suggest that such a procedure "avoids the explanatory inadequacy of correlational methods, and has the theoretical power to model individual differences on various dimensions of cognitive function" (p. 188).

However, information processing studies concerned with the experimental investigation of psychometric tasks have, as previously noted, focused on the identification of possible mechanisms by means of which knowledge is stored and processed. This approach to the investigation of the process of problem solving is characterized by Byrne (1977) as follows: "Ideally we would like to discover what information is stored, in what format, and what mechanisms can search, interpret and use this information" (p. 287).

Latency measures and other estimates based on measures of reaction time may lead to valid models of problem solving processes. They cannot be expected, however, to yield diagnostic information which provides a prescription for direct educational intervention. It was suggested previously that one of the present psychological and educational demands made of theories and tests of intelligence is that they should provide a basis for the improvement of intellectual performance. Procedures which place individuals in different score positions in relation to latency measures on various processing mechanisms may provide a more acceptable description of individual differences than traditional IQ scores for some purposes, but they are equally limited if psychological or educational intervention is the aim.

It is acknowledged that the computer programmer, like any machine operator, can be expected to be interested in the workings of the system he uses, e.g., how the input is encoded, transformed, stored, retrieved, and decoded. "Within an information–processing approach to human cognitive activity, one asks much the same kinds of questions as those used by the user of a computer" (Estes, 1978, p. 3). This explains the preoccupation of many investigators of studies within the framework of information processing and artificial intelligence with the transformation of information and other mechanisms involved in problem solving.

Inherent in this view is a certain danger of machine reductionism, i.e., an attempt to explain information processing as it occurs in humans in terms of computer hardware.

Neisser (1967) considers the limitations of the analogy between cognition and computer hardware:

> The task of the psychologist trying to understand human cognition is analogous to that of a man trying to discover how a computer has been programmed. In particular, if the program seems to store and reuse information, he would like to know by what "routines" or "procedures" this is done. Given this purpose he will not care whether his particular computer stores information on magnetic cores or in thin films; he wants to understand the program, not the 'hardware'. (p. 6)

The above argument applies to other attempts to seek explanations for psychological processes in physical structures. Associationists, Gestaltists, and behaviorists have been unable to explain psychological processes adequately in terms of neurophysiological or environmental mechanisms. Like environmental variables neurological or biochemical processes can be expected to impose limitations on mental functioning, but they are unlikely to provide sufficient explanations for the entire process of mental functioning. In terms of the computer parallel, hardware obviously affects programming, but even the best knowledge of the hardware does not show how the program might meet the requirements of a particular task.

Reductionist methods of any type might provide initial models of the constraints and facilities determining different aspects of the problem solving process, but they provide little information concerning the components of the process itself. Because of this, reductionist models of cognitive processes can be expected to be no more or less useful than hypothetical constructs and intervening variables have been.

What has been lacking in the research attempting to explain problem solving processes are descriptions of the processes by which problems are solved which might provide a direct basis for educational intervention which is tailored to the specific needs of individuals. The "methods of attack," the steps in the solution process, the choices made, and the reasoning strategies employed by the problem solver, need to be described. What the psychological processes actually are is a metaphysical question which cannot be answered on the basis of psychological research. A psychological approach to the study of the problem solving process is concerned with the content rather than with the origins of the phenomenon.

Anderson (1976) concedes:

> The fact that it is not possible to uniquely determine cognitive structures and processes poses a clear limitation on our ability to understand the nature of human intelligence . . . Thus I am proposing a change in our interpretation of what it means to understand the nature of human intelligence. I once thought it could mean unique identification of the structures and processes underlying cognitive behavior. Since that is not possible I propose that we take "understanding the nature of human intelligence" to mean possession of a theory that will enable us to improve human intelligence. (p. 15–16)

A large number of possible, but by no means obvious, elements of the problem solving process have been observed with some consistency. A number of phenomena have been observed repeatedly but interpreted in different ways.

The term, "problem solving process," has traditionally been applied to the characteristics of problem solving performance. In order to obtain information as to how these performance characteristics affect the outcome of problem solving activity, behaviorists focused on situational variables, Gestaltists on built–in mechanisms in the subject, and information processing research mainly on characteristic requirements of the task. All three dimensions are of utmost importance. What is required is a redefinition of the term problem solving process which permits it to cover performance, subject, and task characteristics, and their interactions, simultaneously.

To design an empirical study of the problem solving process is particularly difficult, not only because of the complexity of the mechanisms which might be involved, but because the processes of interest tend to be covert and thus escape the investigator. The first task was therefore to find a means of uncovering some of the components of the problem solving process so that a description of at least some of the operations constituting this complex human behavior could be provided. The pursuit of this aim is facilitated by the present theoretical climate, which once again permits the investigation of psychological processes. Such processes are generated by an actively exploring individual within an interaction system which includes psychological processes, environmental influences, and a variety of individual needs and goals. The interaction of these variables can be expected to result in different outcomes, e.g., differences in problem solving competence, intelligence, etc.

Any research concerned with the question of how people solve problems must be performed within a framework which takes into con-

sideration variables from at least three major sources of expected variation, namely characteristics of the psychological mechanisms which operate during performance, individual differences, and the task. A process model of problem solving should be consistent in terms of all three domains, and should aim to account for interactions between these domains.

As is noted in the following chapters, previous research has tended to emphasize only one of these areas at a time. This is insufficient when the aim is to understand the problem solving process. Incompatibility of theoretical frameworks, design and methodology makes it difficult, if not impossible, to achieve integration by adding together the findings obtained in separate studies from these different perspectives.

What is required is a synthesis of information obtainable in the different domains. A prerequisite for such a synthesis is a research design that allows the investigation of the problem solving process as a comprehensive system. This can only be accomplished if ways are found to represent what is going on during the problem solving process by measures which are sensitive, compatible, and complementary to each domain.

An understanding of the psychological mechanisms operating during problem solving demands the identification of important and replicable problem solving behaviors. Consideration of the task provides a basis for judgments concerning the generality or specificity of the identified problem solving behaviors.

Accounting for individual differences requires the identification of a measure which correlates with various kinds or levels of ability. Concern with the interaction between the process, dimensions of individual differences, and characteristics of the task leads to a consideration of the problem solving process which is comprehensive enough to allow for the investigation of task or person dependent problem solving styles, or both.

To summarize, the research reported here was an attempt to identify empirically and classify the behaviors that individuals exhibit during their attempts to solve a variety of tasks. This required the identification of a set of behaviorally specific components of the problem solving process, which were expected to promise broader applicability across tasks and subjects, a selection of a variety of tasks, and the selection of a variety of individuals. The rationale behind this approach is that individual differences that are observed in the outcomes of test performance might be connected with differences in strategy use.

Broadly, the aims of the study were:

• to develop a usable and replicable classification system on the basis of which problem solving behavior employed by individuals during the problem solving process could be represented;

- to investigate the relationship between variables derived from the classification system, and
- to investigate whether problem solving behaviours and strategies obtained on the basis of the taxonomy would yield groupings of subjects that correlated with various measures of individual differences, i.e., problem solving competence, speed, intelligence, and educational level.

More specifically, the following types of research questions were investigated:

1. What types of problem solving behaviors or strategies do individuals apply during the problem solving process?
2. How do a number of contextual variables affect the problem solving process?
3. In what way are problem solving processes influenced by characteristics of the task?

In one sense this study presents an analysis of the problem solving process into components. In another sense, however, the research attempts to bring about a synthesis in the investigation of human problem solving. Previous research of the problem solving process has tended to be noncumulative, because it dealt with particular aspects of the problem solving process in isolation. The more comprehensive research design used here might help to reduce the present barriers between approaches to the study of problem solving concerned with isolated aspects such as individual differences, process components, competence, task, and other applications.

Finally, this book attempts to put the search for a meaningful conception of intelligence and its manifestation in the cognitive activity of problem solving into one overall context. The purposes of the writer will be achieved to the extent to which the book might encourage more cooperation between competing frameworks, and a greater emphasis on more comprehensive approaches to the investigation of complex cognitive processes.

The content of this book is presented in four parts as follows:

Part 1 contains the introductory Chapters 1 to 4. These contain the rationale and provide a frame of reference for the empirical study on the basis of a discussion of the previous research literature relating to intelligence and problem solving. Chapter 1 sets the broad aims of the book into perspective.

Chapters 2 and 3 present some of the important research findings concerning the nature of intelligence and problem solving. It would seem difficult to appreciate the relationship between such complex concepts without first considering the domains of research each has generated. The literature was reviewed selectively, with the implicit aim on the one hand, of identifying findings from intelligence research which might indicate profitable directions in which the investigation of cognitive processes might proceed, and on the other, of seeking ways in which research into problem solving might contribute to the development of process related theories of intelligence.

Chapter 3 contains an attempt to synthesize the conclusions of the preceding chapters and a discussion of the implications of previous research. An overview of the purpose and design of the empirical study is presented together with a number of research questions.

Part 2, consisting of Chapters 5 to 8, describes and discusses the research methodology and organization of the empirical study. Chapter 5 is concerned with the use of tasks in previous problem solving research, and describes the tasks and the sample of subjects chosen for the present study.

Chapter 6 contains details of the "thinking aloud" methodology, and an attempt is made to differentiate protocol analysis from similar research methods with which it has sometimes been confused.

The development of the taxonomy used as a basis for the classification of problem solving behaviors and strategies is described in Chapter 7. Chapter 8 presents operational definitions of major terms used in this report, and describes the general procedure of data collection.

Part 3 contains Chapters 9 to 12. In these chapters the results of the study are presented and discussed. Converging methods of statistical data analysis are used to establish the utility of performance behaviors as structural components of the problem solving process itself. Chapter 9 reports on the reliability of the taxonomy-based behavior descriptions, and presents findings pertaining to such variables as time on task, strategy preferences, and variety of strategies used in relation to a number of contextual variables. Chapter 10 describes a number of structural components of the problem solving process which were identified by using factor analytic techniques. Separate principal components analyses are performed for each of the tasks.

The major part of this chapter consists of a description of the application of Tucker's (1966) three–mode factor analysis, which provided the means for an investigation of functional aspects of the pattern of preferred problem solving strategies in relation to different tasks, to individual differences, and to interactions between combinations of variables from these domains.

Chapter 11 investigates the utility of the problem solving behaviors and reports the results of a number of multiple discriminant analyses and classification analyses on the amounts of use made of the 18 strategy variables by subjects who were grouped in turn according to achievement in problem solving, speed, level of education, and measured intelligence. It is shown that these variables, which are usually measured by means of scores resulting from performance, are reflected in differential profiles of the actual operations performed by subjects during their work on the task. The results discussed in this chapter suggest that process measures may, in fact, be more sensitive indicators of individual differences than traditional outcome measures.

Chapter 12 contains the report of an initial exploratory attempt to extend the study of structural components of problem solving performance to an investigation of the *dynamics* of the process.

Part 4 consists of Chapter 13, which presents some conclusions and implications of the study. In this final chapter an attempt is made to evaluate the theoretical and practical relevance of the study. The implications of theoretical, empirical and methodological aspects of the research are discussed.

A complete list of references, author and subject indices, and appendices conclude the book.

2 The Conceptualization and Measurement of Intelligence

The aim of the discussion presented in this chapter is not to focus on history, but to raise a number of points relating to emphases which have led to certain dominant approaches in the conceptualization and measurement of intelligence.

These emphases are discussed in varying detail under the following headings: Philosophical Antecedents, Early Scientific Investigations, The Evolution of Methodology, Binet's Conception of Intelligence, The Influence of Factor Analysis, Definitions of Intelligence, Traditional Intelligence Tests, and Modern Developments.

Research efforts in this area have covered a diversity of loosely related topics. A perusal of the extensive literature leaves the impression of an abundance of disconnected, empirical findings, which have yet to be fitted into theoretical contexts. This fragmentation has been commented on, and is reflected in the chapters covering human abilities and related research in the *Annual Review of Psychology* (Ferguson, 1965; Fleishman & Bartlett, 1969; Tyler, 1972; Horn, 1976, 1979; Carroll & Maxwell, 1979; Weiss & Davison, 1981).

PHILOSOPHICAL ANTECEDENTS

The use of the term "intelligence" in psychology is relatively recent. It was, as noted earlier, taken over from everyday language. The word was rarely used in psychological literature prior to the beginning of the 20th century (Spearman, 1923; Tuddenham, 1962; Wechsler, 1958).

However, theories of intelligence have existed since man observed and attempted to explain, initially, human superiority from other species and, later, individual differences in intellectual performance and achievement. Egyptian hieroglyphics suggest that concern for this aspect of human nature has its roots in early history. The writings of Plato (429–348 BC) and Aristotle (384–322 BC) show that sophisticated philosophical theorizing concerning the structure of the human intellect took place at that early stage. The ancient Greek philosophers' focus was on the soul, as the key to the human mind.

Aristotle accounted for dreams, thoughts, and rationality by postulating the existence of multiple souls. Only man possessed the highest soul, "nous," which was seen as controlling reason. The lowest soul, responsible for purely vegatative functions, was regarded as common to all living organisms. In addition to this, animals had a soul which controlled movement. These theories, via Medieval theology and Descartes provided a strong influence on and shaped widely held religious attitudes concerning the nature of man in present day societies.

Hobbes, in the 17th century; Locke, Berkeley and Hume in the 18th century; and James Mill and his son John Stuart Mill in the first part of the 19th century saw reason as the guiding force in man's ability.

Until the middle of the 19th century the interest in the human intellect—regarded as manifesting itself in soul, reason, rationality, etc.—was a philosophical one. Learned discussion focused on how possession of the intellect sets humans apart from other species. Intelligence was conceived as the common feature characterizing members of a higher level species. The possibility of differences in mental ability between individuals was largely ignored. Such variations, even if considered, would obviously have been of no importance in the social order of feudal societies.

EARLY SCIENTIFIC INVESTIGATIONS

The scientific investigation of intelligence did not commence until the middle 19th and early 20th centuries. The different approaches and paradigms of biologists, psychologists, statisticians and others led to a variety of definitions, some of which have yet to be reconciled.

The biologists Darwin (1809–82) and Spencer (1820–1903) identified and described the progressive increase in the flexibility and sophistication of behavior with evolution, by associating the increasing size and apparent complexity of the brain of organisms with increases in their behavior repertoire, and with adaptation to the requirements of different living environments. Spencer (1864) postulated that intelligence evolved gradually, as a result of a phenomenon observed in some species for basic drives to become increasingly differentiated, thus developing into a hierarchy of more specialized capabilities. The latter were found to range from simple sensory reactions to very complex, finely tuned cognitive abilities. More recently developmental psychologists have suggested that a similar kind of development is characteristic in the growth of the human being from birth to adulthood.

The setting up of the first psychological laboratory in Leipzig in 1879 was the result of the endeavor of Wundt and his students to use experimental methods in the investigation of the human mind. More specifically Wundt and his associates sought to investigate elements of the mind, such as sensation and perception, and to search for explanation of how such elements might combine into more complex processes. The emphasis was on the conditions under which mental processes manifest themselves.

Köhler (1927), one of the founders of Gestalt psychology sought to explain "insight," the term he used to describe the capacity shown by members of higher species, particularly by apes and humans, to restructure a given problem situation to their advantage, or to solve a task through recognition of the relationships and interactions between its component parts. Köhler and his coworkers regarded insightful behaviors as more important, and more advanced in relation to evolution, than the acquisition of conditioned reflexes or adaptation resulting from trial and error behaviors.

THE EVOLUTION OF METHODOLOGY

The first experiments conducted to investigate individual differences in a psychological function were probably the reaction time experiments conducted by the German astronomer F. W. Bessel (1784–1846). The earliest scientific attempt to quantify physical and psychological variation between persons was made by Darwin's cousin, Francis Galton (1822–1911), a brilliant mathematician. His *Hereditary Genius* (1871), and *Natural Inheritance* (1889) probably represent the earliest scientifically based reports concerning individual differences in intelligence.

Galton's interest in human development was basically an evolutionary one: "To measure man as he is today with the emphasis, not upon his attainment as the lord of creation, but upon his limitations as the defective ancestor of better generations" (Boring, 1950, p. 483).

Galton studied the variability of psychological functions, e.g., acuity in hearing, reaction time, and color vision, together with that of physical characteristics such as height and weight in his endeavor to understand inheritance and the evolution of mental abilities.

He shared the view of Wundt and his associates that sensory and perceptual processes form the elementary units of all mental activity. In his tests he sought to represent human abilities quantitatively. He was not concerned with the processes that may have been causing these quantitative differences. This approach to the measurement of differences in human ability continued to influence the developers and users of psychological tests well into modern times.

An even more significant influence of Galton's comprehensive investigations of human variation on psychology, and on quantitative research in general, resulted from the statistical methods he utilized to summarize the observations he collected from very large samples. It has been suggested that Galton recorded data for nearly 10,000 individuals (Tuddenham, 1962).

He had access to the statistical methods of the Belgian mathematician Quételet (1796–1874), who had pioneered the extension of the laws of probability—restricted till then to application in games of chance—to investigations which would nowadays be described as anthropological and sociological. Galton's (1889) emphasis on variability led him to supplement Quételet's (1835) concepts of "average man" and "numerical constancy" as scientific representations of human behavior: "It is difficult to understand why statisticians commonly limit their enquiries to averages, and do not revel in more comprehensive views" (p. 62). He discovered the lawfulness of frequency distributions, and postulated that the distribution of intelligence and major physical attributes in the human population can be represented in the manner of the normal curve:

> The law would have been personified by the Greeks and deified, if they had known of it. It reigns with serenity . . . amidst the wildest confusion. The huger the mob and the greater the apparent anarchy, the more perfect is its sway. It is the supreme law of Unreason.
>
> Whenever a large sample of elements is taken in hand and marshalled in order of their magnitude, an unsuspected and most beautiful form of regularity proves to have been latent all along. (p. 66)

Galton's discovery constitutes the origin of the knowledge that values obtained on a variable can be specified statistically in a totally relativistic manner, i.e., on the basis of their position in a frequency distribution of other observations on the same variable. Together with a younger colleague, Pearson, Galton developed the statistical technique of correlation which was used by Spearman (1863–1945) and others in their investigations of general and specific abilities, their organization and interdependencies.

Up to the turn of the century the investigation of variation in mental ability proceeded by means of the study of relatively simple psychophysical variables. J. McK. Cattell (1890), Sharp (1899), Wissler (1901) and their contemporaries assumed individual differences to be a function of variations in the development and association of single sensory and perceptual units.

BINET'S CONCEPTION OF INTELLIGENCE

It was Binet and Simon (1905) who moved the study of differences in the mental abilities of individuals from elementary to more complex variables. Like his contemporaries Binet conceived intelligence as consisting of distinct simpler abilities, which needed to be evaluated separately. But he postulated that intelligence should be represented by a synthesis, in other words by a composite of a number of mental faculties. Tuddenham (1962) describes Binet's idea of intelligence "as a shifting complex of inter-related functions" (p. 490).

Binet himself did not provide any theoretical guidance as to the nature of possible composites or their determinants. Rather, his work was guided by practical requirements:

> Our goal is not at all to study, analyse and to disclose the aptitudes of those who are inferior in intelligence . . . we confine ourselves to evaluating, to measuring their [retarded children's] intelligence in general; we shall establish their intellectual level; and to give an idea of this level we shall compare it to normal children of the same age or of an analogous level. (Binet & Simon, 1905, p. 193)

A number of Binet's contemporaries (e.g., Goddard, 1912 and Terman, 1916), and subsequent developers of ability tests including Wechsler (1939, 1949, 1958, 1967), accepted his method of assessment, and adopted as the rationale for this empirical approach the concept of a single, underlying "entity" of intelligence.

THE INFLUENCE OF FACTOR ANALYSIS

Spearman (1904) observed sizable positive intercorrelations between tests of different abilities. He proposed that these intercorrelations were a reflection of a common or "general" factor underlying performance on the tests. On the basis of factor analysis he claimed to have shown that "higher" abilities depend to a large degree on a common general ability factor "g," and to a smaller degree on a series of, possibly task specific, components "s." Although psychological textbooks generally refer to Spearman's conception of intelligence as "two-factor theory," Spearman's own emphasis seems to have been on "g" rather than on the "s's."

His works reflect little attempt on his part to account for the number and diversity of specific factors in terms of response variables.

Antagonistic to Spearman's theory were those of E. L. Thorndike (1874–1949), L. L. Thurstone (1887–1955), G. H. Thomson (1920, 1939/ 1951), and more recently J. P. Guilford (1959, 1967) and R. B. Cattell (1946, 1963). These factor analysts rejected the model of a universal trait of intelligence underlying all problem solving activity, in favor of a "multiple factor theory" (Thurstone, 1947). Thorndike (1925) developed a theory of multiple "bonds" in which he replaced Spearman's "g" by a large number of independent, more elementary abilities. The theory postulates that the "bonds," which may be corresponding to neurological or physiological connections, i.e., processes, were sampled in varying combinations during different intellectual activities. Thomson (1920, 1939/ 1951) proposed a theory similar to that of Thorndike, but postulated the independent structural components constituting the "bonds" as psychological rather than physiological functions. In Thomson's model, certain bonds, such as learned associations, reflexes, etc. are transferable across tasks.

Thurstone's (1947) contribution was methodological as well as conceptual. He rejected Spearman's "g" in favor of a number of broad group factors, the utility and manifestation of which depend on the requirements of specific tasks. Methodological and theoretical differences between Spearman's and Thurstone's approach are discussed by the latter, as follows:

> There was a quarter of a century of debate about Spearman's single factor method and his postulated general intellective factor g. Throughout that debate . . . the orientation was to Spearman's general factor, and secondary attention was given to the group factors and specific factors which were frankly called "the disturbers of g" . . . The development of multiple factor analysis consisted essentially in asking the fundamental question in a different way . . . for a set of variables, we did not ask whether it supported any one General factor. We asked instead how many factors must be postulated in order to account for the observed correlations . . . and it should then be left as a question of fact in each inquiry whether one of these factors should be regarded as general. (Thurstone, 1952, p. 314)

Thurstone's theory postulates seven basic factors namely verbal, numerical, memory, reasoning, spatial, word fluency ability, and conceptual speed.

Guilford's (1959, 1967) elaborate structural model of intelligence carried Thurstone's work further. He postulates 120 separate abilities, and classifies factors with respect to "operations," "contents," and "products."

Factor analytic procedures have multiplied and continue to be used. They have led to the development of a multitude of tests of intelligence. However, factor analysis remains a tool to summarize data and to reduce the complexities inherent in such data to a limited number of dimensions. From a theoretical point of view the utility of such dimensions will be limited, unless their structure, i.e., the pattern of factor loadings, can be explained in operational terms in relation to the performances of the test takers.

Unfortunately, intelligence tests do not necessarily measure the same constructs. Factors with similar labels may not refer to similar structures. It would not appear justifiable, therefore, to make judgments about a person's intelligence beyond the particular test on which the score was obtained.

At times, test constructors and test users appear to disregard the fact that the application of a mathematical technique, factor analysis, does not guarantee the psychological validity of a particular conception of intelligence. The distinction between mathematically and psychologically determined factors must be kept in mind (Dockrell, 1970; Guilford, 1967; Thomson, 1939/1951; Vernon, 1950). A mathematical factor is obtained as a result of an application of factor analytic procedures to the correlations between a number of items or tests which have been administered to a group of persons. The existence of a psychological factor cannot be inferred automatically from a mathematical factor. A mathematical factor can be interpreted as a psychological factor only if it can be "conceived to be an underlying latent variable along which individuals differ, just as they differ along a test scale" (Guilford, 1967, p. 41).

Most of the research conducted in relation to the factorial structure of intelligence tests has been concerned with their predictive power. Efforts to improve predictive validity by adapting testing procedures continue (e.g., Brown & French, 1979; Carlson & Wiedl, 1979). Much less interest has been shown in the psychological validity of the factors obtained, and in the psychological processes involved, in performance on such tests. There are some exceptions to this, such as studies which have utilized factor analytic techniques to confirm theoretical models of intelligence (e.g. Cattell, 1971; Guilford & Hoepfner, 1971; Horn, 1968; Humphreys, 1979; Jarman & Das, 1977). Despite the theoretical and empirical difficulties which may be affecting such investigations at present (Carroll, 1972, 1980b; Sternberg, 1977b, 1980b), this type of research has contributed, and continues to contribute, to the fact that more recent research has tended to conceive intelligence as a multidetermined construct, the manifestation of which is strongly influenced by highly complex combinations and interactions between cognitive and noncognitive factors that can be internal or external to the individual. However, the traditional view that intellectual ability or abilities can be described only through inference based on the quantitative evaluation of various manifestations of such abilities, has largely survived. This may have been a result of the statistical emphases of earlier theorists. They appear to have provided the justification for Binet, and his successors to the present day, to measure intelligence by summing outcome scores on a varied series of different cognitive tasks. Intelligence has thus been commonly equated with IQ (the "intelligence quotient" first introduced by Stern, 1912), a value derived from pass/fail scores on the items of a test purporting to measure intelligence.

Irrespective of whether test performance is represented by a single score or multiple scores, it is generally interpreted on a normative scale. This means that the individual's score acquires meaning only through comparison with the score(s) of a reference group; usually a large, representative, stratified sample of appropriate age. A major limitation of the traditional norm–referenced intelligence tests is that they do not provide any information about the variables affecting performance, which may have determined a particular score.

DEFINITIONS OF INTELLIGENCE

Attempts to interpret and understand individual differences in intellectual performance and educational achievement from intelligence test scores have led to a general lack of substance in definitions of intelligence: Definitions range from the proverbial ". . . that which intelligence tests measure" (attributed initially to Boring, 1923), and Spearman's (1927) "chronicle of modern intelligence" in which he suggests:

> . . . the chronicle of the modern 'intelligence' has been dramatic. The first act shows it rapidly rising to a dazzling eminence. But in the second, there begin to be heard notes of criticism, which soon swell into an insistent hostile chorus . . . From having naively assumed that its nature is straightway conveyed by its name, they now set out to discover what this nature really is. In the last act the truth stands revealed, that the name really has no definite meaning at all; it shows itself to be nothing more than a hypostatized word, applied indiscriminately to all sorts of things, (p. 24)

to ". . . that which qualified observers (peers, teachers, etc.) describe as intelligence on the basis of repeated observations of behavior in many situations" (Barron & Harrington, 1981, p. 444).

Ignored were the cautions concerning the inherent limitations of intervening variables and hypothetical constructs as explanatory concepts (e.g. Krech, 1950; MacCorquodale & Meehl, 1948; Marx, 1951; O'Neil,

1953), in particular Underwood's (1957) treatise concerning the circularity of response defined models in theoretical research, in which he singled out IQ scores as a prime example:

> The response measure (score on test) is used to infer a hypothetical state or capacity which is called intelligence. Intelligence is responsible for the score on the test. And I think that most psychologists are almost compelled to think of this as some capacity which 'really' exists in the organism, although I repeat that such thinking is not demanded by the operations. (p. 204)

Despite these and other warnings, what started off as a score on a set of heterogeneous items became reified. A person's score on a test measuring a number of abilities came to be regarded as a valid index of his or her general intellectual capacity which ignored that Spearman (1927) had noted: "this general factor "g," like all measurement anywhere, is primarily not any concrete thing, but only a value or magnitude" (p. 75). Later, in the same volume he describes his contribution to the area as follows:

> We have not—as all others—set out from an ill-defined mental entity the "intelligence," and then sought to obtain a quantitative value characterizing this. Instead, we have started from a perfectly defined quantitative value "g," and then have demonstrated what mental entity or entities this really characterizes. The "g" proved to be a factor which enters into the measurements of ability of all kinds, and which is throughout constant for any individual, although varying greatly for different individuals. (p. 411)

A number of more recent investigators have been equally careless about definitions. Jensen (1969), for example, in his well known article in the *Harvard Educational Review,* notes on one page that intelligence is what intelligence tests measure. A few pages later he claims that intelligence is a "biological reality."

The state of affairs reflected in the following quotation is, unfortunately, still valid:

> Theoretical articles usually proceed without an explicit definition . . . Psychological and educational textbooks typically discuss the problems of definition, make reference to common-sense notions about brightness, offer the operational alternative under the heading of intelligence as a hypothetical construct, and then present a sample of theories from Binet through the latest factor analytic conclusions. (Fischer, 1969, p. 668)

Fischer's (1969) definition of intelligence reflects rather well the concept's status of definition in the more recent literature and in present psychological and educational practice:

Intelligence refers to the effectiveness, relative to age peers of the individual's approaches to situations in which competence is highly regarded by culture . . . a person's available frames of reference or meaning networks are the limiting conditions of his possibilities for action. Within this scheme, frames of reference together with their behavioral aspects constitute the approach referred to in the definition. (p. 668)

However, despite the lack of definitional consensus among social scientists and professionals in psychology and education, one would find that most laypersons are of the opinion that they know what intelligence is. Most people believe that they can recognize intelligence, particularly in others.

Sternberg, Conway, Ketron, and Bernstein (1981) conducted a number of investigations into "People's Conceptions of Intelligence." They found that both "experts" and laypersons had similar stereotypes, which they used in the evaluation of the intellectual functioning of self and others, and that the stereotypes bore strong resemblances to certain theoretical definitions of intelligence.

TRADITIONAL INTELLIGENCE TESTS

The potentially damaging effects resulting from the far reaching importance of decisions which are made on the basis of information obtained from individuals' performances on intelligence tests demand that such tests be based on scientific knowledge. The latter would demand that the tests fulfill established theoretical and methodological requirements.

Methodologically, the procedures used in the development of the majority of the established intelligence tests are sound enough, when judged in relation to the standards laid down by the American Psychological Association together with the National Council on Measurement in Education, and generally supported by members of the International Test Commission. Useful overviews of statistical models and procedures of test development include Allen and Yen (1979), Anastasi (1976), Cronbach (1970), Green (1981), Jensen (1980), Lord and Novick (1968), Thorndike (1982), and Weiss and Davison (1981). However, as noted previously, little agreement has been reached, even among psychologists, in their theoretical discussions of the nature of the intelligence measured by such tests.

Although attempts to predict complex intellectual abilities and potential for educational achievement from intelligence test scores have met with limited success, intelligence tests continue to be used for these purposes. Significant but low correlations, mostly around the .30 level (Hunt, Frost,

& Lunneborg, 1973) were obtained when outcome scores from achievement tests and other cognitive tasks were related to IQ scores. Acceptably sized correlation coefficients enhance the predictive validity of the
intelligence test. Failures to obtain substantial correlations, as happens all
too frequently, tend to be blamed on the lack of validity of the intelligence
test. Correlations between outcome measures provide insufficient information for the investigation of possible causes of such findings, which
might lead to the development of more valid tests.

One might have expected that, as a result of their training, psychologists as behavioral scientists would seek to describe and explain, i.e., to
define in behavioral terms, what they are attempting to measure: "The
aim of theoretical psychology is to explain the nature of behavior, taking
that word in a wide sense" (Dodwell, 1970, p. 1).

The majority of tests of general and specific abilities sample behaviors,
but only very few allow for the interpretation of test results in behavioral
terms.

Conceptions of the nature of intelligence have developed historically,
and their various emphases are the result of widely differing attitudes
about its origins (ranging from entirely genetic to entirely environmental),
and about factors determining its growth. More research efforts have
been directed towards the measurement of intelligence than towards the
development of theories concerning the nature of what is being measured.

There has been a tendency to estimate intelligence on the basis of the
performance on variables which are largely determined by culture, educational opportunity, and ideology. Intelligence provides prestige (Fischer,
1969; Spiker & McCandless, 1954; Vernon, 1979, 1981) hence it is understandable that the language, information, and attitudes which are perceived to be dominant among groups enjoying a large amount of prestige
in a society have tended to provide the criteria for the assessment of
intelligence.

The motive underlying Galton's efforts was to improve human ability in
successive generations. Binet's interest was in educational development
and schooling. The developers of the Army Alpha and Beta tests re-
sponded to manpower requirements for the American military forces during World War I (Yoakum & Yerkes, 1920). This tendency of early test
development to be guided by the reason for assessment, rather than by
theoretical conceptions of intelligence, has continued into the present. It
is not surprising, therefore that the content of intelligence tests often
reflects dominant values of the test constructors' own socio-economic
status and political orientation at the time of test construction.

Intelligence tests have tended to focus on school related knowledge and
skills, hence Wesman's (1968) argument for periodic revision of both

intelligence tests and school curricula in order to represent a wider spectrum of the abilities to which a culture has come to give its priorities. In their traditional form, standardized norm–referenced intelligence tests are thus highly sensitive to the relativity of general philosophical attitudes concerning the nature of human beings, and their role expectations in many contexts. According to Anastasi, (1968): "Such tests do reflect, at least partly the concept of intelligence current in the culture in which they were developed" (p. 203).

For more detailed discussions concerning the use and limitations of intelligence testing in changed cultural and social contexts the reader is referred to the papers in a special issue of the *American Psychologist,* entitled *Testing: Concepts, Policy, Practice and Research* (Glaser & Bond, 1981), and to relatively recent publications such as Cronbach (1975), Houts (1977), Jackson (1975), Jensen (1980), Kamin (1974), Karrier (1973), Kearney and McElwain (1976), Ogbu (1978), Vernon (1979, 1981) and Warren (1980).

MODERN DEVELOPMENTS

There are thus a multitude of theories, hypotheses, and intuitions, which have guided, and which continue to guide, research into intelligence. Tuddenham (1962), and more recently, Curtis and Glaser (1981) have traced historically the antecedents of modern conceptions of intelligence and its measurement. Tuddenham's (1962) chapter reflects the interplay and cross fertilization between ideas and developments in methodology. Curtis and Glaser (1981) discuss changes in the conception of intelligence "with times as a function of both our scientific knowledge and the social and cultural setting in which this knowledge is interpreted" (p. 111).

However, few co-ordinated attempts have been made to answer questions of basic theoretical importance. For example, questions which raise issues relating to the kinds of explanations which research should seek, and questions concerning the power and limitations of such explanatory theories have not been investigated.

The ground for the development of a general theoretical basis for such questioning was prepared initially by those who urged interaction and a pooling of research efforts between experimental psychology and psychometrics. Butcher (1968), Cronbach (1957b, 1975), Carroll (1974), Simon (1976), Sternberg (1977b) and others suggested that research in both areas had been accumulating discrete sets of knowledge and methodological expertise for too long. They argued that the findings and methods from experimental psychology should be applied in psychometric research in order to produce a better understanding of the nature of the mechanisms underlying the individual differences reflected in the results of performances on psychometric tests.

Conversely, Bouchard (1968), Hunt, Lunneborg, and Lewis (1975), Simon (1975), and others have emphasized the potential value of systematic investigations of individual differences in cognitive processes. Similar arguments and viewpoints have been brought together by Resnick (1976). Examples of studies in which some such integration has been brought about include Bruner, Goodnow and Austin (1956), Wason and Johnson-Laird (1972) and others who used items from psychometric tests as experimental tasks, and characterized individual differences in the performance on these tasks through analyses of the response patterns and errors.

Whitely (1981) has shown how psychometric latent trait methodology can be combined with information processing methodology to provide new insights into how components of reasoning enter into general intelligence.

Much of the research into the construct of intelligence in the past decade can be characterized by what Pellegrino and Glaser (1979) have called the "cognitive correlates" approach and the "cognitive components" approach. These approaches are neither mutually exclusive nor exhaustive. Both involve the correlation of parameters from information processing tasks with scores obtained on psychometric tests of general or specific abilities. The approaches have different goals.

In the cognitive correlates approach—exemplified by the work of Chiang and Atkinson (1976), Goldberg, Schwartz, and Stewart (1977), Hunt (1978), Hunt, Frost, and Lunneborg (1973), Hunt, Lunneborg, and Lewis (1975), Jensen (1979), Jensen and Munro (1979), Keating and Bobbitt (1978) and Keating, Keniston, Manis, and Bobbitt (1980)—basic cognitive processes are identified which discriminate between high and low scorers on tests of particular abilities. The tendency in these studies is to correlate the performance on simple laboratory type tasks with the scores from psychometric tests.

The cognitive components approach, recommended and used by Carroll (1974), Egan (1979), Pellegrino and Glaser (1980), Simon (1976), Snow (1980) and Sternberg (1977a,b, 1979a,b, 1980a), involves the investigation of complex information processing tasks. Traditional aptitude test items are analyzed with the aim of identifying components of the processes underlying performance. The most ambitious of these attempts is probably Sternberg's (1977a,b, 1980) "componential analysis" of analogical reasoning.

Sternberg (1981b) characterized the different aims of the correlational analyses utilized in the cognitive correlates and components approaches as follows:

> The investigator following the cognitive-correlates approach has no guarantee that there is any relationship at all between components of his or her very simple tasks and performance on complex tests. Hence, this investigator's primary goal is to show a substantial relationship between at least some of the components of simple tasks and on complex tests. The investigator following the cognitive-components approach should be guaranteed, if his or her information processing analysis is correct, that at least some components of his or her complex tasks are related to performance on complex tests. After all, the tasks and the tests are essentially the same! Hence this investigator's primary goal is to show a sensible and interesting pattern of relationships between components of complex tasks and performance on complex tests. The question here, then, is which components correlate rather than whether any components correlate. (p. 2)

In recent years, two quite outstanding theoretical contributions towards more theoretical concerns in rather different, yet complimentary aspects of intelligence research, were made by Glaser, Pellegrino and Lesgold (1977) and by Robert Sternberg (1977a,b). The advances in the conception of intelligence resulting from their work are comparable only with Newell and Simon's (1972) contribution to methodology and procedure which revolutionized psychological research not only in problem solving but with respect to any cognitive process.

Glaser, Pellegrino and Lesgold (1977), in their seminal paper "Some directions for a cognitive psychology" asserted that: "it is strongly recommended that the most significant use of measures of intelligence and aptitude should be not primarily for the purposes of prediction, but for indicating how intellectual performance can be improved" (p. 508).

While this view constitutes a significant shift from the traditional, categorization and selection oriented, raison d'être of measures of intelligence, these authors are providing a basis for a more defensible rationale for the assessment of ability and aptitude. Their message is clear: What is required is a description of the intellectual performance of a testee in operational terms, a description which can form the basis for intervention in order to change performance, i.e., to facilitate an increase in intellectual efficiency.

The type of measurement device which is likely to contribute to improvements in intellectual performance must provide for the interpretation of ability or aptitudes in terms of manipulatible variables which enhance or impede intellectual performance. The first step towards the achievement of such assessment is to analyze individuals' performances per se with a view to identifying those components of the cognitive process itself which might generate the outcome differences observed on the basis of intelligence test performance.

Sternberg's concerns are less applied. His componential analyses of analogical reasoning have grown to a search for a broader theory of human intelligence which utilizes components with varying functions and of differential levels of generality. He distinguishes (Sternberg, 1981a) between two types of process models of intelligence: (1) hierarchical models, which postulate, either explicitly or implicitly, some form of control processes which rule strategy selection and implementation, and execution processes; and (2) nonhierarchical models which are not based on a distinction between "executive and nonexecutive (metacognitive and cognitive) processes" (p. 221). The latter models are characterized by operationally distinct, but highly interdependent component processes which come into operation through mutual, though selective, "activation."

In his own hierarchical "subtheory" of intelligence Sternberg (1980a, 1981a) postulates "lower-order performance, acquisition, transfer and retention components . . . [and] higher-order control processes used for executive planning and decision making in problem solving" (p. 222), but only for "controlled information processing that is under the conscious direction of a given individual" (p. 223).

According to Sternberg's theory, "controlled" information processing comes into operation when the problem solver is faced with "nonentrenched" tasks (Sternberg, 1981b), i.e., problems and domains of thought in which subjects have to reason and form strategies because the processing requirements are too unfamiliar to elicit responses at an automatic level.

During automatic information processing, i.e., processing which is not under the control of the problem solver, Sternberg postulates process components of a single level, as follows:

> For *automatic* information processing that is preconscious and thus not under the conscious direction of the individual, the various kinds of components are also operative, but non-hierarchically. There is no functional psychological distinction in such information processing between executive and non-executive processing. Processing is in the mode of a production system, where all kinds of components function at a single level of analysis. (Sternberg, 1981a, p. 223)

Robert Sternberg was one of the founders of the journal *Intelligence*, a multidisciplinary monthly started by Douglas K. Detterman in 1977. As associate editor of that journal, as coeditor of *Human Intelligence* (Sternberg & Detterman, 1979), and in many papers, Sternberg has been instrumental in disseminating the purposes, directions and insights of the perhaps rather unexpected resurgence of research in the field of human intelligence.

As noted previously, in the study of intelligence few psychologists have attempted to address problems of basic theoretical importance. Sternberg is one of the "few." He has reviewed the psychometric and other approaches and proposed new avenues for research.

In a historic attempt to integrate the fragments of theory development in relation to intelligence Sternberg (1981a) chose an evolutionary model. He identified promising aspects of intelligence research, showed how these might be amenable to particular types of theoretical treatment. He has examined the question of how certain research methods might lead to progress in the understanding of intellectual performance (Sternberg, 1979a,b; 1980b; 1981a,b).

Sternberg professes to be engaged in the "Search for an Intelligent Paradigm for Studying Intelligence" (Sternberg, 1981c).

According to Kuhn (1962), in "normal science" viable theory evolves from cumulative research, while in "revolutionary science" established paradigms are superseded by new ones. He defines a new paradigm as a body of scientific achievement that is

> sufficiently unprecedented to attract an enduring group of adherents away from competing modes of scientific activity . . . [and] sufficiently open-ended to leave all sorts of problems for the redefined group of practitioners to resolve . . . [paradigms provide] models from which spring particular coherent traditions of scientific research. (Kuhn, 1962, p. 10)

Clearly Sternberg, Glaser, Pellegrino and Lesgold, Newell and Simon and others have been creative agents already of such a paradigm. Their work has provided the study of intelligence and its measurement with new guiding principles. They have supplied important prerequisites for new directions in research and new findings.

To summarize, it can be said that the literature of the past decade reflects "an intensive revival of research on the nature of intelligence, and this research has had a decidedly new look" (Resnick, 1981, p. 684).

The psychometric approaches, and their customary use of factor analytic techniques, which had characterized attempts to define the nature of intelligence since the beginning of this century are being replaced by approaches which are aimed at the discovery of cognitive processes which underlie test performance. The latter "new look" approaches differ in emphasis from the former in at least three ways:

1. They focus on the need to define intelligence in behavioral terms, rather than to refine its measurement and predict outcomes.

2. They require that definitions of the nature of intelligence reflect psychologically valid cognitive processes which underlie "intelligent" behaviors.
3. They focus on the malleability and adaptability of human aptitudes, skills and abilities.

This leads them to reject conceptions of a fixed level of intelligence in favor of models in which the assessment of intelligence might provide the basis for adaptive training. The accent is on finding out how the intellectual efficiency of individuals can be increased, rather than on the prediction of future success or failure.

3 Theoretical Frameworks of Problem Solving Research

The aim of this chapter is to describe the present status of problem solving research, and to identify those conceptual structures which may have functioned as models in influential research and debate on the subject.

The body of this chapter is divided into six sections. In the first section, the nature and function of a model of problem solving are discussed briefly and compared with the concept of a model traditional in the physical sciences. The purpose of this section is to provide the reader with a background against which the details of the models to be presented might stand out more clearly.

The four major models which are discussed in this chapter have become so much part of the body of psychological knowledge that one could easily forget that such models are interpretations only of the problem solving process. After a brief introduction to each of the four theoretical frameworks, the following four sections contain descriptions of each of the models in turn.

The concluding section of this chapter contains a summary of the functional significance of these models and points out some of the difficulties which have to be faced by the researcher who works within the interpretative framework of a model.

INTERPRETATIVE FRAMEWORKS

The popular notion of a model in the physical sciences is that it provides a formal symbolic representation of variables and relationships between variables identified on the basis of observation or experimentation in the area of interest. The requirements of models include the characteristics of simplicity and abstraction, and a promise of explanatory and predictive power (Underwood, 1957).

A number of descriptive and predictive models of problem solving have been developed, particularly during the past twenty years (e.g., Atkinson & Shiffrin, 1968; Bower & Trabasso, 1964; Ernst & Newell, 1969; Feigenbaum & Feldman, 1963; Gregg & Simon, 1967; Hunt, Marin, & Stone, 1966; Levine, 1970; Reitman, 1965).

A review of the aims and concerns of previous research into problem solving could have been conducted by a survey of all such models and by a comparison of the areas of agreement and disagreement among them. However, such an approach may have seriously misrepresented the content and flavor of much of the research and debate on problem solving. An examination of the research literature shows that few specific models have stimulated continued discussion and further research (cf. Carroll & Maxwell 1979; Erickson & Jones, 1978; Newell, 1973a; Simon, 1979). Possible explanations for this state of affairs include the fact that research has been quite noncumulative. Separate studies focused on many different aspects of problem solving (e.g., performance differences between individuals, particularly with reference to genetic development and various types of environmental determinants; the structure of the performance itself as best exemplified in the studies of information processing and artificial intelligence; and explanations of problem solving in terms of transfer of training, probability learning, etc.). A wide variety of tasks and problem situations have been used (including anagrams, games, mathematical problems, puzzles of varying difficulty, performance tasks, and everyday personal, scientific, and organizational problems and decision-making), thus making comparison between studies difficult, if not impossible. To suggest that any one or a group of these models provides a valid representation of the current status of knowledge about problem solving processes might lead to wrongly representing research on problem solving as an already well-developed area of empirical knowledge which is founded upon accepted basic concepts and on generally agreed upon methods for the collection and organization of data.

In the physical sciences, most analyses are conducted within frameworks of reasonably well defined theoretical considerations (Braithwaite, 1953). An exception to this occurs at the very early stages of research into unexplained phenomena when new kinds of observations and other data have to be summarized. There are many levels of theories. In its simplest form a theory can be defined as a symbolic system, the main function of which is to integrate a set of wide ranging facts, concepts or variables into a unifying conceptual framework. The elements of the system and the relationship between these elements are defined and interpreted in "shorthand" statements which are descriptive and explanatory, and which make predictions about empirical events. At present, problem solving research is lacking the prototypical theories found in many of the physical sciences. In fact, it is possible that the attempt by some theorists to give their models an appearance which is similar to that of theories in the physical sciences (Greeno & Bjork, 1973; Gregg & Simon, 1967) reduces the usefulness of such models as a means of representing the significant findings of problem solving research more generally. At the present state of knowledge it may be impractical, if not wrong, to represent research into problem solving, and into cognitive processes more generally, as scientific theories analogous to those established in the physical sciences. In general, the focus guiding research into problem solving appears not to have been the discovery and systematic accumulation of empirical knowledge, and certainly not the gradual refinement of seminal models and more comprehensive theories. Rather, most research and discussion has been generated by the identification of, and controversy over, a number of highly provocative concepts (such as "insight," "incubation," computer simulation, etc.) and by the debate over how problem solving ought to be viewed and investigated.

The reported scarcity of general theories and models in previous research, and the claim that formal descriptive models traditionally aspired to in the physical sciences may not suitably represent or interpret contemporary research into problem solving, does not lead to a rejection of the notion of models of problem solving as a means of furthering the research and understanding of the processes involved. On the contrary, if one were to abandon, at least for the present, the above noted conventional definition of a theory as a formal symbolic representation of relationships between variables and adopt, instead, the notion of a theory or model as providing a more general and influential position, with the function of guiding and structuring research, then it becomes evident that there are a number of dominant theoretical positions which have guided much of the research into problem solving.

Important contributors to the history and philosophy of science have stressed that one of the major functions of a model in the development of a science is to persuade others that one way of representing and structuring data is better than any alternative approach (Kuhn, 1962; Polanyi, 1958). Such models serve as "interpretative frameworks" (Polanyi, 1958) and tend to provide their own concepts, their own rules for data collection and structuring, and, of course, their own criteria for deciding which research questions are worthy of investigation.

While the adequacy of such interpretative frameworks is still a matter of dispute (Newell & Simon, 1972; Scheffler, 1967; Sternberg, 1977b), it is noted that even important scientific models are not justified solely by the weight of evidence. One model does not replace another only by reference to universally accepted data. Models and theories are themselves means of interpreting and organizing empirical evidence, and are selected by research workers on the basis of such nonempirical considerations as "simplicity," "fashion," "elegance" or even "theoretical beauty."

Although not developing theories in the tradition of the physical sciences, much of the research into problem solving which has been carried out has been empirical and logical. A small number of "scientific communities" of investigators with similar interpretative frameworks which have guided the investigation of problem solving can be identified. When one defines the term "model" more broadly as an interpretative framework, it becomes evident that a number of models of problem solving exist and that these models appear to have dominated the investigation of problem solving.

Surveying the field from this point of view, four reasonably distinct models of problem solving can be identified as having stimulated problem solving research and as having determined the directions and influenced the designs of such research during this century. Each of these models consists of a set of associated variables and concepts which are organized around a wider conception of what problem solving might be and how it should be investigated.

One might label the four dominant interpretative frameworks which have been influential in problem solving research as the Gestalt model, the behaviorist model, the psychometric model, and the information processing model. In the following four paragraphs the main ideas of these approaches are introduced briefly. This is followed by a more detailed presentation of each model in turn. The latter discussion will include references to significant research exemplifying each theoretical framework.

The Gestalt model owes a considerable debt to philosophy, and its revival to more recent applications of analytic philosophy to psychological issues. It stands as the major nonbehavioral model, and has generated its own quasiempirical research by means of introspection. Important aspects of this model are the assumption of psychophysiological isomorphism, the notion that the activity of problem solving involves some type of reorganisation of relationships, and the claim that successful problem solving results from "insight."

The behaviorist model consists of the set of concepts and claims about problem solving which have arisen from attempts to apply the interpretative framework of learning theory to problem solving. This framework might be described as the stimulus–response, or S–R approach to problem solving. It incorporates within its boundaries the theoretical residue of the operant conditioning movement and other reinforcement centered approaches.

The psychometric model is based on factor analysis and owes much of its impetus to the testing movement and to the development and refinement of factor analytic techniques. This theoretical framework provides the major individual differences model but, at the same time, incorporates some of the present day interest in the structure of cognitive processes. This approach has supplied much of the terminology used in problem solving research. It finds its srongest proponents in applied psychology and in education.

The information processing framework incorporates artificial intelligence models and includes mainly computer based approaches to the study of problem solving. In some ways the information processing model might be seen as a contemporary parallel to the Gestalt model. Both models place great emphasis on problem solving processes. But while the Gestalt model, in its endeavor to reveal the contents of the "black box" and thus to identify the mechanisms of the problem solving process, might be described as subject oriented, the information processing model is essentially task oriented. Within the information processing framework the emphasis is on the isolation of the structural elements of the problem solving processes and on the order of operation. The basic method consists of a detailed task analysis, i.e., the identification of major demand characteristics of the task, which provides the basis for the design of a model, usually a flow diagram, tree model, or computer program of problem solving steps which match the task demands.

In the following sections each one of the above introduced approaches will be discussed in more detail and examples of representative research studies will be presented.

THE GESTALT MODEL

Classical Gestalt psychology is generally regarded as the oldest of the interpretative frameworks within which problem solving was investigated. However, Selz (1913, 1922), a seldom mentioned psychologist of the Würzburg school, had developed a theory of productive thought (Berlyne, 1965; Mandler & Mandler, 1964; Van de Geer & Jaspars, 1966): "He [Selz] strongly believed that creative thought could be explained on the basis of the same principles that are valid for more common forms of thinking" (Van de Geer & Jaspars, 1966, p. 165).

Selz's early stated position thus differed little from later associationist theories (Mednick, 1962) and the position of information processing theorists (Newell, Shaw & Simon, 1962; Newell & Simon, 1972; Taylor, 1960). Selz's thinking was thus well ahead of his time. Unfortunately his work was and is little known, even in his native country, Germany. In his methodology, Selz was also at least one generation ahead of his time. His use of verbal reports "as behavior data which should be explained by a model" (Van de Geer & Jaspars, 1966, p. 164) was much closer to the method of behaviorism and information processing than to the method of classical introspection practiced by the Gestaltists and their Wundtian predecessors.

While proponents of the other three frameworks, which will be discussed in the following sections of this chapter, came to investigate problem solving by way of an interest in associated concepts such as learning, intelligence, and information processing, the Gestalt psychologists, committed to the investigation of how "organisms organize" (Boring, 1957, p. 611) set out to analyze problem solving directly and for its own sake. The Gestaltists' preoccupation with perceptual phenomena and the roots of early psychology influenced their direction of inquiry. Central to this model is the assumption of psychophysiological isomorphism defined by Köhler (1927) as ". . . the thesis that our experiences and the processes which underlie these experiences have the same structure" (p. 201). This assumption was important because it served to *explain* (a concern of the Gestaltist) rather than to merely describe phenomena.

Gestalt psychologists rejected structuralists and S–R notions of a machine-like nervous system and the assumption of the existence of a point for point correspondence between an environmental stimulus and sensory excitation in the cortex. Koffka (1935) maintained that stimulus characteristics which are experienced as similar have correlates in the similarity of cerebral processes, and that consciousness and its accompanying cerebral processes are comparable. He notes:

> This conclusion is based on isomorphism, according to which characteristic aspects of the physiological processes are also characteristic aspects of the corresponding conscious processes. (Koffka, 1935, p. 109)

But in the same book he suggests

> The sensation blue and the corresponding neural event have nothing, absolutely nothing in common (p. 55). . . . If you want to explain all behavior in physiological terms why did you ever introduce the behavioral environment? (p. 52)

Gestalt psychology, founded in Germany around 1920 by Wolfgang Köhler, Kurt Koffka, and Max Wertheimer, was largely a reaction against the atomistic approach of Wundtian psychology. From its beginning, the Gestalt movement commanded wide attention among psychologists. The rise of Nazism caused the leading proponents of Gestalt psychology to leave Germany for the United States of America, where the movement developed further and is still influential, particularly in the areas of social psychology (e.g., Asch, 1958; Festinger, 1957; Heider, 1958; Lewin, 1938) and clinical psychology (Goldstein, 1963; Maslow, 1954, 1968; May, 1967; Perls, 1972; Rodgers, 1942; and others).

According to Wundt (1873), representative of the mainstream associationist position, the task of psychological research was to analyze conscious processes into their elements, and to formulate laws about the connections between such elements. In contrast to this approach, the Gestalt view stressed that experience cannot be described adequately as a sum total of smaller, independent parts. A "Gestalt" (in English, a "structure," "form," or "configuration") was defined as a whole which is greater than the sum of its parts (Wertheimer, 1945). The analysis of a Gestalt of conscious experience into elements would thus negate its essential nature.

One of the postulates of Gestalt psychology was that all organisms have an innate tendency to organize the input from their environment. This tendency is expected to increase in effectiveness proportionally to the organism's position on the phylogenetic scale. The term organization did not refer to the classification of discrete phenomena in the environment, but referred rather to a restructuring of the environment according to certain general principles. Among these principles were the figure/ground principle (i.e., perception of objects or events consists fundamentally of two aspects, namely the figure which has good contour and stands out clearly, and the background which is indistinct and the parts of which are not clearly shaped or patterned), and the laws of form, which postulate that organisms prefer "good," i.e., stable, persisting and recurring, well organized, and closed forms.

Research in the Gestalt tradition (Durkin, 1937; Katona, 1940; Koffka, 1935; Köhler, 1917, 1927; Wertheimer, 1923) focused on the investigation of psychological processes underlying perception and problem solving. Gestaltists account for both areas in similar terms. In either case, the organism is presented with phenomena, the identification, understanding, or solution of which depend on their being organized into a coherently structured "whole" by processes which operate within the organism. In a definition of perception, Day (1969) describes the central principle of Gestalt psychology as follows:

> . . . perception considered in terms of the appearances of things is relationally determined. That is, what is seen, felt or heard is determined not by the

individual properties of things, but by the temporal, spatial, and other relations between them. (p. 54)

The processes operating within the organism may produce a number of alternative organizations of the one phenomenon, as for example in the case of the Necker Cube (Necker, 1832; Day, 1969). Different organizations result from changes in the distribution or the prominence of different parts in a figure/ground relationship.

In the investigation of problem solving the Gestalt approach emphasised the structure of the problem. A proper "understanding" of the parts of the problem was regarded as necessary so that the "forces of organization" could produce a solution. According to this theory the problem solving process consists of transformations which the initial Gestalt of the task undergoes (i.e., the problem solver's perception of the task changes over time), and which eventually lead to a solution.

Gestalt psychologists were selective with respect to the tasks they used. Generally preferred were perceptual types of problems, and tasks which lent themselves to the demonstration of the Gestalt principles of set and organization. Many of the tasks used in problem solving studies conducted within this framework consisted of reasonably simple, practical problems (i.e., problems requiring natural responses) which could be solved in a few operations. Many of the problems required a unique, or "surprise" solution (e.g., Duncker, 1945; Durkin, 1937; Katona, 1940; Luchins, 1942; Luchins & Luchins, 1970; Maier, 1930, 1970; Wertheimer, 1945).

The earliest Gestalt studies of problem solving were conducted by Köhler (1917, 1927). In these studies, chimpanzees were presented with problems, the required solution elements of which were natural to the animals and available to them in the problem solving situation. Although the chimpanzees' problem solving behaviors, as described by Köhler, might appear to be suggestive of trial and error behaviors, Köhler's interpretation of the chimpanzees' responses emphasized that the solution occurred at the point when the animals' reorganization had resulted in the appropriate relational pattern—for example, when Sultan (the chimpanzee) saw the sticks which he could join as a means of making the necessary connection between himself and the bananas hanging beyond his reach. Similar requirements are associated with the solving of problems investigated by Duncker (1945), Maier (1930, 1931a,b, 1940) and others (e.g., the need for a pair of pliers as pendulum weights, to swing one piece of string across to another, etc.).

Gestalt theorists emphasize that "simplistic explanations" (especially associationist or behavioristic ones) were not sufficient to account for the observed phenomena. Major issues under discussion included such concepts as "insight," "discovery," and "understanding." However, the holistic approach with which these concepts were investigated prevented their analysis into more elementary components. In fact, Gestalt psychology failed to provide operational definitions of these constructs and seemed only to establish them as prescientific phenomena.

Köhler (1917, 1927) regarded lack of success in problem solving as biologically determined or as resulting from an inability to integrate previous experience. Later Gestalt psychologists (Katona, 1940; Luchins, 1942; Maier, 1970; Scheerer, 1963; Wertheimer, 1945) concerned themselves especially with phenomena observed to have a restricting effect on the production of an acceptable solution. They were particularly concerned with the interference of habit with flexibility, for instance with "functional fixedness" (i.e., a tendency to think of objects as serving only a limited, e.g., most common or most recent, function), and with "set," which may have been established by previous experience but may be inappropriate to a particular problem situation. Durkin (1937) showed how the solution of more complex puzzles was facilitated by prior experience with simpler ones. This phenomenon had previously been recognized by Köhler (1925). Maier (1930, 1970) investigated the influence of cues on reasoning.

Like Maier, Duncker (1945) emphasized the effects of initial "set" and its "reconstructuring" or "reformulation." He noted that different possible solutions to a problem may vary in value, and analyzed false starts and other unsuccessful attempts of his problem solvers.

A major shortcoming for the empirical study of cognitive processes within the interpretative framework of Gestalt psychology lies in the inaccessibility of the phenomena being investigated. Conclusions from this research are therefore necessarily highly inferential. Another important, though less frequently acknowledged, problem of the Gestalt approach results from the existence of considerable individual differences, which have been largely ignored.

The Gestalt psychologists sought to bridge the gap between subjective experience and the concepts of human functioning as used in the natural sciences. However, as yet little progress has been made in the understanding of the physiological foundations of the mechanisms Gestalt theory proposed, and the postulated isomorphism between environmental processes and their physiological or neurological representation within the subject remains speculation.

As was stated in Chapter 1, the aim of the study reported here is to investigate problem solving as a process, as an interplay between the psychological mechanisms which operate during performance, individual differences and the task. Gestalt thinking may be regarded as having contributed considerably to the conceptualization of this type of research.

Gestalt psychology showed that experimentation is not the only method of investigation. Wundt and his followers assumed that psychological research had to be experimental research. Phenomena were not considered as important enough for investigation if they could not be studied experimentally (Flügel, 1933). Gestalt psychologists introduced the idea of the importance of *qualitative* observation, and, though continuing to encourage experimentation, they rejected the view that measurement is the sole source of valid evidence (Taylor, 1960).

The main means of observation used by the Gestaltists was introspection. Although there are methodological differences between classical introspection and the method of "thinking aloud" protocols used in the present study, a Gestaltist influence cannot be denied, particularly with respect to the previously noted work of Selz (1913, 1922). Selz may have been the initiator of the self report method as utilized in the present study, namely as observation of behavior. Certainly the idea of investigating a *process,* rather than discrete elements of conscious experience, was contributed by Gestalt psychology.

Because of the distinctive style which seemed required in the formulation of problem solving tasks to demonstrate the principles of Gestalt theory, there are many types of tasks to which research in this theoretical framework did not address itself. A more representative sampling of tasks was therefore conducted in the present study.

In conclusion, it might be said that Gestalt theory produced the first attempts to investigate problem solving and other cognitive processes in terms of whole and part-whole relationships. Through this contribution it helped to lay the foundations for later approaches to the investigation of cognitive processes and their components. At the same time, Gestalt psychology has created controversy and provoked opposition. Through this it contributed to a general sharpening of issues by those taking alternative positions.

THE BEHAVIORAL MODEL

The term "behavioral" has been chosen to describe this framework, because underlying many of the concepts and ideas expressed by its protagonists is the notion that problem solving and other higher cognitive processes follow the laws of association and conditioning stressed by the behaviorists. Whereas Gestalt psychology was mainly concerned with perception, behaviorism is first of all a theory of learning.

Problem solving research conducted within the behavioral or S–R framework has focused on the mechanisms of response selection. In contrast to the previously discussed framework of the Gestalt psychologists, whose main concern related to perceptual set, behavioral theory attempted to describe and explain the determinants of the problem solver's response.

Within this interpretative framework the task, instructions, etc., constitute a set of stimuli which can form associations, of varying probability of occurrence and strength, with sets of responses and mediating variables. The probability and strength of each association are determined by basic learning principles, which postulate that the responses which are most frequently reinforced are most strongly associated with the stimuli and are therefore most likely to be elicited.

The interpretation of problem solving within a behavioral framework emphasises trial and error behavior, habit family hierarchies, responses established by operant conditioning, chains of associations and transfer of learning. Investigators and theorists tended to focus on one or two S–R pairs in reasonably simple situations in which the above mechanisms were seen to be operating.

The concept of trial and error behavior was introduced into animal psychology by C. L. Morgan (1894) and E. L. Thorndike (1898, 1917). Referring to human behavior, Woodworth and Schlosberg (1954), who maintain that the term goes back to Alexander Bain (1855, 1870), state that

> Given a genuine problem, there must be some exploratory activity, more or less in amount, higher or lower in intellectual level. The much used phrase 'trial and error' ought logically to mean the same as exploration or searching for a goal. (p.818)

S–R theorists suggest that in tasks in which it is impossible to predict possible results of each of a variety of alternative stimulus–response associations, the problem solver has to rely on the feedback provided by trial and error activity. Davis (1966) suggested a binary classification of problem solving tasks depending on whether they elicit "implicit or covert trial and error behavior," i.e., depending on whether the problem solver is able or unable to estimate outcomes of the response alternatives available to him or her. Davis (1973) goes as far as to suggest the operation of

> . . . implicit trial and error, in Maier's pendulum, two-string and hatrack problems, Luchins' water-jar problems, a gold-dust version of the water-jar task (Restle and J. H. Davis, 1962), Duncker's (1945) candle problem and ball transfer or pea-transfer problem (Raaheim, 1963, Saugstad and Raaheim, 1960). (p.47)

The results of early information processing type studies of concept identification (e.g., Bourne, 1966; Bruner, Goodnow, & Austin, 1956;

Hunt, 1962), hypothesis testing (Bower & Trabasso, 1964), and rule learning (Haygood & Bourne, 1965) were interpreted in the behavioral framework of problem solving on the basis of the selective reinforcement of correct concept responses, hypotheses, and rules.

Other tasks interpreted as problem solving on the basis of trial and error included probability-learning tasks (Kendler & Kendler, 1962; Stevenson & Odom, 1965) and maze learning (Erickson, 1962). The habit-hierarchy concept (Hull, 1952) can provide an elegant model of problem solving, and might provide a justification for the order in which a problem solver produces responses, a measure of the originality of such responses, and, more generally, the difficulty level of the problem.

A simplified description of the concept is provided by Davis (1973) as follows:

> We may say that the problem stimuli (objects and instructions) elicit a hierarchy of solution responses. The strength or position of each response in the hierarchy is directly related to S's reinforcement history; . . . The order in which S "thinks of" or tries various responses is directly related to their position in the hierarchy—strongest, least original responses being tested first . . . The sequential testing and rejecting of response alternatives may be said to rearrange the S's original hierarchy of response alternatives by strengthening the initially weak, correct alternative. (pp.48–49)

Maltzman (1955) and later Gagné (1962, 1964) elaborated Hull's model of habit-hierarchy by the inclusion of provisions for temporal habit-hierarchies of a complex and compound nature. A given set of stimuli might thus elicit a hierarchy of hierarchies. Conversely, Maltzman's framework also allows for the case in which several stimuli are assumed to elicit the same response. Entire habit–hierarchies are strengthened, weakened, and restructured relative to other compound hierarchies according to reinforcement contingencies. In a number of experiments, response hierarchies have been demonstrated by using anagram tasks (e.g., Davis & Manske, 1968; Mayzner & Tresselt, 1962).

The utility of the principles of operant conditioning as an explanation of problem solving, even in quite complex situations, is exemplified by Cofer (1961), Dulany (1968), Kendler and Kendler (1961, 1962), Skinner (1966), Staats (1968), and others. These investigators define problem solving in terms of the functioning of previously acquired stimulus–response associations, and sequences of responses. Most of this work relies on verbal sequences. Staats (1968) and Staats and Staats (1963) explained the production of novel associations and "creative scientific behavior" (Staats, 1968) in terms of the simultaneous occurrence of two stimuli, which are unrelated to each other, and each of which had been related to a response by previous reinforcement. The simultaneous occurrence of the two stimuli is assumed to elicit a novel response combination. Quite complex cognitive behavior sequences are assumed to have been established by chaining (Skinner, 1966; Staats, 1968), i.e., simple S–R relationships produce response sequences which, themselves serving as stimuli, combine with other response sequences to elicit more complex sequences, etc. As in Maltzman's system, each step is assumed to involve hierarchies of alternative responses.

Previous experience with the same or a similar task may facilitate or impair the production of a solution. Transfer of training in the context of problem solving tended to be investigated by using procedures for paired–associates (Osgood, 1949). A considerable number of principles and variables pertaining to this mechanism have been postulated. Houston (1976) reviewed this research and noted its potential contribution to the investigation of such constructs as stimulus and response similarity and task difficulty and their influence on problem solving. Other theorists like Gagné (1962, 1964, 1965), and more recently Skinner (1974), have focused on transfer of training as one of the most important constructs in problem solving.

One of the shortcomings of the behavioral approach is that all interpretations of research findings are based on the assumption that complex cognitive processes like problem solving follow the same, admittedly powerful, laws of conditioning as do simple examples of learned behavior. The carving up of the problem solving process into small portions of conditioned responses has resulted in many specific laws of simplified S–R relationships, but has failed to lead to comprehensive models and more complete descriptions. Aspects and elements of problem solving, especially in relation to environmental variables, were investigated. This approach had little to say about the structure of the process as a whole, as it was impossible to "reconnect" the aspects of behavior described in separation. While the Gestaltists' undefined and unanalyzed concepts such as insight, fixation, and cognitive organization were too vague, the S–R mechanisms postulated by behaviorists provided too simple an explanation. The tasks used were simple; many of them were irrelevant.

The central concern of the behaviorist's theoretical framework is the explanation of the process by which the organism acquires the appropriate response to a stimulus. A major concern in the present study was to attempt to explain the relationship between the psychological mechanisms taking place during the problem solving process and the task. Despite this apparent congruence of aims, the extreme positivism of the behaviorist approach would have made a study of essentially covert cognitive processes impossible within the S–R framework. On the other hand, the important behaviorist concepts such as the goal gradient (Hull, 1952), habit family hierarchy (Hull, 1934; Maltzman, 1953, 1955), and generalization (Osgood, 1953) have considerable relevance as explanations of problem solving. Perhaps the most important contribution to the present study stemming from S–R theories resulted from the insistence of this approach on operationally defined variables. The units of observation in the present study are objectively definable and observable problem solving behaviors. Every effort has been made to restrict the categories of the taxonomy which was prepared for the classification of problem solving behaviors to low inference variables.

THE PSYCHOMETRIC MODEL

Psychometric studies and models tend to focus on the products of behavior rather than on the performance itself. The traditional emphasis was to improve the predictive power of measures. Although the research findings resulting from this approach can provide useful information which is related to but not identical with aspects of the processes involved in performance, psychometric models are based on correlations. No matter at how high a level of sophistication the statistical analyses are performed, test scores, with few exceptions (e.g., Guilford, 1967), do not provide information concerning the variety of strategies which may have been used by individuals obtaining particular performance scores.

Research conducted within this framework has tended to link problem solving behavior with intelligence factors. A frequently applied procedure had been to focus on mainly unidimensional problem solving phenomena or strategies, e.g., success/failure, age, or socioeconomic status (Duncan, Featherman, & Duncan, 1968; Tyler, 1965), and to correlate the position on measures of these criteria with performance or intelligence characteristics. Where such correlations are shown to be significant, it is presumed that the intelligence characteristics—e.g., crystallized and fluid intelligence (Cattell, 1963, 1966), level 1 and level 2 strategies (Jensen, 1969, 1973b; Longstreth, 1978), certain factors identified by Guilford's (1967) model—in some sense influence or predetermine the subject's problem solving performance.

Two major explanations might be proposed for the predominance of psychometric and other product oriented studies, particularly during the early and middle parts of this century.

First, psychometric tests appeared to provide an expedient means of obtaining information about groups of individuals. These tests were pioneered in the early part of this century (Binet & Simon, 1905), in fact "1915 to 1939 can perhaps be called the boom period in test development" (Thorndike & Hagen, 1969). The general faith in the results of standardized tests, and the difficulties inherent in other methods of assessment at a time when large groups of army personnel needed to be tested, coincided with the development of increasingly sophisticated statistical methods based on correlation.

A second explanation of the popularity of the psychometric approach in the study of abilities may be that the concentration on analyses of the products of the performance of subjects on standardized tests was a response to the behaviorists' demand that psychological research be restricted to overt and quantifiable aspects of behavior, and to their call to discontinue the study of "consciousness" (Watson, 1930).

Not only research concerned with individual differences, but also studies which sought to define aspects of cognitive behavior, were based on the analysis of test scores. Factor analytic techniques were applied to the test results in order to determine additive components of cognitive activity. The most influential contributions originating from this type of research have been those associated with names such as Burt, Cattell, Guilford, Spearman, Thomson, and Thurstone.

On the basis of correlations between test scores, Guilford (1959, 1967) produced his Structure–of–Intellect model, in which he postulates five intellectual operations (cognition, memory, convergent production, and evaluation) and 24 categories of information. The latter categories are further cross classified in terms of four content categories (figural, symbolic, semantic, behavioral) and six product categories (units, classes, relations, systems, transformations, and implications). The model may thus be represented as a $5 \times 4 \times 6$ cube containing 120 cells.

Psychometric theories began to lose prestige during the late 1960s and 1970s, not only as a result of the civil rights movement in the USA, but also because of the increasing realization that definitions and explanations of cognitive processes generated from test scores are no more valid and generalizable than the tests on the basis of which they were obtained.

In addition to this it must be noted that even in analyses of valid observations, obtained results in a given domain do not necessarily explain that domain. This was pointed out by Thurstone (1947), Cattell (1946, 1957), McNemar (1962), and others. Such early warning that factor analytic constructs can serve only as a preliminary step towards the explanation of phenomena was widely ignored.

There are, however, a number of potential advantages in the use of factor analysis, even in process oriented research. While lacking the explanatory power required for the development of theory, the descriptive results obtained from factor analyses can make important contributions to the planning of investigations.

If one accepts the assumption of correlation, based on the work of

Spearman and Pearson, that two measures taken on a given sample and showing a high degree of association may be regarded as to some extent measuring the same phenomenon or construct (and conversely, that if two acceptably reliable measures are not significantly associated, they are measuring different phenomena), factor analysis can facilitate the selection of a set of variables for further investigation which includes a maximum amount of the information of concern, in a minimum number of constructs. The reduction of the number of variables to be analyzed might be expected to result in a more comprehensive and careful investigation of the more limited set of variables.

A further advantage of factor analytic techniques results from the fact that they provide opportunities for the assessment of the extent to which a given variable may be related to more than one factor; perhaps to more factors than are expected or desirable.

Although to date most psychometric research has been concerned with traits, and "the approach has had little to say about processes or conditions for problem solving" (Forehand, 1966, p. 357), its potential contribution to the study of the structure of the processes involved in problem solving is substantial. The development of research designs which combine the psychometric approach, with its emphasis on objective measurement, with theoretical concepts and experimental techniques from other orientations, suggested long ago by Cronbach (1957b), Guilford (1961), Green (1964), and Forehand (1966), is being proposed with increasing frequency, more recently (e.g., Carroll, 1974, 1976, 1978; Cronbach, 1975; Messick, 1972; Sternberg, 1977a,b). The contents of publications such as the multidisciplinary journal *Intelligence,* which began in 1977, has perhaps been the most prominent vehicle of witness to the fact that these proposals are being accepted at last. Studies such as Allison (1960), Dunham, Guilford, and Hoepfner (1968), and more recently Hunt, Frost, and Lunneborg (1973), Lunneborg (1974), Hunt, Lunneborg, and Lewis (1975), Whitely (1976, 1977), and the work of R. J. Sternberg (1977b, 1978, 1979a) provide impressive evidence of the potential of research which combines psychometrics with other approaches.

In the present study considerable use was made of this approach. Individual differences in problem solving competence and intelligence, and individual differences in the use of problem solving behaviors or strategies were analyzed by means of factor analytic procedures. Factor analyses served to summarize the data collected in the present study. It also provided the means for the investigation of the relationships and mutual interaction of variables from the three major dimensions of the problem solving process, the psychological components of the process of performance, individual differences, and the task.

THE INFORMATION PROCESSING MODEL

Of more recent origin than the preceding three approaches to the study of problem solving is the framework of information processing research.

Research and technical developments reported in the mid 1950s and early 1960s are frequently regarded as having marked a turning point as regards research into cognitive processes (Green, 1966; Forehand, 1966; Newell & Simon, 1972; Radford & Burton, 1974).

The behaviorists were extending their aims to include serious analyses of mediating processes (Hebb, 1960; MacCorquodale & Meehl, 1948; Spence & Spence, 1968; Woodworth & Schlosberg, 1954). The publication of Bruner, Goodnow and Austin's studies of concept formation in 1956 made a tremendous contribution to methodology, not only because their research design permitted the inference of cognitive strategies from observed behaviors and from verbal reports, but also because, though conducting their studies against a background of psychological theories, they did not permit any specific theory of cognition to restrict them in their endeavor to describe and to analyze the strategies used by their subjects. Bruner, Goodnow and Austin's stress on the relevance of task characteristics in concept formation, their suggestion that subjects utilize cues from the environment, previous experience, etc., and their definition of strategies used by subjects emphasized the need for more careful investigations of the features of both subject and task in the problem solving situation, and of the mechanisms operating during the problem solving process. The work of these investigators generated a host of variables and hypotheses. Bourne (1966) listed about 40 classes of variables which he suggested to have been investigated as a result of Bruner, Goodnow, & Austin (1956). Other investigators (e.g., Dienes & Jeeves, 1965; Wason, 1960; Wason & Johnson-Laird, 1972) have attempted to integrate the work of Bruner et al. with a number of theoretical positions and extended their methodology to other fields.

Perhaps comparable to the tremendous impact behaviorism had on psychology and on behavioral sciences more generally, was the impact produced by information theory (Cherry, 1957; Frick, 1959; Shannon, 1948; Wiener, 1948) and its redefinition of many psychological phenomena in terms of systems theory (Koch, 1959). The concepts and measures of the statistical theory of selective information (information theory) have become so much part of psychology and other behavioral sciences that it would be difficult to delineate the direct contribution of the theory. The terminology and jargon of information processing and artificial intelligence research was drawn from information theory, for example, individuals and environments are described as information sources, performance becomes information processing, memory is described as information storage, and sense organs have become communication channels. By providing a language which facilitated the representation of models of human performance in terms of cybernetic concepts, information theory offered a new and effective tool for the analysis of behavior sequences and systems.

The work of Miller (1956, 1960), Broadbent (1958), and others, who drew attention to the limits of human processing capacity, and Chomsky's models for the description of language processes (Chomsky, 1956, 1965; Allen & Van Buren, 1971), provided important input to the study of cognitive processes.

Burt (1962, 1968), Mace (1965), and others (cf. Radford, 1974) observed that "psychology is regaining consciousness" (Mace, 1965, p. 1). Like the Gestalt psychologists and their predecessors, information processing theorists rely strongly on verbal reports to obtain data about cognitive processes. Unlike classical introspectionism, however, "protocol analysis" does not require the subject to undergo the elaborate training required by Wundt and the Gestaltists, nor is its aim to report the "facts" of conscious experience. The aim of protocol analysis is to provide data about the *operations* subjects perform when they solve problems. This method is therefore more similar to that of Selz (1913, 1922) than to the method of introspection as used by the other early psychologists.

The development and increasing availability of computers led to the notion of their potential utility to model complex human behavior (e.g., Feigenbaum, 1962; Feigenbaum & Feldman, 1963; Hunt, 1970; Reitman, 1965; Simon & Newell, 1958; Weizenbaum, 1976).

The major concern of research conducted within this framework was to provide descriptive models of problem solving behaviors during the problem solving process, one of the goals being to represent the problem solving process and other cognitive activities graphically as a tree or other network of successive steps. The computer program provided a method for the specification of the detail required by this type of model, and in addition to this provided the opportunity to test the sufficiency of the specifications.

Newell et al. (1962) suggested the maze to be a useful model of various kinds of problem solving activity. For example, the task of the individual attempting to discover the proof for a theorem may be regarded as that of finding one of the paths through a complex maze. The maze begins with one or more of the axioms, ends in the specified theorem, and consists of all possible paths which might be taken. The authors suggest that the maze model provides a basis for the estimation of the difficulty of a particular problem or type of problems, the size of the maze that must be searched providing the unit of measurement.

The work of Newell and Simon and their Information Processing Theory (Newell & Simon, 1972) constitutes a major breakthrough in the study of problem solving, and in research into cognitive processes in general. The major aim of this research was to construct simulation models which would allow the testing of the theory of problem solving behavior. Data from problem solving protocols provided the basis both for the construction of theory and for the design of the simulation model of the processes exhibited by the subject, which was used to test the theory. The framework for Newell and Simon's theory is basically determined by the importance of two dimensions of the problem solving process: "(1) the demands of the task environment and (2) psychology of the subject" (Newell & Simon, 1972, p. 55).

The theory specifies the interaction between variables from these two dimensions. It postulates that the subject's response to a problem is determined by his or her perception of the stimulus and the feedback received from the environment as a result of behavior. The "task environment" is defined as

> . . . an environment coupled with a goal, problem or task—the one for which the motivation of the subject is assumed. It is the task that defines a point of view about an environment, and that, in fact, allows an environment to be delimited. (Newell & Simon, 1972, p. 55)

The psychology of the subject determines the internal representation of the task environment or the "problem space." The latter term refers to the psychological environment in which the problem solving activity takes place. Newell and Simon (1972) note that the subject's "problem space" includes

> . . . not only his actual behaviors, but the set of possible behaviors from which these are drawn; and not only his overt behaviors, but also the behaviors he considers in his thinking that don't correspond to possible overt behaviors . . . This is not a space that can yet be pointed to and described as an objective fact . . . An attempt at describing it amounts, again, to a representation of the task environment—the subject's representation in this case. (p. 59)

According to Newell and Simon's (1972) theory, human problem solving takes place within the problem space by means of a search. Successful problem solving is described as searching selectively through a maze of possibilities and reducing it to manageable proportions (Simon, 1969). By accounting for such factors as subject related constraints, goal, and task environment, Newell and Simon's theory permits the formulation of hypotheses concerning the subject's internal representation of his or her problem space, where the representation of the problem space is equated with a model of the process of problem solving as it relates to the particular subject. Within this framework chess playing, for example, would be described as follows: subject related constraints include memory restrictions, limitations of serial processing, etc.; the goal is to place the opponent's king into a checkmate position; and the task environment consists of the chess board, the rules and the possibilities available to the player. The player's problem space, therefore, consists of his internal representation of the chess board with all possible moves and configurations of the chess pieces, which he evaluates and manipulates on the basis of their expediency for placing the king in checkmate.

The model presumes that the subject is motivated by the goal, and is capable of identifying and executing the behaviors demanded by the situation, the basic premise being that the capabilities of man are adaptive to the situation.

Simon and Newell and their co-workers have investigated their information processing theory in relation to a number of different tasks. Most frequently analyzed types of problems were board games, crypt arithmetic (in which the subject is asked to solve an equation in which numbers have been substituted by letters), and puzzles such as the Tower of Hanoi.

Simon and Newell found that among the variables influencing human problem solving processes, only a few gross characteristics are invariant over subjects and tasks. These variables relate to limitations of the human information processing system, mainly in relation to short-term memory capacity and processing speed, e.g., limited speed of transfer from short-term memory to long-term memory (Greeno, 1973; Hayes & Simon, 1974; Newell & Simon, 1972; Simon, 1969, 1975).

Computer based research has tended to develop in two reasonably distinct directions: (1) studies which aim to simulate the human subject as a problem solver (e.g., Johnson, 1964; Newell & Simon, 1972; Reitman, 1965), and (2) research oriented to finding efficient algorithms for the solution of tasks (e.g., Arbib, 1969; Bannerji, 1969; Minsky, 1968, 1963; Nilsson, 1971).

Despite the difference between a model aimed at the simulation of human problem solving behavior, and one which is designed to develop a useful program, i.e., a usable system, for the solving of problems, the separation between the two approaches, which have been referred to as the "simulation mode" and the "performance mode" of artificial intelligence research (Weizenbaum, 1976), is not absolute. Examples of purposeful or unintentional combinations of both modes include the work by Hogarth (1974), Newell, Shaw and Simon (1963), and Smetana (1975).

The research cited in the preceding pages, particularly the contributions of Newell and Simon, has led to a variety of other investigations within the information processing framework.

Newell, Simon, and their co-workers noted from their early publications on (Newell et al., 1958a,b) that models of behavior represented as computer programs are expected to be highly specific, because they are representative of the behavior of one individual in one problem situation. A change in either subject or task will result in a change of the program. This phenomenon may explain the lack of cumulative theoretical research and the fact that the dominant impression gained by a reviewer of the literature published during the last decade is of the sheer number and variety of single studies which have been conducted. There is little coherence and no overlap (Erickson & Jones, 1978).

Puzzles, mathematical problems, system representation, and decision making provided the major environments for investigation, mainly by computer simulation. The flavor of the literature and the variety of problem situations which have been employed might best be conveyed by some examples of the types of tasks investigated.

The puzzle-type tasks included anagrams (Newell & Simon, 1972), analogies (Rumelhart & Abrahamson, 1973; Sternberg, 1975, 1978), syllogisms (Revlis, 1975), crypt arithmetic (Newell & Simon, 1972), three-term series (Huttenlocher, 1968; Quinton & Fellows, 1975), Tower of Hanoi (Simon, 1975), missionaries and cannibals (Brée, 1975a; Jeffries, Polson, Razran, & Atwood, 1977; Simon & Reed, 1976), and chess playing (Chase & Simon, 1973; De Groot, 1965; Newell et al., 1958a; Newell & Simon, 1972; Simon & Reed, 1976).

Simpler but more realistic tasks included arithmetic problems (Greeno, 1977, 1978a,b; Hayes, 1973; Kieras & Greeno, 1975; Mayer & Greeno, 1975; Smith, 1973), geometry problems (Brée, 1975b; Gelernter, 1963), and the fitting of mathematical functions (Gerwin, 1974; Huesman & Cheng, 1973), physics (Chi, Feltovich & Glaser, 1981; Chi, Glaser & Rees, 1981; Larkin, McDermott, Simon & Simon, 1980; Larkin & Reif, 1979; Reif & Heller, 1982; Simon & Simon, 1978), engineering (Bhaskar & Simon, 1977; Bundy, 1978; De Kleer, 1977), chemistry (Feigenbaum, 1977). Other tasks from the real life situation include studies of electronic trouble shooting (Brown & Burton, 1975; Rasmussen & Jensen, 1974; Stallman & Sussman, 1976; Sussman & Brown, 1974), information retrieval (Smetana, 1975), computer programming (Gould, 1975; Mayer, 1975; Miller, 1974; Sackman, 1970), decision making in management (Clarkson, 1962; Kuehn & Hamburger, 1963; Smith, 1968), and diagnosis in medicine and psychiatry (Berner, Hamilton, & Best, 1974; Geach, 1974; Kleinmuntz, 1968; Sussman, 1973).

Many of the information processing studies and models are interesting, but their task and subject specificity make it impossible to make generalizations from them. Newell (1973b) himself, in a paper entitled "You can't play twenty questions with nature and win," criticized the "phenomena-driven" approach of information processing research. He bemoans the lack of orderliness in the growth of knowledge in cognitive psychology, which he blames on the noncumulative research of many separate phenomena. These investigations have generated a large number of follow-up experiments, often conducted in a framework of dichotomous hypotheses. Newell recommended that models of cognitive processing should aim for a greater degree of completeness, including more precise specifications of alternative strategies and control structures. He maintains that computer simulation provides a means to achieve this.

Computer simulation does not necessarily provide a panacea for the present dilemma. Careful simulation may lead to precise specifications of certain processes, at times even to the simulation of hierarchical structures, but, utilizing the above discussed methodologies, it will rarely result in a model of simulated processes which are analogous to either the only, optimal, or even the most frequently operating processes underlying performance of a task. Cohen (1977) suggests an interesting parallel:

> The assumptions made in designing a computer simulation are just as likely to be arbitrary and selective as the assumptions made in constructing a psychological model. In essence, the problem of separating out structure from strategy, the basic control structure from the optional operations, is very similar to the problem of distinguishing between competence and performance. (p. 221)

Cohen's terms "control structure" and "optional operations" might be understood to describe the demand characteristics of the task and the problem solving behaviors displayed by the individual, respectively. Information processing research has been task oriented. The emphasis has been on the control structure, i.e., the demand characteristics of the task. Despite early suggestions that

> . . . important similarities may be expected among the programs which represent the behavior of the same individual in different situations, or among those which represent the behavior of different individuals in the same situations. On the basis of these similarities, a more general theory of the kind of behavior under study may be developed. (Taylor, 1967, p. 485)

and despite the attention drawn to the need to investigate information processing with reference to individual differences (e.g., Anderson, 1976; Duncan, 1959; Gagné, 1966; Resnick, 1976), the major emphasis of research within the information processing framework has to date been on the development of solution models which are tailored as carefully as possible to the demand criteria of the task.

One of the major concerns shared by information processing theorists and earlier theoretical positions relates to the form with which information is received, stored, transmitted, etc. The literature, particularly in the area of modern psycholinguistics, gives an impression that specifications of information processing and storage are frequently viewed as ends in themselves (e.g., Castellan, Pisoni, & Potts, 1977). What appears to be ignored is that the nature of the information processing which takes place during cognitive activity, and its structure, might be expected to have decisive effects on the utility of the processes to facilitate certain outcomes. Studies focusing on the internal representation of problems (e.g., Hayes & Simon, 1974; Reed, 1977; Reed, Ernst, & Bannerji, 1974) suggest that a person's interpretation or representation of a problem, in other words the structure of the problem solving process, is not dictated by the formal task structure. To date little published research is available concerning the relationship between processing variables and individual differences, or the combined interaction of both of these with task characteristics. To investigate these relationships is the aim of the present study.

CONCLUSIONS

An important conclusion, which can be reached from a comparison of the research into problem solving conducted within the four interpretative frameworks presented above, is that each approach has resulted in extensive additions to theoretical and empirical knowledge. Although they pursue diverse aims, there are obvious signs of mutual complementation and increasing cross–fertilization.

Especially in relation to the study of individual differences, the psychometric and the information processing approaches are finding some rapprochement (e.g., Carroll, 1976; Hunt, 1976; Keating & Bobbitt, 1978; Hunt, Lunneborg & Lewis, 1975; Resnick, 1976; Sternberg, 1977b, 1978, 1979a).

The differences between the four interpretative frameworks discussed here are not so much differences in theoretical approach to the area of problem solving as a whole, but differences in the content, i.e., focus, of the research. The psychometric and behavioral approaches to the study of problem solving have tended to stress the product or results of performance. Gestalt and information processing theories emphasize the processes which take place when individuals work on problems. Both these approaches place major importance on the investigation of the structure of the task. Behaviorists and Gestalt psychologists place strong emphasis on problem definition. Gestalt psychology, having stressed its central importance more clearly than the behavioral approach, has made a major contribution in the preparation of the ground for the developments which later occurred within the framework of information processing theory.

On the basis of their central emphases, the here discussed four approaches to the study of problem solving were found to fall into three groups: (1) subject oriented research, emphasizing the variables which originate from the problem solver (exemplified best by the psychometric approach, and to some degree by the behavioral approach), (2) task oriented research, emphasizing variables originating from the characteristics of the task itself (best exemplified by the information processing approach), and (3) research originating from the contextual setting of the task (exemplified mainly by the Gestalt approach).

If one were to identify any one characteristic which all the approaches described in this chapter have in common, one might suggest that all four models seem to be based on an assumption that the significant variation in problem solving is a function of variation along a single dimension, i.e., performance.

Within the Gestalt framework this dimension consists of the reorganization of the initial perception of the task. In the behavioral framework this performance relates to various contextual variables. In psychometrics performance related to individual differences, and in the information processing approach it reflected the characteristic requirements of the task.

An assumption of unidimensionality makes it possible, for example, for an investigator of psychometric persuasion to evaluate problem solving performance rather than to describe it. This assumption also allows the investigation of problem solving on the basis of task structure, or reinforcement patterns in terms of dichotomous hypotheses. The research conducted within the context of one of the above discussed models does not have to take into consideration the multitude of conceivable problem solving variables, but can be confined to reasonably simple comparisons between competing alternatives. The model thus serves to organize and simplify the research design, and provides the basis for the interpretation of the obtained results.

Unlike major models provided by the physical sciences, the models of problem solving do not tend to compete with each other as alternative representations and interpretations of the same established set of data. Since there are only few, if any, generally accepted data about problem solving, the models compete with each other solely as alternative views of the activity itself and of the manner in which problem solving should be investigated. This is the reason why few logical and empirical connections between the models exist, and why research in the area has been largely non-cumulative. There is no way in which empirical evidence can be used to demonstrate the greater validity or the superiority of one model over another. Nor it is possible to claim that one model may have generated more research than another because, as was shown in the preceding discussion, advocates of the different models were not necessarily in agreement with respect to what constitutes appropriate research. Fundamentally, each model makes a claim about how problem solving should be understood and investigated.

This chapter did not present a complete analysis of the relationship of problem solving research to the development of theory. Only the major approaches to the investigation of problem solving have been discussed in relation to broad interpretative frameworks, and many details and specific points of view within these frameworks have been ignored. The aim of the above presentation has not been to provide a comprehensive review of all problem solving research, rather it has been to show that different interpretative frameworks focus on different principles. For this reason it is unlikely that the application of one of these theoretical frameworks would turn out to be superior to any other when the aim of the research is to investigate the problem solving process more generally, and from a broader front.

Further research conducted within one of the previously discussed interpretative frameworks might, at best, be expected to result in the gaining of slight increases in understanding of the phenomena involved within narrow aspects of the problem solving process, and this has, in fact, been the result of the majority of studies.

The position at the present time is that, as a result of the tendency of the majority of research being conducted within relatively narrow frameworks, differences in findings resulted from the variation in the aims which particular studies were designed to achieve.

Before research can be expected to make a more comprehensive contribution to the understanding of the major principles of the phenomena of interest, a basis has to be found from which a combination of the aims of previously separately investigated areas can be explored together. There is an obvious necessity for attempts to design research studies which concern themselves with the widest possible range of phenomena relating to problem solving. Extensive studies of behavior, task and subject variations, and their interaction have to be made. This type of research, if it can be accomplished, may provide some prospect of finding models which can be expected to be superior to those which have been designed to focus on specific aspects. The term "superior" is used here to refer to the potential contributions such models might make to the generation of future research, and to the gaining of a more comprehensive description and understanding of the problem solving process.

Ideally, a theory of problem solving should offer a broad conception of the problem solving process which encompasses, at least, the dimensions of the problem solving behaviors themselves, the possible influences of task characteristics, and individual differences. The majority of studies which were discussed in this chapter focused on one particular aspect of the phenomenon. In the past 20 years, researchers appear not to have aimed to provide a complete description of the problem solving process. Perhaps the time for grand theories (Levy, 1970) had run out for a while. More circumscribed theories of specific aspects of problem solving met the needs of the behaviorist and the information processing theorists better than a complete description of the total process, a prerequisite for which would have to be a definition of the phenomenon as an entity. The conceptualization of a cognitive process as an entity, however, was made difficult as a result of the domination of the behaviorist approach in psychological research. In addition to this, well circumscribed theories can be expected to lend themselves more readily to computer validation than can broad conceptions.

To return to a more comprehensive approach of broad conceptions of human problem solving behavior can be expected to lead to a discovery of what important questions investigators of the problem solving process should ask, and to suggest the form which the answers to such questions should take.

Some of the more comprehensive theories, particularly those presented by Gestalt psychologists and psychometricians, were presented at a level of generality which presents difficulties for empirical research. There was a tendency in Gestalt psychology and information processing research to base theories on analogies to systems rather than on the analysis of observations. What is necessary is to identify overt behaviors which may provide the basis for descriptive and explanatory theories, which, in turn, can be validated in relation to other overt behaviors.

A feature which characterizes much of the behaviorist and information processing research has been its focus on extremely complex mechanisms. Instead of attempting to explain what individuals actually do when they solve problems, the aim has tended to be to account for complex mechanisms, such as behavior hierarchies, stimulus generalization, or information coding, storage, and transformation. The theoretical significance of these mechanisms is not denied. They represent factors in terms of which individuals may well differ, and in relation to which a given subject might change over time and task situations. Theories based on these complex mechanisms may well account for observed events, but they have served to describe and explain hypothetical constructs, rather than observable behaviors. Lacking the necessary physiological and neurological knowledge, we have, at present, no way of knowing whether the postulated constructs exist. The value of postulating hypothetical constructs lies in the fact that predictions can be made about phenomena which are yet to be fully explained. However, unless testable propositions concerning the hypothetical constructs are forthcoming, this type of research fails to contribute to an understanding of the phenomena in question.

Instead of providing promising sources of testable propositions, hypothetical constructs in problem solving research conducted within all the major theoretical frameworks discussed in this chapter have tended to link analogy (and at times, speculation) with observed phenomena. Defining the psychological phenomena which take place during problem solving as neurophysiological or machine structures does not make it possible to relate these psychological processes to other variables, e.g., the task or other environmental differences. It is unlikely that the use of hypothetical constructs will lead to the identification of testable propositions about the problem solving process which would not also be identified if problem solving performance were defined as behavior.

Our understanding of the problem solving process is in its beginnings. Therefore, descriptive as well as explanatory research is required at the present stage. To base research into problem solving processes on descriptions of actual problem solving behaviors makes theory development more difficult than to postulate explanatory constructs. However, basing research on behavior descriptions will assure that any propositions which might be made as a result of such research are, in fact, testable and exclude speculations about unobservable phenomena.

Behavior descriptions are, by definition, observable. Their great advantage is that they may be used either as explanatory variables, or as the phenomena to be explained. Hypothetical constructs serve explanatory purposes only, and they may lead to explanations of phenomena which might eventually be shown not to exist.

To summarize, it is suggested that a more comprehensive approach to the investigation of the problem solving process is required, and that this approach should be based on a definition of the psychological mechanisms that take place during problem solving, in terms of identifiable problem solving *behaviors*. Such an approach permits the linking of variables from the psychological process domain with other variables and thus makes a more comprehensive study of the problem solving process possible. This type of research design carries the promise of descriptive as well as explanatory information, and the derivation of testable propositions, concerning at least some of the phenomena of this important and complex human behavior.

Basing intelligence research on identifiable problem solving behaviors can be expected to provide bridges between previously unrelatable research efforts concerned with separate aspects of problem solving by supplying a focus for the simultaneous evaluation and possible integration of much of the previous noncumulative research. Most important, it would move the debate about problem solving into an arena which might exclude speculation about unobservables.

4 The Implications of Previous Research and the Empirical Study

The three preceding chapters were designed to provide a context for the description of an empirical study. Chapter 1 contained the rationale for the study, which it relates to historic and present trends in the conceptualization of problem solving and intelligence more generally. Chapters 2 and 3 provided selective reviews of historical and current psychological research relating to intelligence and problem solving respectively. The emphasis in both chapters was on the evolution of major theoretical viewpoints, rather than on historical developments.

After a synthesis of the conclusions and a discussion of the implications of the two preceding chapters, this chapter summarizes the purposes, design and limitations of a comprehensive empirical study, the report and discussion of which constitutes the content of the remaining chapters of this book.

IMPLICATIONS OF PREVIOUS RESEARCH

Two interesting observations will have been made by the reader of the preceding chapters: (1) The literature of the last two decades reflects the revival of an intense interest in both intelligence and problem solving, (2) The scientific studies of both phenomena, though separate for many decades, appear to share common origins.

Problem solving and the intellect have been dominant areas of concern in 19th century philosophy and in early 20th century psychology as characteristic elements in the functioning of humans. However, the fundamental question which was not answered—which was in fact scarcely addressed—concerns the nature of the processes which constitute such a departure from the functioning of other animals.

As noted previously, Aristotle had postulated the existence of "nous," the soul which allows humans mental operations that other organisms are denied. The assumption of a unique, probably nonphysical entity and essence of human life was taken over by psychologists, and is likely to have contributed considerably to the lack of extensive study of cognitive processes per se. As a single, unique entity, the mind had implications for the life and behavior of those who possessed it, but there was no access to it. Scientific study of actual cognitive processes was therefore not possible.

This did not lead, as is sometimes suggested, to a trivialization of mental phenomena. However, by reducing mental functioning to manifestations of one essence, the early philosophers and psychologists blocked for themselves access to anything below the surface of the phenomena which were covered by a single word such as soul, mind, intellect, etc., and were therefore regarded as unanalyzable.

Eventually, the conception of the intellect changed, and from this change arose the need for new definitions of intelligence and problem solving. The mind, which had been regarded as something like a storage vessel for information, came to be viewed as an organ for the processing of information. Problem solving, reading, and other cognitive activities became recognized as complex mental activities worthy of study for their own sake. Despite this, research has not yet provided comprehensive descriptions of such complex mental processes.

Various aspects of problem solving have been investigated in isolation. As was shown in Chapter 3, many points are being made repeatedly by different investigators. A body of frequently observed, yet by no means generally accepted, "facts" concerning problem solving appears to be building up. For example, it appears now to have been generally acknowledged that the process of problem solving involves a number of stages or phases. Various stages have been postulated. However, different theorists tend to explain cognitive processes in different ways. No one approach appears to be more promising than the others when a general description and understanding of the process is desired.

The Gestalt approach was mainly philosophical. The constructs under investigation were ill-defined and inaccessible to empirical study. Much of the research relating to problem solving appears to have been concerned with attempts to identify the conditions which lead to insight. Insightful behavior was regarded as intelligent by Köhler. "Productive thinking" was regarded as insightful (Wertheimer, 1945).

The behaviorists, in their commitment to "objective" measures of overt behaviors, emphasized the manipulation of problem solving processes and the understanding of influences of environmental controls on performance. Explanations were sought for the mechanisms by which elements of the problem solving environment combine into more complex compounds. In general, behaviorists did not aim to describe the content of the psychological processes which take place during problem solving, but tended to postulate hypothetical constructs and intervening variables.

Factors of intelligence, the relationships between the performances on certain tasks, and the skill factors of various types, repeatedly identified in factor analytic studies have certainly made a significant contribution to problem solving research. But the general restriction of this approach to performance measures, i.e., the outcome of problem solving activity, has left unasked such questions as "What types of activities or processes operated during performance?" or "How could one measure the variables which might be responsible for observed differences in performance?" The latent variables which were postulated could not be observed directly. It was not possible, therefore, to describe them operationally or to combine them with other variables.

Information processing and artificial intelligence research moved from the investigation of problem solving on the basis of relationships between isolated elements of the process to focus on the contents of the process, i.e., the components of the process as sequential units. Attempts were made to map the problem solving processes (represented as computer programs) of individuals on the basis of perceived solution requirements of the task. Even this approach has not revealed sufficient information about the problem solving process. It resulted in a large number of task specific, and frequently subject specific models. Although there seem to be more commonalities than differences among these models, little attempt appears to have been made to differentiate processes as they relate to different products of problem solving.

There has been a tendency to disregard the variability and complexity of intelligence and the varieties of problem solving behaviors. The complexities and multiplicities of both concepts and their interrelationship have been largely ignored.

After roughly sixty years of conceptual separation, the past decade has brought an increasing convergence of research from the two fields. One cause for this convergence may be that, at roughly the same time, both intelligence and problem solving have once again become part of the mainstream of research concerned with human cognition, learning and development. Suddenly, interest was shown in the experimental literature, which contains an abundance of laboratory studies of problem solving. Research in psychology and education identified definite relationships between specific aspects of problem solving and intelligence, and between intelligence and academic performance. Sufficient evidence accumulated to encourage further research.

Three forces in cognitive psychology have been particularly relevant in the above noted renewed convergence of the areas of problem solving and intelligence:

1. In experimental psychology there has been a shift towards the investigation of increasingly complex forms of cognition, and of operations which may be enhanced through training.
2. This increasing concern with more complex tasks has occurred at a time when technological developments, especially in the field of electronics and the computer industry have made available the means to model a variety of such processes.
3. Finally, and possibly most important, there has been a return to an acceptability of the study of mental processes, as exemplified in the following quotation:

The basic reason for studying cognitive processes has become as clear as the reason for studying anything else: because they are there. Our knowledge of the world must be somehow developed from the stimulus input . . . cognitive processes surely exist, so it can hardly be unscientific to study them. (Neisser, 1967, p. 5)

There has been an important shift in psychological and educational research over the past decade or so. This shift has been towards a concern with the content and structure of cognitive processes rather than in the outcomes of performance.

Like biologists, the early psychologists aimed to explain phenomena as entities. Psychology as a modern science is concerned with interdependencies among variables, rather than with their physical nature. To understand behavior means to be able to account for differences between variables and sets of variables under varying conditions. The latter requires delving below the surface manifestations of phenomena to discover their nature.

Technological developments during the past twenty years have led to radical changes not only in research methodology and techniques of data analysis but in the substance of scientific investigations in all areas. The availability of computer modelling in cognitive research has led to expectations of flow-charts and systems diagrams of increasingly sophisticated intellectual processes. It has certainly contributed to the development of the "new look" (Resnick, 1981) which is reflected in the preoccupation with the structure of processes in recent research relating to intelligence and to other areas of cognition.

The focus on process rather than on outcome of performance has been confined largely to theoretical research. There is no reason for a continuation of this state of affairs. Information pertaining to the components of cognitive processes and their interrelationships is equally important for developments in applied areas such as psychological assessment and training, developmental and educational psychology, learning and teaching, management and industry, etc.

Another important shift has been "the trend away from strict, artificial, simplifying laboratory experimentation" (De Groot, 1966, p. 20), which began with the information processing and artificial intelligence studies of the 1960s.

Information processing and artificial intelligence research were able to analyze problems and specify task demands by a careful matching of monitored or simulated problem solving behaviors employed by single subjects in relation to specific tasks. While the results of this type of research were of considerably greater direct behavioral relevance than those of previous approaches, none of these approaches served to reveal much information about the processes which might operate during problem solving more generally; in other words, they did not explain how people actually solve problems.

PURPOSE OF THE EMPIRICAL STUDY

The following chapters of this book contain the report of an investigation of intelligence incarnated in the performance of problem solving.

Both the aims and the methods of this study differ in a number of respects from those more frequently encountered in the traditional and more recent research literature concerning human intelligence.

First, the aim of the study was to seek a systematic description of cognitive processes underlying intelligent performance rather than the prediction of future performance or the testing of strict hypotheses concerning particular cognitive constructs or events.

Second, the investigator purposely chose neither a strictly psychometric nor a systems approach as a framework for the study. The latter, and a computer simulation approach were considered initially, but put aside in favor of an empirical approach. It seemed premature to search for rules governing the functions of the system producing behavioral outcomes without first having identified components of the system in behavioral terms.

Third, an endeavor was made to minimize control and other artificial aspects of traditional experimental research, and to operate in an experimental setting that was as close to real-life as possible.

Fourth, data for the study were derived from "thinking aloud" protocols. This methodology was taken over from information processing research, particularly from Newell and Simon (1972) but used in a novel way. The analysis of protocols on the basis of three-second intervals introduced a new rigor resulting in increased completeness and reliability of the data. A more important departure from the traditional uses of protocol analysis lies in its application in the present study. In information processing and systems research protocol analysis has been used to derive qualitative information. In the present study this method of data collection is utilized to yield both qualitative and quantitative information. Its application in conjunction with psychometric techniques of any kind is an innovation.

Fifth, the "thinking aloud" protocols were analyzed on the basis of an empirically based classification system of observable problem solving behaviors. Because of its crucial importance in the generation of data for the study, the reliability of protocol interpretation and coding was carefully investigated.

Last but not least, the prospective findings of the study were expected to be valuable and to contribute to psychological knowledge to the extent to which they succeed in providing adequate, systematic descriptions of manipulatible components of the process of problem solving per se. It was envisaged that, if replicable and successful, the findings of this study might be used in investigations of the rules of the system, i.e., truly theoretical research, on one hand, and on the other, the formation of new and more valid conceptions of intelligence which might extend the knowledge and broaden the scope of psychometricians. From this perspective the present study is expected to contribute to a bridging between the two approaches.

The major purpose of the investigation reported here is to explore problem solving more comprehensively, and to seek information concerning its dimensionality. A number of behaviorally specific components of the psychological mechanisms which operate during the problem solving process are identified and related to other variables. Important areas are identified which might lead to the development of hypotheses for further investigation.

Although no formal hypotheses are stated, a number of research questions are posed. These questions concern the interrelationship of variables originating from the three major sources of variation during the problem solving process, the task, the subject, and the environment.

More specifically, the research questions relate to the manner in which subjects interacted with the task. The focus of attention in the study is on the problem solving behaviors and strategies used by 89 subjects in their attempts to solve 12 different tasks.

DESIGN OF THE EMPIRICAL STUDY

The methodology used is described and discussed in detail in Chapters 5 to 8. Only a few explanatory and summarizing remarks will be made at this stage to provide the reader with an overview.

Conceptually, this study has drawn from the findings of a large number of research studies, representing previously discussed interpretative frameworks. The strongest influence, both in conceptualization and methodologically, was exerted by the position reflected in information processing research, in particular by the work of Newell and Simon (1972). Gestalt psychology strengthened the interest in process oriented research. The behaviorist framework was responsible for the concern to use low inference measures in the present study. Psychometrics contributed the interest in individual differences, and factor analytic procedures appealed as a method of data reduction and analysis.

The work of Ericsson and Simon (1980), Newell, Shaw and Simon (1958a), Newell and Simon (1972), Ericsson (1975), Buswell (1956), Krutetskii (1976), and others provided convincing recommendation for the utilization of the "thinking aloud" procedure as a promising means to externalize at least some of the generally covert behaviors operating during the problem solving process.

It was assumed that the "thinking aloud" protocols would provide information about the problem solving behaviors and strategies used by the subjects and would therefore provide some insights into the problem solving process. Also, it was assumed that the task type and certain subject characteristics might affect the problem solvers' strategies, and that such an effect, if found, would be reflected in the "thinking aloud" protocols.

The dimensions examined in this study were selected on the basis of their perceived relevance in the problem solving context. The research literature, designers of psychological tests, educational and organizational psychologists, and others have stressed the importance of such variables as competence, speed, intelligence, level of education, and, of course, the characteristics of the task; and their relationship to cognitive activity and performance. An understanding of the operation of such factors in the problem solving context can be expected to lead to an improvement in predictive and diagnostic measures, as well as to the development of methods aimed at producing more effective problem solving behaviors.

The subject characteristics, the influence of which was investigated in the present exploratory study, were therefore represented by the variables of problem solving competence, speed, educational level and an estimate of measured intelligence. For most of the analyses two levels were assigned to each of these three variables, although three levels were assigned to the competence variable for some analyses.

By requesting each individual to solve a number of different tasks, and by grouping subjects on the basis of a number of criterion variables, i.e., competence, speed, intelligence, it became possible to compare the effects of various levels of these variables on the problem solving behaviors used during the problem solving process. Monitoring the problem solvers' progressive behaviors and strategies in sequence provided further information about the process. Attempts were made to analyze the problem solving behaviors emerging from the protocols in terms of aggregate frequencies of the types of strategies used overall, and on the basis of their sequential pattern of occurrence. The latter analyses allowed some initial exploration of the dependency between different problem solving behaviors.

The "thinking aloud" protocols and the subjects' positions on the criterion variables were analyzed in relation to the questions raised for the study. The most time–consuming aspect of the study was the analysis of the protocols to obtain the data on the basis of which the problem solving process was to be investigated. This analysis involved the following major steps:

1. The complete cassette recorded "thinking aloud" protocols were transcribed verbatim, keeping all behavior sequences, including pauses, intact.
2. The transcribed protocols were divided into three-second units.
3. Each three-second unit was classified on the basis of a previously prepared taxonomy of 18 empirically obtained problem solving behaviors. This procedure yielded a total of 41,960 problem solving responses for the 89 subjects' attempts to solve 12 tasks.
4. The protocols from ten randomly selected subjects (i.e. 4598 three-second response units) were scored by two independent judges so that the reliability of the taxonomy could be assessed.

RESEARCH QUESTIONS

The major questions posed for this study in Chapter 1 were investigated as follows:

Question 1: What types of problem solving behaviors or strategies do individuals apply during the problem solving process?

The design of the present study implies that problem solvers themselves might provide some information about the methods and behaviors they employ during their attempts to solve problems. The benefit of determining empirically the types of problem solving strategies used by subjects lies not only in the potentially increased understanding of the processes involved, but in the possibility of identifying means by which problem solving ability might be improved. Identification of strategies provides basic information about the ways in which problem solvers interact with the task. For example, whether they are attentive to the instructions; whether they are creative, convergent, or divergent thinkers; whether they make appropriate use of the given input information; whether they anticipate the possible outcomes of their hypotheses; and whether they refer to their memory in order to apply their own background experience to the given problem.

An answer to Question 1 is thus contained in the application of the taxonomy which was developed on the basis of empirically identified problem solving behaviors. Preferences for certain strategies were identified in relation to individual subjects and tasks by calculating the frequency with which each strategy was used by each subject while working on each task. Use of problem solving behaviors was also investigated for each subject as a proportion of the total number of problem solving behaviors exhibited by that subject in relation to a particular task.

Question 2: How do a number of external criterion variables (i.e., level of education, problem solving competence, speed, and measured intelligence) affect the problem solving process?

The investigation of this question is of particular importance to the possible teaching of problem solving skills and to educational planning in general. If problem solving ability and levels of intellectual functioning, for example, could be operationally defined in terms of problem solving behaviors and strategies, useful information might be obtained about hitherto inaccessible cognitive processes and the factors which might influence them.

Individual differences in problem solving performance and correlates of problem solving ability and measured intelligence have been investigated in the past; but little is known about the actual behaviors and strategies which might underlie these performance differences, and about the manner in which such processes may differ between individuals with varying characteristics.

Question 2 was therefore explored by comparisons of the problem solving behaviors used by solvers with those employed by nonsolvers and by those subjects who decided to discontinue the task prematurely. The patterns of problem solving behaviors of fast and slow working subjects were compared in a similar manner. Measured intelligence was used as a classification variable rather than as a criterion; first because of the coarseness of the estimate of this criterion; second because of the smaller number of subjects taking part in the study whose IQ estimate placed them outside the average (i.e. mean $\pm$ 1SD region); and third because of gross variations in the distributions of the dependent variables.

In the descriptive analysis of the sequential data some comparisons between extreme IQ groups were included. To answer Question 2 the frequencies of use made of each behavior were compared for the 12 tasks for subjects of different problem solving competence, education, estimated intelligence and speed. The variety of different strategies used was investigated as well as the frequency with which the strategies were employed. Multiple discriminant functions were computed to ascertain whether specific sets of problem solving behaviors would be able to discriminate between the criterion groups.

Question 3: In what way are problem solving processes influenced by characteristics of the task?

The problem solving process consists of the interaction between the problem solver and the task which the problem solver attempts to solve. Because of this, characteristics of the task, such as its type, length, difficulty, etc., can be expected to exert considerable influence on the problem solving processes. Although certain differences between tasks, for example between verbal and performance items, are generally accepted and regarded as obvious, their differential effects on problem solving behaviors have not been investigated. An understanding of the effect of task specific characteristics on problem solving behavior might lead to the addition of an operational definition of the concept of task difficulty level to the psychometric one, and might thus provide a basis for the identification and teaching of effective strategies for the solving of different types of problems.

To answer Question 3 the total amounts of use made of each behavior category and the transition behaviors for all subjects were compared between the 12 tasks. Other explorations of the influence of the task included comparisons of the first principal components obtained from task specific analyses, comparisons of preferred problem solving behaviors, and comparison of preference ranks and average usages of problem solving behaviors between the 12 tasks. These analyses provided some means to determine whether the processes of problem solving were differentially affected by the characteristics of the task. In other words, it was possible to investigate whether the task alone determines the problem solving behaviors and strategies.

The criterion variables of problem solving competence, speed, and measured intelligence were investigated in combination by means of $3 \times 2 \times 2$ analysis of variance of the mean frequencies of usage of the different behavior categories across all tasks.

Finally three-mode factor analysis for subjects $\times$ strategies $\times$ tasks was performed to investigate the problem solving process in a more comprehensive way.

The above discussed questions were explored mainly in relation to aggregates of the amount of use made of various problem solving behaviors by each subject on each task. The concern was to investigate certain structural components of the problem solving process and to establish their relative importance. In an attempt to analyze the dynamics of the problem solving process, an initial attempt was made to investigate behavior sequences as they occurred.

It was assumed that the further the occurrences of sequential problem solving behaviors are removed from one another in time during the problem solving process, the lower is their dependency. Because of this, pairs of sequential behaviors immediately following one another were summarized as pairs making up the elements of one-dependent transition matrices, which were then analyzed on the basis of the Markoff-chain model.

For each of the 12 tasks, three major types of comparisons of the transition matrices were made:

1. The overall transition matrices made up of the sequential pairs of problem solving behaviors were compared for groups of subjects of varying problem solving competence, speed, and measured intelligence.
2. The patterns of transition behaviors were compared along the time dimension for the total sample and the above mentioned criterion grouping in two ways:
   a. The overall trends in the occurrence of the behavior sequences were investigated and compared for the beginning, middle, and end periods of the problem solving process.
   b. The same three-second segments were compared with regard to the relative contributions made by specific behavior sequences to changes in the pattern of strategy usage over time.
3. The rate of changes in problem solving behaviors and strategies over time and the relative amounts of repetitive behaviors were investigated in relation to individual and group differences.

The methodology and rationale of the study are discussed where relevant throughout this report. Particular attention is paid to the utility of protocol analysis for the investigation of cognitive processes, its strengths, and weaknesses as a means of obtaining information about the problem solving process, in Chapters 6 and 13.

It was recognized that every attempt should be made to design research in such a way that it might yield reproducible findings across a variety of situations. In the present study, the problem solving process was explored in relation to a number of different tasks and with a comparatively large number of subjects. In addition to this, and following the concern of Harris (1967), Campbell and Fiske (1959), and others, a number of different statistical methods were used to analyze the data, the aim of the latter being a modest attempt to increase the reliability of the findings as far as they are determined by the chosen method of data analysis. Matters affecting the reliability of the study as a whole, in particular with reference to the taxonomy of problem solving behaviors used in this study, are discussed in more detail in Chapters 7 and 13.

To summarize, it might be said that in the study reported here the problem solving process is explored by means of a research design which focuses on actual problem solving behaviors, and which allows the investigation of behaviors and strategies as they occur in relation to different tasks and subject characteristics.

The approach taken is novel, because although these components of problem solving have previously been investigated in isolation, they have not been explored in combination, so that all relevant dimensions of the problem solving situation could be explored independently but simultaneously, and in relation to one another. The comprehensive approach to the investigation of the problem solving process used in the present study is facilitated by the use made of the "thinking aloud" methodology, and by the application of multivariate statistical procedures, in particular by the availability of three-mode factor analysis. Strategy use is investigated as it is affected by both task and subject variables.

LIMITATIONS OF THE STUDY

The present study is an exploratory one. Its findings are presented as initial empirically derived information about the problem solving process and should be examined by further research. The study has many limitations indeed. Although these are discussed in Chapter 13, some are noted here in order to provide the reader with a limiting framework which might guide the evaluation of the utility and the generalizability of the findings and conclusions contained in specific chapters.

The aim of the study is to make an initial attempt to account for generally observed performance differences in cognitive tasks of the type frequently presented as IQ test items, in terms of variables which characterize the problem solving performance of individuals.

The generalizability of any findings obtained in the study, no matter how well supported, is limited not only because of the lack of representativeness of the samples of individuals and tasks, but more important, because the study is limited to cognitive variables.

The concept "intelligence," even if narrowed to its problem solving aspects, would certainly include variables from other domains in addition to the cognitive component behaviors which constitute the process of problem solving. Personality, interest, motivational, social and environmental determinants of the problem solving performance have been ignored in this study.

The importance of these variables is recognized, and it is accepted that their effect on the problem solving process provides research questions of high priority. In the present study it is also assumed that all subjects had the same goal, namely to solve each task presented to them. It is acknowledged that individual differences in the strength of each problem solver's goal, which are determined by previous experiences, interests, and other motivational variables, interact in complex ways with the task requirements and affect performance.

The procedure of requiring subjects to solve all problems in one session, and the presentation of tasks in the same set order, while providing some control of the experimental situation, may have affected the findings.

A number of the limitations of this study have resulted directly from the chosen method of data collection and analysis. Most important, the validity of the findings of the study are limited by the validity of the "thinking aloud" methodology and protocol analysis as sources of data about the problem solving process. The contents of the protocols are restricted to what subjects were able to verbalize about their behaviors and strategies during the problem solving process. Other behaviors, of which the problem solver was not aware or which were not expressed, may have occurred. The methodology precluded the detection of parallel processes. This matter is discussed further in subsequent chapters.

The validity of the study depends on the ability and willingness of the subjects to cooperate in the research by verbalizing their problem solving behavior, on the investigator's ability to train the subjects in the "thinking aloud" technique, and on the reliability of the taxonomy of problem solving behaviors, on the basis of which responses are classified.

Another limitation stems from the fact that the majority of responses were categorized by one investigator only. While every effort was made to remain objective, the possibility that bias may have had some effect on the categorization of responses cannot be denied. The reliability of the taxonomy was assessed, however, and the results of this part of the study are reported at the beginning of Chapter 9.

A further limitation of the study results from the selection of the subjects. The sample size is limited. Eighty-nine volunteer subjects performed all 12 tasks, and the population consisted of one class of Year 11, Year 12, first year university and second year Teachers College students. All subjects were older adolescents or adults. Reasons for this choice are discussed in Chapter 5. No consideration was given to developmental variables affecting the problem solving process. Future research will have to be concerned with the question of whether the findings of this study will hold for different age groups, and describe how patterns of preferred strategy use might change during development.

The findings of this exploratory study must be interpreted as tentative until they can be replicated with better and more representative samples. However, the purpose of the research is to explore empirically in a more comprehensive and in-depth way the problem solving process than has been done in previous research. A major aim is to provide a means of describing and quantifying at least some of the components of the problem solving process. The results of this study were compared with those of other studies of the problem solving process. Areas of considerable agreement were identified. Despite its limitations the present study is, therefore, expected to make a useful contribution to the design of future research into problem solving and intelligence.

METHODS AND ORGANIZATION OF THE STUDY

5 The Tasks and the Sample

This chapter discusses the tasks and the selection of subjects in the present study within the framework of previous research, perceived needs, and constraints of research in the area as a whole.

After a brief description and justification for the use of the Block Design test, the use of tasks in the problem solving literature is summarized and the implications of the present state of affairs are discussed. A presentation of the basic considerations leading to the choice of the problem solving items in the present study follows, with a description of each individual task. The sample of subjects is described in the latter part of this chapter.

THE BLOCK DESIGN TEST

Different methods have been used to determine the degree to which subtests of the Wechsler tests measure "g," i.e., general intelligence. These include second order factor analysis (Cohen, 1959), hierarchical factor analysis (Wallbrown, Blaha, Wallbrown, & Engin, 1975), and principal component analysis (Kaufman, 1975). The Block Design test has stood up extremely well in these and other studies.

The WAIS Block Design test (Wechsler, 1955) was used to obtain an approximate estimate of the level of general intellectual functioning for each subject in the study. The reason for including a measure of general ability was to allow for some monitoring of possible patterns in problem solving activity that might be directly related to different levels of intelligence as assessed traditionally. Time constraints prevented a more complete and valid assessment of measured intelligence. Considerable cooperation had been required of each subject taking part in the study, and every effort had to be made to restrict time requirements. The administration of further WAIS subtests would have been at the cost of the problem solving data.

Initially, it had been planned to follow the frequently used procedure (for supporting literature, see Silverstein, 1970, 1974, 1982) of administering the WAIS Vocabulary test together with the Block Design test. This was not done, as it was expected that for the purposes of the study, Vocabulary, a measure of "crystallized" intelligence, i.e., a task basically assessing education and acculturation (Cattell, 1963; Horn, 1968; Horn & Cattell, 1966), would not add much to the measure of "fluid" intelligence, i.e., problem solving ability.

Wechsler's Block Design test is based on Kohs' Block Test, which was offered by its originator as a comprehensive non-verbal measure of ability (Kohs, 1920). Kohs (1923) suggests that the following aspects are among those which contribute to performance on the test: a clear understanding of the pattern to be produced, the trying out of various combinations under the influence and direction of the required pattern, and judgment based on the comparison of the completed pattern with the model. He suggests that the degree to which intelligence involves such operations as analysis, combination and discrimination, deliberation and completion, and evaluation and judgment, determine the extent to which block design tasks can be regarded as measures of intelligence.

Adaptations of Kohs' test are included in many intelligence scales. Wechsler's Block Design tests have generally been found to conform to all criteria of a "good" test (Matarazzo, 1972, p. 212; Wechsler, 1958, p. 58). Wechsler's Block Design tests correlate well with a variety of criterion measures, with Full Scale IQ, and with most of the sub-tests of WAIS, WISC, and WISC-R. The WAIS Block Design test's correlation with the Comprehension, Information and Vocabulary sub-scales of the above mentioned Wechsler tests is considerably higher than the correlation between pairs of verbal tests themselves (Wechsler, 1958).

Kohs (1923) provides a correlation between Binet IQ and Block Design score of $r = .82$ ($PE = 0.01$), for 366 cases. Correlations reported in the more recent literature between WAIS Block Design scores and Wechsler or Binet Full Scale IQ tend to be in the range between .6 and .8 (Matarazzo, 1972; Sattler, 1974).

The WAIS Block Design test was administered individually to each subject, and scored according to the directions provided by Wechsler (1955).

THE USE OF TASKS
IN PROBLEM SOLVING RESEARCH

A considerable impediment to progress in the research area concerned with human problem solving processes results from the fact that insufficient attention has been given to the problem task itself. This observation has been made by a number of investigators and reviewers of the area during the past 25 years (Davis, 1966; Duncan, 1959; Fleishman, 1982; Johnson, 1972; Kendler & Kendler, 1962; Lorge, Fox, Davitz & Brenner, 1958; Scandura & Brainerd, 1978; Speedie, Treffinger, & Houtz, 1976).

By virtue of the fact that it provides the stimulus for the subject's problem solving behavior, the task is an essential, and possibly central, component in each problem solving study. Nevertheless, a review of the literature suggests that tasks appear to have been considered as relatively peripheral to the major research aims. Many tasks which have been used might be regarded as insignificant and irrelevant, and seem to have been chosen haphazardly. Few investigators made attempts to justify their choices or to supply a rationale concerning the representativeness of the tasks used.

The lack of any generally acceptable taxonomy of tasks or task attributes also presents a problem in other areas of psychological research (Fleishman, 1982; Melton, 1964). There has been a tendency to treat the experimental task as though its sole purpose were to distract the subject while variables, presumably unrelated to the task, are being observed—or as though it could be utilized as a completely in-active entity, on the basis of which performance data can be obtained. "Traditionally, the psychologist has been interested primarily in what is left when the process has been stripped of what is specific to the particular task in hand" (Scandura, 1977, p. 2).

Not only has there been little concern for the nature of the tasks used in investigations, but the relationship between tasks and the effects the choice of a particular task might have had on the experiment, have generally been ignored. Even in the stimulus sets utilized in traditional research into concept formation (for reviews, see Erickson & Jones, 1978; Mervis & Rosch, 1981; Neimark & Santa, 1975), "attributes are combined arbitrarily to form items" (Mervis & Rosch, 1981, p. 91).

More recent research using computers to isolate components of complex cognitive processes has succeeded in identifying appropriate heuristics for the solving of specific problems. The tasks used in this type of research include chess playing, logic theorem proving, crypt arithmetic, and sentence analysis, as well as more traditional tasks like the Tower of

Hanoi and the Cannibals and Missionaries puzzles in a variety of transformations. This type of research has, as was noted previously, resulted in a prolific number of largely independent theories, which explain problem solving processes on the basis of the particular heuristics by means of which individuals or computer programs solved specific tasks adequately. In many cases much attention is devoted to various possible models of task structure, but no suggestion is made that there might be a unique or most appropriate structure of tasks, on the basis of which a taxonomy could be developed.

In fact, in cases where a task has been successfully analyzed into structural, perhaps even hierarchical elements, it is possible to show that the observed task structure is only one among a number of possible structures which would fit the particular task. On the basis of artificial intelligence and other computer simulation studies, one might actually wonder how many different structures a researcher would be expected to identify in his endeavor to account for the attempts of a particular population of subjects to solve a given task.

Few attempts have been made to obtain an understanding of how the task per se, affects human behavior. Attempts to justify why a particular task was chosen initially are rare, despite Cronbach's (1957b) suggestion that

> the important matter is not to establish laws which apply loosely to a random, unorganized selection of situations, . . . the important matter is to discover the organization among the situations, so that we can describe situational differences as systematically as we describe individual differences. (p. 677)

and Brunswik's (1956) recommendation that concepts of sampling from differential psychology be applied to the choice of stimuli and conditions because

> examining treatment conditions as a statistical universe is a possible way to advance experimental thinking (p. 38) . . . in fact proper sampling of situations and problems may in the end be more important than proper sampling of subjects, considering the fact that individuals are probably on the whole more alike than are situations among one another. (p. 39)

Referring to Brunswik's criticisms of the ad hoc selection of treatments, Edwards (1971) writes:

> He saw that psychology is not only about people who emit behavior—it is also, perhaps more importantly, about the tasks which elicit that behavior. That is, he saw that the task-relevant characteristics of the environment are a

necessary part of every process theory in psychology . . . even now many deeply sophisticated theorists fail to recognize how much effort they spend in modelling the task, and how little effort they spend in modelling the behavior of the subject in the task . . . My own guess is that most successful models now available are successful exactly because of their success in describing tasks, not people. (p. 640)

These views were strongly supported by others, for example, Gagné (1977), Stevenson (1972), and by Fleishman and his co-workers. Fleishman (1982) suggests "Psychologists must be as attentive to the sampling of tasks as they are to the sampling of subjects" (p. 823).

The small number of published studies of problem solving which have concerned themselves with the task per se can be summarized according to their major emphases under the following five categories:

a. Attempts to provide criteria for task selection;
b. Comparisons of different methods of task presentation;
c. Studies of effects resulting from the variation of certain task elements;
d. Statistical studies;
e. Information processing research.

Each of these approaches will be considered briefly and evaluated in terms of its possible utility in providing a basis for the sampling of tasks in the present study.

Approach a, which sets out to provide criteria for task selection by considering at least some task attributes, is exemplified by the work of Marks (1951) and Ray (1955). Postulating a functional relationship between the task itself and the behavior of the problem solver, Marks (1951) notes, "the core of the theory is awareness by S of the elements. To the extent that he is aware, S [the subject] will be likely to solve P [the problem]" (p. 74). He suggests that problem solving research should utilize tasks which are:

• plausible (i.e., stimulate interest)
• complex (i.e., elicit problem solving behavior)
• structured (i.e., allow quantification and recasting in other contexts)
• solvable (by which Ray means single solution tasks).

Ray's (1955) paper is the result of probably the earliest and most comprehensive review of tasks used in problem solving research. Restricting himself to nonverbal, i.e., performance tasks, he lists most of the tasks which were described in the psychological literature between 1935 and 1955, thus providing a pool of tasks for experimenters. Each task is described in terms of what is given, what is required, and where applicable "hints," the latter being a listing of cues.

Like Marks (1951), Ray (1955) sets up a number of criteria (which he does not justify) for the suitability of tasks in problem solving studies. These can be summarized as follows:

- Tasks should be "reasonably complex" (Ray, 1955, p. 34):
  should require several responses;
  should allow for more than one hypothesis concerning how to solve the problem;
  should allow for the application of trial and error procedures;
  should require more time than that needed for a single brief act.
- Tasks should be clear:
  a clear description of the problem should be available;
  a solution should be classifiable as successful or unsuccessful;
  in most cases some physical equipment should be used.
- Tasks should require either one of two procedures:
  to discover the operation that changes the given situation into the desired situation;
  to predict the solution from the given situation and the method of proceeding from the given to the desired situation.
- Solutions should be scorable along a continuum.

Ray (1955) assesses the effectiveness of his deliberations by concluding:

> It is possible to offer a set of attributes which may be found useful in problem solving tasks, although none of the tasks considered in the paper meet the complete list. In fact, it may be doubted that any one task ever will exhibit all of them, and some of them are certainly unsuited to certain kinds of investigations. . . . (p. 141)

The establishment of criteria for attributes of problems and the use of such criteria in task selection does not meet the requirements of a classification system for tasks. The issue is avoided by the provision of a selective screen. Restricting the types of problems which might be used in research does not lead to a taxonomy of tasks, nor will it contribute to the type of generalization of findings that is desirable for the results of studies of problem solving processes. A further difficulty lies in the fact that the establishment of criteria and the judgment of whether a given task meets a particular set of criteria depend heavily on subjective decisions made by investigators from study to study. On the other hand, the criteria listed provide a checklist of desirable attributes, which may well contribute to the selection of tasks that might facilitate the investigation of complex human behavior.

The literature contains a number of studies comparing different methods of task presentation. The studies of this type in which the basic concern was the task itself, approach b, were mainly conducted during the 1950s. Studies concerned with variations in the level of concreteness of the task include those of Saugstad (1957), Gibb (1956), the studies published by Lorge and his coworkers during 1955, and Cobb and Brenneise (1952).

Lorge and his coworkers (Lorge, Fox, Davitz, & Brenner, 1958; Lorge & Solomon, 1955) presented the "Mined Road Problem" at seven different levels of reality (i.e., verbal description, photograph, miniature scale model without manipulation and with varying amounts of manipulation). Level of reality was found to have little effect on problem solving performance.

The general aim of these studies was to observe the effects of different methods of administration on the solution of the same problem. The investigators were not concerned with comparisons between different tasks.

The third type of research into the task per se, approach c, was concerned with effects resulting from the variation of certain task elements. This type of study, while again not concerned with task classification, tended to illustrate more than approaches a and b the importance of the particular task. Duncan (1959) summarizes the results of these studies as follows:

> In contrast to the experiments on methods of problem presentation, studies of variation among problem elements consistently reported at least some significant, occasionally powerful effects in problem solving performance. Thus performance on a problem may or may not be influenced by contextual variables such as methods of presentation, that do not change relationships among elements of a problem. But changes of a problem's internal structure usually influence performance, even in cases where the problem remains, in some physical sense, the same. (p. 410)

Examples for approach c are Bennedetti's (1956) study aimed at identifying those aspects of Luchins' water jar problem that might be contributing to the rigidity of responses given by subjects, and Battig's (1957) study of such variables as word length and frequency of usage of specific letters and their effect on the success in word games. Duncan (1959) reviewed a number of studies in which an increasing degree of disorder of digit presentation was found related to an increase in the number of computation errors.

Statistical studies, i.e., approach d, are exemplified on the one hand by the use of traditional item analysis procedures in test development, which provide indices of task difficulty and power of discrimination, and on the other hand by approaches such as that provided by Davis (1961), who classified tasks according to a distribution of solution times: "Under standard conditions a particular problem should consistently yield a characteristic distribution of solution times for samples of subjects from the same parent population" (p. 20).

In contrast to approaches a, b, and c, none of the proponents of the statistical approach, d, considers task requirements, meaning, or structure. Instead, task difficulty is totally determined by the sample of individuals to whom the task is presented. This approach to establishing relative differences between tasks has thus been based on normative information, without attempting to explain psychologically why some problems might be more difficult than others. The legitimacy and utility of the statistical approach would depend on the aim of the research.

The task, per se, has been of serious concern in information processing research, approach e, from its beginning. Reitman (1965), Davis (1966), Bourne, Ekstrand, and Dominowski (1971), Johnson (1972), Speedie, Treffinger, and Houtz (1976), and others claimed that all tasks can be described within three dimensions, namely the task environment, type of outcome, and task complexity.

Task environment characteristics refer to the ambiguity of tasks. Well defined problems, in which the requirements are clear, as for example in anagram tasks, are preferred by these researchers. Examples of ill defined tasks are divergent production tasks (Guilford, 1967). The type of outcome refers to the number of possible solutions, i.e., single versus multiple solution tasks. Task complexity depends on the maximum number of logical steps which may be necessary to reach a solution. These were regarded as either controlled, i.e., inherent in the directions, or uncontrolled, i.e., dependent on the subject's interpretation of the problem.

Characteristics of the behavior of the problem solver in information processing research tends to be related to the amount of experience (previous learning of specific information) and to problem solving processes which could generally be summarized under the traditionally applied headings of preparation, production, and evaluation.

Speedie, Treffinger, and Houtz (1976) regard the task environment as independent of subject behavior. Their approach to task description is similar but less subjective and restricted than approach a.

With the exception of the statistical approach, all the above discussed considerations of the task per se are totally distinct from the use to be made of such tasks in the study of behavior. There is no suggestion that human behavior patterns themselves might provide a basis for the study of experimental tasks.

While there appears to be a complete lack of concern for the tasks themselves in experimental psychology and in psychometrics, the roots of a framework for the classification of tasks may be observed in industrial and social psychology.

Fleishman (1975, 1982) discusses general problems related to the development of taxonomies of tasks which are applicable to human performance. He summarizes different models and rationales which have been used in the definition of task characteristics according to four categories, which he regards as mutually exclusive and exhaustive. His proposed four categories are: a behavior descriptive approach, a behavior requirements approach, an ability requirements approach, and a task characteristics approach.

The behavior descriptive approach is based on what the subject actually does while performing the task, e.g., pushing buttons, setting dials, moving chess pieces. The emphasis is not on what tasks require subjects to do, or on what should be done ideally, but rather on the subject's actual behavior while working on the task. This approach has been used specifically in research on job characteristics and job analysis in industrial psychology (e.g., Dunnette, 1976; McCormick, 1965).

The behavior requirements approach emphasizes the identification of behaviors or skills that are assumed to be required in order to achieve criterion levels of performance (e.g., Altman, 1966; Fleishman, 1975; Gagné, 1964; Miller, 1966; Steiner, 1966).

The ability requirements approach focuses on the abilities or other personal characteristics which are required for successful task completion (Ferguson, 1956; Fleishman, 1975; Hare, 1962). This approach differs from the behavior requirements approach mainly, "in terms of concept derivation and level of description. The ability concepts are empirically derived through factor analytic studies and are treated as more basic units than the behavior requirement functions" (Fleishman, 1975, p. 1130).

The task characteristics approach "treats the task as a set of conditions that elicit performance" (Fleishman, 1975, p. 1130). Its dimensions refer primarily to the physical nature of the task stimuli and the instructions (Hackman, 1970; McGrath & Altman, 1966).

In terms of the above presented categories a considerable number of studies in the area of human problem solving have tended to follow the second and third approaches, neither of which appear to be concerned with the task itself. The behavior descriptive approach might be expected to contribute most if the aim of the research is to identify the processes and behaviors actually used by subjects during problem solving. A combination of the behavior descriptive and the task characteristics approaches may hold the greatest potential to contribute to the understanding of how tasks influence problem solving behaviors.

To summarize, it can be said that studies of problem solving, historically, have rarely used several different tasks in one study. This was probably due to the fact that investigators were not interested in the task per se, but regarded it as a means only of obtaining data concerning the phenomena of major interest, thus denying the effects the characteristics of the task might have on the observed phenomena.

Information processing research attempted to map cognitive processes on the basis of characteristic solution requirements of the task but, apart from Newell and Simon (1972) and Sternberg (1975, 1977a,b), few investigators combined several different tasks in one study.

The aim of the present study is to investigate problem solving within a tripartite framework, namely in relation to variables making up the performance itself, those originating from individual differences, and variables resulting from task differences. The task is thus regarded as an essential and central component of the problem solving process.

In the absence of a general taxonomy of tasks in the published literature, an endeavor was made in the present study to choose tasks from a variety of areas, which might be regarded as representative of the types of tasks individuals are frequently required to solve. Taking heed, therefore, of the published studies which have been particularly concerned with the characterization and choice of tasks (e.g., Fleishman, 1975; Hackman, 1970; Marks, 1951; Ray, 1955), and after trying out some 40 tasks in preliminary trials of the "thinking aloud" methodology, a subjective, though reasonably informed, choice was made by the investigator in the selection of the 12 tasks for the present study.

PROBLEM SOLVING TASKS
USED IN THE PRESENT STUDY

Most problem solving studies have been conducted on the basis of one task. The basic reason for the decision to use a number of different tasks in the present investigation was to go beyond previous research and to allow for at least some generalizability of the findings. It is recognized that the tasks are not a random sample of all possible tasks, and that they cannot be regarded as a representative sample of a definable population of tasks. Rather, the different tasks can be interpreted as providing a variety of situations in which problem solving behaviors are observed and possibly replicated.

The problem solving tasks chosen for the study consist of 12 self contained items. No attempt was made to select tasks according to difficulty, but care was taken to select items which were expected to require varying amounts of time, both to read and to solve. Verbal and performance tasks are included.

Tasks from a variety of problem solving situations were chosen for the present study because such different tasks could be expected to emphasize possible types of problem solving strategies by eliciting different problem solving responses. This does not imply that the strategies used in these tasks are the only or the most relevant strategies available in human problem solving. Nor is it presumed that different types of problem solving activity, in fact, exist. It is merely suggested that the tasks provide examples of different ways in which problem solving may manifest itself. A priori, the tasks of the present study provide examples of different problems, not examples of different kinds of problem solving activity.

It has been shown in the literature (Chase & Simon, 1973; De Groot, 1965; Reitman, 1976) that the observation of persons during the playing of games can offer an opportunity for the study of problem solving under conditions of high subject motivation. The decision not to use games to provide the stimulus situation for the present study was made because it was considered that the playing of games differs from other problem solving situations in at least two important ways. First, the subject's problem solving behavior is influenced to a considerable degree by the actions of his opponent, whose goals tend to be opposed to those of the subject. Second, in most games moves are irreversible. A "bad" hypothesis or a wrong move may therefore have lasting negative effects. This is not the case in most other problem solving situations, where unsuccessful strategies tend not to be disastrous but, as a rule, result in a waste of time only.

A constraint in the selection of tasks for the present investigation was that they had to be readily soluble. The aim was to investigate problem solving strategies used in relation to a number of different tasks. Yet each subject was required to complete all tasks in one session so that the influence of extraneous variables could be reduced. A total time of one to two hours was regarded as not too fatiguing for motivated senior high school and tertiary students, especially with tasks of varying content.

In the absence of a generally acceptable task taxonomy, many different groupings of the tasks are possible. Verbal versus performance tasks, intelligence test items versus achievement tasks, single solution versus open-ended problems, are only some of the ways in which the tasks could be categorized.

As one of the aims of the present study was to make some initial investigation into the possibility of grouping tasks on the basis of their strategy requirements, no commitment to any grouping model was made initially. Problems are therefore discussed in arbitrary groupings.

A full listing of the tasks, including their exact wording and the order of presentation, is provided in Appendix A. In the following section, a brief description and justification for the choice of each of the stimulus situations for problem solving activity in the present study is presented. Abbreviated labels, which are explained in Appendix A, are used in referring to each task in this text.

Five of the twelve tasks were items from individual intelligence tests. Four of these tasks were *Similarities* items from the *Wechsler Adult Intelligence Scale* (WAIS) (Wechsler, 1955). Tasks 8 [Poem/Statue], 9 [Praise/Punishment], 10 [Fly/Tree], and 11 [Wood/Alcohol] are WAIS Similarities items 10 to 13 inclusively.

This type of task forms part of many individual and group intelligence tests. It requires the subject to recognize and to identify common elements of each pair of concepts presented and, at higher levels, to provide a single concept or abstraction which covers both the concepts. This type of task samples the ability to discriminate between superficial and essential aspects of likeness and samples concrete and abstract thinking.

Wechsler (1958) noted that the responses he obtained from subjects to his similarities items contained useful qualitative information concerning individual differences in thought processes. He and others suggested that similarities items are among the most reliable measures of intellectual ability, and that they provide the kind of task "which has been recognized by all investigators as containing a great amount of g" (Matarazzo, 1972, p. 206).

Similarities items are easily administered and they are generally found to have an interest appeal for the average adult.

Matarazzo (1972) notes that Wechsler's Similarities test

> is often designated as a test of abstraction or concept formation, and to the extent that it calls for perception of broad, common, or universal elements between the terms compared, its designation as such is altogether justified. But it should be remembered that the mere presence of a universal element does not in itself and of itself constitute conceptualized relationship. The essence of a concept requires a generalization or deduction drawn from particulars, and one is never quite sure whether a subject in giving a superior (2 credit) response has actually done just that. (p. 488)

The latter scoring difficulty did not apply in the evaluation of responses in the present study because both 1 credit and 2 credit responses were scored as achievement or competence category A, i.e., correct or nearly correct solution.

The other intelligence test item was Task 1 [Binet], a reasoning task designed for superior adults. It originated from the Stanford-Binet Intelligence Scale (Terman & Merrill, 1961, p. 148), where it occurs as item 5,

Superior Adult III, Reasoning II. Task 3 [15 × 30], though much simpler, is also an *arithmetical reasoning* task. This item is hardly a "problem" in the sense of the other tasks. To perform this task the subject needs only to understand the task requirement, recall a method or formula, and execute the manipulation of the simple numbers correctly.

Calculation has traditionally contributed the core of any elementary school mathematics curriculum. The interest of psychologists in the learning, teaching, and assessment of calculation skills dates back at least to Thorndike's (1927) work, *The Psychology of Arithmetic* and continues as an important area of research (e.g., Gelman & Gallistel, 1978; Krutetskii, 1976; Resnick & Ford, 1981).

The inclusion of this type of item in the present study is justified on two main grounds. First, most intelligence tests include items which require arithmetical reasoning on the premise that the ability to solve such problems provides an indication of mental alertness (Matarazzo, 1972; Wechsler, 1958). Second, even adult subjects tend to regard arithmetic questions as relatively legitimate tasks. While such tasks may elicit reactions of embarrassment resulting from the subject's perceived or real lack of proficiency, computation tasks are rarely regarded as irrelevant or unfair.

The computation skills required for Tasks 1 and 3 do not exceed those required of students at the upper primary school level, and they resemble the types of computations required of adults in day-to-day life.

The fact that a large number of the simple tasks which form the body of most omnibus intelligence tests discriminate effectively between individuals of different general ability shows that an in depth study of the processes involved in the completion of such tasks is warranted. The suggestion to investigate IQ type items as experimental tasks has frequently been made in the research literature (Carroll, 1974; Cronbach, 1957b; Das, Kirby, & Jarman, 1975; Estes, 1974; Hunt, Frost, & Lunneborg, 1973; Messick, 1973).

Carroll (1974) called for the provision of a general methodology for the interpretation of *Psychometric Tests as Cognitive Tasks* (Carroll, 1974), leading to a characterization, but not necessarily to a classification, of task dimensions determined by factor analysis according to a model of cognitive processes. Carroll's suggested method is initially based on subjective judgment rather than on hard data, as he advises investigators to start with a model of cognitive processes suggested by recent theories and experimental reports, and then to interpret and characterize the factor analytic results on the basis of this model. An advantage of Carroll's approach is that it generates large numbers of hypotheses concerning a multitude of processes which might be expected to contribute to a single psychometric test item. The disadvantage for the present study would have been that Carroll's major concern, like that of most other investigators and theorists in this area, is to identify the source of individual differences on the basis of cognitive processes rather than to explain these processes in relation to a variety of tasks.

Tasks 4 [Pebbles] and 5 [Platform] were taken from De Bono (1967). These *puzzle-type* problems were regarded as particularly appropriate for the present study because the solutions of such tasks tend to be somewhat novel and therefore require some original thinking. At the same time these problems do not require specialized knowledge. The two particular tasks utilized in the present study were regarded as representing reasonably well distanced positions on a possible abstract/concrete continuum of the De Bono tasks, and were thus expected to contribute to the variation between stimulus situations.

The three *performance tasks* were Task 2 [: : :], taken from Scheerer (1963), and Tasks 6 [6m → 4Δ] and 7 [9m → 1h] adapted from Wertheimer (1945) and De Bono (1967).

In the research cited, these tasks were not used to explain information processing, but to investigate Gestalt principles. Katona (1940), for example, taught his subjects different solutions or gave different hints, and then compared "intuitive" and "logical" solutions in relation to such variables as time required, retention, and transfer of skills.

Like the verbal De Bono tasks, these tasks have the character of puzzles. The subject cannot rely on the retrieval of previous experience, but must proceed by reasoning or by trial and error. It was assumed that these performance tasks would elicit a mixture of perceptual and manipulative activity, and would therefore provide a dimension not contained in the verbal tasks. In this way they were expected to contribute positively to the investigation of possible general strategy patterns across tasks.

It is possible, however, that the fact that manipulation was permitted restricts the utility of these tasks for protocol analysis. Thomas (1974) found that manipulative problems tended to elicit "a fairly rapid series of moves with little verbal commentary" (p. 258). Thomas' observation, which differed from the experiences of other researchers (Greeno, 1976; Newell & Simon, 1972; Simon, 1976; Simon & Kotovsky, 1963), and from the results obtained in the present study, may be explainable by the fact that Thomas had purposely not trained his subjects in the "thinking aloud" method.

Task 12 [8TB/2] was noted informally and its origin could not be established. Initial pilot trials identified this task as a particularly difficult one. Its inclusion in the present study resulted from the fact that subjects in the pilot study found it particularly easy to "think aloud" in this task. There was little need for prompting by the examiners. Also, quite subjectively perceived, a certain similarity between Tasks 12 and 1 seemed of potential interest for a comparison of strategies used across tasks. Both tasks require a similar type of computational manipulation, but more importantly they require that critical choices be made.

To summarize, it can be said that in the absence of a relevant or generally accepted model for the classification of tasks, the stimulus items for the present study were selected in such a way that a variety of problems would be encountered. Items which had previously been used in the literature were preferred. Intelligence test items, in particular, were favored in response to Carroll's (1974) paper, urging the use of such items in research on "psychometric tests as cognitive tasks." Care was taken to choose tasks which required no specialized knowledge, and to exclude items which were likely to be solved on the basis of previous learning of similar tasks.

The items included in the final set of tasks for the present study consist of 12 discrete items, which are dissimilar enough not to be solved by direct transfer of training from earlier to later administered tasks. This assumption is supported by evidence gathered in the pilot study, when various randomizations of task presentation were tried out.

A major criterion in the selection of tasks was provided by the desire to present subjects with problems which they would not be expected to perceive as either unfair or as irrelevant. It was recognized that the successful application of the "thinking aloud" procedure requires a high degree of motivation on the part of each subject taking part in the study.

THE SAMPLE

The initial sample consisted of 58 male and 58 female students who volunteered after a talk on intellectual efficiency, to take part in a study of problem-solving which included training in the procedure of "thinking aloud". Forty of the subjects were Year 11, and 20 were Year 12 students all attending a large metropolitan high school. Twenty were second year students in a tertiary course leading to a degree in education as specialist primary school teachers, and 36 subjects were first year psychology students from an educationally prestigious, large university.

The data presented in this book are confined to the results obtained from only 89 of the total sample of 116 subjects, these 89 subjects having completed all requirements of the present study. The final sample of 89 young adults consisted of 39 males and 50 females. Thirty-one subjects (12 males and 19 females) were Year 11, and 16 subjects (10 males and 6 females) were Year 12 high school students. Twenty subjects (5 males and 15 females) were teachers' college students in their second year of training, and 22 subjects (12 males and 10 females) were first year psychology students. The age of the subjects ranged from 16 years to 23 years, the mean age being 18 years and 5 months, with a standard deviation of 2 years. All subjects spoke English as their dominant language.

Older adolescents and adults were chosen as subjects for several reasons. First, as was noted previously, the study is an exploratory one, and the methodology required considerable motivation and stamina on the part of the subjects. Senior high school and tertiary students were chosen because it was assumed that their continuous involvement with problem solving tasks of different kinds would make the requirements of the study more meaningful to these subjects than to other sections of the community, and that the subjects' motivation to participate and persevere in the required tasks would be increased. Also, it was necessary to obtain subjects of a reasonable level of reading proficiency, and with the maturity to comprehend and follow the somewhat unusual procedure of "thinking aloud". In addition to this, the investigator's aim was to initially identify typical problem solving behaviors of students, rather than to study the development of problem solving skills or differential behavior patterns in a wider population.

Sex was not investigated as a separate variable because the sample was regarded as too small already in relation to the number of variables under investigation. Further support for the decision to ignore the sex variable in the present study was gained from the fact that the research literature does not provide any evidence which might suggest significant sex differences between adults in problem solving relating to the types of tasks used here (Maccoby & Jacklin, 1974; Petersen, 1978; Stafford, 1972; Waber, 1976).

Since the main object of the study was to attempt to perform an initial and exploratory investigation of the problem solving process by studying some of the interrelationships between strategy, task and subject variables, it was not considered necessary to attempt to draw a random sample, or a sample which would be representative of any one particular group in the population. It was considered important, however, to obtain maximal cooperation from each subject taking part in the study, and to attempt to make the sample as varied as possible with respect to the measures employed in the study. To ensure the latter, subjects from varying ethnic backgrounds were included in the study.

Previous research concerned with the processes involved in human problem solving was mainly conducted with single or considerably smaller numbers of subjects. The present study, in fact, utilizes a larger group of subjects than has been reported in the literature to date.

One disadvantage of providing a highly detailed analysis of the problem solving behavior of a relatively small and homogeneous sample in a limited number of task situations is that the findings cannot be generalized.

On the other hand, large-scale investigations can fail to identify individual and group differences, or differences between experimental situations. Robinson's (1972) advice regarding the choice between large and small-scale studies in the area of verbal behavior, ". . . if there are general laws governing verbal behavior . . . they will be manifest with a few subjects as clearly as with many . . ." (p. 201), was considered applicable to the present research endeavor. Some constraints on the size of the sample were imposed by the time involved in gathering data from verbal protocols.

An alternative design to the one chosen in this study would have been to reduce the number of tasks. This latter strategy was rejected because it was considered that it would have resulted in an undesirable diminution of the opportunity to investigate task related variables and would therefore have reduced the possibility of isolating certain general trends across tasks. In addition to this, it was regarded as unlikely that a random sample of subjects would have resulted in a group of subjects of sufficiently high motivation to cooperate in the study.

It is recognized that the nature of the present sample and its size imply that the findings of the present exploratory investigation can be generalized only with caution and are therefore of limited utility. However, as argued by Kish (1959), this does not preclude the legitimate application of statistical analyses to the data collected. This point is further discussed in Chapter 9.

In summary, it can be said that there is no presumption that the group of subjects studied here is necessarily typical of any larger sample or that generalizations can be made to other populations not studied here. The central interest is in the process of problem solving, as revealed by the study of the problem solving behavior of 89 senior high school and tertiary students.

If the present exploratory study results in the development of a replicable technique for the identification of characteristics of problem solving processes, it will make possible the design of more reliable procedures for the collection of data from more representative samples.

PROCEDURE

Each subject attended two small group sessions in which training to think aloud was given. During the following week, subjects were presented with the 12 tasks, in the same predetermined order, in one individual testing session without time restriction.

For each task in turn, the directions were presented typed on a sheet of paper, and the subject was asked to begin work on each task by reading the directions aloud. The experimenter's role during the testing session was merely to hand to the subject one stimulus sheet after another, to encourage continued "thinking aloud". The experimenter was directed to prod after a period of silence lasting approximately 10 seconds, and to monitor the cassette recorder. Each problem solving session was recorded in its entirety. The WAIS Block Design test was administered at the end of each problem solving session.

After verbatim transcription of the 1068 problem solving protocols, the content of each of these was divided into three-second intervals. The content of each interval was subsequently classified according to a taxonomy of problem solving behaviors, previously developed and validated by the author. This analysis yielded 41960 responses, i.e., three-second units, each of which could be described by one of 18 strategy variables. For each subject and task, the data consisted of the amounts of time (measured in three-second units) spent, using each of the 18 mutually exclusive and all inclusive problem solving strategies.

6

The "Thinking Aloud" Methodology

DATA GENERATION

In this chapter, an attempt is made to justify the use of the "thinking aloud" methodology for the collection of data by distinguishing it from other verbal report procedures with which it has sometimes been confused.

The central problem in the design of a methodology for the investigation of complex cognitive performance like problem solving, decision making, memory retrieval, or reading, is that the processes involved in such performances are mainly covert.

Data generation in experimental and applied research in such areas has tended to utilize one of two methods, either stimulus–response, i.e., input–outcome, or process tracing procedures. Input–outcome studies of problem solving and intelligence have tended to focus on characteristics of either the subject (e.g., motivation, ability), the task (e.g., different methods of presentation, difficulty), or on variables in the problem situation which might be expected to influence the subject's responses. In stimulus–response or input–outcome research, investigators might hypothesize intervening variables, or make other inferences from observed responses to the processes underlying performance, but they do not aim to trace the process of performance per se. In other words, no attempt is made to identify what the subject actually does during the act of problem solving.

As was suggested previously, the problem solving process might be represented as a succession of events or behaviors. The first aim in the present study was to find a methodology which would be capable of providing a source for the description of at least some of the sequential elements of the problem solving process. Subsequent aims related to the investigation of whether certain elements or processes occur in any general pattern in relation to different subjects or tasks. The term pattern is used here to refer to any consistencies in problem solving behaviors or strategies which might be identified in the population of possible behaviors, i.e., possible elements of the problem solving process available to the problem solver.

It was necessary, therefore, to describe, in addition to the outcomes of the subjects' problem solving performances on each task, processes operating during that performance. The latter aim was oriented less towards a quantitative assessment of the phenomena under investigation than towards the identification of certain qualitative features of the process. A major methodological problem in the study was to find a way of identifying such qualitative features. Because problem solving behaviors are essentially covert, it was necessary to utilize a methodology which would somehow externalize this process and at the same time result in minimal interruption of it.

Although an "ideal" process of sequential operations might theoretically be assumed on the basis of the structure of the problem itself, at least for some well defined tasks like mathematical problems, this "ideal" process may bear little resemblance to the structural elements which operate when individuals solve problems. Processes which are presumed to operate on the basis of task requirements alone must be regarded as incomplete as they fail to take person and environment related process determinants into consideration. Different individuals might attend differently to the same task. They may differ in their amounts of consideration and reflection on different solution possibilities, their utilization of external or internal cues, or perhaps in the capacity or use of memory storage and retrieval processes. A methodology was therefore required which permits the monitoring of the process itself by which input is transformed into output, in other words, a process tracing method.

A review of published problem solving research showed that little is known about possible relationships between the products of problem solving, i.e., the solution, and the processes involved in achieving these products. Measures such as the quality of a solution or the time required to achieve it, while useful in the description of individual differences and sometimes in the study of task requirements, do not permit inferences about the particular path an individual took to reach a solution. "To study problem solving processes we must devise ways of getting subjects to generate observable sequences of behavior" (Kilpatrick, 1967, p. 4).

PROCESS TRACING

A number of investigators attempted to externalize covert processes by designing materials which were expected to reveal the choices of strategies made by individuals during their work towards a solution to a problem.

Lazerte (1933) devised an "envelope test" which was expected to monitor each step in the problem solving process as the subject selected one of several alternative problem solving strategies written on different envelopes. After choosing one of the strategies, the subject finds contained in the envelope another set of envelopes providing further alternative problem solving behaviors. This procedure continues until a solution to the problem has been achieved. Lazerte's method was modified and extended by a number of later investigators. It became known as the "Tab Item" technique, mainly as a result of Rimoldi's (1955) adaptation in which he provided subjects with alternative questions and answers. Similar methods which were essentially based on Lazerte's idea were used in the study of problem solving processes by Glaser, Damrin, and Gardner (1954), Cross and Gaier (1955), Buswell (1956), Rimoldi, Devanne, and Haley (1961), and many others. Rimoldi, Fogliatto, Erdmann, and Donnelly (1964) provide a review of its use. An important contribution to further development of the method and to its extension to other fields of psychological research was made, for instance, by McGuire and Babbott (1965) who designed a branching test of medical diagnosis in which the problem is modified as the testee proceeds, and by Elstein, Shulman, and Sprafka (1978) in their investigation of the clinical reasoning of physicians.

All applications of Lazerte's method, no matter how elaborate their design, restrict the strategies available to the problem solver. The subject is presented with a list of predetermined steps, rather than required to generate his or her own procedure. While the method might be useful for highly defined, simple problems, and in learning situations, it does not provide a valid source of information for investigations into the processes taking place during problem solving. The identification of available options and the decision of which alternatives to follow, i.e., each step, are part of the process of complex cognitive behavior and are essential components of any attempt to provide a description of problem solving processes. In a study of such processes the "envelope," "Tab Item," and similar methods must be rejected on the basis of the interference they cause with the processes to be monitored, by the introduction of predetermined steps or property lists of the process under investigation.

Another major disadvantage of any method involving direct questioning of the subject results from social interaction aspects of question and answer methodologies. The social situation in which research is conducted must be expected to influence any psychological investigation. The quality of the rapport which exists between experimenter and subject can affect both the kind and amount of information the subject is prepared to provide. A cooperative subject may try to please the experimenter, and may thus influence the results in a number of different ways. The subject may supply what he or she regards as socially acceptable responses. Some of the questions posed may not be relevant to the problem solving behaviors utilized by particular persons. Also, in order to provide answers, the subject may draw on types of behaviors conventionally regarded as important, but which are not part of the subject's normal repertoire. Fill-in information might be provided in response to questions which the subject is unable to answer from memory.

Other frequently used process tracing procedures are the behavior protocol and directed interviews or reports. In the behavior protocol method, the investigator endeavors to monitor and record the subject's reactions and behaviors during the performance of a task. The data generated by this method constitute the investigator's perception of the components of the performance.

Directed interviews or reports are obtained through questioning, or by instructing subjects prior to task performance to observe and report on certain aspects or operations of their performance. The "envelope" and "tab item" methods result in directed reports.

Three techniques which force the subject to make his or her own decisions concerning which alternative problem solving behaviors are available at each given point, and which appear to require a minimum of interference on the part of the investigator, stand out in the research literature. They are the methods of introspection, retrospection, and "thinking aloud." The subject's verbalizations are either tape-recorded or written for protocol analysis at a later time.

INTROSPECTION

The method of introspection, as used in much of the earlier work in psychology to study the "contents of consciousness" requires the subject to report about "internal" processes as they occur. An example for this type of approach is provided by the paper by Maier (1931b) entitled "The solution of a problem and its appearance in consciousness," in which the author poses the following questions:

a. Does the solution develop from a nucleus or does it appear as a completed whole?
b. What is the conscious experience of an individual just before the solution is found?
c. Is the reasoner conscious of the different factors which aid in bringing about the solution? (p. 181).

The earliest psychological experiments relied on introspection, which James (1890) defined as "looking into our minds and reporting what we there discover" (p. 185), and which he expected to provide the basis for psychological research "first, and foremost, and always" (Vol. I, p. 185). Wundt regarded immediate experience as the subject matter of psychology. Psychological methodology, therefore, had to reveal immediate experiencing. "Classical introspection," as developed by Wundt (1924) and his followers, involved a highly systematic analysis of "mental processes" into elements and required thorough and exacting training of subjects in the method (Boring, 1953). Although James and Wundt differed somewhat in their definitions of introspection and while the Würzburg School modified Wundt's method, all applications of introspection encourage subjects to interpret sensations and other experiences, and to make inferences about the processes occurring during problem solving. Thus, a description is obtained by the investigator of the subject's interpretation of what took place during problem solving. The danger of rationalization is great, as the subject is instructed to report his or her inferences about the psychological and physiological processes taking place during performance, i.e., to report on certain specified "mental events" (Humphrey, 1951). Methodologically, directed reports differ little from introspection. The latter is, in fact, a procedure of directed reporting, the only difference being that classical introspection was restricted in its contents to closely specified mental phenomena.

RETROSPECTION

Use of the method of retrospection requires the subject totally or partially to complete a task, and then to describe the strategies used. A description of the problem solving process obtained by this method would be based on the actions and thoughts the subject can remember to have occurred during problem solving. Ghiselin (1952) compiled a number of retrospective reports by musicians, writers, and other artists about their creative processes. Hadamard (1945) and Wertheimer (1959) obtained retrospective accounts of scientists' and mathematicians' problem solving. The data generated by this method are determined by the subject's retrospective perception of reactions and behaviors during task performance.

The research literature contains little evidence to recommend this method. Katona (1940) observed that subjects, even after solving a series of similar problems, were unable to state how they had proceeded. The same was found by Hendrix (1947), Szekeley (1950), and Ghiselin (1952). Studies frequently cited in support of the method of retrospection (e.g., Saugstad, 1958; Stinessen, 1973, 1974; Wittrock, 1966) were found to require subjects not to recall how they had proceeded during problem solving, but to state the general principles, in other words a rule, leading to a solution of the given problem.

This use of the method of retrospection has much in common with introspection, as it relies on the subject's subjective interpretation of the process under investigation. Even when retrospection is used as by Katona (1940), Hendrix (1947), and others, the dangers of rationalization by the subject, while possibly less than in the case of introspection, are nonetheless important sources of error. Also, "Retrospective accounts leave much more opportunity for the subject to mix current knowledge with past knowledge, making reliable inference from the protocol difficult" (Newell & Simon, 1972, p. 184). Neither method includes specific directions for the analysis of data derived by its use. To leave the identification of evidence for the occurrence of strategies to the subject's own judgment, as in both introspection and retrospection, makes both methods highly subjective.

PROTOCOL ANALYSIS

The "thinking aloud" technique, frequently referred to as "protocol analysis," was used by Binet (1903), Claparède (1934), Duncker (1945), Bloom and Broder (1950), and many early investigators. It gained popularity in problem solving studies during the 1960s (Miller, Galanter, & Pribram, 1960), and was refined particularly by De Groot (1965) in his studies of chess playing. Use of the method in information processing research (Dörner, 1973; Greeno, 1976; Krutetskii, 1976; Lüer, 1973; Newell & Simon, 1972; Paige & Simon, 1966; Simon, 1976), has led to its utilization in many related areas of psychological research, for instance decision making (Payne, 1975), ability test performance (Merz, 1969), various studies of concept formation (Dominowski, 1974; Huesmann & Cheng; 1973; Kotovsky & Simon, 1973), and in clinical psychology (Kleinmuntz,

1968). The areas of application of the "thinking aloud" method appear to be increasing still, and include areas of more applied psychological research, e.g., industrial process control (Bainbridge, 1974; Bainbridge, Beishon, Hemming, & Splaine, 1974), trouble shooting (Rasmussen & Jensen, 1974), and computer programming (Brooks, 1975).

Introspection and retrospection require the subject to analyze the composition of thought processes, i.e., a breakdown into sensations, images, and feelings; "thinking aloud" requires no more than that the subjects during their problem solving activity provide an account of what they are doing, i.e., say out aloud everything that comes into their minds while they are working on the task. The subjects thus report problem solving behaviors, rather than mental states. The subjects are encouraged to state what they are doing, what is being searched for, plans and hypotheses, and which aspects or relations of the task catch their attention. The subjects are not permitted to theorize about their own behavior. The following quotations characterize the method:

> . . . only to report the information and intentions that are within his current sphere of conscious awareness. All theorizing about the causes and consequences of the subject's knowledge state is carried out by the experimenters, not by the subject. (Newell & Simon, 1972, p. 184)

> . . . while the introspector makes himself—as—thinking the object of his attention, the subject who is thinking aloud remains immediately directed to the problem, so to speak allowing his activity to become verbal. (Duncker, 1945, p. 2)

Training is commonly given to subjects before the study begins so that during problem solving they can "think aloud" in an ongoing manner and without time delay. Research studies tend to suggest that interference to the problem solving process due to the "thinking aloud" method might be reduced and minimized by giving subjects sufficient practice, and by ensuring that the experimenter does not say more than absolutely necessary. The experimenter must not direct the subject's approach, ask leading questions, reinforce, etc., while subjects are "thinking aloud." It is, of course, essential that a standard procedure be applied from subject to subject and for all tasks.

The data are contained in a protocol, nowadays a verbatim transcript of a tape recording of each subject's verbalizations of his problem solving behaviors. Inferences concerning possible processes are made on the basis of the protocols by the investigator at a later stage. As in the method of introspection and unlike the method of retrospection, there is no time lapse in the "thinking aloud" method between the occurrence of the problem solving behavior and the reporting.

In a comparative study of introspective and "thinking aloud" protocols, Benjafield (1969) found the two conditions to differ. He observed that the "thinking aloud" protocols were more complete and contained more information than the introspective protocols. More important, the "thinking aloud" protocols were found to "differ from introspective protocols by being more present-oriented, having a more elliptical form, and containing more indefinite referents" (p. 83). Benjafield argues that "thinking aloud" constitutes an externalization of "inner speech" (Luria, 1961; Vygotsky, 1962).

On the basis of this model "thinking aloud" might be regarded as a quite natural activity, which constitutes no more than the vocalization of the already present inner speech, i.e., language covertly utilized by individuals to plan and organize their thinking. If one assumes, however, that cognitive processes do not occur as "inner language," "thinking aloud" procedures would involve the additional task of translation of such processes into words.

Considerable controversy has surrounded all process tracing methods, largely as a result of the behaviorists' generalized criticism of introspective methods.

Major arguments against the generation of data on the basis of verbalization relate to questions of objectivity, validity, reliability, completeness, and distortion.

A number of critics of the method have viewed "thinking aloud" as a form of nonretrospective introspection, and have attacked it on the same grounds as classical introspection.

Claparède (1934) strongly advocated "thinking aloud" but noted some of the limitations of the method by suggesting that thinking may tend to inhibit speech, that thinking may be so rapid and unorganized that speech may not be able to keep up with it or reflect it precisely, and that subjects may remain silent just when the experimenter would most like to know what is going on.

Duncker (1945), although a strong proponent of the method, warns that "a protocol is relatively reliable only for what it positively contains, but not for what it omits" (p. 11).

It must be accepted, of course, that the analysis of "thinking aloud" protocols does not provide a complete description of the problem solving process. It is, however, a method which permits the externalization of certain covert processes, and thereby provides the investigator with an initial tool. Although data derived from "thinking aloud" protocols might be used to show that certain strategies are contingent on one another, processing of a parallel nature cannot be investigated on the basis of such protocols alone. A combination of protocol analysis and experimental procedures would be required for this. As suggested by Miller, Galanter, and Pribram (1960), the important aspect of this difficulty lies not so much in the collection of the data on the basis of "thinking aloud" protocols, but in careful interpretation of the data.

More serious is the danger that the subject might proceed to solve a problem differently when asked to "think aloud" than he or she would when solving it silently (Claparède, 1934; Kilpatrick, 1967; Neisser, 1963).

RESEARCH

The research literature does not appear to contain reports of studies which were specifically designed to investigate differences in the structure of the problem solving process as reflected by subjects' plans, strategies, and stages on the way to solution, or the structure of solutions associated with the instruction to "think aloud."

In general the literature tends to deny the existence of major negative effects. In fact, there is some support for the view that "thinking aloud" might improve problem solving performance. Hafner (1957) gave individual performance tests to two matched groups of children. He reported that the "thinking aloud" group made significantly fewer moves to achieve solutions than the nonverbalizing group. This study also reports a tendency for the "thinking aloud" group to take less time and to obtain a slightly higher proportion of correct solutions. However, differences in the latter two variables failed to reach significance. Marks (1951) found that "thinking aloud" facilitated problem solving performance. He reports a correlation of .83 between performance and "thinking aloud." Similar supportive evidence was presented by Byers and Davidson (1967), Davis (1968), and Benjafield (1969).

A study which has frequently been cited erroneously in support of the assumption that "thinking aloud" enhances problem solving performance, was reported by Gagné and Smith (1962). In this study four groups of adolescents were presented with the Tower of Hanoi problem. Two of the groups were required to "think aloud" during their attempts to solve the problem. Gagné and Smith (1962) observed that "requiring subjects to verbalize during practice has the effect of making them think of new reasons for their moves, and thus facilitates both the discovery of general principles and their employment in successive problems" (p. 18).

These investigators found "thinking aloud" to be linked with significantly superior performance on the basis of shorter solution times, fewer moves required, and greater success in formulating a solution principle at the end of the task. However, as the above quotation indicates, in this study the requirement to think aloud was confounded with the requirement to justify each step. The influence of "thinking aloud" itself on performance can therefore not be assessed on the basis of Gagné and Smith's (1962) study.

A negative influence of "thinking aloud" has been reported by Brunk, Collister, Swift, and Stayton (1958), who found that "thinking aloud" on one of two concept formation tasks had the effect of lowering the correlation between the two tasks. The report of these authors contains insufficient detail to identify whether "thinking aloud" provided assistance or an impediment.

There is considerable research evidence, however, from studies in which outcomes of problem solving activity were compared under similar circumstances with and without the instruction to "think aloud," to suggest that the additional task of "thinking aloud" does not greatly affect problem solving. Roth (1966) reported no differences in solution time, the number of correct solutions, and the dominant mode of imagery (identified on the basis of a questionnaire) in reasoning tasks between subjects obliged to "think aloud" and those not required to do so. Dansereau and Gregg (1966) found that multi-digit multiplication problems were solved equally fast "thinking aloud" as silently. They suggested that "verbalization adds external memory aids" (p. 78), but came to the conclusion that in their study the positive and negative effects of "thinking aloud" balanced each other, as the gains in memory compensated for losses in processing speed.

RECENT FINDINGS

Newell and Simon (1972) compared the number and structure of solutions to tasks, requiring the creation of proofs in logic, produced by 10 subjects who had been instructed to "think aloud," with solutions to the same tasks obtained by different investigators at Yale University for 64 subjects under conditions without verbalizations. Detailed analyses and careful comparisons of the structures of the solutions failed to show reliable differences between the two groups. Although the small number of subjects in the "thinking aloud" condition did not permit a reliable comparison in terms of gross measures of performance outcome, the data did not suggest the presence of such differences.

No differences were found between subjects in the "thinking aloud" group and those in a similar nonverbalizing group in a comparison of performances in a concept formation task (Dominowski, 1974). Weisberg and Suls (1973) found no difference in the proportion solving Duncker's (1945) candle problem between a "think aloud" group and a similar control group.

More than any other utilization of the method, Newell and Simon's (1972) investigation of problem solving, which was based on data generated by "thinking aloud" protocols, regained scientific respectability for protocol analysis. At the same time, it led to a re-opening of discussions on the utility of the method for scientific research.

Two major papers reviewing the use of verbal protocols as a research methodology published in recent years were those of Nisbett and Wilson (1977) and Ericsson and Simon (1980).

Nisbett and Wilson (1977) emphasize dangers inherent in verbal reports, because of the possibility of "Telling More Than We Can Know." Much of the paper concerns issues relating to classical introspection rather than to mere "thinking aloud" during the problem solving. The authors suggest that:

> when people attempt to report on their cognitive processes, that is, on the processes mediating the effects of a stimulus on a response, they do not do so on the basis of any true introspection. Instead, their reports are based on a priori, implicit causal theories, or judgments about the extent to which a particular stimulus is a plausible cause of a given response. This suggests that though people may not be able to observe directly their cognitive processes, they will sometimes be able to report accurately about them. Accurate reports will occur when influential stimuli are salient and are plausible causes of the responses they produce, and will not occur when stimuli are not salient or are not plausible causes. (p. 231)

The above cited quotation clearly indicates the subject of contention to be the inference of cognitive processes in introspection. The same is true for the Evans and Wason (1976), Evans (1976) versus Quinton and Fellows (1975) argument. In the studies under discussion subjects were required to find reasons for their solutions or to justify the correctness of alternatives presented to them. The "thinking aloud" procedure per se, though it might well be applied in combination with introspection (e.g., Gagné & Smith, 1962; Davis, 1968), is not designed to elicit explanations or justifications of overt behavior, but rather to provide a record of the individual's problem solving behaviors. "Thinking aloud" "is therefore closely related to the observational techniques used in ethology, where a blow-by-blow record of the behavior of an animal or group of animals is used as the basic form of data" (Byrne, 1977, p. 289).

Nisbett and Wilson (1977) found that experimental subjects were generally unaware of perceptual and affective processes which may have led to their judgments and changes in attitude. However, when asked to describe certain psychological processes, they mentioned processes which they believed might or should have occurred, rather than behaviors they had perceived to have actually occurred. A large number of the studies cited by Nisbett and Wilson in support of their criticisms involved retrospective reports.

Rationalization and editing on the part of the subject, though less common than during introspection and retrospection, constitute a danger during "thinking aloud." Carefully designed instructions to ensure that subjects verbalize continuously rather than retrospectively, and verbalize behaviors rather than interpretations of their actions, can be expected to reduce these dangers. Because "thinking aloud" is an ongoing process during problem solving, it might be assumed that in most cases the time required for rationalization may not be available to the subject. The latter point has implications for the selection of subjects in studies using "thinking aloud" methodology. This matter will be discussed later in this chapter.

THE UTILITY OF "THINKING ALOUD"

The utility of "thinking aloud" as a method and its distinction from classical introspection, was stressed by Duncker (1945), Bakan (1954), Burt (1962, 1968), McKellar (1962), Newell and Simon (1972), Wason and Johnson-Laird (1972), Radford (1974), Byrne (1977), and particularly by Krutetskii (1976). Influenced possibly by Newell et al.'s (1958) emphatic statement that "thinking aloud is just as truly behavior as is circling a correct answer on a paper-and-pencil test" (p. 156), these authors provide strong support for the acceptance of "thinking aloud" protocols as a source of scientific data, and for the use of the method in studies concerned with the processes of human problem solving.

At the same time all the above mentioned authors and others reiterate Duncker's (1945) early warning that problem solving protocols do not provide a means of assessing the complete problem solving process.

Stephenson (1968) defended the method by providing opponents of self report techniques with the following example:

> The psychologist, observing a man reading a book, cannot tell by nonsubjective methods what the reader has on his mind as he reads. Observation of his eye movements, his absorption in this or that within the pages of the book, will never tell us whether he is counting the words, or day dreaming, or reading with one set of feelings and identifications or another. (p. 500)

Common sense would suggest that the psychologist should question the man. The reply might not contain a completely adequate description of the total situation, but it is likely to provide more information than is otherwise available. The same is true for the design of a study of problem solving processes. The "thinking aloud" method can be expected to provide access to some information which is not otherwise obtainable at present. In addition to this, a number of safeguards might be introduced in an endeavor to make the protocols as valid, as reliable, and as comprehensive as possible.

The "thinking aloud" technique does not require additional memory capacity and minimizes the danger that subjects might confuse past and present behaviors or stages during problem solving. This means that the method is applicable to long as well as to short tasks, and that highly complex problems can be analyzed. The findings of the research literature lead to the conclusion that there is sufficient evidence to justify the assumption that the additional requirement of continuous verbalization imposed by the "thinking aloud" methodology is unlikely to provide a negative influence on problem solving, no matter whether the "thinking aloud" process per se is interpreted as merely the vocalization of "inner speech" (Benjafield, 1969; Luria, 1961; Vygotsky, 1962) or as the translation of a nonverbal process into speech (Huttenlocher, 1976; Klinger, 1971; Perfetti, 1976). Johnson (1964) noted that some subjects were more fluent in their "thinking aloud" than others. He interpreted these differences by suggesting that some individuals, perhaps highly verbal persons, would "think aloud" automatically, while others would have to make a conscious effort to transform thought into verbalization. Research on this latter theoretical problem is of importance, but the present discussion has to be restricted to the products of the "thinking aloud" methodology, and thus excludes attempts to explain the process itself.

Criticisms of verbal report methods were probably best met in a more recent thorough paper by Ericsson and Simon (1980). On the basis of a broad review of the literature, these authors presented strong arguments for the use of "thinking aloud" protocols in cognitive research. Supporting some of Nisbett and Wilson's (1977) arguments in relation to introspection and retrospection, Ericsson and Simon (1980) suggest that the validity and the reliability of "thinking aloud" protocols may depend on the nature of both the task and the reporting itself. They argue that "thinking aloud" is more valid and reliable than introspection and retrospection because the information it yields is concurrent with the operation of the processes being described and that, at each stage of the problem solving process, the protocols draw on the contents of short-term memory only. This view neither denies nor contradicts the two generally agreed on major limitations of verbal protocols: one, that they include only those events and operations of which the subject is aware at the time, and two, that they are sensitive only to sequential operations, and do not permit any more than vague inferences concerning parallel processes which might be taking place.

Neisser (1963) postulated the requirement of a higher degree of attention and an increased organization of thought during problem solving to stem from "thinking aloud" procedures. If this were so, "thinking aloud" may well have a facilitating effect on the solving of a task. Reorganization of ideas and strategies is to be expected to occur frequently during problem solving activity. The fact that some of it may occur because the subject is expected to verbalize, should not be regarded as a contaminating factor in a study in which all subjects are given uniform training and instructions to verbalize. The degree to which "thinking aloud" procedures may result in an increase of problem solving efficiency, and the adequacy of the verbalizations as a data source for a description of the complete problem solving process, were outside the framework of the present study.

It is recognized, however, that the use of the "thinking aloud" protocol as a source of data has a number of implications. The information obtained by this method differs from materials typically obtained in psychological research. However, the more objective methods, especially as used in experimental studies, limit research to output behaviors.

An obvious source of reservations concerning self report methods of any kind is provided by findings from research relating to human perception and selective memory. Interference effects can operate retroactively and proactively. This means that information may be lost as a result of confusion originating from either preceding or succeeding operations.

Another important memory related loss of awareness of operations can be explained in relation to what has been described as the Zeigarnik effect (Zeigarnik & Lewin, 1927). This effect describes the tendency of persons to forget events relating to the achievement of goals and subgoals once they have been accomplished.

During problem solving, the investigator might observe the subject to be struggling with certain aspects of the task. Questioning after the problem has been solved might show the subject to have forgotten all about his or her efforts. This forgetting may, in fact, not be "covering up." The memory of laborious effort in pursuit of the solution may have become masked completely by the accomplishment of the goal. The Zeigarnik effect is understood to operate as a clearance mechanism for information traces which are no longer relevant.

Distortion may occur. Although the "thinking aloud" method can be expected to result in less bias than, for example, retrospection (since forgetting and distortion can be expected to increase over time), the information obtained from "thinking aloud" protocols is obviously not free from bias. People's memories operate in relation to previous experiences, beliefs, and assumptions. If reasoning is essentially an equilibrium seeking process, subjects might try to make sense of a given incident or behavior by reporting their interpretation rather than what they actually observe. The work of Gibson (1969), Vernon (1970, 1971), and others has shown clearly that the products of an individual's perceptions are influenced by the individual's frame of reference, which in turn is affected not only by variables in the immediate situation, but by past experience, attitudes, values, etc. In Herbart's (Klein, 1970) terms, individuals "apperceive" events in relation to their accumulated experience. Or, as expressed by Piaget (1953), they "assimilate" what they perceive to their existing cognitive schemata, and where this is not possible, "accommodation," i.e., an alteration of the conceptual framework, may take place.

The evidence for occurrences of the above described processes underlines the need for the investigator who is considering the use of self report data to determine to what extent the subject's report is related to "real" events. Dulany (1968), in an ingeniously designed study of verbal conditioning, combined self report with experimental evidence, thus providing a test of the reality of the self report data on the basis of their systematic interrelation with observed behavioral phenomena. There are many instances in which the investigator will not be in a position to make a Dulany type judgment. However, by choosing variables, the operation of which can be determined and observed, i.e., behavioral variables, the probability of misinterpretation as a result of self report is reduced. Further, it is important that the investigator ensures that the subject's "thinking aloud" is continuous, that as little use as possible is made of retrospections, and leading questions are avoided so as not to suggest processes or interpretations to the subject.

There are a number of fairly obvious ways in which "thinking aloud" might be encouraged and facilitated. Naturally, it will help if the subject can be put at ease, which is aided by being seated comfortably in a reasonably congenial environment, by the provision of some understanding of the purpose of the study, and by allowing each subject adequate time for problem solving activity. The results of pilot sessions which were conducted prior to the present study to explore certain variables of the "thinking aloud" methodology had shown that the success of the methodology, measured in terms of the completeness of the protocols, depended on the amounts of time available, as well as on the amounts of prompting (i.e., encouraging the subject to continue), which again takes time.

Another set of reservations concerning the adequacy of data derived from "thinking aloud" may relate to mechanisms originating from the social situation in which the data are collected, e.g., will the problem solver produce "socially acceptable" responses?

The total thrust of the psychological literature is to suggest that the individual who is motivated by a strong need for approval is quite different from the person who is unafraid to be judged and does not need to tailor his self presentation to the presumed wishes of his audience. (Davis, 1969, pp. 155–156)

In the present study the "thinking aloud" data were obtained by cassette recording each subject's activity in the presence of an investigator. To some degree this makes "thinking aloud" into a social situation, i.e., the investigator's presence can be expected to influence the products of the "thinking aloud" activity. If the method is to be applied with success, it is important therefore that the interpersonal climate of the problem solving situation enables the problem solver to indicate his or her perceived reactions truthfully, i.e., to indicate concerns, frustrations, criticisms, etc., in addition to behavior or strategy descriptions. When expressions of displeasure, doubt, ignorance, or inadequacy are understood to be not only acceptable, but encouraged and valued by the investigator, it can be expected that the subjects are less likely to feel that they must invent behaviors, which may not have occurred, or pretend to be confident about a way to proceed to solution of a task, when perhaps only vague ideas presented themselves.

The above suggested precautions are not designed to suggest that, as is sometimes suggested, if subjects can be highly motivated to cooperate, this alone will increase the accuracy of their self report. Too much eagerness to please may lead the subject to attempt to satisfy what he or she perceives to be the investigator's interest. Weiss (1968), for example, in a study in the area of applied social research, found that the tendency to give socially acceptable answers increases when interviewers, in their own judgment, had better rapport with subjects.

Although a number of methodological points relating to the use of "thinking aloud" protocols have been discussed in the literature, it is clear that there are still many issues on which further research is required. In the meantime, the use of the method in the present exploratory study must be regarded as a heuristic which is expected to provide a basis for the description of initially covert processes which might subsequently be tested.

"Thinking aloud" protocols are most unlikely to ever correspond exactly to or include all cognitive activity taking place during the problem solving process. It would seem equally unlikely, however, that an analysis of such protocols would fail to provide some new insights into the processes involved. In this study it is assumed that the "thinking aloud" verbalizations of subjects correspond closely to at least some of the usually covert problem solving behaviors. An attempt is made to identify categories of verbalization, reflecting homogeneous types of behaviors such as intentions, plans, difficulties, repetitions, etc., and phases or

stages during the problem solving process, by comparing their occurrences, sequences, and interactions across a number of different tasks
and for different individuals.

Previous investigators appear to have given little consideration to the
suitability of subjects. The absolute requirement of high motivation on the
part of the cooperating subjects has been stressed previously. In addition
to this Huttenlocher (1976) warns: "A person may be able to represent
certain information in thought and to solve problems involving that information, without necessarily being able to formulate messages that could
convey that information to others" (p. 267).

Even in very early studies it was observed that subjects frequently had
difficulty in expressing their thoughts verbally during problem solving
(Durkin, 1937; Ruger, 1910). Marked differences between subjects in the
spontaneity and completeness of "thinking aloud" products were also
noted by Claparède (1934) and De Groot (1965). Johnson (1964) observed
individual differences in the fluency with which "thinking aloud" occurred. Pretesting of subjects will facilitate the selection of individuals
with high verbal skills, if these are regarded as necessary. However, a
review of the literature would suggest that carefully planned and imple-
mented training of subjects may be a more essential requirement than high
verbal skills. A provision for prompting to verbalize, to prevent periods of
prolonged silence, would have to be incorporated.

The choice of task may influence the adequacy of the procedure. It was
noted previously that the "thinking aloud" methodology does not restrict
the length or complexity of the task. On the other hand, Thomas (1971,
1974) suggested that performance tasks might not provide adequate
"thinking aloud" protocols.

In most early studies the problems and puzzles used required the
manipulation of objects. Durkin (1937) reports that many of his subjects
were of the opinion that thinking and manipulation, though both aimed at
the solution of the problem, were distinctly separate, alternative activities. It was suggested that manipulation must be regarded as basically
a perceptual motor activity which does not lend itself to verbalization.
Therefore to force subjects to form an internal representation of the task,
which might permit transformation and lead to more adequate verbalization of the problem solving activity, a number of experimenters designed
tasks in which manipulation was constrained to some degree (Durkin,
1937) or completely eliminated (Benjafield, 1971).

On the basis of the literature to date the virtues of different tasks in
studies utilizing "thinking aloud" cannot be assessed. As has been noted
previously, research concerned with problem solving and intelligence has
been noncumulative. The diversity of tasks used has been so great that it
is difficult to compare these studies. An additional difficulty, which pre-

vents the drawing of general conclusions, results from the fact that few studies provide details of the precise instructions given to subjects concerning the "thinking aloud" required of them. A reason for this may have been, as suggested by De Groot (1966), that many investigators have "had a bad conscience about using introspective data, and as a result used them poorly . . . Even Duncker apparently preferred not to be too explicit about his use of introspective data" (p. 21).

Among the methods applied in previous research studies of human problem solving, the "thinking aloud" procedure appeared to be the most promising method for the investigation of the problem solving process in the present study. The following paragraphs provide a summary of the advantages of the method which determined its selection for the present study as the most suitable choice of methodology for the identification of strategies during problem solving.

"Thinking aloud" protocols permit the derivation of data representing actual problem solving behaviors and not interpretations or theorizations about such behaviors. Protocol analysis does not rely on subjective inference, i.e., the a priori specification of the relevant problem solving behaviors or the sequences in which they occur. It therefore allows for an empirical investigation of the process.

The data are closely related to the task. The delay between the occurrence of the problem solving behaviors and their being reported is minimal. The dangers of editing and rationalization, as well as those of confusing memory and ongoing activity or behavior, are therefore considerably reduced. The method is not restricted to tasks of short duration. Long and highly complex tasks can be used because subjects are not forced to rely on memory as in the method of retrospection.

Subjects do not need to infer processes. The protocols are analyzed by the researcher for evidence of consistent patterns of problem solving strategies.

The major advantages of the "thinking aloud" method, however, are that it is relatively easy to learn and that it can be highly productive. As long as the subjects are motivated to cooperate, and if they understand what is required of them—not only to solve the problem but to verbalize what is in their minds while doing so—and as long as the data obtained by application of the method are interpreted within a framework which accepts the limitations of the method, "thinking aloud" protocols can provide access to thought processes. A particular virtue of the procedure is that details of temporal sequence and even pauses are reflected: "Protocols provide us with a very valuable window onto our thought processes. Though the scope of that window is not infinite, it is wider than most of the other windows available" (Hayes & Flower, 1981, p. 18).

As was suggested by Miller et al. (1960), the problem of the "thinking aloud" method lies not so much in the collection of the data, but in knowing what to do with them. The analysis of the products of "thinking aloud" requires objectivity on the part of the researcher. This can be attained by the provision of two or more investigators to analyze the protocols independently, and by the requirement of high inter-analyst reliability. Objective data analysis is possible, according to Buswell (1956) and Newell and Simon (1972), if behavior categories and processes are determined from the data rather than imposed on the data.

A framework for the classification of the data obtained from "thinking aloud" protocols and details of its development are presented in the next chapter.

7

The Development of a Classification System of Problem Solving Strategies

This chapter contains the description of a set of concepts that might serve as a taxonomy for the coding of frequently used problem solving strategies, and in this way contribute towards a framework within which an initial attempt to investigate the dynamics of the problem solving process itself might be made.

The development of a scheme for the analysis of problem solving behaviors is described from its origin as a set of vaguely defined stages derived from the literature to its current form as a modest taxonomy, which allows the representation and quantification of aspects of the problem solving process on the basis of recorded sequences of verbally reported problem solving behaviors.

OBSERVER BIAS

The design of any study aimed to analyze behavior is based on both conscious and inadvertent decisions, which strongly influence what is observed. What is observed depends on the position of the observer. Standing at the foot of a mountain or at the side of a lake allows for the observation of details as regards shape, color, vegetation, etc. From a little distance these phenomena can be observed in relation to one another and as part of the same landscape. To the passenger in an airplane the same mountain and lake form part of a much more comprehensive pattern of landscape organization, but detail is masked. Whichever position is chosen by the observer will influence what is explored and what is noticed.

In the same manner manifestations of human behaviors can be expected to differ according to the position which is chosen for observation. The aim may be to observe single acts, or to investigate possible links between a number of behaviors, or even to stand back further in an attempt to search for more comprehensive patterns into which such behaviors might be organized. No matter how carefully designed, the chosen scheme for both data collection and data analysis will influence not only what the investigator observes, but will to some degree determine the regularities and laws which might be identified.

An attempt will be made to explain the rationale for the final taxonomy, and to report the major decisions made during its construction and evolution.

At the outset, two points must be stressed. First, the taxonomy developed and utilized in the present study is just one of many which could have been developed, depending on the position and situation of the observer of the phenomena under discussion. Second, it is recognized that a major shortcoming of the study stems from the method of data collection decided upon. This shortcoming results from the well known, and previously stressed fact that "a protocol is relatively reliable only for what it positively contains, but not for what it omits" (Duncker, 1945, p. 11). The "thinking aloud" methodology, its limits and its advantages were discussed in the previous chapter. The concern of the present chapter is not with the method of data collection, but rather with the development of a framework for the classification of problem solving behaviors.

HISTORICAL STAGES

The research literature served as a first source of information concerning such behaviors. While the bulk of previous studies have been concerned with outcomes of problem solving behaviors, the dynamics of the process itself have been of interest to some researchers at least since Helmholtz (1894). Although this research has been noncumulative, the studies could be summarized vaguely in one or the other of the following three types: (a) studies concerned with mental content, i.e., "the conscious content of experiential data, which is in the mind at any given time" (Chaplin, 1968, p. 290); (b) research concerned with task analysis and attempts to provide models for the solution process, usually in the form of a computer program, and (c) attempts to describe or to characterize problem solving behaviors or processes per se.

Studies of the latter type were expected to provide a pool of the most relevant input data in the initial stage of the development of a taxonomy of problem solving behaviors. A survey of these studies showed that a variety of approaches have been used in attempts to identify more or less generalizable stages or phases during the problem solving process. All of the stages or phases under investigation appear to be based on, or somehow to incorporate the work of Wallas (1926), which in turn was probably based on Helmholtz's (1894) proposed stages of:

1. previous investigation of the problem in all directions;
2. not consciously thinking of the problem;
3. appearance of the "happy idea."

Basing his work on introspections of famous "creators," Wallas (1926) proposed the following four-stage model:

1. *Preparation*—subject becomes involved with the problem and searches for and accumulates relevant information.
2. *Incubation*—a time during which there is no conscious effort to deal with the problem, but although the subject is not aware of it, work on the problem continues.
3. *Illumination*—which follows if incubation is successful.
4. *Verification*—some elaboration of reality testing of the solution.

Ghiselin (1952), describing creative processes reported by 39 world-famous personalities, gives some support to the same stages, without, however, making any generalizations concerning the order in which these stages occur.

It is of interest to note that the above stages, which were empirically but not experimentally based (Wallas, 1926), have been supported by a number of investigators since then and were in the 1970s still considered to be of major importance by some investigators and textbook writers (e.g., Aiken, 1973; Anderson, 1975; Skemp, 1971). Table 7.1 presents typical examples of research supporting a generalized stage concept as a relatively invariant sequence of events during human problem solving.

A series of studies in which an attempt was made to identify Wallas' stages experimentally (Patrick, 1937, 1938, 1941) supported the relevance of stages, but found their sequence to vary. The latter finding was supported by Eidhoven and Vinacke (1952) who concluded that ". . . the stages are not stages at all, but processes which occur during creation. They blend together and go along concurrently" (p. 168).

A similar view is expressed by Johnson (1972): "Problem-solving processes, like other psychological processes are functionally interdependent in that the conclusion of one initiates the next; but the first does not always cease when the second commences" (p. 146).

TABLE 7.1
Examples of Research Concerned With Generalized Sequential
Stages of Problem-Solving

HELMHOLTZ (1894)
1. Investigation of *P* in all directions
2. Not consciously thinking about P
3. Appearance of 'happy idea'

DEWEY (1910)
1. Felt difficulty
2. Location and definition
3. Possible solutions
4. Reasoning
5. Acceptance or rejection

WALLAS (1926)
1. Preparation
2. Incubation
3. Illumination
4. Verification

ROSSMAN (1931)
1. Observation of difficulty
2. Analysis of the need
3. Survey information
4. Proposed solutions
5. Birth of the new idea
6. Experimentation to test out promising
   solution; perfection by repeating
   some or all previous steps

YOUNG (1940)
1. Assembly of material
2. Assimilation of material
3. Incubation
4. Birth of the idea
5. Development to usefulness

POLYA (1945)
1. Production
2. Incubation
3. Illumination

HUTCHINSON (1949)
1. Preparation
2. Frustration
3. Insight
4. Verification

MAWARDI (1960)
1. Abstract thoughts   (A)
2. Instrumental thoughts   (I)
3. Metaphonic ideas   (M)
4. Orientation   (O)

OSBORN (1963)
1. Think up all aspects
2. Select sub problem
3. Gather data
4. Select relevant data
5. Think up possible help
6. Select attacks
7. Think up possible tests
8. Select soundest test
9. Imagine all possibilities
10. Decide final answer

SKEMP (1971)
1. Assimilation
2. Accommodation

NEWELL AND SIMON (1972)
1. Input translation
2. Internal representation
3. Method selection
4. Implement and monitor
5. Reformulate

JOHNSON (1972)
1. Seek information
2. Represent and transform
3. Organize and reorganize
4. Judgmental processes

ANDERSON (1975)
1. Preparation and production
2. Incubation and Eureka or AHA
   experience

STERNBERG (1980a)
1. Encoding
2. Inference
3. Mapping
4. Application
5. Justification (verification)
6. Response (communication)

Other criteria for the classification of problem solving processes have been used (e.g., Mawardi, 1960). Newell, Shaw, and Simon (1962) found it useful to distinguish two processing stages only; namely "solution generating processes", i.e., "searching for possible solutions"; and "verifying processes", i.e., "processes for determining whether a solution proposal is in fact a solution" (p. 72).

With a somewhat different aim, Osborn (1963) also distinguishes between "idea-creation" and "idea-evaluation." Concerned less with an explanation of the processes involved, than with the recommendation of brainstorming as a technique, Osborn's ten-stage model (1963) suggests an alternating of stages of creative thought (stages 1, 3, 5, 7, and 9) and stages of evaluative thought (stages 2, 4, 6, 8, and 10) as follows:

1. Think up all phases of the problem;
2. select the sub-problem to be attacked;
3. think up what data might help;
4. select the most likely sources of data;
5. dream up all possible ideas as keys to the problem;
6. select the ideas most likely to lead to a solution;
7. think up all possible ways to test;
8. select the soundest ways to test;
9. imagine all possible contingencies;
10. decide on the final answer (p. 207–208).

Osborn's work and that of others aiming to improve problem solving performance (e.g., Ashton, 1962; Guilford, 1967; Crutchfield & Covington, 1965; Davis, 1969; Myers & Torrance, 1964) owe a considerable debt to the work of Polya (1945, 1954, 1957), who provided teachers with a set of basic rules for the teaching of heuristic methods, particularly applicable to mathematical problem solving.

CONTENT VERSUS MECHANISMS

A distinction is sometimes made between the "content" of the problem solving process, in this book defined by the problem solving behaviors or strategies which individuals employ while working on a task, and the "mechanisms" by which these behaviors take place, i.e., originate, are maintained, and are transformed. In many discussions of the problem solving process, both content and mechanisms are subsumed under a single category, usually referred to as "process." Although process, content, and mechanisms are parts of a general phenomenon, there are good reasons for the use of different terms. In principle, because a large number of problem solving behaviors are within the subject's own experience, an individual can be expected to be able to report accurately about the content of a large proportion of the problem solving process. It is acknowledged, of course, that such variables as the experimental situation, memory constraints, motivational characteristics, and linguistic fluency may set limits to the adequacy of such reports. However, the mechanisms of the problem solving process, i.e., "all the processes by which sensory input is transformed, reduced, elaborated, stored, recovered and used" (Neisser, 1967, p. 4), are not typically available to self observation, but require inferences to be made. Different methods of self report and their utility and limitations were discussed in the previous chapter. Suffice it here to state that the present study is concerned with the behavioral content of the problem solving process rather than with neurological or biochemical mechanisms.

In their article in the *Annual Review of Psychology,* Posner and McLeod (1982) provide evidence for the continuing importance in the contemporary literature of research aimed at the identification of elementary cognitive operations, their coordination in a range of theoretical systems, and the search for links between them and neurological structures. Yet, at the moment there exists no agreed upon definition of what constitutes an "elementary" cognitive operation (Chase, 1978; Posner & McLeod, 1982).

A NEW TAXONOMY

The decision was made not to base the classification of the problem solving behaviors manifested in the protocols obtained in the present study on one of the already existing frameworks, but to attempt to devise a new taxonomy. A reason for this was the concern that an available framework might restrict the information which might be gained in the present study. It was felt that even though a new taxonomy would have to be crude at this stage, it could be expected to contribute new and fruitful insights.

Another reason for not utilizing one of the previously listed classification systems was that all of these systems tended to suggest a large number of high inference variables. "The term 'inference' refers to the process intervening between the objective behavior seen or heard, and the coding of this behavior on an observational instrument" (Rosenshine, 1971, p. 19). To be useful, a taxonomy of problem solving behaviors must lead to low inference measures of the processes involved. This criterion can be reached if the items contained in the taxonomy focus on specific, relatively objectively defined, observable behaviors. To meet these needs, the rationale was to proceed empirically and to derive a taxonomy from the protocols of the problem solvers' expressed thoughts and behaviors, rather than to force on to these empirical records a classification or framework derived from an untried theory or a set of higher inference variables suggested by a previous investigator.

A rough summary list of stages which could be defined under low inference conditions frequently recurring in the literature was prepared. A pilot study was conducted in which 10 adult subjects of superior measured intelligence attempted to solve eight different tasks using the "thinking aloud" technique. Cassette recordings of the complete "thinking aloud" protocols of each subject were transcribed verbatim. Attempts to apply the list of stages prepared from the literature to a number of protocols from the pilot study showed clearly that, despite their apparent general plausibility and despite any positive contributions that, for instance, Polya's and Osborn's stages might be found to make to the teaching of problem solving skills, most of the stages, phases, and heuristics as presented in the literature were of limited usefulness in attempts to characterize the problem solving behaviors of the subjects in the pilot study. Many of the categories of the summary list were unoccupied as it was impossible to judge whether the subjects exhibited behaviors even remotely resembling some of the items. For example, no subject appeared to have used "experimentation to test out the most promising solution by repeating some or all of the previous steps" (Rossman, 1931, step 6) or to have attempted "to think up all possible help" (Osborn, 1963, step 5). Many of the items obtained from the literature were not defined clearly enough for reliable coding.

To obtain a better impression of problem solving behaviors which were in fact used, the protocols obtained in the pilot study were analyzed a second time. This time behaviors suggestive of stages, heuristics, etc., were identified and noted on cards as they occurred. A list of 70 behavior items was prepared and arranged in a form that allowed a rough count to be taken of the number of times each behavior occurred.

The construction of this more comprehensive system was undertaken in keeping with the overall aim of the study to identify, from careful investigation of the problem solving protocols, the behaviors actually used by individuals during problem solving, and then to investigate the applicability of these behaviors across different subjects and tasks. In this way, the thorough investigation of the protocols themselves provided the basis for the identification of the actual problem solving behaviors, and their arrangement into a taxonomy of discrete behaviors. The items making up the taxonomy were not predetermined, but determined by the subjects' verbalizations. The observation of the expression of a particular behavior thus provided the proof for its existence.

Since a taxonomy has to display a certain amount of parsimony, it cannot include every observed behavior. The problem was to select those behaviors which could be expected to provide pay-off in subsequent analyses. Future pay-offs are difficult to estimate on the basis of an exploratory study. It was decided, therefore, to risk error in the direction of generosity rather than in parsimony, and to allow for pruning at a later stage.

The previously referred to list of 70 observed behaviors was scanned, therefore, for behaviors that appeared promising. Behaviors included in a modified list produced at this point were chosen on the following basis:

1. These behaviors occurred more frequently than others across subjects and tasks in the pilot study;
2. these behaviors could be identified relatively easily and reliably, and were therefore easy to code;
3. these behaviors appeared of logical interest to the investigator, both as a result of their similarity to phenomena described in the previous research literature and their apparent empirical relevance.

As was noted earlier, the decision to rely on "thinking aloud" protocols of problem solving behaviors restricts the taxonomy to those behaviors which were verbalized. Only what is observed can be analyzed. It is necessary to refrain from making judgments about phenomena which have not been externalized. Objective data analysis from "thinking aloud" protocols is possible, according to Newell and Simon (1972), if behavior categories and processes are determined from the data, rather than imposed on the data. The subject's expression of a particular behavior served as the criterion for the existence of that behavior.

HEURISTICS VERSUS COMPLEX PROCESSES

Careful inspection of the list of 50 items showed a small number of redundancies. More important, it was noted that items could quite easily be grouped logically. A considerable number of items described the reading of directions or the stimulus passage, i.e., input related behaviors. Others were strongly solution related. Some items related to emotional variables, some to critical and judgmental responses. Some behaviors were more idiosyncratic than others. It also became evident that from a behavior analytic point of view many items fell into one of two distinct categories; heuristics and descriptions of more complex processes resulting from associations and transformations of information.

The complex processes include processes which integrate what has been done; they also affect the orientation of the problem solving process. Frequently, they are steps of processes which are not necessarily clearly distinguished from prior or subsequent steps. In a sense these steps might be regarded as continuous, as woven throughout the total problem solving process. It was observed that subjects, as they approached each task and applied heuristics, to some extent also clarified the task for themselves. In the case of Task 1 [Binet], for example, most subjects recognized from the beginning that the task involved some mathematical operations, and that the solution would be the result of these mathematical manipulations.

The distinction between heuristics and complex processes is not only useful, but essential to an operational approach to the tracing of problem solving processes. The heuristics in the process of problem solving are the behaviors which the problem solver applies, i.e., the operations through which the individual tries out and establishes links between the given task and a solution. These behaviors might be regarded either as directly available in the individual's skills repertoire or as behaviors which could be suggested or taught to the individual. On the other hand the complex process is defined here as the relation between the individual's progress in his or her attempts towards a solution, which includes the sum of, and the interaction between, the heuristics and their effects, and the state of the process at different points. The occurrence of complex processes is unlikely to be under the control of the individual, and cannot be suggested or taught directly.

From an operational point of view these two types of processes might correspond to two consecutive but interrelated levels of abstraction. The heuristics domain is established on the basis of operations performed on the data base, i.e., the directions or the stimulus passage, and also covers the operations performed on the products of transformations. The complex process domain operates as a set of selective associations and tranformations resulting from judgments made by individuals in relation to their progress and the perceived reality state of the solution process.

These two types of distinct processes, both of which occurred in the problem solving protocols of all subjects in the pilot study, could be compared to the information processing and Gestalt approaches. Defined and programmable heuristics are part of the repertoire of the individual, who, after searching for the relevant ones, controls and operates the situation. On the other hand there are complex processes, which take place while the problem solver seems unaware, for the occurrence of which the individual has to be ready but seems unable to control directly.

Heuristics provide an excellent characterization of the problem solving activities investigated by information processing researchers. They display the structure of the responses to a variety of task demands. The goal of this research was to describe how the solver should proceed to solve the problem. The aim in the present study is not to identify simply what the solver must know or do to be successful, but to describe *how* problems are solved. Heuristics therefore describe only part of the process; they describe operations at certain points. Another set of essential components has to be related to a series of associations and transformations that compound and transform information in some way, thus making it available for further application of heuristics at a more advanced point. The problem solving process may be viewed as an interaction of heuristics and complex processes which are mutually interdependent, quite possibly each determining the pay-off of the other in terms of immediately contingent processes and in terms of reaching a meaningful solution.

THE ROOT MODEL

The finding that the problem solving behaviors obtained from the protocols could be grouped logically, and that within larger categories items were frequently dichotomous, prompted the consideration of a ROOT type model to facilitate the classification of the items obtained from the protocols as discrete and mostly dichotomous variables. The total taxonomy model is shown in Fig. 7.1.

The root model suggests in diagramatic form a structure or organization for major components of the problem solving process which were observed in the present empirical study. The model reflects a number of elements which act and interact in the process of problem solving.

It was mentioned previously for example that a particular behavior item would either be related to the problem input, i.e., the stimulus passage containing directions or the problem itself, or that it would not be related to information contained in the input. This accounted for the first branching of the root, into major branches labelled Directions/Stimulus Passage related, Solution related, Self related, Judgmental, Unrelated, and Memory related activity. The major numerical codes were used to describe each behavior contained in the model. The major branches were labelled 100, 200, . . . 600. Heuristic processes were represented as left subbranches and coded as 10s; more complex processes presupposing associations and transformations were represented as right subbranches and designated as 20s. Specific items within these subbranches were labelled as units.

The first root is coded 100, and represents stimulus oriented behaviors. This includes all operations which originate from the task as presented to and perceived by the problem solver. It is important to remember that, no matter in what form the task is presented, what determines the subject's

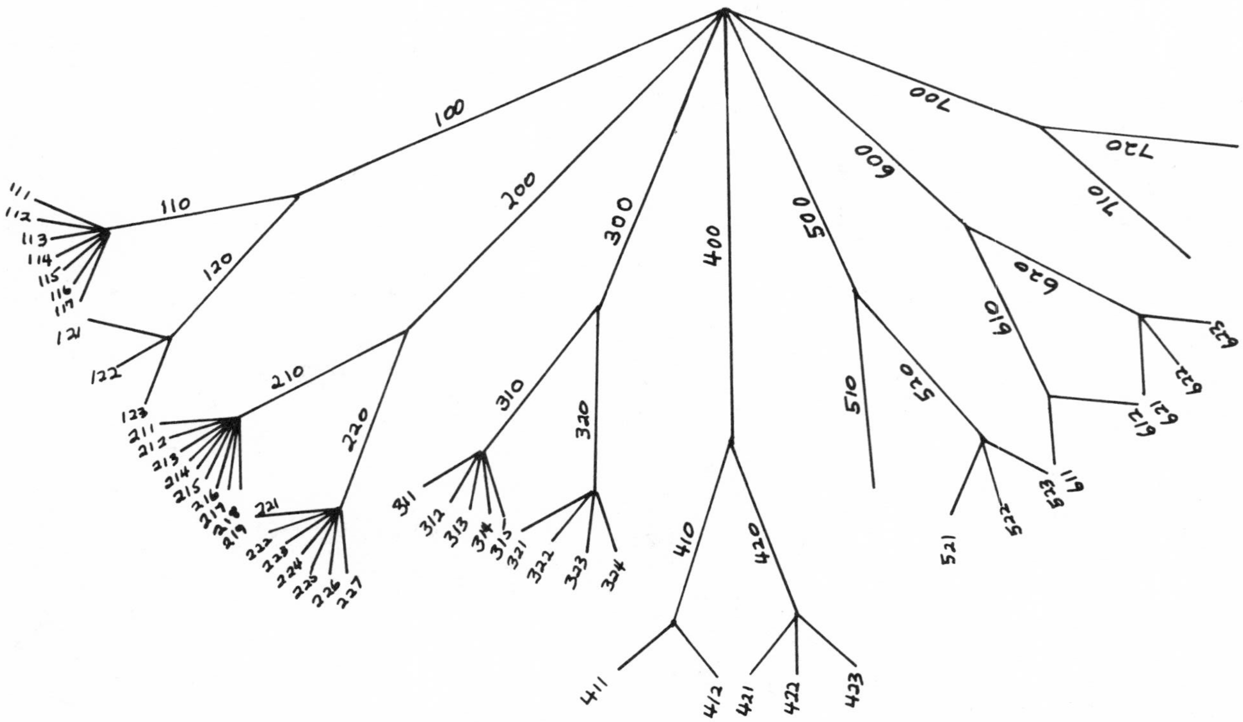

FIG. 7.1. The root model.

reactions to the task, and the stimulus passage oriented problem solving behaviors, will be the subject's own perception or representation of what has been presented.

The left subbranch of root 100 is labelled 110 and contains a number of Directions/Stimulus Passage related heuristics (e.g., First reading, i.e., 111; rereading, i.e., 112; summarizing or chunking of input information, i.e., 117). The first right subbranch of root 100 is coded 120 and contains specific complex processes like the recognition of problem requirements (code 121), or identification of boundaries or constraints contained in the problem directions (coded 122). Three-digit numbers serve as symbols for all codes.

Root 600, for example, represents memory processes. These include not only the problem solver's previous experiences and knowledge of the problem itself, but also previously learned problem solving strategies, conventions, and sets. Again, what is important in relation to memory determined operations is not what the individual may be expected to remember, but what he or she is able to, or chooses to, select from memory at a particular point during the problem solving process. The complete taxonomy is presented in summary form in Table 7.2, and in detail in Table B.1 in Appendix B.

PROTOCOL ANALYSIS

The taxonomy was applied to data collected in the pilot study and to new data in the following manner: The transcribed verbatim protocols were divided into a series of three-second interval units in sequential order of occurrence. Each three-second unit was then coded according to the taxonomy. The choice of the three-second interval as the basic unit was based on empirical evidence provided in the literature (Amidon & Flanders, 1967; Flanders, 1965; Rosenshine, 1971) which suggests that such a time interval may provide an optimal indication of behavior over time with regard to both reliability of judgment, and the detection of sudden changes of behavior. Three-second time intervals are easily determined. The identifiable beginning and end of these naturally occurring units provide a basis for reliable protocol analysis.

This use of the taxonomy allows for the investigation of the number and variety of problem solving behaviors by each individual and in each task, as well as across tasks, and for the measurement of the frequencies with which a given behavior occurs within and across problems. It also provides an indication of how certain behaviors are linked together over time. The system permits the separate recording of key processes and of phenomena whose positions may be relatively unimportant in the process sequence.

TABLE 7.2

Summary of the Taxonomy of Problem Solving Behaviors

	Response Category		Code	
D:	Directions/Instructions/Stimulus Passage - related activity		100	
	D_H	Survey of given information		110
	D_C	Identification of problem/or its parts from given information		120
S:	Solution - directed activity		200	
	S_H	Heuristics		210
	S_C	Reasoning		220
PERS:	Self-related activity/Reference to self		300	
	$PERS_H$	Idiosyncratic operations		310
	$PERS_C$	Emotional reactions		320
J:	Critical evaluation/judgment		400	
	J_H	Critical assessment/verification		410
	J_C	Judgment/evaluation		420
P:	Pause		500	
	P_H	Activity filled pause		510
	P_C	Silence		520
M:	Memory		600	
	M_H	Attempts to use memory		610
	M_C	"Insight"		620
C:	Changing the conditions of the problem		700	

As an illustration of the use of the taxonomy as a coding system, part of a sample protocol and its coding is given below. The vertical strokes indicate the three-second units.

111

Subject 201 (Task 2): "Without raising the pencilⅠ from the paper draw four
111   111   321
straight lines whichⅠ include all nine dotsⅠ —Oh I don't know about this oneⅠ
117   211
—four straight lines which include all dotsⅠ —now if I went fromⅠ top left to
215   215   215   411
bottomⅠ up to the top oneⅠ —top left— upⅠ there that's twoⅠ —no that doesn't
421   211   215
workⅠ —so I'll try top leftⅠ to bottom leftⅠ . . ."

Sequence of responses (codes):

111, 111, 111, 321, 117, 211, 215, 215, 215, 411, 421, 211, 215, . . .

The coding of the above passage can be interpreted as follows:

Subject 201, a second year teachers college student began, as instructed, with reading the problem aloud (coded 111) from the typed sheet containing the stimulus passage. He utilized the first three three-second intervals for this first reading. After a comment conveying personal feelings relating to the perceived difficulty of the task (coded 321), the main points of the stimulus passage are picked out (coded 117), and a first plan is tested (coded 211). This activity continues over the next three time units. This ongoing activity is coded 215. "There that's two" is a standing back to assess progress (coded 411) which is followed by a critical judgment of the adequacy of the attempted plan for solution (coded 421). Another plan is tried (coded 211) which extends to the next trial (coded 215).

The sequence of codes traces the process of problem solving. It shows at a glance which problem solving strategies were used by the subject, as well as the order and frequency with which they were used. Because a relatively small number of major codes are used to represent a variety of problem solving behaviors, the approaches of several subjects to the same task, and the approaches applied by one subject to several different tasks, can be compared.

OPERATIONAL DEFINITIONS

In the following section a detailed explanation of each item of the taxonomy is presented. Items which are self-explanatory such as "First reading" are listed without explanation.

The basic requirement for scientific research is a set of phenomena which have been operationally defined. Underwood (1957) asserts "An operational definition is one which specifies the meaning of the concept by denoting the measuring operations" (p. 51). and suggests that "a criterion of whether or not a so-called empirical concept is a scientific concept is whether or not it has been operationally defined" (p. 52).

Operational definitions do not go very far towards an explication of the important variables or functional relationships of the phenomena they define. A definition in operational terms is not a theory, nor is it scientific in itself, but it provides the essential basis for the measurements which make possible initially the identification of the phenomena for subsequent scientific investigation. Operations defining a particular phenomenon serve to differentiate it from other phenomena.

An attempt will be made to precede operational definitions by literary ones, i.e., dictionary type definitions. It is accepted that the operational definition alone must specify the phenomenon to be investigated. A literary definition, however, may help to provide the reader with a better introduction to the general nature of the phenomenon to be observed, and may thus provide a frame of reference for the operational definition.

All phenomena, i.e., problem solving behaviors, under consideration in the present study are subject responses. The use of different tasks might be interpreted as replications, i.e., validations of the research rather than as stimulus manipulations. The differentiation between phenomena must therefore rest on the response measures.[1]

As stated above, operational definitions must provide a basis for the establishment of reliable differences between all items of the taxonomy. The presence or non-occurrence of a certain behavior are two conditions resulting from differences in problem solving behavior.

The definitions provided here must of necessity be regarded as provisional, as the phenomena of concern have not previously been investigated scientifically. A preliminary objective, therefore, of a study like the present one, is to explore whether certain components of the problem solving process can be operationally defined, so that further work can be done to demonstrate the conditions under which these phenomena vary and ways in which they are interrelated.

The names for the categories, and the levels of their mutual exclusiveness are not completely satisfactory at this stage. They are, however, the best the investigator was able to formulate at present. Better labels for some of the items will have to be found. In the meantime the names of phenomena do not affect their definition and measurement.

Code 100:   Directions/Stimulus Passage Directed Activity

Responses and associations made by the problem solver in relation to information found within the directions, instructions, or stimulus passage. The subject concentrates on the specifications of the task in two ways:

---

1. "If the same stimulus manipulations are used, phenomena are differentiated by different response measures if, and only if, these response measures are poorly correlated. . . . Obviously, if these response measures correlate highly there is no basis for distinguishing two phenomena. But, since they do not correlate highly, scientific analysis is aided by insisting upon definition of independent phenomena" (Underwood, 1957, p. 78)

Code 110: Survey of Given Information

This code includes the accumulation of information which may lead to solution from the directions or instructions. This has been described as follows:

> The initial phase can be described as *exposure,* a period in which the environment is perceived. (Taylor, 1971, p. 194)

> The very first cognitive act, when a subject attends to a problem. (Goor, 1974, p. 113)

> Observation of a need or difficulty. (Rossman, 1931, p. 57).

> Intensive analysis of the problem (Dreistadt, 1969, p. 159).

Guilford (1967) referred to this activity as the "input stage," and presented a flow chart illustrating how at some points during the problem solving process one might return to it.

"Preparation" (Wallas, 1926; and others) basing their concept of "stages" on Helmholtz (1894) called this activity "preparation." It includes the gathering of data or information from the problem specifications: "Where the subject becomes involved with the problem and searches for and accumulates relevant information" (Wallas, 1926, p. 191).

111: *First reading of directions or instructions.*

112: *Rereading or repetition of instructions.* This can occur and reoccur at any stage during the problem solving process.

113: *Task segmentation or chunking.* That is, summarizing or picking out the main points. An activity understood in terms of G. A. Miller's contribution to information processing:

> By organizing the stimulus output simultaneously into several dimensions and successively into a sequence of chunks, we manage to break (or at least stretch) the informational bottle-neck . . . the process of recoding . . .deserves much more explicit attention than it has received . . . Recoding procedures are a constant concern to clinicians, social psychologists, linguists and anthropologists . . . I anticipate that we will find a very orderly set of relations describing what now seems an uncharted wilderness of individual differences. (Miller, 1956, pp. 95–96)

114: *Brief reference to the directions or the text of the stimulus passage.* This includes the scanning of the passage and references to it to check parts of the input.

115: *Questions to the examiner (clarification only). Trying to understand.*

116: *Attempts to absorb, rehearse, and memorize directions.*

117: *Analysis of input into major sections, rephrasing of text or instructions.*

Code 120: Identification of the Problem or Its Parts from Given Information

In addition to focusing on the information provided in the stimulus passage, the subject adds another dimension by defining the problem or talking about the purpose of parts of the directions or about the directions in relation to the problem.

The subject synthesizes information from the instructions or stimulus passage and locates crucial aspects of the task. Essentially, this stage involves the process of comprehending the problem, its givens and goals, and its rules for moving from givens to goals (Burack, 1950; Johnson, 1955).

It has been suggested that forming an appropriate initial conception of the problem is the most vital and difficult prerequisite for solving real world problems.

As described by Wallas (1926) this problem solving behavior is made up of systematic conscious analyses of the problem just prior to initial attempts to develop a hypothesis.

121: *Recognition that the problem exists.*

122: *Identification of boundaries and constraints.*

123: *Definition of the problem or parts thereof.*

Example: So she'd not want to marry the old man, but she's got no chance to pick a white pebble. (De Bono, 1967, p. 121)

Code 200: Solution Directed Activity

Problem solving behaviors which are aimed or intended to produce, or to approach the production of a solution to a given task are included in this code. Focus is not on the directions or stimulus passage but on the solution(s) to the task, i.e., "solution generating process . . . as distinct from processes for determining if a solution proposal is in fact a solution" (Newell, Shaw, & Simon, 1962, p. 72).

Code 210: Heuristics (Repertoire Operations)

Operations which can be taught, or applied upon a suggestion from others are coded 210.

211: *Generating plan or hypothesis.* The part of "preparation when thought is changing rapidly and the subject is perceiving new ideas" (Wallas, 1926, p. 81), or the "phase of explosion" (Taylor, 1971, p. 194). It includes at least one of the following behaviors: starting a new hypothesis or working on a new plan; generating plans or hypotheses without developing them further or testing them; or free association of ideas for solution without working on a specific one.

Examples: Or perhaps she can paint a pebble white . . .

Let me try to put the triangles side by side . . .

I'll draw from top left to bottom left . . .

212: *Trial and error.* Random application of solving behaviors to "see what happens." NO hypothesis or plan.

213: *Start procedure again.* Return to former hypothesis without adding to it or changing it.

214: *Compare and relate.* Attempts to identify common features among parts by inspection and association of two or more variables (objects, ideas, events) to note similarities and differences. Synthesis of several bits of information contained in the task (stimulus passage) by comparison or classification, or association of task information with extraneous matter.

Examples: It's like . . . ; It goes best with . . .
         If . . . then . . . ; It's the same as . . .

215: *Continuing activity.* Working on a previously stated hypothesis without obvious elaboration. Execution of idea.
Once a hypothesis or plan is proposed, it has to be tested out. This activity involves putting the idea or plan into action to see what happens.

(This classification was created to allow for separate coding of new ideas, plans, hypotheses, and continuing activity.) In a chain of reasoning presenting a series of separate hypotheses, each new hypothesis would be coded 211. The code 215 applies to application, i.e., thinking out of a plan or hypothesis under current investigation. (219 applies to the actual execution of detail.) Sternberg (1975) advises that models of stages or component processes of problem solving must allow for the reentering of a previously executed stage and cautions that, "One must be careful not to label repetitions of the same component process as separate processes. This error is especially likely to occur if other processes intervene" (p. 124).

216: *Random application of general or previously learned rule.* Closely related to 212, but not really trial and error activity. Attempts to apply "the first rule which comes into mind" without consideration of its applicability to the task. "Thoughtless" application of previously learned rule without consideration of consequences.

> Example: Choosing a mathematical operation at random and attempting to apply it without having made an attempt to find out what is required by the task.

217: *Modification of plan or hypothesis.*   This activity is always preceded by critical judgment (400).

218: *Survey or summarization of what has been done.*   Former trials, hypotheses, and other activities are listed, compared, or interpreted. (Critical comments and conclusions regarding the suitability of certain actions are classified under judgment [400]).

219: *Calculation/working out details.*   This includes the manipulation of numbers by application of mathematical operations. The physical execution of, for instance, a plan to achieve the balancing of a number of objects (matches) under specified conditions.

Code 220: Reasoning

This behavior involves complex cognitive processes like transformation and transposition; analysis and synthesis; recall, recognition, and reconstruction; as well as prediction.

221: *Recognition of important aspects or requirements of a solution.* This category contains responses which indicate that the subject has understood important aspects or prerequisites of solution, i.e., the identification of specific or additional problems which have to be overcome before proceeding to solution.

222: *Application of relevant rule.* The recognized solution requirements are related to a broader category or to a major idea which shares a common set of rules.

223: *Elimination.* Identification of unsuitable or faulty paths to solution.

Example: The way to go about it is not by . . .
Marrying the old man is not the answer . . .

224: *Search for concealed aspects.* Attempt to identify possible deceptive variables, in a non-judgmental manner.

Example: Is there a trick involved?

225: *Reasonable approximation of a possible solution.* Correct reasoning resulting in the "wrong" answer due to a minor error in calculation.

Unusual but acceptable solution to a defined problem. Intermediate, not part solution.

Code 300: Person (Self) Related Activity

These behaviors refer to idiosyncratic responses of a somewhat intuitive or introspective nature. The subject provides information not only in relation to the current status of the task but includes personal, noncognitive variables. The responses coded in this category present a glimpse of the complex interplay between the integrity of the problem solver as a person with emotional reactions and a need for self protection, and as a task oriented provider of a solution.

Schachtel (1959) presented a perceptual theory in which creativity was associated with the ability to perceive a stimulus and to refer to it "in itself" without reference to himself as the perceiver. Creativity was defined as "the art of seeing the familiar fully in its inexhaustible being, without using it autocentrically for purposes of *remaining embedded* in it and reassured by it" (Schachtel, 1959, p. 184).

It is the "autocentricity" and "embeddedness" referred to above, which seem to characterize responses coded 300.

Code 310: Idiosyncratic Operations

Overtly self-involved rather than task oriented activity is included in this code.

311: *Intuitive prediction of solution of part problem.* Suggestion of solution not preceded by preliminary thinking out, i.e., search for plan, etc., but immediate decisions without obvious consideration of consequences. "I think . . ." was frequently used in connection with this. Frequently reference was made to a personal experience.

312: *Imagery.* Report of visualization of the problem situation or of part thereof. Attempts to visualize the task situation.

313: *Introspection.* As a result of self observation, the subject describes, assesses, or interprets his or her own experience.
Attempted explanations of the variables operating during problem solving are given by the problem solver.

Example: My mind is strained trying to take this in . . .

There is a search going on in my long term memory . . .

314: *Retrospection.* Post hoc report and/or interpretation of the problem solving activity by the subject.

Example: I tried to imagine both objects . . .

Worked by trial and error method first, then . . .

315: *Justification.* The subject gives reasons for his or her problem solving responses.

Example: I did . . . because . . .

Because I don't know how to divide, I used to take away . . .

Code 320: Emotional Reactions

Expressions of feelings and attitudes to the task and the task situation are in this code. Also included are statements expressing self-criticism; any comment which the subject makes referring to his or her own ability, personality, mood, etc.

321: *Comment relating to difficulty or ease of task.* Statements coded in this category refer to the subject's personal perceptions of the ease or difficulty level of the task.

Example: Who on earth has invented this task . . .
I am confused, I feel stupid . . .
This is a difficult one . . .

322: *Frustration.* Expression of negative feelings about the task or the solving activity. References to "mental blockage," swearing, etc.

Example: This is really frustrating . . .

I'll tell you what I'm going to do with this . . .

323: *Lack of motivation.* Expression of desire to avoid or postpone solving of the task. Refusal to continue.

Example: Could I do this later?
Do I really have to go on?
I'll skip that one . . .

324: *Positive emotional reaction.* Expression of a feeling of accomplishment, pleasure, excitement, or relief.

Code 400: Critical Evaluation/Judgment

This code includes assessing criterion satisfaction, i.e., correctness, suitability, adequacy, desirability, etc., of input, solving activity, or solution. Implied is a kind of sensitivity to error or discrepancy on the one hand and assessment of relative adequacy in relation to more or less defined standards or criteria. This type of response has the character of an assessment based on a means-end relationship; it is a matter of seeing whether what is done "works well."

In the educational literature the type of response classified here tends to be subsumed under "critical thinking," a broadly applied category, which is regarded to be "higher" on a taxonomy of objectives than, for example, "comprehension" (Sanders, 1966), and is similar in meaning to the "evaluation" stage in Bloom's (1956) *Taxonomy of Educational Objectives*. It is similar to Dewey's (1933) concept of "reflective thinking" which also encompasses a wide range of activities.

Problem solving behaviors classifiable under category 400 involve judgments of statements and behaviors on the basis of a priori criteria. Such behaviors include the subject's assessment of the appropriateness and correctness of his or her own problem solving activities for the purpose of accepting or rejecting, continuing or discontinuing the particular activity. This definition is based on those by Smith (1953) and Ennis (1967, 1971), though unlike Smith's "critical thinking," the activity as defined for the present study does not include attempts at interpreting the meaning of behaviors and statements.

Code 410: Critical Assessment/Verification

Behaviors aimed at checking what has been done are coded 410.

411: *Assessment of the adequacy, suitability, etc., of progress.*   Solution or any part of the process of problem solving.

Example: Now let's see, how well does this fit?
           Have I used more than 4 lines?
           First I count whether I have enough matches.

412: *Recalculation.*   Checking mathematical calculations.

Code 420: Judgment/Evaluation

Decisions concerning how satisfactory previously applied behaviors were are included in Code 420. "This is logically differentiated from productive thought in that typically nothing is produced . . . merely an evaluation or categorizing of an object of thought" (Johnson, 1955, p. 51).

421: *Self correction (not self criticism, i.e., 321).*   Resulting from the assessment of the adequacy of the previously executed step or strategy.

Example: That was wrong . . .
           I should have divided first . . .

422: *Reservation re solution.*   Recognition of wrong move or failure, without a suggestion to remediate the failure.

423: *Questioning of consequences.*   Of a step, action, or solution.

Code 500: Pause

Different kinds of pauses occur, ranging from complete silence for short or long periods, i.e., pauses during which the experimenter engages in some prodding, to pauses in problem solving activity during which the subject engages in task irrelevant conversation or other activity.

Pauses occurred in all "thinking aloud" protocols. They must be regarded as the "missing data" of this methodology. In other words, the protocol contains no evidence on what behaviors or operations were taking place at this stage. They cannot be regarded as residuals, however, as it is most likely that they mask continuations of the same types of behaviors as were observed before and after the pause occurrence.

Code 510: Activity Filled Pause

This code is used to classify comments which cannot be interpreted as bearing a relationship to the task or problem solving activity.

Code 520: Silence

521: *Complete silence.*

522: *Examiner prodding.*   After a period of silence lasting approximately ten seconds.

Example: Please think aloud.
                 What are you thinking?

523: *Fill-in on the part of the subject.*   The subject uses meaningless words or phrases to fill-in silences.

Example: Well . . . , I mean . . . , Let's see . . . , etc.

Code 600: Memory Related Activity

Responses classified in this category contain attempts on the part of the subject to recall or link up with previously experienced similar situations or tasks.

Code 610: Attempts to Utilize Memory

The subject tries to establish associations with task relevant previous knowledge or experiences.

611: *Attempts to recall.*   Previous experience with same or similar tasks.

612: *Attempts to associate.*   Comparing or relating the task or aspects of the task to experiences outside the immediate task environment.

Code 620: Insight

Defined by English and English (1958) as "the process by which the meaning, significance, pattern or use becomes clear, or the understanding thus gained", and defined by Greeno (1977) as "immediate understanding of a relationship, . . . sudden occurrence of solution" (p. 43).

In Gestalt theory, insight was originally described as occurring suddenly, and as a novel reaction not based on previous experience. In its use in the present taxonomy, the term still implies an all or none reaction (i.e., the subject understands or does not understand), but such a reaction may appear gradually. For sudden insight the term illumination (Wallas, 1926) is preferred. Gobits (1975), making a distinction between insight as a product and insight as a process, defines the latter "operationally as knowledge of relations between structures" (p. 1). The latter would appear somewhat difficult to observe.

Insight can result in final or part solutions. It may also uncover major solution paths. All of these could be triggered by one or several components of the task or the problem situation. Where it leads to final solutions, insight is perceived as having a quality of spontaneity about it. In instances in which it does not lead to sudden solution, it may result in redirections of problem solving activity, or in radical alterations and new short term goals in the efforts of the problem solver.

621: *Illumination.*   That is, sudden recognition of a solution or part thereof.

622: *Sudden association.*

Example: . . . feeling I've seen this before . . .

623: *Memory flash.*

Code 700: Changing the Conditions of the Problem

Code 710: Illicit Use of Tools

The subject requests access to or use of external aids or tools.

Example: I want to draw a diagram of the situation . . .

15 times 30 . . . in your head . . . could I do it on paper?

Code 720: Violation and Expansion

Suggesting a hypothesis or solution which violates the conditions of the task is coded 720.

Example: Can the rules be changed?

Expansion, i.e., arriving at a solution or performing an operation in such a manner that the original meaning of the directions or stimulus passage is expanded, lengthened, or otherwise altered is also included in the code.

Example: The girl really wanted to marry the money lender . . .

REDUCTION OF CATEGORIES

All categories of the taxonomy were used for coding in the pilot study. Because of rare use and/or extremely skewed distributions, some categories were omitted as a result of the pilot study. In general, a category was combined with others, or omitted if no logical combination was possible, or if few subjects exhibited the behavior.

In his recent important article concerning "Systems for Describing Human Tasks," Fleishman (1982) showed that, to be useful, taxonomies in psychology as in other sciences have to contain "a rather large and steadily increasing set of categories" (p. 832). He concludes:

> The increasing fragmentation of categories while perhaps complicating life, is consistent with empirical work on the interrelationships among human task performances. More importantly, if nature is more complex than we would like it to be *we need to take steps to organize and to conceptualize it in ways in which it is more manageable.* (Fleishman, 1982, p. 832)[2]

The present study complied with the latter suggestion in two ways: (1) The study of the nature of intelligence was made more manageable by the investigation of its manifestation in the process of problem solving; and (2) The taxonomy of problem solving behaviors developed on the basis of the pilot study was reduced drastically for this initial investigation of the problem solving process.

---

2. Italics inserted by the present author.

The 50–behavior taxonomy was thus reduced to one containing only 18 variables. This reduction in variables was not unexpected, as a number of behaviors had in fact been included because of their being of possible rather than of probable interest. After all, it had been decided to risk error in the direction of generosity rather than in that of parsimony.

Initially the problem solving behaviors occurring in each three-second interval were coded by the investigator. To assess the reliability of the taxonomy produced on the basis of the pilot study, two other independent coders, a male recent graduate in psychology, and a female second year psychology student were trained in the use of the taxonomy. Neither had previously been connected with the project, but both were interested in finding out more about problem solving strategies. The coders were trained by the investigator in separate sessions, on the basis of a some-what more extensive version of the set of definitions provided above. The criterion for training was to classify correctly (correct being defined here as "in agreement with the judgments of the investigator") 80% of the items presented in one protocol.

A random sample of 10 protocols from the pilot study were chosen, and the coders classified these independently. The reliability of judgment between the two coders was established by calculating a Pearson's product moment correlation coefficient. The reliabilities calculated separately for the 10 protocols ranged from .82 to .93. This level of agreement compares favourably with inter scorer reliabilities reported in the literature (Quealy, 1969; Squire, 1964).

It was observed that coders were more inconsistent in their judgments of infrequently encountered behaviors than in frequently encountered ones. This tendency seems understandable if one considers the complexity of the task of giving consideration to 50 strategies more or less simultaneously. Of the 50 items included in the taxonomy, 18 were used with sufficient frequency and were coded reliably enough to be retained for further investigation in the present study. The reliability of the final taxonomy was investigated more thoroughly. The results of this investigation are presented at the beginning of Chapter 9.

In the following section details are provided concerning the manner in which items were combined or deleted. This information is presented according to the major codes used and in the order of occurrence of the items under discussion in the taxonomy.

Within the larger category of 110, "Directions Directed Activity"; item 115, "Questions to the examiner" was among the most rarely used items and was combined with items 114, "Brief reference to text" and 116, "Attempts to absorb, rehearse, or memorize directions"; thus creating a new variable, i.e., new variable 4 (NV4), which describes activities in which the subject displays Directions/Stimulus Passage Directed Activity (Code 100) by making efforts to apply heuristics to the given information.

Items 113, "Task segmentation or chunking" and 117, "Analysis of input into major sections" were shown to present considerable inconsistency in coding, and were combined into one category (NV3) defining, summarizing, and chunking of the given information.

Code 120, "Identification of the Problem or its Parts from Given Information," was used as one category because the amount of use made of items 121, 122, and 123 separately failed to reach the criterion of use by 25 per cent of the subjects in the study.

In the major category 210, "Solution Directed Heuristics"; items 212, "Trial and error," 213, "Start procedure again," and 216, "Random application of . . . rule," were combined on a logical basis into (NV8), "Trial and Error Activity." In the same manner items 214, "Compare and relate" and 218, "Survey or review . . ." were combined. Item 217, "Modification of plan or hypothesis," proved difficult to distinguish from the "generation of a new hypothesis," item 211, and was therefore deleted.

Insufficient use made of the separate items of major category 220, "Reasoning," led to a combination (NV12). The same applies to the combination of items 311 to 314 (i.e., "Intuitive prediction of solution," "Imagery," "Introspection," and "Retrospection") as "Self-involved operations" (NV13), and items 321 to 324 ("Comment relating to difficulty/ ease of task," "Frustration," "Lack of motivation," "Positive emotional reaction") as "Emotional reactions" (NV15).

"Judgment and Verification" (Code 400), "Pause" (Code 500), and "Memory Related Activity" (Code 600) were used as gross classifications because of the relatively small number of responses observed for individual items in these sections of the taxonomy.

The major division, "Changing the Conditions of the Problem" (Code 700) was used by two subjects only, and was therefore deleted from the taxonomy for the present study.

The 18 variables deemed to occur with sufficient frequency and coded reliably enough to warrant further investigation in the present study are summarized in Table 7.3.

Of the 18 variables retained for further analysis in the present study, only three represent Gestalt type complex processes, 10 denote heuristics and four are representative of behaviors in broader categories combining both heuristics and complex states. Five variables are stimulus passage oriented, and six are solution oriented.

All the variables in the original taxonomy described positive problem solving behaviors, i.e., behaviors the use of which would be expected to facilitate solution. It is understood that not all heuristics which subjects

TABLE 7.3
List of 18 Problem Solving Variables
Retained for Further Investigation

New Variable NV		Taxonomy Code	Heuristic	Complex	Abbreviated Description
1		111	√		First reading
2		112	√		Rereading
3	Stimulus passage oriented	113+117	√		Chunk/ Summarize
4		114+115+116	√		Ref. to text/ Scan/Check Attempts to understand
5		121-123		√	Identif. of problem or part from given info.
6		130	√	√	Negative
7		211	√		Plan/Hypoth.
8		212+213+216	√		Trial & Error
9	Solution oriented	214+218	√		Compare and Relate, Review former trials
10		215	√	√	Continuing activity
11		219	√		Calculate/Detail
12		221-225		√	Reasoning
13		311-314	√		Self-involved
14	Self- oriented emotional	315	√		Justification
15		321-324		√	Emotional reaction
16		411-423	√	√	Judg./Verific.
17		500			Pause
18		600	√	√	Memory related

apply are necessarily useful or relevant in terms of leading to a solution. Some subjects misread or misunderstand problems, or make errors of other kinds. It might be argued that an adequate coding system should be flexible enough to accommodate deviations from "ideal" behaviors.

In the development of the present taxonomy it was noted that the nonjudgmental approach chosen paid off in that all but one type of behavior was codable under the proposed system. The behaviors which were found to be difficult to accommodate in a taxonomy containing positive behaviors only related to instances where the subject directed his or her attention to perceptually salient, but solution irrelevant, input information, and as a result of this tended to fail to consider other important information provided in the directions or the stimulus passage. To make a complete coding of all behaviors observed in the problem solving protocols possible, one additional code was created under the major category of Directions/Stimulus Passage Directed Behaviors (Code 100). Code 130 provides for the coding of the above detailed nonrelevant or inappropriate use made of input information.

A further study of the reliability of the coding based on the taxonomy was conducted, this time using the reduced list of 18 variables. The results of this study are presented in Chapter 9. It is suggested that the level of consistency with which the 50 behaviors and the 18 final variables were used by different coders would justify consideration of the taxonomy as a reliable basis for the analysis and categorization of problem solving protocols.

SUMMARY

To summarize, it can be said that the original aim in the development of the taxonomy was to classify the problem solving behaviors which individuals appear to use, and then to investigate whether characteristic strategy patterns can be identified. In the evolution of the taxonomy, however, many problem solving behaviors were combined, and others added in order to make the classification workable and to characterize performance more completely.

The resulting taxonomy of 18 problem solving behaviors can be regarded as providing low inference measures because this set of items focuses on specific, objectively defined and observable behaviors which can be quantified and recorded as frequency counts.

A difference between the taxonomy presented here, and the stages, phases, and other classifications postulated in a number of previous research studies concerned with the tracing of problem solving processes lies in the fact that the present taxonomy was designed to be, and represents, a template only, which might facilitate some initial gauging of certain elements of the problem solving process. The 18 variables investigated here are expected to provide the means to obtain no more than a first impression, a distant glimpse of possible structural components of a highly complex system.

The manner in which the taxonomy is presented does not assume that behaviors occur in a given sequence, or that every problem solver uses a given number of heuristics. Certain categories, in particular the division into heuristics and more complex states, may be found to correspond to certain stages or phases of problem solving described in the published literature, but no prejudging has taken place here as regards the order and universality with which such behaviors occur.

A tendency can be observed in the research literature to convert logical classification schemes into psychological realities by assuming that one or the other offers an invariant characterization of behavior. No such power is attributed to the present taxonomy. The latter is, in fact, regarded as a first step only, namely to have provided a repertoire of concepts, as called for by Estes (1976), Allport (1975), Anderson (1976), Sternberg (1977b), Fleishman (1982), and others, so that the process of problem solving might be investigated.

Finally, a relatively simple subset of 18 problem solving behaviors, i.e., operations performed by individuals during problem solving, was chosen to provide a taxonomy for an initial but comprehensive investigation of the problem solving process.

Operations performed by most individuals on almost all tasks, no matter how frequently or how rarely, can be expected to be relatively enduring, and may thus be regarded as part of the structure of the problem solving process. This approach shares the assumption "fundamental to all information processing models, that they incorporate a certain number of elementary processes or operations a concatenation of which can produce complex behavior" (Posner & McLeod, 1982, pp. 478–479).

However, as is discussed further in Chapter 13, the present author's view is that the problem solving process is not purely a concatenation of its component parts, but that it involves very complex, possibly multidimensional, interactions between components.

8

Definition of Terms and General Procedure of Data Collection and Analysis

DEFINITION OF TERMS

The definitions of key terms used in this study are presented in three consecutive sections as follows: general terms, terms related to the gathering of data, and terms relating to the interpretation of the data.

General Definitions

The following definitions are intended to introduce the general framework within which the study was conceptualized.

Problem solving. The lack of a generally acceptable definition of this term in the literature, and the broad and apparently indefinite scope of its use, led Ernst and Newell (1969) to note that "Behind this vagueness . . . lies the absence of a science of problem solving that would support the definition of a technical term" (p. 1).

Traditionally, the term problem solving has been used to describe the behaviors applied by a motivated subject, attempting to achieve a goal, usually in an unfamiliar context, after initial lack of success (Johnson, 1972). Definitions of the term tend to maintain that a problem exists where an individual is confronted by a "difficulty" (Dewey, 1933), a "gap" (Bartlett, 1958; Köhler, 1927), a "conflict" (Duncker, 1945), and "disequilibrium" (Piaget, 1968), or a "deviation" from a familiar situation (Raaheim, 1974). While this type of description would seem to be equally suitable to define such terms as searching, understanding, or learning, "much contemporary research continues to reflect the basic Gestalt view that problem solving, by virtue of its emphasis on response discovery is something apart from learning" (Erickson & Jones, 1978, p. 62).

Historically and up to the present day the term problem solving has been used with considerably greater frequency in reference to the outcomes or products, in particular the success/failure aspect of the activity, than to the process per se.

Problem solving as a process became the focus of research with the weakening of interest of research workers in the perceptual and experiential aspects of thought, as they had been pursued by Associationists and Gestalt psychologists.

As was noted in the introductory chapters, the Gestalt approach to research into problem solving might be described as subject oriented. The more recent, important contributions of the information processing and artificial intelligence studies, though concerned with the investigation of the problem solving process itself, focused primarily on the demand characteristics and structure of certain problem solving tasks (e.g., Newell & Simon, 1972; Scandura, 1973, 1977; Wickelgren, 1974).

The term problem solving can refer to all those overt and covert activities which take place to reach a solution or otherwise accomplish a goal or purpose in the problem solving situation.

For the purposes of the present study, the term problem solving is used to describe broadly the results of the interaction of components from the following five domains of variables:

a. the problem or task, T
b. the problem solver or subject, S
c. the situational circumstances or the environment in which the problem is presented or presents itself, E
d. the behaviors or processes which take place between the point of initial contact with the problem by S and the solution produced by S, X
e. the solution or product of the problem solving activity, P.

Regardless of the type of problem or the manner in which task (T), subject (S), environment (E), and process (X) variables interact, the product (P), whatever form it might take, is always a function of the interaction of variables from the remaining domains. This relationship can be expressed more parsimoniously by the mathematical function

$$P_{(T)} = f(T + S + E + X)$$

where every variable may be represented by a number of domain components.

In the present study the product P is, however, not the dependent variable. Instead, the aim is to investigate structural components of the problem solving process X, which in turn must be expected to be a function of variables from the remaining domains, hence

$$X = f(T + S + P + E).$$

Although it is accepted that during problem solving the above suggested sets of variables may interact in many intricate ways, it seems legitimate and necessary to define each of them separately.

Problem or task: These terms are used interchangeably in the research literature and in the present study. The term problem has traditionally served as a label for a variety of phenomena ranging from mathematical tasks to problems in real life. A common characteristic of all problems seems to be that they involve an aim which the problem solver wishes to accomplish, the means for which (i.e., the required knowledge, skills, techniques, or behaviors) are not at his or her disposal.

To be confronted with a problem means to be faced with a difficulty or an obstacle which cannot be solved or dealt with in an already known or habitual manner. A reasonably general yet meaningful description of a problem or task might thus be that it may arise from any stimulus situation in which an appropriate response is not readily available.

This definition is similar to many explanations of the term found in the research literature. Dewey (1933) described a problem as

- whatever—no matter how slight and commonplace in character—perplexes and challenges the mind so that it makes belief at all uncertain (Dewey, 1933, p. 13);
- a question for which there is at the moment no answer is a problem (Skinner, 1966, p. 225);
- a problem arises when a person is motivated toward a goal and his first attempt to reach it is unrewarding (Johnson, 1972, p. 133);
- a stimulus situation for which an organism does not have a ready response (Davis, 1973, p. 12);
- a system has a problem when it has or has been given a description of something but does not yet have anything that satisfies the description (Reitman, 1965, p. 126).

The definition of a problem as a phenomenon which may arise in any stimulus situation in which an appropriate response is not readily available, is broad enough to cover physical, emotional, intellectual, and social problems. It can refer to problems of varying complexity, to defined and ill-defined tasks, to structured and unstructured problems. It serves to prevent the problem solver from avoiding or ignoring the problem, but does not require the individual to recognise the task "objectively." The "objective" problem is the task as perceived by the individual. This position allows for the fact that what is a problem for one person may not be one for another. The latter individual, in this case, does have an appropriate response readily available in a stimulus situation which may present a problem for the former person. In summary, it is suggested that the above presented definition of the term problem or task subsumes all types of problems, without, however, obscuring the differences which may exist in different problem solving situations.

A further point of definition may require clarification. It would follow from the above presented definition that a problem which does not elicit any reaction from the individual, or a task which has been solved would cease to be a problem. The English language unfortunately does not provide an alternative term to cover these types of situations. Frequently occurring tasks, such as the simple arithmetic "problem" $1 + 1 = 2$, which elicit well rehearsed, often automatic responses, do not fall into the problem category defined above. Other languages provide alternative terms for these "problems" (e.g., in German one would use "die Aufgabe," and in French "la tâche") which permit a clearer distinction between a "problem" which requires at least some effort in terms of productive thinking on the part of the subject, and what may be described as a simple exercise or routine stimulus–response association. The term "problem" as used in this study does not include simple stimuli presented for automatic response.

Problem situation: This concept was first used by Wertheimer (1923), who regarded it as consisting of two ingredients. These are the aim or solution, i.e., "that which is demanded," and the stimulus or materials, knowledge, skills, etc., i.e., "that which is given." The process of problem solving commences when what is given is brought into association with that which is demanded. This will include, for example, considerations of how the givens might lead to a solution. The "functional value" (Duncker, 1945; Köhler, 1917) of the givens might be assessed as done by, for example, Köhler in the case of the sticks utilized by the chimpanzee to reach the bananas.

Subject: This term refers to the individual who is attempting to solve a problem. The problem solver cannot be considered to be a neutral agent. All variables—many of them unknown, some known but not yet measurable, others constant—which determine the subject's behavior make up this domain. Obvious examples of these variables are motivation; memory; intelligence; general background and experience, including experience with problems of a certain type; and social and personality variables.

Environment: The total problem solving environment includes physical, psychological, and sociological variables. The physical environment provides many of the perceptual cues and memory associations which might be used by the problem solver to define, analyze, and understand the problem, and to enlarge the set of available approaches to the task.

Physical, psychological, and sociological variables and factors resulting from their interaction may, on the other hand, place certain constraints on the task, the solution, or the problem solving activity, and directly or indirectly influence the process as a whole. The problem environment contains, of course, the experimenter with all his or her characteristics. Task directions, definitions, etc., form part of the problem or task.

Process: In the research literature problem solving, like learning, is often referred to as a process. Yet the evidence for the occurrence of this process is based on an examination of the end product, performance. The outcome of problem solving, i.e., the results of the process (or processes), not the processes themselves, are described.

Although little is known of what occurs during "the unseen operations by which solutions are reached" (Johnson, 1972, p. 133), the term process will, in the present study, not be used merely as a label for mental events which have not been understood (Davis, 1973), but will refer to the behaviors which can be observed while the subject is engaged in problem solving activity in accordance with the definition presented by Davis (1961):

> The problem solving process, which begins with the presentation of the problem, is terminated when the subject arrives at a correct solution, when he arrives at an incorrect solution he believes correct, or when the experimenter ends the experimental session. (p. 20)

The process or processes which occur in time between the subject's perception of the problem and the presentation of a solution must by definition be dynamic. Behavior over time implies activity, i.e., change. Because of their occurrence and change over time, processes differ from structures.

Product or solution: These terms are used interchangeably for the result of the problem solving activity. The term product would appear to be more suitable for research purposes because of the connotation of the term solution. One would, generally, expect a solution to be "correct." In the present study both terms are used for the results or outcome of the problem solving attempted by subjects. The terms apply to both "correct" or "incorrect" outcomes.

Problem solving behavior or operation and problem solving strategy: Again, these terms are used interchangeably to denote any response, or any part of a response pattern which is observed during the subject's problem solving activity, i.e., can be identified on the basis of the subject's problem solving protocol. It is acknowledged that many behaviors are unobservable, and will therefore not be contained in the protocol. The difference in processing rate per time unit between thought and speech and the inability of speech to reflect parallel processes result in the fact that the "thinking aloud" protocol contains a reduced version of the problem solving process, no matter how perfect the experimental conditions.

Strictly speaking, the use of the term "strategy" should perhaps have been restricted to dynamic processes involved in performance, which are made up of several operations or behaviors. On the other hand, the repeated use of a specific operation over time may well be conceived as a strategy rather than an operation.

Posner and McLeod (1982), reviewing information processing models "in search of elementary operations" in cognition, have come to similar conclusions, and suggest:

> Dynamic processes that perform specific operations we call "strategies." The idea is that elementary mental operations may be assembled into sequences and combinations that represent the strategy developed for a particular task. It is often difficult to determine whether the elementary mental operations isolated are strategies or whether they are structures. (p. 480)

These authors also note problems in the reverse situation and point out that sequences of operations, i.e., "strategies," may turn into relatively enduring structural components of a cognitive process:

> The chess master who has developed a strategy for the analysis of the chessboard over many years of practice may be unable to modify. Thus it becomes more structural in character. Indeed high levels of skills seem to be characterised by the development of a structural basis for what in most of us is a painfully assembled strategy. (p. 480)

Terms Related to Data Gathering

Definitions of the following terms are provided in an endeavor to increase the clarity of the description of the method of data gathering summarized later in this chapter.

Stimulus passage: This term refers to a single sheet of paper containing a diagram, a typed sentence, paragraph, or paragraphs presenting the subject with the task. For example, in the case of Task 2 [:::], the stimulus passage contained the instructions and a representation of the nine-dot pattern. The stimulus passages provided the means by which the subject was acquainted with each task. A separate stimulus passage was prepared for each of the twelve tasks. The beginning of each task consisted of the subject being handed the appropriate stimulus passage, and required to read it aloud.

Verbalization or "thinking aloud": The terms are used interchangeably to refer to the subject's verbal expressions and descriptions of his or her ongoing problem solving activity. Chapter 6 provides a more detailed description and discussion of the method.

Protocol: The verbatim transcript of a cassette recording made of all verbalizations produced by subjects during the problem solving session. The protocol contains a complete record of the description of the problem solving provided by the subject's "thinking aloud." It also contains evidence of any other verbal or verbally reported activities which occurred. A protocol, then, provides a description, keeping time sequence intact, of problem solving performance as it occurs. On the other hand not every description of performance on a task constitutes a protocol. A description of a task consisting of goals and outcomes is not sufficient. The problem solving protocols provide information not only concerning the answers subjects provided, but also, and more important, they provide an indication of the sequence in which problem solving behaviors occurred. Subjects may ask questions, refer back to the stimulus passage, compute, etc., in a particular order.

Process components were identified on the basis of the amounts of use made by each subject of certain problem solving behaviors or strategies, and by investigating transition sequences of these behaviors at various temporal stages of the problem solving activity.

Behavior or strategy use was measured by dividing each protocol into sequential intervals of three seconds' duration, and by then classifying each three-second unit according to the predetermined taxonomy described in Chapter 7.

Terms Relating to Data Interpretation

The following terms were used in the classification of problem solving behaviors, and in the subsequent interpretation of the data obtained from the protocols.

Taxonomy of problem solving behaviors: This term refers to a set of behavior categories which was prepared to form a basis for the classification of problem solving behaviors from the obtained protocols.

The taxonomy was designed in the form of a *root system* in which each main category is represented by a major root. Each major root is divided into left and right branches, representing heuristics and more complex problem solving processes respectively. The root system type of taxonomy permits the categorization of certain problem solving behaviors as discrete entities, yet represents the problem solving process as a whole as a complex system of interacting component behaviors, i.e., an intricate network consisting of intertwined roots and branches. The root system provides the means for flexible and multiple coding of problem solving behaviors in the sense that it allows for separate coding of behavior components or fragments, and for the combining of less frequently observed behavior components into broader categories simultaneously. As a detailed description of the taxonomy and its development is provided in Chapter 7, only the main roots will be defined here. Figure 7.1 shows a graphic representation of the system.

Stimulus passage directed activity (Code 100):   Reading Figure 7.1 from the left, these types of behaviors are represented by the first main root of the root system. Problem solving behaviors classified by this root focus on the information contained within the stimulus passage or task directions.

The left branches of this root (Code 110) describe responses in which the subject concentrates on the specifications of the task, and surveys the given information by behaviors such as reading, rereading, references to the text, the repetition of instructions, text related questions, etc.

The right branches of the first root (Code 120) represent more complex stimulus passage directed activity including behaviors such as attempts to identify the problem or parts thereof from the given information, e.g., to identify certain boundaries or constraints contained in the task, to define parts of the task, etc.

Solution directed activity (Code 200):   The second main root from the left in the root system does not represent stimulus passage oriented behaviors, but focuses on the solution of the problem. The left branching parts of this root (Code 210) describe a repertoire of heuristics including the following types of responses: the search for a plan or hypothesis, trial and error strategies, the comparison or relating of different parts of the problem, the application of a previously learned rule, calculations, etc. The right branches of this root (Code 220) contain more complex solution directed behaviors which have resulted from the transformation and restructuring of sets of ideas, e.g., the recognition of important aspects or requirements of the solution, the identification of solution components, etc.

Self related behaviors (Code 300): The responses categorized here are somewhat idiosyncratic and intuitive in nature. The left branches of this root (Code 310) include introspection, retrospection, and imagery. The right branches tend to represent emotional responses including expressions of personal adequacy or inadequacy, comments on the perceived ease or difficulty of the task, frustration, lack of motivation, etc.

Judgment and verification (Code 400): Involves critical review and judgment of both already executed and planned behaviors and ideas. Some operations classified here simply interrupt the problem solving process when an error or a wrong reaction is spotted. Responses of critical assessment include the suitability, adequacy of certain responses, parts of the directions, progress, etc. Examples of left branching behaviors (Code 410) are checking and recalculation. Right branches (Code 420) include self correction, reservations concerning a method of proceeding or a solution, the recognition of a wrong move, and the estimating or questioning of the consequences of planned steps.

Pause (Code 500): Refers to silence and to the expression of fill-in words (e.g., well, . . . I mean, let's see . . .) on the part of the subject (Code 520), as well as to pauses in task related activity during which the subject appears to stall for time by making irrelevant comments (Code 510). While a number of pauses could be interpreted in relation to antecedent and subsequent behaviors, this has not been attempted within the framework of the present study which concentrated on low inference behaviors. The provision of a classification category for pauses is regarded as an important aspect of the taxonomy, however, not only because of its value for potential analysis in future research but, more important, because the preservation of pauses makes an essential contribution to the provision of a close approximation to the sequence and time relationships of components of the problem solving process.

Memory (Code 600): Left branches of this root (Code 610) represent the subject's attempts to recall previous similar situations or relevant experiences, i.e., attempts to establish associations with appropriate previous knowledge. The right branches (Code 620) describe complex memory involved responses such as the sudden recognition of a solution or part thereof, sudden associations, memory flashes, and responses such as "I have a feeling I've seen this before."

Task difficulty: This term is used in its psychometric sense. The relative difficulty levels of the 12 tasks used in the present study were determined by the frequency with which the problems were solved by subjects. A ranking of tasks in order of facility is provided in Table 9.5.

Competence or achievement: The terms problem solving competence and achievement are used interchangeably to describe the outcome of the problem solving activity. This variable was subdivided into two (i.e., solvers versus nonsolvers) or three (i.e., correct or nearly correct solution, gives up, wrong solution) levels and the relevant results chapters contain an indication of the number of levels used in each instance.

Speed of problem solving refers to the time taken, measured in three-second units, by the subject to work on the task. *Fast* workers took less than median time. *Slow* workers took median time or more. Median problem solving time was calculated for each task separately.

Measured intelligence: An estimate of measured intelligence (IQ) was obtained for each subject by individual administration of the Block Design Test from WAIS. Scaled scores, calculated as directed by the WAIS manual for each subject, were used in relation to this variable throughout the study.

GENERAL PROCEDURE

Data Collection

The problem solving data were collected in individual interviews conducted in the mornings, during July and August 1978. Each institution from which the subjects were selected made available one or two quiet rooms somewhat removed from the area where classes and lectures were being held. Approximately three quarters of the interviews were conducted by the investigator. The other interviews were conducted by two clerical assistants, who had been trained in the administration of the WAIS Block Design Test, and who were trained to act as uninvolved technicians, i.e., to monitor the cassette recording of the sessions, to establish rapport, and to make use of one of a number of prescribed prompts whenever the subject paused for longer than a period of ten seconds. To estimate the latter amount of time the technician was issued with a watch containing a second hand.

As an initial contact with each of the institutions from which subjects were selected, the investigator presented a short talk to groups of students who had gathered for either a lecture in psychology, or, in the case of schools, for a class assembly. Following these presentations, the investigator answered questions of clarification. The talk emphasized the need for research into cognitive processing and described the aims of the project as an attempt to explore *how* people go about solving problems, rather than whether they are able to solve them. Volunteer subjects were invited to place their names on a list after the session.

Each volunteer subject served in a further introductory group session, and in one individual practice session, followed by the experimental session.

During the group session the aims of the research were repeated, and the "thinking aloud" methodology was explained and discussed with the potential subjects. A stimulus passage containing a practice problem was given to each subject, and part of a demonstration tape recording, in which the "thinking aloud" method was used to solve the practice problem, was played several times. Individual interview times were arranged with the subjects during this session.

The second practice session placed the subject in a one-to-one situation with the experimenter. The purpose of this interview was three-fold: (1) to ascertain the subject's understanding of the "thinking aloud" methodology, (2) to provide actual practice in the procedure, and (3) to establish rapport and to provide a warmup trial for the actual data gathering session. The experimental session followed this practice session after an interlude of approximately five minutes of light conversation between the experimenter and the subject, designed to put the subject at ease. After all twelve tasks had been attempted in sequence, and after a further short period of light conversation, the WAIS Block Design Test was administered. Most subjects completed the entire interview in approximately two hours, although the variation between subjects was considerable.

No time limits were imposed on the subjects in their work on each task. The major reason for this decision was the consideration that a speed requirement might lead the subject to attempt to solve the tasks by means of minimal moves and to eliminate as many redundant moves as possible.

The tasks were typed on single sheets of paper, one task appearing on each page. These pages are referred to as the stimulus passages. The twelve tasks were administered, one after the other, without time limit to all subjects in the same order. Details of the contents of the tasks and the order of their presentation are provided in Chapter 5. At the beginning of each task the subject was handed the appropriate stimulus passage by the experimenter and requested to, "start off by reading the stimulus passage aloud." The total experimental session, with the exception of the administration of the WAIS Block Design Test, was recorded on cassette.

In keeping with the requirements of the "thinking aloud" methodology, the cassette recordings included each subject's description of his or her problem solving activity, together with expressions of emotions, verbal interactions between the subject and the experimenter, and extraneous noises which occurred during the experimental session.

Three factors can be expected to have had a facilitating influence on the continuity of the subjects' "thinking aloud" activity. These were the use of the demonstration tape recording in the initial group practice session, the practice tasks preceding the experimental session, and the experimenter's promptings (e.g., "keep thinking aloud," or "what are you doing now?") which were given following each period of silence lasting approximately ten seconds.

To organize the data, the cassette recordings were transcribed verbatim and in order of time sequence divided into a series of three-second intervals. The latter was achieved by using a metronome in conjunction with the cassette recordings of the subjects' verbalizations during problem solving and the typed protocols.

The choice of the three-second interval as a unit is based on the empirical evidence provided by Flanders (1965) and Amidon and Flanders (1967). These studies suggest that the three-second interval may provide the best indication of behavior over time with regard to both the reliability of judgment, and the detection of sudden changes of behavior.

The basic data for the present study are thus provided by three-second interval units, which are easily determined. The units occur naturally. They have an identifiable beginning and end and are easily agreed upon whether viewed by the subject or by another person.

The subjects' behavior during each three-second interval was next classified according to the previously described root system taxonomy. The problem solving protocols of a random sample of ten subjects were classified by two judges. The results of this investigation of the reliability of the classification procedure are presented at the beginning of Chapter 9.

Data Analysis

Apart from the previously mentioned investigation of the reliability of the taxonomy based behavior descriptions, four different types of analyses of the data were carried out: (1) Problem solving speed and the variety of problem solving strategies used were compared for subjects of varying problem solving achievement and measured intelligence. (2) Certain structural components of the problem solving process were investigated on the basis of the total amounts of use made by subjects of particular problem solving behaviors. A three–mode factor analysis (Tucker & Messick, 1963; Tucker, 1964, 1966) was performed to investigate possible functional relationships between preferred problem solving strategies, tasks, and individual differences between subjects. The results of this analysis were related to patterns identified by performing principal components analyses for each of the tasks separately. (3) Multiple discriminant functions were computed to investigate the utility of the process variables in the identification of individual and group differences in relation to problem solving competence, speed, level of education, and general ability. (4) In a set of analyses, designed to preserve at least some of the time sequences in which component behaviors of the problem solving process occurred, the data were summarized in the form of one-dependent transition matrices, i.e., matrices whose elements are pairs of subsequent behaviors. The transition matrices obtained for the different tasks and for contrasting groups of subjects were then compared on the basis of a Markoff–chain model (Kruskal, 1978). Comparisons were made of overall trends over different periods of problem solving time. The relative contributions made by specific behavior sequences to changes in the pattern of strategy use over time were investigated, and the rate of shifts from one problem solving strategy to another and the relative amounts of repetitive behaviors were compared over time.

PRESENTATION OF RESULTS AND DISCUSSION OF FINDINGS

9 Global Observations Relating to the Outcome of Problem Solving Performance

The aim of the empirical study reported here is to investigate the problem solving process by taking into consideration variables from at least three major sources of variation, namely characteristics of the psychological mechanisms which operate during performance, individual differences, and the task. A taxonomy of problem solving behaviors, the development and contents of which were described in Chapter 7, provides the basis for the organization of the data.

This first chapter of the results section begins with a description of the reliability of the behavior classifications, both in terms of their replicability and their appropriateness as a general tool. Coder agreement is assessed separately for strategies, tasks, and subjects, and for the total number of coding decisions made across the protocols of 12 tasks obtained from a random sample of ten subjects. In the following sections of this chapter, speed of performance, strategy preferences, and the variety of problem solving strategies used are discussed in relation to a number of contextual variables. Like all chapters in this section, the chapter concludes with a summary of findings.

As described previously, the verbatim "thinking aloud" protocols for each of the 89 subjects were cassette recorded, timed in units of three-second intervals and categorized according to the final taxonomy of 18 explicitly defined, mutually exclusive, all inclusive problem solving behaviors.

Problem solving behavior observed on the 12 experimental tasks per subject yielded, as can be seen in Table 9.9, a total of 41,960 responses, i.e., 41,960 three-second intervals or 34.97 hours of problem solving protocols. The results of an investigation of the reliability of the taxonomy based bahavior descriptions will be presented first.

THE RELIABILITY OF THE TAXONOMY BASED
BEHAVIOR DESCRIPTIONS

A number of statistically related but conceptually different types of reliability could be examined in the present study. As the procedures required to establish these reliabilities differ according to what is being assessed, the definitions of a number of terms have to be clarified initially.

In the present chapter, the general concept of *reliability* refers to the methodology of categorizing problem solving behaviors according to a taxonomy of 18 strategy variables. The two major reliabilities of interest refer (a) to the replicability of the behavior categorizations on the basis of the taxonomy, and (b) to the appropriateness of the taxonomy as a general tool, i.e., its stability across subjects and different tasks.

The latter type of reliability provides information concerning the consistency with which a strategy might describe operations used across tasks, subjects, or both. This reliability can be represented by a *stability coefficient* (Medley & Mitzel, 1958, 1963), which can be obtained by correlating the categorizations of strategy use made by the same coder for various pairs of tasks.

The aim of the present exploratory study was to investigate possible relationships between strategy, task, and subject variables. A conceptualization and discussion of the reliability of the method in terms of the stability of the strategy variables would therefore lead to circularity and must be regarded as inappropriate at this stage.

The correlation between the categorizations made by different coders in relation to the same task is referred to as a *coefficient of coder agreement*. This coefficient provides an index of the objectivity of the method of categorization of problem solving behaviors. In other words, it provides information concerning the "reliability" of the coders, and relates therefore to the replicability of behavior categorizations on the basis of the taxonomy.

A high level of agreement between coders must be regarded as a crucial requirement for the validity of the present methodology. A low coefficient of coder agreement would cause any interpretation of obtained results to be questionable. Observer disagreement acts as a limiting factor not only on the reliability, but also on the validity of findings in an observational study.

Coder Agreement

To assess the degree of reproducibility, i.e., the objectivity with which the taxonomy of problem solving behaviors could be applied by two independent coders, a temporary assistant (a final year psychology student who was new to the project and not acquainted with the aims of the study) was trained to use the taxonomy on a number of protocols obtained in a pilot study which had been conducted prior to the present investigation. He then, completely independently from the investigator, coded the problem solving protocols of a random sample of ten subjects.

The codings obtained by the investigator were compared with those obtained by the assistant coder for all 12 tasks of each of the randomly chosen ten subjects.

Agreement between the coders was assessed in several ways. Table 9.1 shows the proportions and percentages of agreement for each subject and task separately, for each subject across tasks, and for each task across subjects for all coding decisions made across the 12 tasks for the ten subjects contained in the random sample.

Of the 4598 coding decisions made by each coder, i.e., the number of three-second intervals coded across the 12 tasks for the ten subjects contained in the random sample, 4187 coding decisions were identical. In other words, the two coders agreed a total of 91.06% of the time. The average percentages of agreement for tasks across subjects and for each subject across tasks were 90.04% (*SD* = 3.44%) and 90.36% (*SD* = 3.43%) respectively.

These proportions of agreement between coders were high, and compared favorably with those between judges in other observational studies (e.g., Ames, 1965; Goor, 1974; Jacobsen, 1973; Olshavsky, 1976; Quealy, 1969; Smith, 1964).

Although the literature shows that the investigators of large numbers of studies were satisfied to assess interjudge reliabilities by computing the percentage of instances in which two decision makers agreed, this approach might be regarded as somewhat inadequate.

The practice of using simple percentage of agreement between coders has two major shortcomings. Firstly, the interpretation of percentage of coder agreement may be ambiguous when, as in the present study, some cells contain very low frequencies while other strategies occur relatively frequently. For example, if the coders agreed in two out of three instances of occurrence of one strategy and in 19 out of 20 instances of another strategy, percentages of 66.67 and 95.00 respectively are obtained. The percentages of agreement do not reflect the fact that in both cases the coders differ in only one decision. Table 9.1 contains a number of examples of this type of ambiguity. Using proportions of agreement instead of percentages reduces this problem to some extent.

The other shortcoming of the measures of percentage and proportion agreement is that neither method provides separate consideration of the amount of agreement which might be expected by chance.

Scott (1955) argued that the above measures may be inflated by chance

TABLE
Coder Agreements for the Protocols

Task	116 Prop.	116 %	121 Prop.	121 %	201 Prop.	201 %	210 Prop.	210 %	521 Prop.	521 %
1 [Binet]	$\frac{21}{23}$	91.30	$\frac{32}{35}$	91.43	$\frac{18}{20}$	90.00	$\frac{24}{26}$	92.31	$\frac{22}{27}$	81.48
2 [:::]	$\frac{34}{40}$	85.00	$\frac{11}{14}$	78.57	$\frac{43}{46}$	93.48	$\frac{137}{143}$	95.80	$\frac{11}{16}$	68.75
3 [15×30]	$\frac{4}{4}$	100.00	$\frac{8}{8}$	100.00	$\frac{9}{9}$	100.00	$\frac{10}{11}$	90.91	$\frac{4}{5}$	80.00
4 [Pebbles]	$\frac{79}{80}$	98.75	$\frac{71}{75}$	94.67	$\frac{54}{63}$	85.71	$\frac{54}{56}$	96.43	$\frac{28}{36}$	77.78
5 [Platform]	$\frac{79}{80}$	98.75	$\frac{51}{54}$	94.44	$\frac{47}{50}$	94.00	$\frac{49}{49}$	100.00	$\frac{14}{15}$	93.33
6 [6m→4Δ]	$\frac{20}{21}$	95.24	$\frac{47}{51}$	92.16	$\frac{78}{85}$	91.76	$\frac{140}{152}$	92.11	$\frac{28}{32}$	87.50
7 [9m→1h]	$\frac{35}{43}$	81.40	$\frac{35}{40}$	87.50	$\frac{27}{37}$	72.97	$\frac{30}{34}$	88.24	$\frac{20}{25}$	80.00
8 [Poem/St]	$\frac{2}{2}$	100.00	$\frac{3}{3}$	100.00	$\frac{13}{16}$	81.25	$\frac{12}{14}$	85.71	$\frac{2}{3}$	66.67
9 [Praise/P]	$\frac{8}{11}$	72.73	$\frac{21}{24}$	87.50	$\frac{18}{19}$	94.74	$\frac{34}{41}$	82.93	$\frac{10}{12}$	83.33
10 [Fly/Tree]	$\frac{10}{11}$	90.91	$\frac{6}{6}$	100.00	$\frac{19}{19}$	100.00	$\frac{31}{35}$	88.57	$\frac{3}{5}$	60.00
11 [Wood/Alc.]	$\frac{14}{16}$	87.50	$\frac{16}{16}$	100.00	$\frac{18}{19}$	94.74	$\frac{34}{37}$	91.89	$\frac{13}{15}$	86.67
12 [8TB/2]	$\frac{80}{85}$	94.12	$\frac{30}{31}$	96.77	$\frac{38}{40}$	95.00	$\frac{47}{48}$	97.92	$\frac{9}{11}$	81.82
Total	$\frac{386}{416}$	92.79	$\frac{331}{357}$	92.72	$\frac{382}{423}$	90.31	$\frac{602}{646}$	93.19	$\frac{164}{202}$	81.19

agreement. He proposed a coefficient π, which is designed to estimate the extent to which chance agreement is exceeded when the judgments of two coders are compared:

$$\pi = \frac{Po - Pc}{1 - Pc}$$

where $Po = \frac{1}{N}\sum_{i=1}^{c} n_{ii}$ refers to nominal agreement for C categories $(C=2)$

and $Pc = \sum_{i=1}^{c} Pi^2$ is the chance agreement for C categories, and Pi is the

proportion of judgments made by all observers for the ith category.

A number of adaptations and extensions of Scott's π have been pro-

9.1
of Ten Randomly Chosen Subjects

Subject 524		527		529		531		610		Total	
Prop.	%	Prop.	%	Prop.	%	Prop.	%	Prop.	%	Prop.	%
$\frac{49}{63}$	77.78	$\frac{11}{15}$	73.33	$\frac{44}{49}$	89.80	$\frac{109}{122}$	89.34	$\frac{37}{42}$	88.10	$\frac{367}{422}$	86.97
$\frac{48}{62}$	77.42	$\frac{101}{110}$	91.82	$\frac{44}{49}$	89.80	$\frac{76}{83}$	91.57	$\frac{29}{33}$	87.88	$\frac{534}{596}$	89.60
$\frac{50}{60}$	83.33	$\frac{17}{23}$	73.91	$\frac{8}{9}$	88.89	$\frac{11}{11}$	100.00	$\frac{6}{8}$	75.00	$\frac{127}{148}$	85.81
$\frac{88}{91}$	96.70	$\frac{62}{65}$	95.38	$\frac{34}{35}$	97.14	$\frac{52}{56}$	92.86	$\frac{58}{58}$	100.00	$\frac{580}{615}$	94.31
$\frac{91}{94}$	96.81	$\frac{28}{30}$	93.33	$\frac{45}{48}$	93.75	$\frac{67}{68}$	98.53	$\frac{51}{55}$	92.73	$\frac{522}{543}$	96.13
$\frac{25}{31}$	80.65	$\frac{52}{57}$	91.23	$\frac{145}{145}$	100.00	$\frac{93}{103}$	90.29	$\frac{56}{63}$	88.89	$\frac{684}{740}$	92.43
$\frac{20}{21}$	95.24	$\frac{54}{57}$	94.74	$\frac{47}{48}$	97.92	$\frac{34}{38}$	89.47	$\frac{9}{17}$	52.94	$\frac{311}{360}$	86.39
$\frac{7}{7}$	100.00	$\frac{43}{48}$	89.58	$\frac{40}{44}$	90.91	$\frac{8}{9}$	88.89	$\frac{6}{7}$	85.71	$\frac{136}{153}$	88.89
$\frac{20}{22}$	90.91	$\frac{9}{13}$	69.23	$\frac{12}{15}$	80.00	$\frac{24}{26}$	92.31	$\frac{5}{5}$	100.00	$\frac{161}{188}$	85.64
$\frac{5}{6}$	83.33	$\frac{2}{2}$	100.00	$\frac{26}{32}$	81.25	$\frac{5}{5}$	100.00	$\frac{4}{4}$	100.00	$\frac{111}{125}$	88.80
$\frac{16}{17}$	94.12	$\frac{35}{36}$	97.22	$\frac{46}{48}$	95.83	$\frac{21}{22}$	95.45	$\frac{3}{4}$	75.00	$\frac{216}{230}$	93.91
$\frac{23}{27}$	95.19	$\frac{11}{12}$	91.67	$\frac{52}{66}$	78.79	$\frac{106}{112}$	94.64	$\frac{42}{46}$	91.30	$\frac{438}{478}$	91.63
$\frac{442}{501}$	88.22	$\frac{425}{468}$	90.81	$\frac{543}{588}$	92.35	$\frac{606}{655}$	92.52	$\frac{306}{342}$	89.47	$\frac{4187}{4598}$	91.06

posed (Cohen, 1960; Emmer, 1972; Flanders, 1967; Garrett, 1972; Light, 1971). All of these coefficients are interpretable as the proportion of agreement between judges after allowance for chance.

Cohen's (1960) K coefficient was regarded as most appropriate for the establishment of levels of intercoder agreement in the present study. Scott's π method assumes that the proportional distributions of marginals for each pair of judgments are symmetrical and approximately equal to the average proportional distributions of marginals obtained from all judgments. The codings obtained in the present study do not meet this assumption, as coders were in no way restricted in the amount of use they made of the various categories.

Cohen's (1960) K coefficient is very similar to Scott's (1955) π, but Pc, i.e., chance agreement, is defined differently. Pc is based on observed marginals rather than on predetermined or expected marginal distributions. Cohen does not assume that the distribution of proportions over the categories for the population is known or equal for the coders.

Nominal agreement for C categories ($C \geq 2$), Po, is computed in the same manner as Scott's Po, but Pc, chance agreement, is obtained as follows:

$$Pc = \frac{1}{N^2} \sum_{i=1}^{C} (n_{i+})(n+i)$$

$$K = \frac{Po - Pc}{1 - Pc}$$

or in terms of frequencies

$$K = \frac{Po - Pc}{N - Pc}$$

The above formula was used in the computation of the coefficients of agreement, i.e., reliability coefficient K, which are presented in the last column of Table 9.2.

The K coefficient computed here is based on the assumption that all disagreements between coders are of equal importance. This treatment was regarded as preferable to Cohen's (1968) "Weighted Kappa" at the current state of knowledge concerning the differential importance of the strategy variables. Any decision procedure to determine a procedure of weighting the variables would have been highly subjective at the present time.

Table 9.2 shows coder agreement data for each strategy and Cohen's (1960) K coefficients for each task separately and for the total coding decisions made across all tasks.

The K values ranged from 0.81 to 0.96, indicating a very high proportion of agreements between the coders. Chance expectancies are given only for the agreements as the other values are immaterial for the assessment of coder agreement.

Table 9.3 shows details of agreements and discrepancies of judgment between the coders for each strategy variable summed across all tasks. The columns of the table represent the categorizations made by coder A and the rows represent those made by coder B. The diagonal cells show the frequencies of agreement between both coders for each strategy.

The overall K coefficient of 0.912 obtained by comparing the coders' judgments across all tasks for the ten subjects which had been randomly selected for the reliability study shows that 91% of the joint judgments were agreements, chance being excluded.

These results suggest that problem solving behaviors investigated in the present study can be regarded as having been assessed reliably and that the taxonomy of problem solving strategies which was prepared for the present study yielded highly consistent judgments and can be regarded as providing a tool for reproducible assessments of observed problem solving strategies.

SPEED OF PERFORMANCE

As was reported previously, the design of the study placed no limitation on the amounts of time available for work on each of the tasks. In the analyses which will be discussed in the following sections, the measure of speed of problem solving for each task was provided by the number of three-second intervals used by the subject.

In the solving of intellectual tasks speed of performance is often considered a characteristic of individuals with high ability. Over many years there has been an emphasis on measuring academic potential in terms of learning or response rate depending on whether the test related to the learning of new material or to the recall of previously learned information.

Most psychometric tests estimate intellectual ability in terms of both the correctness and the speed with which a given task is completed. In many group administered intelligence tests, for example, testees are required to provide correct answers to as many test items of increasing difficulty as possible within a given time span. The resulting IQ scores, therefore, are dependent on the speed of information processing as well as on the correctness of the response. Individuals who respond more slowly tackle fewer items and receive a lower score than those who answer a larger number of items in the same time span. Hunt, Lunneborg, and Lewis (1975), for example, have pointed out that

> although a verbal intelligence test is directly a measure of what people know, it is indirectly a way of identifying people who can code and manipulate verbal stimuli rapidly in situations in which knowledge per se is not a major factor. (p. 223)

Other studies using a variety of tasks have found a significant relationship between psychometric estimates of general ability and response times (Goldberg, Schwartz, & Stewart, 1977; Hunt, Frost, & Lunneborg, 1973; Hunt, Lunneborg, & Lewis, 1975). Amounts of increase in response or processing time with increasing level of complexity of items in a test also have been shown to be related to measures of intelligence (Eysenck, 1967; Scott, 1940; Spiegel & Bryant, 1978).

TABLE 9.2
Reliability Data Relating to Coder Agreement

Task	Strategy Variable	Number of Occurrences	Number Both Coders Agreed	Agreement Expected by Chance	Percent Agreement	Reliability Coefficient K (Kappa)
	1	50	50	6.0	100.0	
	2	9	4	0.1	44.4	
	3	21	17	1.2	81.0	
	4	11	9	0.3	81.8	
	5	5	4	0.1	80.0	
	6	0	0	0	0	
	7	65	56	10.2	86.2	0.849
	8	13	13	0.6	100.0	
1 [Binet]	9	30	27	2.6	90.0	
	10	24	24	1.4	100.0	
	11	119	100	30.2	84.0	
	12	0	0	0	0	
	13	4	2	0.0	50.0	
	14	11	7	0.2	63.6	
	15	19	19	0.9	100.0	
	16	32	28	2.3	87.5	
	17	1	1	0.0	100.0	
	18	8	6	0.2	75.0	
	1	30	30	1.5	100.0	
	2	13	9	0.2	69.2	
	3	16	14	0.5	87.5	
	4	14	14	0.5	100.0	
	5	8	6	0.1	75.0	
	6	0	0	0	0	

2 [::::]					
7	129	116	26.4	89.9	0.878
8	75	72	9.9	96.0	
9	28	21	1.2	75.0	
10	101	93	16.3	92.1	
11	24	18	0.9	75.0	
12	4	4	0.0	100.0	
13	5	4	0.1	80.0	
14	12	7	0.2	58.3	
15	20	17	0.7	85.0	
16	112	103	21.4	92.0	
17	5	5	0.1	100.0	
18	0	0	0	0	
1	24	24	3.9	100.0	
2	1	1	0.0	100.0	
3	10	9	0.6	90.0	
4	0	0	0	0	
5	2	0	0	0	
6	0	0	0	0	
7	8	8	0.6	100.0	
8	0	0	0	0	
9	0	0	0	0	
3 [15 × 30]					
10	0	0	0	0	
11	70	62	29.3	88.6	0.812
12	0	0	0	0	
13	9	9	0.6	100.0	
14	3	2	0.1	66.7	
15	14	6	0.7	42.9	
16	5	4	0.4	80.0	
17	2	2	0.0	100.0	
18	0	0	0	0	

(Continued)

TABLE 9.2 (Continued)

Task	Strategy Variable	Number of Occurrences	Number Both Coders Agreed	Agreement Expected by Chance	Percent Agreement	Reliability Coefficient K (Kappa)
	1	240	240	94.1	100.0	
	2	53	49	4.2	92.5	
	3	47	38	3.1	80.9	
	4	20	19	0.7	95.0	
	5	33	32	2.1	97.0	
	6	0	0	0	0	
	7	101	78	13.3	77.2	
	8	3	3	0.0	100.0	
	9	0	0	0	0	
	10	24	24	1.0	100.0	0.895
	11	0	0	0	0	
	12	13	10	0.8	76.9	
	13	8	8	0.1	100.0	
	14	23	19	0.8 ·	82.6	
	15	17	15	0.5	88.2	
	16	19	15	0.6	78.9	
	17	13	13	0.3	100.0	
	18	1	0	0	0	
4 [Pebbles]	1	104	104	20.1	100.0	
	2	113	113	23.7	100.0	
	3	42	41	3.2	97.6	
	4	31	29	1.8	93.5	
	5	11	11	0.2	100.0	
	6	0	0	0	0	

5 [Platform]					0.962
7	72	70	9.4	97.2	
8	1	1	0.0	100.0	
9	0	0	0	0	
10	51	50	4.7	98.0	
11	2	2	0.0	100.0	
12	3	2	0.0	66.7	
13	41	39	2.9	95.1	
14	17	17	0.5	100.0	
15	15	8	0.3	53.3	
16	25	23	1.4	92.0	
17	12	12	0.3	100.0	
18	3	3	0.0	100.0	
1	23	23	0.7	100.0	
2	32	31	1.3	96.9	
3	19	18	0.6	94.7	
4	43	32	1.9	74.4	
5	14	12	0.3	85.7	
6	0	0	0	0	
7	159	155	35.9	97.5	
8	103	94	13.2	91.3	
6 [6m→4△] 9	9	4	0.1	44.4	0.922
10	110	104	15.6	94.5	
11	6	6	0.1	100.0	
12	10	10	0.1	100.0	
13	5	5	0.0	100.0	
14	33	30	1.4	90.9	
15	20	18	0.5	90.0	
16	134	129	24.3	96.3	
17	4	4	0.0	100.0	
18	16	15	0.3	93.8	

(Continued)

TABLE 9.2 (Continued)

Task	Strategy Variable	Number of Occurrences	Number Both Coders Agreed	Agreement Expected by Chance	Percent Agreement	Reliability Coefficient K (Kappa)
	1	27	27	2.0	100.0	
	2	77	77	17.3	100.0	
	3	10	9	0.3	90.0	
	4	19	13	0.7	68.4	
	5	11	11	0.3	100.0	
	6	2	2	0.0	100.0	
	7	57	50	8.9	87.7	
	8	27	21	1.7	77.8	
	9	5	0	0	0	0.845
	10	25	22	2.2	88.0	
	11	0	0	0	0	
	12	2	2	0.0	100.0	
	13	2	1	0.0	50.0	
	14	12	11	0.4	91.7	
	15	16	9	0.5	56.3	
	16	55	47	8.6	85.5	
	17	7	7	0.3	100.0	
	18	6	2	0.0	33.3	
T7 [9m→1h]	1	14	14	1.4	100.0	
	2	14	12	1.1	85.7	
	3	1	1	0.0	100.0	
	4	14	12	1.1	85.7	
	5	0	0	0	0	
	6	0	0	0	0	

T8 [Poem/Statue]					
7	12	8	0.7	66.7	
8	0	0	0	0	
9	40	32	9.2	80.0	
10	1	0	0	0	0.868
11	37	37	10.4	100.0	
12	2	2	0.0	100.0	
13	7	7	0.3	100.0	
14	0	0	0	0	
15	3	3	0.1	100.0	
16	6	6	0.2	100.0	
17	2	2	0.0	100.0	
18	0	0	0	0	
T9 [Praise/P]					
1	17	17	1.5	100.0	
2	7	5	0.2	71.4	
3	0	0	0	0	
4	5	4	0.1	80.0	
5	0	0	0	0	
6	2	1	0.1	50.0	
7	13	12	1.0	92.3	
8	2	1	0.0	50.0	
9	50	43	11.7	86.0	0.838
10	22	16	2.1	72.7	
11	44	40	9.8	90.9	
12	6	6	0.4	100.0	
13	2	1	0.0	50.0	
14	5	4	0.1	80.0	
15	2	1	0.0	50.0	
16	6	6	0.2	100.0	
17	5	5	0.3	100.0	
18	0	0	0	0	

(Continued)

TABLE 9.2 *(Continued)*

Task	Strategy Variable	Number of Occurrences	Number Both Coders Agreed	Agreement Expected by Chance	Percent Agreement	Reliability Coefficient K (Kappa)
	1	14	14	1.6	100.0	
	2	0	0	0	0	
	3	2	2	0.0	100.0	
	4	1	1	0.0	100.0	
	5	0	0	0	0	
	6	0	0	0	0	
	7	23	22	4.2	95.7	
	8	2	2	0.1	100.0	
	9	22	19	3.9	86.4	0.880
	10	20	20	4.0	100.0	
	11	18	13	2.0	72.2	
	12	1	1	0.0	100.0	
	13	11	11	1.0	100.0	
	14	1	0	0	0	
	15	3	3	0.1	100.0	
	16	7	4	0.3	57.1	
	17	0	0	0	0	
	18	0	0	0	0	
T10 [Fly/Tree]	1	10	10	0.4	100.0	
	2	1	1	0.0	100.0	
	3	2	2	0.0	100.0	
	4	2	1	0.0	50.0	
	5	0	0	0	0	
	6	2	2	0.0	100.0	

	Index					Density
T11 [Wood/Alc.]	7	33	33	4.9	100.0	0.919
	8	2	2	0.0	100.0	
	9	56	52	13.2	92.9	
	10	6	6	0.2	100.0	
	11	72	71	23.8	98.6	
	12	4	4	0.1	100.0	
	13	7	6	0.2	85.7	
	14	5	2	0.0	40.0	
	15	14	13	0.9	92.9	
	16	14	10	0.7	71.4	
	17	0	0	0	0	
	18	0	0	0	0	
T12 [8TB/2]	1	41	41	3.5	100.0	0.906
	2	28	26	1.5	92.9	
	3	25	25	1.4	100.0	
	4	22	21	1.2	95.5	
	5	6	4	0.1	66.7	
	6	10	10	0.3	100.0	
	7	126	113	29.8	89.7	
	8	10	10	0.3	100.0	
	9	2	2	0.2	100.0	
	10	92	87	17.5	94.6	
	11	5	0	0	0	
	12	4	4	0.0	100.0	
	13	16	15	0.5	93.8	
	14	21	18	0.8	85.7	
	15	7	6	0.1	85.7	
	16	44	42	4.2	95.5	
	17	3	3	0.1	100.0	
	18	16	16	0.4	100.0	

(Continued)

TABLE 9.2 (Continued)

Task	Strategy Variable	Number of Occurrences	Number Both Coders Agreed	Agreement Expected by Chance	Percent Agreement	Reliability Coefficient K (Kappa)
	1	594	594	77.3	100.0	
	2	348	328	25.4	94.3	
	3	195	176	8.2	90.3	
	4	182	155	6.9	85.2	
	5	90	80	1.9	88.9	
	6	16	15	0.2	93.8	
	7	798	721	133.1	90.4	
	8	238	219	12.8	92.0	
All tasks	9	242	200	12.0	82.6	0.912
	10	476	446	49.1	93.7	
	11	397	349	32.6	87.9	
	12	49	45	0.8	91.8	
	13	117	108	3.2	92.3	
	14	143	117	4.0	81.8	
	15	150	118	4.4	78.7	
	16	459	417	46.9	90.8	
	17	54	54	1.1	100.0	
	18	50	38	0.4	76.0	

TABLE 9.3

Coder Agreements and Discrepancies for each Strategy Across All Tasks for Ten Subjects

										Coder A										
Strategy	1	2	3	4	5	6	7	8	9	10	11	12	13	14	15	16	17	18	Total
1	594																		594
2	2	328	6	3	2		1				3				2				348
3	1	1	176	5	5						1			2					195
4	1	1	4	155	3	6	2		1	1	2				1	2		1	182
5			1	1	80	2	3		1		1			2		3			90
6						15										1			16
7			3		1	7	721	8	7	8	1	22	4			13	2		798
8		1					8	219		5	3		2						238
9		3				5	6	4	200	1	9	3		3		8			242
10					1	6	3	6	1	446	4	4	1			1	7		476
11			3		1		8	6	12	4	349	2	4	1	1	6	8		397
12												45	2			2			49
13		1			1		1	1			1		108	1			1		117
14				3	1		3		2	4	1		1	117	4	4	2	1	143
15				1			1		1	1	1				118	19	7	1	150
16			1	1	1		4	2	2	4	6	1	2	4	9	417	4		459
17																	54		54
18							4	2							1		5	38	50
Total	598	335	194	173	96	42	767	248	227	474	378	78	124	128	135	470	91	40	4598

Coder B

181

Reaction time studies have shown that "One of the basic tenets of human performance is that man is slow when he is uncertain" (Chase, 1978, p. 25).

Kaufman (1979a) found that speed of correct responding is highly related to problem solving ability, and notes:

> It is important to remember that quick performance is not just related to behavior or personality, but also bears a clear relationship to problem solving ability. Children who solve . . . problems quickly do better . . . than do youngsters who solve them more slowly. (p. 39)

Questions have been asked, however, concerning the origins of the role played by speed in intellectual performance. Is speed a noncognitive variable or a cognitive variable? It is undeniable that personality, motivation, interest, and other factors as well as environmental variables, can influence the speed with which an individual solves problems. Cognitive style (Kagan, 1966) and anxiety would obviously provide major influences on the speed with which the individual responds.

After finding that speed of performance and success in problem solving are highly correlated across different age levels, Kaufman (1979b) justifies the allocation of bonus points for speed in the Wechsler tests, and suggests:

> The fact that quick responders are better problem solvers than slow responders implies that performance time is an intellectual attribute and deserves to contribute to an individual's Performance and Full Scale IQ. (p. 596)

but cautions:

> The trend supports speed as an aspect of intellect, but for any particular child, a slow performance time may be due to non-intellective factors such as anxiety, motor difficulties, or a reflective cognitive style. (pp. 596–597)

The relationship between the amounts of time taken by subjects in their work on each task in the present study and intelligence and achievement were briefly investigated.

SPEED, INTELLIGENCE, AND ACHIEVEMENT

The amounts of time taken for work on each problem (measured in three-second units) were correlated with intelligence (measured by WAIS Block Design [BD] scaled score) and with the total time taken for all problems for each subject in the total sample and for groups of different levels of achievement. Achievement levels were defined in two ways, first in terms of three categories as follows: Level A contained subjects whose solutions to the problem under consideration were correct or nearly correct, level B covered the subjects who gave up, and level C for subjects who produced a wrong solution. In the second set of analyses only two levels of achievement, "correct or nearly correct," and "gives up or wrong solution," were used.

The correlations of the time taken and BD scores across all subjects for each task resulted in only two significant ($p \leq .01$) but relatively low correlations. Time taken for Task 3 [15 × 30] was found to correlate negatively with the intelligence measure ($r = -.30$), while in the case of Task 7 [9m→lh] a positive correlation ($r = .35$) was obtained. A post hoc explanation of this is that the longer a subject might take to solve an easy problem of the type of Task 3, the less ability he or she might be expected to have. Conversely, in the case of Task 7, it might be expected that brighter individuals might persevere longer with a task whose solution might be regarded as a challenge.

Relating the times taken with the BD scores for the subjects grouped according to their level of achievement in each task resulted in only one significant correlation (Task 12 [8TB/2] $r = .38$) for achievement level A, i.e., subjects who solved or nearly solved the task, suggesting that the brighter these subjects were the faster they solved the task. This is not an unexpected finding in the case of a task whose solution required basically convergent thinking. For the group who gave up or whose solutions were incorrect, significant correlations were obtained in the cases of Task 7 [9m→lh], $r = .41$, Task 8 [Poem/St] $r = .42$, Task 9 [Praise/Punishment] $r = .36$, Task 10 [Fly/Tree] $r = .29$, and Task 12 [8TB/2] $r = .30$. None of the achievement groups yielded a significant correlation between speed of work and intelligence for Task 3 [15 × 30]. The discrepancy between this finding and the above noted significant correlation obtained for this task when times taken and BD scores were correlated across all the subjects can be explained as a decrease in the correlation coefficient due to the reduction of variance between the subjects resulting from the splitting of the total sample into subsamples.

Separate analyses for the group of subjects who gave up and those whose problem solving activity resulted in an incorrect solution showed significant results for Tasks 7 ($r = .32$), 8 ($r = .48$), 10 ($r = .30$), and 12 ($r = .28$) for the latter group. This means that the more intelligent the subjects of this group were, the faster they reached the (incorrect) solution.

The time taken and BD scores of the subjects who gave up produced significant and moderately high to substantial correlations for Tasks 2 (r

TABLE 9.4

Significant Correlations (p < .05) Between BD Score
and Time Taken on Task

| | | | | Task | | | | |
Group	2	3	5	7	8	9	10	12
All Subjects		-.30		.35				
Achievement A								
Achievement B	.32		.52	.41		.72		.38
Achievement C				.32	.48		.30	.28
Achievement B + C				.41	.42	.36	.29	.30

= .32), 5 (r = .52), 7 (r = .41), and 9 (r = .72). These tasks might be regarded as problems which could be expected to elicit a certain amount of innovative, creative behavior in certain individuals. It would therefore be reasonable to suggest that more intelligent subjects, who were unsuccessful in their attempts to solve these problems, may have tried to spend more time on the problems in the hope of finding a solution than less intelligent subjects.

The above discussed correlation coefficients are summarized in Table 9.4.

Only in the group of subjects who abandoned the task before solving it (achievement level B) was there a tendency for the size of the correlation coefficients to be increased for the more difficult tasks. The pattern is, however, not a systematic one. This might suggest that the amounts of variance which might be explained by the speed–intelligence relationship do not appear to increase with increasing task difficulty.

The observation that the relationship between perseverance with the problem and intelligence in group B, who abandoned the task before solving it, is restricted to work on the more difficult problems may be explained by the not unexpected finding that the tendency to abandon the task tends itself to be a function of task complexity (see Table 9.5 for details relating to task difficulty).

The relatively low correlations between the measure of intelligence and time taken to solve the problems in the present study may have resulted from the fact that the Block Design test, used as a measure of general intelligence, is a timed test, while time in the problem solving tasks was unrestricted. One might expect problem solving times to be more highly related to the Block Design scores if the former had been timed also.

It is important to remember that the size of the correlation coefficient "r" is strongly influenced by the variability in the correlated scores. "The greater the variability, the higher the correlation, other things being equal. If the variability of either X or Y were zero, the correlation would be zero"

TABLE 9.5
Ranking of Tasks According to Facility

Rank	Task	Content	% Solvers Achievement Level A	% Nonsolvers Achievement Levels B and C	% Giving Up Achievement Level B
1	T 3	15 × 30	89	11	1
2	T 8	Poem/St.	73	27	7
3	T10	Fly/Tree	63	37	10
4	T 9	Praise/P	45	55	15
5	T 1	Binet	40	60	11
6	T 4	Pebbles	35	65	17
7	T11	Wood/Alc.	27	73	22
8	T 6	6m → 4△	25	75	34
9	T 7	9m → 1h	22	78	34
10	T 5	Platform	21	79	26
11	T 2	⦂⦂	19	81	43
12	T12	8TB/2	7	93	26

(Guilford & Fruchter, 1978, p. 324). The variability of the WAIS BD scores was relatively small in the present sample, which represented a restricted range of general ability. A reduced correlation between this variable and others was therefore to be expected.

The rather superficial estimate of general ability provided by the WAIS Block Design score (see Chapter 5 for details) was included in the present study in an attempt to introduce at least a small measure of control of potential differences in the observed problem solving behaviors that may be a direct function of the level of intellectual functioning. General ability may therefore be regarded as basically a categorical variable of auxiliary importance in this study in which, apart from the strategies themselves, the variables of competency and speed were of primary concern.

To make use of the general ability variable in its intended manner, subjects were categorized into intelligence classifications established by Wechsler (1949, 1958, 1974) on the basis of the IQ estimates obtained from the BD scores. The manuals accompanying the Wechsler tests provide details of the relation of IQs and scaled scores obtained from individual subtests. This information made it possible to classify the subjects for the present purposes.

Comparison of Ability Groups

Table 9.6 shows the distribution of the present sample in comparison with the standardization samples of WAIS (Wechsler, 1958) and WISC-R (Wechsler, 1974), and the theoretical normal curve.

It must be stressed that the numbers in the present study are small

TABLE 9.6

Comparison of the Distribution of the Present Sample with those Used in the
WAIS and WISC-R Standardizations and the Theoretical Normal Curve

Group Present Study	Wechsler IQ	Classification	Normal Curve	Percent Included WAIS	Percent Included WISC-R	Present Study	Present Study
1	130 and above	Very Superior	2.2	2.2	2.3	6.7	6
2	120 - 129	Superior	6.7	6.7	7.4	6.7	6
3	110 - 119	High Average (Bright)[b]	16.1	16.1	16.5	30.0	27
4	90 - 109	Average	50.0	50.0	49.4	46.0	41
5[a]	80 - 89	Low Average (Dull)[b]	16.1	16.1	16.2	10.0	9
-	70 - 79	Borderline	6.7	6.7	6.0	-	-
-	69 and below	Mentally Deficient[b]	2.2	2.2	2.2	-	-

[a]The IQ estimates of subjects classified as Group 5 in the present study were 85 and below. The sample did not include subjects with IQ estimates below the level of 84.

[b]The terms "High Average (Bright)," "Low Average (Dull)," and "Mentally Deficient" correspond to the terms "Bright Normal," "Dull Normal," and "Mentally Defective," respectively, used by Wechsler in the WAIS, WPPSI and WISC (1949) manuals.

NOTE: Table 9.6 was adapted from Tables 12 and 8 respectively of the WAIS (Wechsler, 1958, p. 20) and WISC-R (Wechsler, 1974, p. 26) manuals.

TABLE 9.7

Mean Times and Standard Deviations for Five Ability Groups, Irrespective of Achievement

Task	BD 1		BD 2		BD 3		BD 4		BD 5	
	$\overline{X}$	SD	$\overline{X}$	SD	$\overline{X}$	SD	$\overline{X}$	SD	$\overline{X}$	SD
1	27.00	4.55	33.33	9.10	43.74	32.59	47.73	65.51	47.78	25.09
2	79.00	47.25	81.33	48.03	69.41	50.52	70.54	37.12	40.44	24.94
3	5.67	2.98	4.83	1.46	10.85	10.37	11.12	8.38	21.67	15.11
4	73.17	36.50	75.50	36.94	68.78	34.58	68.37	32.16	62.67	21.97
5	53.33	24.29	68.50	21.31	59.26	25.92	59.59	23.10	58.00	31.45
6	62.67	31.11	82.33	32.36	47.48	36.60	68.73	36.08	52.00	30.00
7	52.17	26.13	81.33	40.86	42.40	26.03	40.46	21.18	26.56	12.25
8	37.17	23.74	26.67	16.83	20.31	19.17	20.65	18.75	20.11	11.56
9	28.17	16.46	25.33	17.97	17.78	11.34	16.68	9.45	17.67	9.20
10	15.83	11.75	16.83	10.64	15.81	13.31	18.20	14.98	13.22	9.04
11	20.00	10.34	13.83	7.15	18.69	10.71	18.85	11.25	17.44	7.93
12	51.67	26.77	69.33	33.17	64.22	35.04	45.51	23.76	33.89	22.17

TABLE
Average Times Spent on Each Task

| | Achievement | | | | | | Achievement A Ability | | | | |
| | A | | B | | C | | | | | | |
Task	$\overline{X}$	SD	$\overline{X}$	SD	$\overline{X}$	SD	Very Sup.	Superior	High Av.	Average	Low Av.
1	41.67	33.67	78.80	38.67	32.98	20.33	26.6	33.0	51.6	35.1	(37.0)
2	54.65	43.24	76.18	37.15	67.68	48.52	27.5	86.5	67.9	52.0	(15.0)
3	11.05	10.35	20.9			8.36	5.7	4.6	10.6	9.6	23.3
4	59.57	19.29	83.33	30.67	71.22	37.45	(26.0)	41.0	57.3	63.2	52.8
5	52.26	27.33	58.87	21.69	62.06	24.67	67.5	(99.0)	40.0	45.6	58.0
6	50.23	36.01	71.97	31.21	54.48	38.71	45.7	(57.0)	40.7	93.0	–
7	35.20	26.93	54.10	29.00	38.74	22.16	66.0	(80)	18.4	47.4	21.0
8	18.32	16.49	29.67	10.98	33.89	23.0	24.0	26.7	17.5	14.5	12.4
9	16.38	11.97	22.15	12.52	20.00	10.78	11.5	27.4	16.7	14.3	11.0
10	12.09	12.94	21.44	9.23	26.17	10.51	15.4	14.2	· 9.7	13.4	9.5
11	10.21	7.54	24.20	9.69	20.60	9.66	13.7	(5.0)	10.9	10.3	(16.0)
12	62.67	34.34	62.30	27.71	43.45	29.18	(27.0)		63.5	(45.0)	

Note: Values in brackets refer to the results obtained from only one person.

indeed, and that an impression only may be gained in this exploration of possible tendencies of variables which might, at best, provide some indication of directions for future research. The description of the observed relationship between general ability and the time taken for tasks will therefore be brief.

Table 9.7 shows the mean times and standard deviations irrespective of outcome of the problem solving activity for the five ability groups for each task. The mean times taken across tasks did not differ significantly between the five ability groups ($F_{4,55} = 0.54$, $p > .05$), nor did the variability. A one way analysis of variance performed on the standard deviations of the tasks between ability groups resulted in $F_{4,55} = 0.68$ ($p > .05$).

In terms of the mean times taken across subjects for the total of 12 tasks, competence of problem solving as defined in the present study and general ability grouping were shown to be independent of one another ($\chi^2 = 1.84$, $df = 8$, NS). This finding provides further support for the tendency indicated by the previously discussed low correlations between BD scores and achievement.

Separate χ^2 tests were conducted for each task of 5×3 contingency tables testing the hypothesis that the time each of the five ability groups tended to spend on the task was independent of their achieved level of three problem solving competencies. All $12\chi^2$ values obtained in this way were significant ($p \leq .01$), which resulted in the rejection of the original hypothesis, because it was shown that in all 12 tasks the times spent by different ability groups differed for the three levels of competence.

Table 9.8 shows the mean numbers of three-second units spent on each task by various criterion groups. It was found that, irrespective of ability level, problem solvers, i.e. achievement level A, tended to spend

9.8
by Different Criterion Groups

	Achievement B Ability					Achievement C Ability			
Very Sup.	Superior	High Av.	Average	Low Av.	Very Sup.	Superior	High Av.	Average	Low Av.
–	(29.0)	(68.0)	84.3	76.7	(29.0)	(39.0)	37.7	35.5	32.6
96.0	100.0	69.8	69.3	62.7	113.5	57.5	70.3	77.9	32.2
–	–	–	23.0	–	–	(6.0)	–	23.2	–
(73.0)	94.0	73.2	88.3	77.0	88.3	91.5	66.6	70.1	73.0
80.0	68.0	69.7	53.3	44.0	35.0	54.0	61.8	65.7	72.0
79.7	106.7	93.2	70.6	64.6	–	34.5	32.8	64.0	36.3
57.3	96.0	52.6	42.7	35.0	(9.0)	–	46.1	34.7	21.0
–	–	23.5	33.0	–	63.5	–	35.5	25.6	29.8
(37.0)	–	13.5	19.2	–	36.3	(15.0)	19.7	18.9	21.0
–	–	24.5	20.5	20.7	(18.0)	(30.0)	29.1	28.4	9.5
(23.0)	–	23.1	24.0	22.0	28.0	15.6	23.0	20.6	15.0
64.0	96.0	66.5	53.2	38.5	45.5	56.0	63.7	37.8	32.6

significantly less time ($p < .01$) than nonsolvers, achievement level C, and those abandoning the task before solving it, i.e. achievement level B. This might suggest that failure to solve a task may be less related to insufficiency of time than to an inadequate apportioning of time to task relevant activities. This suggestion is examined further in Chapter 11, where further support for such reasoning will be provided by the results of the discriminant function analyses.

The variable of speed in problem solving was investigated at two levels in the present study. Each subject was classified as "fast" or "slow" on the basis of whether the number of three-second units spent in working on a given task was equal to, below, or above the group's median time spent on that task. Speed of problem solving was found to be unrelated to the task variable within each of the five ability groups.

The relationship between speed and type of task was investigated separately for each ability level, by comparing the numbers of fast and slow individuals in the 12 tasks. The following χ^2 values were obtained:

Ability Group	WAIS:BD SS	WAIS IQ EQU.	Wechsler Classification	χ^2 (df = 11)
1	≥16	≥130	Very Superior	11.25
2	14–15	120–129	Superior	15.85
3	12–13	110–119	High Average	3.99
4	8–11	90–109	Average	9.65
5	≤7	≤85	Low Average	18.40

To reach significance at the .05 level with 11 degrees of freedom, a χ^2 value of at least 19.68 is required. The lowest ability group, group 5, comes closer to this value than any of the other groups. Inspection of the frequencies revealed a tendency of the members of this group to work mainly on the easier tasks, working relatively slowly as may be expected of individuals with less natural ability, and to take a guess at a solution or to abandon the difficult tasks after a relatively brief period. This resulted in considerably larger numbers of slow subjects in the cells for easier tasks and larger numbers of fast subjects in the categories of the difficult tasks.

χ^2 were performed for each task to test the hypothesis that achievement level, i.e., the outcome of the problem solving activity, is independent of the time spent on the task.

After comparison of the frequencies in 2 × 3 (i.e., 2 levels of speed × 3 levels of achievement) contingency tables, the original hypothesis was accepted (p > .05) for Tasks 1 [Binet], 2 [⦂⦂], 3 [15 × 30], 4 [Pebbles], 5 [Platform], 7 [9m→1h], and 12 [8TB/2]. In other words, analyses of the time spent on these tasks provide no evidence that the achievement level resulting from the problem solving activity is influenced by the speed of problem solving.

In the case of Task 6 [6m→4Δ] and in all of the similarities items, i.e. Tasks 8 to 11 inclusive, the original hypothesis was rejected, and it was shown ($p < .05$) that for these tasks achievement level was related to speed of problem solving. Inspection of the frequencies showed a consistent tendency across the tasks for solvers (i.e., achievement level A) to be fast workers, while competence level C, consisting of subjects who failed to solve the problem correctly, tended to contain a larger number of slow subjects.

The independence of frequencies in 2 × 2 contingency tables, i.e., subjects classified according to speed (fast versus slow) and two levels of competence: those who solved the task correctly (i.e., category A) versus the combination of subjects who abandoned the task prematurely and those who failed the task (i.e., categories B and C) was tested.

For Task 3 [15 × 30] and the similarities items, Tasks 8 to 11 inclusive, χ^2 tests showed that competence level was not independent of speed.

In each of these tasks a significantly larger number of solvers (competence level A) came from fast working groups than from slow groups. The following χ^2 were obtained for these tasks:

Task	χ^2 (df = 2)	p
3. [15 × 30]	5.89	<.05
8. [Poem/Statue]	7.55	<.01
9. [Praise/Punish.]	8.20	<.01
10. [Fly/Tree]	7.69	<.01
11. [Wood/Alcohol]	13.61	<.01

χ^2 values obtained from the analyses of 2 × 2 contingency tables for the other tasks failed to reach significance at the $p = .05$ level. Problem solving achievement and speed were thus shown to be related in tasks which, with the exception of Task 11 [Wood/Alc.], were the easiest tasks in the study. These results suggest that problem solving competence and speed of work may be related in the case of easy but not difficult tasks. A reason for this may be that easier tasks require a smaller or more predictable number of problem solving strategies. Fast solving can be expected to have resulted from solvers having applied correct or adequate strategies more or less from the beginning, while nonsolvers may not have been equally competent in their selection of the appropriate strategies. This type of reasoning finds further support in the findings—to be discussed later in this chapter—that solvers were found to have significantly lower mean variety scores, i.e., that they applied fewer different strategies, than nonsolvers, and that easy tasks, in general, elicited a smaller number of different strategies.

STRATEGY PREFERENCES

Preferences in strategy use for subjects and tasks were assessed on the basis of the frequencies with which certain behavior categories were used.

A first test of whether the previously identified 18 problem solving behaviors were applied consistently and similarly across different tasks was performed by comparing individual task and overall frequencies of use made of each behavior category. This approach makes it possible to identify which specific behaviors, if any, may have been of particular importance in the solving of different tasks.

As subjects were allowed unlimited amounts of time to solve the problems in the present study, the total and average times taken to solve the tasks differed both between subjects and between tasks. Some of the tasks were found to be more difficult than others, i.e., they required a greater number of three-second units than others. Some subjects worked faster than others. Reference to the observed raw score frequencies of the time units does not permit direct comparison of similarities and differences in patterns of strategy use across tasks and subjects.

A number of analyses were performed, therefore, on both the raw frequencies of strategy use (in units of three seconds) and on the frequencies for each strategy as a proportion of the total problem solving time spent by a given subject on a given task. The conversion of each subject's raw frequencies to proportions of total time spent on a given task results in a loss of information concerning the influence of differential task lengths and difficulty levels, and a disregard for ability differences between subjects on patterns of strategy use.

On the other hand the expression of amounts of strategy use as a

TABLE
Frequency of Use of Problem

Strategy	Data Base	Task 1 N	%	Task 2 N	%	Task 3 N	%	Task 4 N	%	Task 5 N	%	Task 6 N	%
1	Raw	471*	13.0	222	3.7	190*	19.4	2147*	35.1	914*	17.6	216	4.0
	Prop.	1642*	18.4	550	6.2	2783*	31.3	3612*	40.6	1857*	20.9	567	6.4
2	Raw	185	5.1	185	3.1	6	0.6	1043*	17.0	1104*	21.3	196	3.6
	Prop.	336	3.8	342	3.8	29	0.3	1203*	13.5	1841*	20.7	348	3.9
3	Raw	191	5.3	141	2.4	40	4.1	424	6.9	310	6.0	185	3.4
	Prop.	491	5.5	226	2.5	393	4.4	588	6.6	493	5.5	273	3.1
4	Raw	58	1.6	107	1.8	7	0.7	184	3.0	286	5.5	244	4.5
	Prop.	117	1.3	199	2.2	45	0.5	222	2.5	481	5.4	450	5.1
5	Raw	45	1.2	109	1.8	3	0.3	308	5.0	188	3.6	108	2.0
	Prop.	104	1.2	148	1.7	40	0.5	415	4.7	331	3.7	202	2.3
6	Raw	0	—	14	0.2	1	0.1	57	0.9	36	0.7	38	0.7
	Prop.	—	—	64	0.7	14	0.2	97	1.1	70	0.8	99	1.1
7	Raw	499*	13.8	1276*	21.3	48	4.9	753*	12.3	666*	12.8	1107*	20.4
	Prop.	1040*	11.7	1705*	19.2	385	4.3	1018*	11.4	1054*	11.8	1589*	17.9
8	Raw	147	4.1	1234*	20.6	18	1.8	22	0.4	39	0.8	1072*	19.7
	Prop.	252	2.8	1757*	19.7	102	1.2	30	0.3	57	0.6	1687*	19.0
9	Raw	425*	11.7	45	0.8	7	0.7	3	0.05	15	0.3	29	0.5
	Prop.	974*	11.0	41	0.5	32	0.4	4	0.04	21	0.2	36	0.4
10	Raw	239	6.6	1041*	17.4	10	1.0	404	6.6	559*	10.8	722*	13.3
	Prop.	608	6.8	1573*	17.0	38	0.4	621	7.0	943*	10.6	1220*	13.7
11	Raw	904*	25.0	71	1.2	439*	44.8	10	0.2	20	0.4	94	1.7
	Prop.	2464*	27.7	102	1.2	3789*	42.6	13	0.2	26	0.3	187	2.1
12	Raw	44	1.2	51	0.9	27	2.8	84	1.4	78	1.5	72	1.3
	Prop.	112	1.3	74	0.8	292	3.3	116	1.3	118	1.3	109	1.2
13	Raw	45	1.2	112	1.9	62	6.3	114	1.9	345	6.6	86	1.6
	Prop.	75	0.9	152	1.7	331	3.7	169	1.9	574	7.0	124	1.4
14	Raw	40	1.1	104	1.7	22	2.3	197	3.2	173	3.3	141	2.6
	Prop.	101	1.1	134	1.5	129	1.5	272	3.1	274	3.1	194	2.2
15	Raw	88	2.4	119	2.0	33	3.4	70	1.1	65	1.3	143	2.6
	Prop.	163	1.8	185	2.1	188	2.1	105	1.2	112	1.3	235	2.6
16	Raw	179	4.9	959*	16.0	48	4.9	239	3.9	331	6.4	893*	16.4
	Prop.	307	3.5	1226*	13.8	190	2.1	308	3.5	525	5.9	1339*	15.1
17	Raw	52	1.4	80	1.3	11	1.1	45	0.7	41	0.8	33	0.6
	Prop.	106	1.2	136	1.5	89	1.0	71	0.8	67	0.8	74	0.8
18	Raw	8	0.2	122	2.0	8	0.8	17	0.3	26	0.5	60	1.1
	Prop.	9	0.1	288	3.2	31	0.3	39	0.4	56	0.6	168	1.9
TOTAL	Raw	3620		5992		980		6121		5196		5439	

proportion of percentage of total problem solving time permits investigations of the relative importance of certain strategies and strategy patterns across different tasks, and the possible identification of generally relevent behaviors across subjects and tasks.

In the reporting of the results, tables and other references will be labelled as "raw data" or "proportion data" depending on whether raw frequencies of three-second units or ipsatized scores are under discussion.

Table 9.9 provides a frequency distribution of the categorized problem solving behaviors according to each of the 12 experimental tasks. The 18 problem solving strategies and the 12 tasks make up the rows and columns respectively of Table 9.9. In addition to the raw frequencies of the 18 problem solving behaviors, the percentage of use was calculated for each

9.9
Solving Strategies Across Tasks

| Task 7 | | Task 8 | | Task 9 | | Task 10 | | Task 11 | | Task 12 | | Total |
N	%	N	%	N	%	N	%	N	%	N	%	N
242	6.5	146	8.0	130	8.2	123	8.4	114	7.0	226	5.2	5141*
898*	10.1	1344*	15.1	1277*	13.8	1644*	18.5	1207*	13.6	1127*	12.7	18458*
565*	15.1	95	5.2	22	1.4	33	2.3	28	1.7	283	6.5	3745
1466*	16.5	464	5.2	104	1.2	197	2.2	128	1.4	591	6.6	7047
94	2.5	21	1.2	19	1.2	22	1.5	25	1.5	252	5.8	1724
237	2.7	134	1.5	139	1.6	177	2.0	188	2.1	452	5.1	3790
166	4.4	98	5.4	40	2.5	33	2.3	8	0.5	135	3.1	1366
457	5.1	690	7.8	259	2.9	334	3.8	77	0.9	304	3.4	3633
79	2.1	1	0.1	1	0.1	5	0.3	1	0.1	80	1.9	928
207	2.3	13	0.1	4	0.05	54	0.6	4	0.04	151	1.7	1672
13	0.4	80	4.4	64	4.0	23	1.6	30	1.8	44	1.0	400
76	0.9	216	2.4	316	3.5	127	1.4	152	1.7	109	1.2	1338
717*	19.2	226*	12.4	209*	12.2	183*	12.5	199*	12.2	1008*	23.3	6891*
1614*	18.1	759	8.5	994*	11.2	733	8.2	935*	10.5	1810*	20.3	13635*
377	10.1	21	1.2	21	1.1	13	0.9	21	1.3	172	4.0	3157
690	7.8	71	0.8	63	0.7	40	0.5	134	1.5	295	3.3	5178
13	0.4	318*	17.4	338*	21.3	361*	24.7	440*	27.0	21	0.5	2015
19	0.2	1690*	19.0	1938*	21.8	2291*	25.8	2273*	25.5	31	0.3	9349
549*	14.7	107	5.9	155	9.2	90	6.2	96	5.9	1103*	25.5	5075
1144*	12.9	377	4.2	725	8.2	366	4.1	443	5.0	2200*	24.7	10257
33	0.9	443*	24.3	408*	25.6	314*	21.5	435*	26.7	31	0.7	3202
83	0.9	1963*	22.1	1896*	21.3	1615*	18.2	2152*	24.2	73	0.8	14364*
29	0.8	38	2.1	38	2.4	30	2.1	15	0.9	42	1.0	548
86	1.0	147	1.7	266	3.0	184	2.1	84	0.9	89	1.0	1677
40	1.1	49	2.7	28	1.8	42	2.9	46	2.8	176	4.1	1145
78	0.9	130	1.5	115	1.3	157	1.8	196	2.2	338	3.8	2438
130	3.5	36	2.0	32	2.0	38	2.6	27	1.7	172	4.0	1112
277	3.1	165	1.9	188	2.1	134	1.5	175	2.0	312	3.5	2353
127	3.4	36	2.0	19	1.2	36	2.5	52	3.2	64	1.5	852
307	3.5	155	1.7	82	0.9	243	2.7	307	3.4	118	1.3	2199
509*	13.6	83	4.5	72	4.5	73	5.0	74	4.5	447*	10.3	3907
1061*	11.9	356	4.0	413	4.6	380	4.3	330	3.7	771	8.7	7206
43	1.2	16	0.9	8	0.5	14	1.0	12	0.7	36	0.8	391
169	1.9	144	1.6	101	1.1	113	1.3	87	1.0	80	0.9	1236
17	0.5	13	0.7	16	1.0	30	2.1	8	0.5	36	0.8	361
32	0.4	84	1.0	71	0.8	111	1.2	31	0.4	48	0.5	969
3743		1827		1620		1463		1631		4328		41960

task for both raw and proportion data. The results based on the proportion data are printed in italics below those based on the raw frequencies. The last column of the table shows the sum of frequencies and the total percentage of use for each strategy collapsed across tasks. The figures in italics in the last column represent the sums of observations for the 18 strategies expressed as percentages of total times across all subjects and tasks, and the total percentage of use based on the proportion data (i.e., the "percentage" of percentages).

In this manner the most and least frequently used strategies can be identified for both real time and relative usage.

Inspection of Table 9.9 shows that real (raw) and relative (proportion) frequency of use of specific problem solving behaviors varied across the different tasks. No single problem solving strategy was used with equal frequency across all tasks. Preference trends are revealed by the row totals.

On the basis of the raw frequencies strategy 7 (Code 211: Plan/Hypothesis) was the most frequently used strategy over all tasks. It was used 16.4% of the total problem solving time, this value having been obtained by summing the responses of all subjects across all tasks. The next strategies according to raw frequency use were strategies 1 (Code 111: First reading) and 10 (Code 215: Continuing activity).

When the assessment of frequency of use is based on the percentage data, strategy 1 (Code 111: First reading) with 17.3% of total use becomes the most frequently used strategy, which is followed by strategies 11 (Code 219: Calculation/Detail) and 7 (Code 211: Plan/Hypothesis) which were used 13.5% and 12.8% respectively.

The observation of the relatively more frequent use of strategy 1 (Code 111: First reading) in the percentage data is understandable. In the current research design use of this strategy was mandatory for all tasks. The strategy was therefore expected to emerge as an important one. Its apparently lesser importance when assessed on the basis of raw frequency data would have resulted from its being flooded by other strategies in longer and more difficult tasks. As was noted previously, the expression of the frequencies of strategy usage as percentages of total time spent by a given subject on a given task has the effect of masking differential task difficulties (especially in terms of length of time required) and subject abilities.

Rank orders of the total use made of each strategy (total use being calculated by summing the frequencies of use for each strategy across all subjects) were established in two ways.

Kendall's coefficient of Concordance[1], "W" (Maxwell, 1975), was computed for the rankings within tasks and the rankings across tasks for both the sums of raw scores and the amounts of use made of each strategy as a sum of the percentages of each subject's total time spent on a given task.

W provides a measure of overall correlation for k rankings of the same n objects or situations, and is defined as

---

1. The coefficient W is the ratio of the obtained S to the maximum value S can attain. The latter would obtain if every object were given the same rank by each judge and no ties were allowed. This maximum value of S can readily be shown to be $k^2 (n^3 - n)/12$, for $(n^2 - 1)/12$ is the variance of the first natural numbers, $n(n^2 - n)/12 = (n^3 - n)/12$ is the sum of their squares about their mean, while $k^2 (n^3 - n)/12$ is the sum of the squares of k times each rank about k times their mean.

The coefficient W varies from 0 to $+1$, signifying complete randomness in the k rankings to complete agreement between the rankings. (Maxwell, 1975, pp. 119–120).

$$W = \frac{S}{k^2(n^3 - n)/12} = \frac{12S}{k^2(n^3 - n)}$$

where, in the present context, S is the sum of the squares of the deviations of the total of the ranks obtained by each task (in the case of within tasks analysis of strategies, i.e., across tasks rankings), or each strategy (in the case of within strategy analysis of task ranks of each category) from the average of the respective task or strategy totals. Table 9.10 gives the obtained coefficients of concordance and the levels of their significance.

The significance of W was tested by means of the F-distribution after application of a correction for continuity, i.e., an adjusted value for W, W', which is given by Maxwell (1975, p. 120) by the formula

$$W' = \frac{12(S-1)}{k^2(n^3 - n) + 24}$$

and the computation of a variance ratio by use of the formula

$$F = \frac{(k-1)W'}{1 - W'}$$

Degrees of freedom were computed as follows:

$$N_1 = (n-1) - (2/k)$$
$$N_2 = (k-1)[(n-1) - (2/k)]$$

TABLE 9.10
Kendall's Coefficient of Concordance Values and Significance

Test	Raw Data	Proportion Data
1. Are the rankings (established within each variable + across tasks) random within tasks? ($k=18, n=12$)	$W = 0.4096$ $W' = 0.4095$ $W' = F_{11.89/202.13} = 11.7905$ $\chi^2_{11} = 88.47$ $p < .001$	$W = 0.055$ $W' = 0.055$ $F_{10.89/185.13} = 0.9894$ $\chi^2_{11} = 10.89$ NS
2. Are the rankings (established within each task) random across tasks? ($k=12, n=18$)	$W = 0.5549$ $W' = 0.5549$ $F_{16.83/185.13} = 13.7135$ $\chi^2_{17} = 113.2$ $p < .001$	$W = 0.4605$ $W' = 0.4604$ $F_{16.83/185.13} = 9.3864$ $\chi^2_{17} = 86.11$ $p < .001$

It has been suggested that when N is larger than 7, W' is approximately distributed as chi square (Siegel, 1956, p. 236), with $df = N-1$

$$\chi^2 = \frac{S}{(1/12)kn(n+1)} = k(n-1)W$$

The χ^2 values were computed according to the above formula and are included in Table 9.10.

The significant W values obtained for both the rankings within tasks (Test 1, Table 9.10) and within strategies (Test 2, Table 9.10) based on the raw data and for the within strategies based on proportion scores were found to have a probability of occurrence of less than $p < .001$. These very low probabilities justify the rejection of the null hypothesis that the amounts of use of various strategies in one task are unrelated to the use in the other tasks. The highly significant values of W show that there was considerable agreement between tasks in relation to the rankings of the use of various strategies, in other words, that subjects tended to essentially display a similar pattern of overall strategy use across tasks.

The finding of a very small and non-significant W for the within tasks ranks based on the proportion data can be interpreted as suggesting that the rankings of the proportions of strategy use across tasks are unrelated to the rankings of strategies within tasks. This finding is not surprising if one remembers that the expression of the use made by subjects of a strategy as a proportion of the subject's total time on the task results in the abolition of differential lengths and, therefore, difficulties of the tasks. One would, therefore, not expect systematic strategy use within task patterns.

Converting the amount of use made of each strategy into a percentage of total problem solving time was not expected to reduce the between tasks differences in strategy use, e.g., performance tasks requiring less reading.

In summary, Kendall's coefficient of concordance indicates the extent of association between the set of 18 problem solving strategies and the 12 task situations in which they were applied by providing a measure of overall correlation. The W values obtained in the present study show a high degree of agreement in the pattern of strategy use across tasks.

USE OF STRATEGIES BY TASK TYPE

Inspection of the columns in Table 9.9 reveals that the frequencies of use of the strategies varied between tasks, and that there was a tendency for some strategies not to be used for some tasks. The frequencies marked with asterisks in Table 9.9 provide an indication of apparent trends in strategy preferences for task types.

Summed across all tasks and all subjects it appears that the solution directed strategies (Code 200) were used most frequently, as about 50% of all responses fell into categories of this type. Stimulus passage directed responses made up 30% of the total responses.

Strategy 1 (Code 111: First reading), which overall accounted for the largest amount of time spent when the problem solving behaviors were described as proportions of total problem solving times, appeared to be of lesser relevance in the nonverbal tasks. This finding seems noteworthy, particularly if one remembers that the reading requirements of the stimulus passage in terms of lines, number of words, syllables, etc., of the similarities items, i.e., Tasks 8 [Poem/Statue], 9 [Praise/Punishment], 10 [Fly/Tree], and 11 [Wood/Alcohol] were less than the amount of reading required by the stimulus passages describing the performance Tasks 2 [∶∶∶], 6 [6m→4Δ], and 7 [9m→1h]. An explanation of this apparent contradiction might be that even during the first reading of the stimulus passage, subjects tend to begin their attempts to work on the task. If the task is a performance one this is more difficult and would thus be expected to occur less frequently. One would therefore expect the first reading, of even a short verbal problem, to occupy proportionally more time than the reading of a performance task with somewhat longer instructions.

The findings of the analysis of raw frequencies for the same variable show that in addition to the tasks with the longest stimulus passages, i.e., Tasks 1 [Binet], 4 [Pebbles], and 5 [Platform]; Task 3 [15 × 30] showed the first reading to be of particular relevance. This finding was as expected for Tasks 1, 4, and 5. The relevance of the first reading variable of a short and easy task like Task 3 [15 × 30] suggests that more than a first reading may have been involved, and further supports the above explanation. Further reference to this phenomenon is made in Chapter 11, when the results of the discriminant analyses are discussed. Strategies 2 (Rereading) and 3 (Chunk/Summarize stimulus passage information) were used most frequently for the problems when the stimulus passages failed to provide direct access to solution paths. Tasks 4 [Pebbles], 5 [Platform], and 7 [9m→1h] could be characterized as requiring a certain amount of divergent thinking before a path towards solution can be initiated. Support for this type of reasoning can be found by noting the difference between Tasks 6 [6m→4Δ], and 7 [9m→1h] with respect to the relevance of these strategies. Both tasks are performance tasks, the medium in both cases being matches.

Task 6 would for most subjects require a certain amount of manipulation, or Trial and Error activity, i.e., Strategy 8, which cannot take place simultaneously with Strategy 1 (First reading). The stimulus passage of Task 7 [9m→1h], when first encountered appeared to most subjects nonsensical and would therefore have been more likely to have triggered off some considerations of plans and hypotheses than Trial and Error manipulation of the matches. Strategy 7 (Code 211: Plan/Hypothesis) appears to have had little applicability to Task 3 [15 × 30], both in absolute raw score frequencies and relatively speaking, i.e., when computed for each subject as a proportion of time spent on this task. Strategy 7 was used only 4–5% of the time. However, it was identified as the most frequently used strategy when raw frequencies were summed across all tasks, and its frequency of use was roughly proportional to task difficulty. The overall use of Strategy 16 (Code 400: Judgment/Verification) was considerably greater in the performance than in the verbal tasks. When the frequencies of use were analyzed in relation to achievement, this variable was one which discriminated particularly strongly between solvers and nonsolvers in most tasks.

THE VARIETY OF STRATEGIES USED

The variety of strategies used was measured for each subject by counting the number of discrete strategies used for each given task. Strategies used repeatedly were counted only once per task.

In an attempt to assess individual differences between subjects, the mean number of different strategies used was calculated across the 12 tasks for each subject. The mean variety scores obtained in this manner for each of the subjects ranged from 5.00 to 9.54 ($\bar{X}_{\text{Means}} = 7.05$, $SD_{\text{Means}} = 0.97$), with the standard deviations for individuals ranging from 1.58 to 4.82 ($\bar{X}_{SD} = 3.21$, $SD_{SD} = 0.62$). These values show little variation between the subjects in relation to the variety of strategies applied in their attempts to solve the 12 tasks. It was, therefore, regarded as legitimate to sum the number of different strategies used across the total group of subjects for each task. A mean variety of strategies score was calculated across subjects for each of the 12 tasks. The data for each task are thus treated as independent replications of the problem solving process.

In Table 9.11 the tasks are ranked according to the mean variety of strategies used—standard deviations and levels of facility are given also. There is a significant and not unexpected tendency for the more difficult tasks to require the application of a larger variety of strategies. For the 12 tasks the Spearman rank order correlation between the mean variety scores of strategy use and task difficulty, the latter measured by the proportion of subjects achieving a correct solution to the task, is

$$r_s = 1 - \frac{6(148)}{(12)^3 - 12} = .48$$

This means that 23.38% of the variation between the two variables is explained by their relationship.

TABLE 9.11

Mean Variety of Strategy Scores, Standard Deviations and Levels of
Facility for the Tasks

		Variety of Strategies Used		Facility
Rank	Task	Mean	SD	% Solvers
1	6 (m→4△)	9.75	2.42	25
2	5 (Platform)	9.37	2.46	21
3	2 (⸬)	9.33	2.60	19
4	4 (Pebbles)	9.01	2.31	35
5	12 (8TB/2)	8.82	2.70	7
6	7 (9m→1h)	8.61	2.40	22
7	1 (Binet)	7.62	2.55	40
8	8 (Poem/Statue)	6.15	2.75	73
9	11 (Wood/Alc.)	5.58	2.32	27
10	9 (Praise/P.)	5.56	2.07	45
11	10 (Fly/Tree)	5.55	2.60	63
12	3 (15×30)	3.94	1.94	89

The following section reports the results of statistical computations including analysis of variance procedures, which were applied in a preliminary attempt to investigate, ex post facto, possible relationships between the dependent variable variety of strategy use and a number of independent variables which were represented in the problem solving performances of different subgroupings of the population under investigation.

The investigation of an area of behavior as complex as that of problem solving necessitates the employment of techniques of data analysis which not only take into account a number of variables at a time, but which permit the consideration of possibly quite subtle interactions between such variables. The decision was made to use multiple classification analysis of variance because of the lack of other statistical tools for analyses of this type that might be more appropriate for the data collected in the present study, although two of the assumptions underlying analysis of variance procedures cannot be regarded as fulfilled by the present data.

The variances within the subgroups were shown to be highly homogeneous (cf. Table 9.12), thus safeguarding the mathematical appropriateness of the statistical tests. In relation to the other two assumptions reliance was placed on the

increasing evidence, that even though fairly significant departures from strict theoretical assumptions may exist, analysis of variance is sufficiently "robust" that it will still yield results, which may be meaningfully interpreted. (Popham & Sirotnik, 1973, p. 166)

TABLE
Mean Variety of Strategies Used

| | Achievement Level | | | | | | Time | | | | | | |
| | A (Pass) | | B (Gives up) | | C (Fail) | | Fast | | Slow | | Group 1 (Very Superior) | | Group 2 (Superior) |
Task	X̄	SD	X̄	SD	X̄	SD	X̄	SD	X̄	SD	X̄	SD	X̄	SD
1	7.36	2.23	10.30	2.05	7.29	2.49	5.85	1.57	9.51	1.93	7.17	1.17	7.83	1.72
2	8.53	2.70	9.55	2.23	9.45	2.85	7.81	2.37	10.89	1.61	9.50	3.99	8.67	2.50
3	3.77	1.89	7.00	(N=1)	5.11	1.73	2.65	0.82	5.23	2.33	2.83	1.17	2.67	0.82
4	8.87	2.40	9.87	2.09	8.79	2.25	7.47	1.63	8.69	3.05	8.50	1.64	9.33	1.51
5	8.96	1.97	9.37	2.45	9.55	2.65	7.80	1.78	10.89	1.87	9.00	1.55	10.17	2.71
6	9.36	2.51	10.53	2.03	9.35	2.46	8.16	2.03	11.31	1.58	10.33	1.63	9.83	1.47
7	7.05	2.38	9.57	1.93	8.67	2.29	7.12	2.01	10.28	1.50	8.67	2.50	9.33	3.20
8	5.47	2.49	7.17	1.77	8.11	2.69	4.47	1.85	7.73	2.50	8.33	2.07	7.67	3.83
9	6.10	1.92	6.56	2.45	4.71	1.82	5.61	1.96	5.86	2.30	5.83	1.47	6.17	3.19
10	5.98	2.66	4.56	1.34	4.92	2.53	5.70	2.77	5.50	2.51	5.33	2.16	5.50	3.02
11	5.35	2.81	5.27	2.26	5.84	2.08	5.17	2.34	6.40	1.94	6.67	3.20	5.00	1.79
12	9.33	2.13	10.09	2.84	8.29	2.53	7.39	2.20	10.41	2.29	8.00	1.67	9.67	3.78
Mean	7.17		8.32		7.51		6.27		8.56		7.51		7.65	
Var.	3.41		4.37		3.49		2.74		5.35		4.33		5.05	

and the view of others like Winer (1971) and Stanley (1968) who have provided supportive evidence for the robustness of analysis of variance procedures.

The present study is an exploratory one only, the measures for which were obtained from discrete populations (i.e., Year 11, Year 12, Teachers' College, and University students who volunteered for the study at the required time), rather than from samples representing specified populations.

The aim was to look at the utility of a set of problem solving variables as descriptors of process variables which could be investigated further, rather than the utility of these variables as predictors of performance or as means to make causal inferences. In fact, the reason for the use of significance tests in the present study as a whole was to indicate the importance of certain trends in the observations made rather than to evaluate the generalizability of the results of variables, the measurement of which in the present exploratory study was qualitative rather than quantitative.

The independent variables selected as criteria for the establishment of subgroups of the population under investigation were problem solving achievement, time spent on the task, i.e., speed, and level of intellectual functioning. Table 9.12 shows the means and standard deviations for each task of the variety of strategies used by the different criterion groups.

Educational Level

Prior to the investigation of possible relationships between the variety of strategies used and the above mentioned independent variables, the possi-

9.12
by Different Criterion Groups

Intelligence							Educational Level				(A priori groups)			
Group 3 (High Average)		Group 4 (Average)		Group 5 (Low Average)		Tertiary				Secondary					
						(University)		(Teachers' C)		(Year 11)		(Year 12)			
$\bar{X}$	SD	$\bar{X}$	SD	$\bar{X}$	SD	$\bar{X}$	SD	$\bar{X}$	SD	$\bar{X}$	SD	$\bar{X}$	SD		
7.44	2.67	7.71	2.68	8.11	3.10	8.55	2.41	7.25	2.22	7.65	2.97	6.75	1.91		
9.22	2.55	9.78	2.30	8.33	3.04	10.14	2.21	9.45	2.56	8.48	2.42	9.69	3.20		
3.67	1.98	4.20	2.05	5.11	1.62	3.82	4.15	3.15	1.14	4.55	2.23	3.94	1.69		
9.00	2.65	9.05	2.11	8.78	2.86	10.00	2.05	9.00	2.20	8.52	2.35	8.63	2.50		
9.19	2.86	9.56	2.20	8.89	2.89	9.27	2.25	9.30	1.98	9.97	2.44	10.38	3.16		
9.11	2.53	10.22	2.52	9.33	2.24	9.86	2.73	9.20	2.38	9.61	2.33	10.56	2.16		
8.70	2.64	8.78	2.17	7.33	2.00	9.32	2.25	8.95	2.21	8.74	2.22	6.94	2.57		
5.56	3.12	5.90	2.40	5.67	1.73	6.09	3.01	7.20	3.43	5.61	2.12	5.94	2.35		
6.00	2.11	5.61	2.23	4.00	1.32	6.63	2.40	5.15	2.08	5.29	1.60	5.00	1.86		
6.07	2.83	5.34	2.74	4.22	1.39	6.14	3.15	6.15	2.66	5.03	2.07	5.00	2.50		
5.89	2.38	5.80	2.24	4.78	1.72	6.09	1.82	6.00	2.46	5.39	1.94	4.94	2.48		
9.85	2.73	8.44	2.44	7.22	2.68	9.82	2.08	9.05	1.70	7.77	3.03	9.19	3.27		
7.48		7.53		6.81		7.98		7.49		7.22		7.25			
3.90		4.21		3.81		4.46		4.12		3.72		5.53			

bility of a confounding effect on the independent variables was investigated by the a priori group membership which made up the total population. As was mentioned previously, the total population originated from four a priori groups of different educational levels. In this context the educational level of the subject refers to the subject's area of origin, i.e., the subject pool; in the present study secondary school Year 11, Year 12, University, or Teachers' College student.

A one-way analysis of variance of the unweighted mean variety scores for each task across the subjects in the four a priori groups showed no significant difference between the four groups ($F_{3,44} = 0.40$. To reach significance at the level of $p = .05$ with three degrees of freedom in the numerator and 44 degrees of freedom in the denominator, the F-value would have had to be 2.82). This result justified the use of the subjects from the four educational levels of origin as one total population in the subsequent analyses of the relationship between the dependent variable of variety of strategies used and the above specified independent variables.

In terms of the mean variety of strategies used across the 12 tasks, educational level was found to be independent of problem solving achievement, the latter being measured at the three levels previously specified. A 3 × 4 (achievement × a priori group) contingency table analysis yielded a χ_6^2 of 3.20. To be significant at the level of $p = .05$ with six degrees of freedom a χ^2 value of at least 12.59 is required.

Educational level and level of intellectual functioning, the latter having been estimated by scaled scores on the WAIS Block Design test and categorized into levels according to Wechsler's (1949, 1958, 1974) Intelligence Classification, were also found to be independent in relation to the mean variety of strategy use (χ^2_{12} = 16.43. With 12 degrees of freedom, the χ^2 value at the p = .05 level of significance has to reach a value of 21.03).

In relation to the variety of strategies used, educational level and time spent on the task were independent also (χ^2_{33} = 17.94. With 33 degrees of freedom χ^2 has to reach a value of 43.77 to be significant at the p = .05 level).

Table 9.12 shows the mean numbers of different strategies used and the standard deviations for achievement, time, intelligence level, and educational level criterion groups for each task. Inspection of this table shows that not only the standard deviations between subjects within tasks, but also the variances of the mean variety scores between tasks are highly homogeneous for the competence, intelligence, and educational level criteria.

Achievement: On the basis of the variety of problem solving strategies used, no significant differences were found between the mean variety scores for each task in the three achievement levels ($F_{2,33}$ = 1.10. At the p = .05 level of significance for $2/33$ degrees of freedom an F value of at least 3.29 is required).

Speed: Slow subjects, i.e., those using more than median time, used a significantly larger variety of strategies than fast subjects, who worked for the median amount of time or less on each given task (t = 6.07, df = 11, p < .001).

Intelligence: No significant differences were found in the mean variety of different strategies used between subjects operating at varying levels of intelligence.

On the basis of the average number of different strategies used across all tasks, level of achievement was found not to be influenced by the speed of problem solving, i.e., the time spent on the task (χ^2 = 0.24 df 2).

After the preliminary consideration of broad trends, based on the mean variety score of strategy use for each task reported above, an overall analysis of variance was conducted which took greater cognizance of the variety of strategies used by individual subjects within various criterion groups.

Ability, Achievement, Speed

The purpose of this analysis was to analyze the basic pattern of the variety of strategy use with regard to level of general intellectual functioning, competence (i.e., achievement) in problem solving and the time taken

TABLE 9.13
Summary of Analysis of Variance of Variety of Strategies Used

Source of Variation	SS	df	MS	F	p
General Ability (A)	80.85	4	20.21	2.89	<.05
Competence in PS (C)	419.60	2	209.80	29.97	<.001
Speed of work (S)	362.27	1	362.27	51.75	<.001
A × C	62.84	8	7.86	1.12	NS
A × S	64.18	4	16.05	2.29	NS
C × S	20.25	2	10.13	1.45	NS
A × C × S	33.80	8	4.23	0.60	NS
Within Cell (Error)	7267.95	1038	7.00		

for the task, and the possibility of higher order interactions between these variables. The results of this type of exploratory analysis may be useful for the evaluation of general ability–problem solving competence–speed of work patterns, and for the development of teaching methods which are tailored to the needs of individuals or small groups.

Table 9.13 presents a summary of the results of this $5 \times 3 \times 2$ analysis of variance. Unequal cell frequencies were dealt with by adopting the model suggested by Winer (1971) for $p \times q$ factorial design to the $5 \times 3 \times 2$ factorial case. The sums of squares for the main effects and interactions were obtained by multiplying the sums of squares obtained in the usual manner after averaging the numbers of different strategies used by all subjects in a given intelligence group (A) at a given competence level (C) and speed of work (S), by the harmonic mean of the numbers of subjects per ACS cell. The degrees of freedom for the sum of squares for error $(SS_{within\ cell})$ were determined by summing the sum of subjects in each ACS cell and subtracting the number of the cells making up the ACS table (i.e., $\Sigma\Sigma\eta ij - pqr = 1058 - 30 = 1028$). As A, C, and S are fixed factors, the proper denominator for all F tests in this analysis is the error mean square, $MS_{within\ cell}$.

The three main effects, i.e., general ability, competence in problem solving, and speed are significant. All three influenced the variety of strategies utilized in the work on the given tasks. None of the interactions tested between the main effects were significant at or beyond the $p \leq .05$ level, although the general ability $\times$ speed $(A \times S)$ interaction with its $\pm$ of 2.29 came within 0.08 of reaching significance at the $p = .05$ level.

General ability (A) is a classification variable included in the present study to explain or control potential variability in the variety of problem solving strategies used, which may be a function of the level of intellectual functioning.

The separate and combined relationships of the independent variables, competence in problem solving and speed, variables C and S, with the dependent variable variety of strategies used, were the factors of primary interest.

The interpretation of the significant effect of speed (S) is not difficult as this variable occurred at only two levels in the present study. Fast working subjects used consistently fewer different strategies than the slow group.

The interpretation of the findings relating to general ability (A), and competence (C), is less straightforward as these variables occur at five and three levels respectively. Inspection of the means and the marginal totals in the analysis of variance tables suggested that subjects operating at the three higher levels of intelligence, i.e., high average, superior, and very superior, tended to use a greater variety of strategies than those subjects classified to be of average or low average intelligence.

From inspection of the variety of strategy values for the competence variable (C), it appeared likely that competence level B, which consists of subjects who abandoned the task before completion, tended to display the largest amount of variety in strategy use. Competence level A, containing the subjects who produced a correct solution to the given task, appeared to show the least amount of variety in strategy use.

An attempt was made to substantiate statistically the above described impressions concerning the three main effects. The Newman–Keuls technique (Winer, 1971) was used for a posteriori tests, since no consideration had been given to specific contrasts of interest prior to the completion of the analysis.

Table 9.14 shows the results of the application of the Newman–Keuls test to all pairwise differences for the three main effects and for the $A \times S$ interaction effect by presenting the obtained levels of significance. This table confirms the impressions gained from inspection of the treatment sums and means.

It may be of interest to focus some attention on the interaction effect between general ability and speed $(A \times S)$, for which an F value approaching significance at the $p = .05$ level was obtained.

Figure 9.1 illustrates the relationship between these variables by showing that fast and slow speed of work tended to affect the mean variety of strategy use, averaged across the 12 tasks, quite differently at different levels of general ability.

The graph shows that speed of work has a substantial effect on the number of different strategies used for the three highest and the lowest ability groups. The Newman–Keuls test applied to the cell means of the AS summary table provided a statistical indication of the interaction effect by testing the differences between the levels of the speed factor (S) for each level of the general ability (A) dimension. The results of these

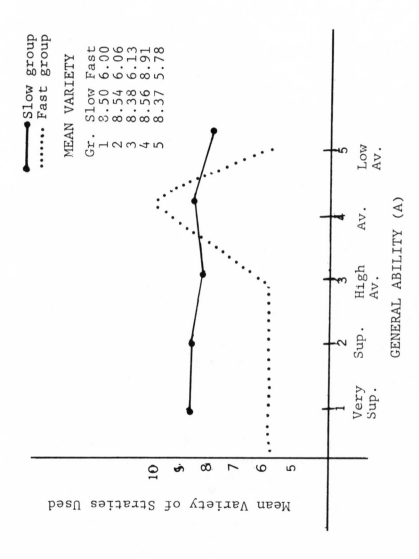

FIG. 9.1.   Speed × general ability interaction for the variety of strategies used.

TABLE 9.14

Significance Levels Obtained from Newman-Keuls A Posteriori
Comparisons of Group Means

Variable		Pairwise Contrasts				Legend	
General Ability		A2	A3	A4	A5	A1	very superior
(A)	A1	.01	.05	.01	.05	A2	superior
	A2		.05	.01	.01	A3	high average
	A3			.05	.05	A4	average
	A4				NS	A5	low average
Competence		C2		C3		C1	correct solution
(C)	C1	.01		.01		C2	gives up
	C2			.01		C3	fail
General Ability		A2	A3	A4	A5	(p values for the	
×	A1	NS	NS	.01	NS	significance of	
Speed	A2		NS	.01	NS	differences of speed	
(A × S)	A3			.01	NS	levels (S) between	
	A4				.01	various ability levels	
						(A).	

analyses are included in Table 9.14 and confirm the impression conveyed
by Figure 9.1 that speed might be expected to make a significant difference to the variety of strategies used only for the above and below average groups.

For the subjects operating at an average level of general ability, i.e.,
group 4, the difference, if any, between slow and fast working subjects is
negligible. As it is generally assumed that close to 70% of the population
fall into the category of average intellectual functioning, it follows that for
most persons the number of different strategies used in attempts to solve
problems is not related to the speed with which they work. For these
subjects speed of work might be expected, therefore, to determine the
number of tasks they are able to tackle in a given time, rather than the
likelihood of their solving the tasks. For the groups operating at the other
four levels of general ability, the time allowed on each cognitive task
determines, as in the case of subjects in the average ability group, the
number of tasks which can be attempted in a given time. In addition to
this, however, the amount of time allowed for each task might determine
success on a given task because slow solvers might require a greater
variety of strategies than fast ones to solve the task. The use of a greater
variety of strategies by slow workers may be the result of a tendency on
the part of these subjects to use different methods in their problem solving. On the other hand, it is possible that slow subjects tend to try out a
larger number of different strategies before they come to utilize the most

suitable ones. Further research into this area is recommended as greater knowledge of factors influencing individual differences in the relationship between speed of work and strategy use in problem solving would lead to more efficient methods of assessment and training in most areas of cognitive activity. Educational administrators and others involved in educational planning in such areas as ability grouping would also benefit from this type of research.

SUMMARY OF FINDINGS

The major findings presented in this chapter can be summarized as follows:

The empirically derived taxonomy of problem solving behaviors yielded highly consistent behavior descriptions for all strategies and tasks.

The importance of this finding lies not only in the reliability, i.e., the replicability of the assessments of these behaviors but also in the fact that the identified behaviors provide a means of investigating problem solving processes in a variety of different tasks. Over 4598 coding decisions made for a random sample of ten subjects, coder agreement was 91%, chance being excluded.

Time on task was investigated in relation to problem solving competence, measured intelligence, and tasks. The following tendencies were observed:

- Summing time on task for each subject across all tasks, it was found that, disregarding intelligence level, solvers tended to spend significantly less time than nonsolvers and those subjects who gave up.
- Comparisons between tasks showed that in all 12 tasks, the times spent by different ability groups differed for the three levels of problem solving competence. In the case of more complex, and hence more difficult tasks, more intelligent subjects worked faster, irrespective of the correctness of the solutions they produced. Solvers worked faster than nonsolvers. more intelligent nonsolvers whose problem solving resulted in incorrect solutions, worked faster than less intelligent subjects in the same group. The findings of the study thus support previous research, cited in this chapter, which had shown a strong positive correlation between intelligence and speed of problem solving.
- In the group of subjects who gave up, more intelligent subjects tended to persevere longer in more difficult tasks. In the case of easier tasks,

no significant relationship between intelligence level and perseverance on the task was found in this group. This is not surprising, since
the easier tasks in the study tended to be shorter than the more
difficult ones.

- Over all subjects speed was found to be a function of task complexity.
  In analyses which disregarded intelligence level, a statistically
  significant relationship between problem solving achievement and
  speed was found in the case of easy but not in relation to more
  difficult tasks.

The investigation of ranked strategy preferences showed that subjects
tended to display similar overall patterns of strategy preferences across
tasks. Solution directed strategies were used most frequently, i.e., 50% of
the time, while stimulus passage directed activities made up about 30% of
the total responses. Variations in the amounts of use made of specific
strategies appeared to be related to the type of task.

The variety of strategies used was investigated in relation to subjects
and tasks. More difficult tasks were found to require the application of a
larger variety of strategies. Solvers tended to use a smaller variety of
strategies than nonsolvers. Fast solvers used the smallest variety of different strategies.

All other things being equal, slow subjects used a significantly larger
variety of strategies than fast subjects. As noted earlier, slow performance can be a reflection of insecurity. Slow problem solvers tried out a
greater number of strategies, while fast subjects were able to choose
appropriate strategies in relatively shorter times.

An overall analysis of variance of ability, achievement, and speed
showed all three main effects to be influencing the variety of strategies
utilized in the work on the given tasks. Although none of the interactions
were found to be statistically significant, a tendency was observed for
subjects operating at the three highest levels of intelligence (i.e., high
average, superior, and very superior) to use a greater variety of strategies
than those subjects classified to be of average or low average intelligence.

In relation to problem solving achievement, the largest variety of strategies was used by subjects who abandoned the task before completion,
while solvers showed the least amount of variety.

In summary, it can be said that solvers worked faster than nonsolvers,
and used fewer different strategies. More intelligent subjects, irrespective
of achievement, worked faster than less intelligent subjects, on more
difficult tasks. Disregarding intelligence, the relationship between
achievement and speed was found to be statistically significant in the case
of easy tasks only. Differences in levels of education were not reflected in
the variables discussed in this chapter. Year 11 and Year 12 High School

and first and second year tertiary students, who made up the samples, provided a narrow age range and relatively homogeneous academic endeavor. It may not be surprising, therefore, to find that educational achievement, as defined in the present study, was found to be independent of such global performance characteristics such as time on task, strategy preferences, and variety of strategies used. As is shown in later chapters, particularly Chapter 11, the components of the problem solving process itself are shown, in this study, to provide a more sensitive and valid reflection of differences in problem solving between subjects of varying levels of education than the outcome measures discussed here.

10 Structural Components of the Problem Solving Process

The previous chapter provided global information concerning the use made of the strategies by groups of individuals across a variety of tasks. This approach was useful when the aim was to describe characteristics of the outcome of performance, such as the time taken to solve problems and the type and the variety of problem solving strategies applied by different groups of subjects. The present chapter describes the results of attempts made to identify and classify certain attributes of the problem solving process itself.

It is shown that some information concerning structural components of the problem solving process can be obtained by using factor analytic techniques. Separate principal components analyses were performed for each of the tasks on the taxonomy derived problem solving behaviors. However, the major part of this chapter consists of a presentation of the results of the application of Tucker's (1966) three–mode factor analysis, which provided the means for an investigation of functional aspects of the pattern of preferred problem solving strategies in relation to different tasks, to individual differences, and to interactions between combinations of variables from these domains.

The literature provides evidence that investigators attempting to discover general principles of behavior have essentially utilized one of two types of research strategy. Allport (1942) referred to these as the nomothetic or group average approach and the ideographic or clinical approach. The latter approach is concerned with the explanation of unique phenomena, for example, the characteristics of individual cases, which cannot be fitted into a general scientific framework. The nomothetic research leads to the postulation of general laws.

Definite limitations are inherent in both types of strategy if the aim of the research is to discover generalizable behavior patterns. Taking a group average to represent the entire group, thus treating individual differences as random error, may result in a masking of important trends of variation in the data. Where individual differences are large and systematic, the mean value is not representative of the performance of the group, or even of any member of the group (Sidman, 1952). It is possible, for example, that an investigator who reports no effect of a variable on performance is actually dealing with several types of subjects, some for whom the variable has a facilitating effect and some for whom it is disruptive. However, separate analyses of the data obtained from individual subjects can become extremely cumbersome, and may make the identification of group trends difficult if not impossible.

There is a need for a methodology which permits the systematization of obtained individual differences and at the same time provides an opportunity to apply averaging procedures only to the degree to which they appear justified by communalities in patterns of behavior.

Tucker's (1963, 1964, 1966) three–mode factor analysis, on the basis of a theorem by Eckart and Young (1936), works with cross products rather than correlations, thus retaining information about means and variances. This factor analytic technique can achieve the above suggested type of integration of nomothetic and ideographic research designs. This method can be used, for example, to investigate whether it is meaningful to hypothesize a single set of problem solving behaviors for a given task, or whether one must deal with some finite number of patterns of problem solving behavior which is, hopefully, smaller than the number of individuals attempting to solve the task.

An aim of the present study is to attempt to discover possible functional aspects of the patterns of preferred problem solving strategies in relation to specific situations, i.e., tasks, and to take into consideration the interaction of both these problem solving dimensions in combination with variables resulting from individual differences. This type of investigation can be expected to lead to a description of the problem solving process, and might, in effect, lead to predictions of the types of strategies which might be used by a subject with a given set of characteristics in attempts to solve a particular type of task.

To be of scientific value, research findings are, of course, expected to allow for generalization across a larger number of persons rather than for an individual. There is a possibility of identifying groups of subjects, whose problem solving behavior might be described in terms of particular types of relationships between their displayed pattern of strategy use and variables inherent in the task situation. The following section, then, describes the results of attempts to search, in a systematic way, for such interactions between subject, task, and strategy variables in the description of the problem solving process.

Another dimension of interest, the analysis of which became possible on the basis of the data collected in the present study, was to attempt to categorize tasks on the basis of the similarity of problem solving strategies elicited across subjects. This could have been achieved by factor analyzing a matrix made up of the intercorrelations between all possible pairs of tasks. A high correlation between a pair would mean that similar problem solving strategies were elicited by both tasks. A factor thus represents a set of tasks which evoke similar problem solving behaviors.

Tucker's (1966) three–mode factor analysis provides a statistical tool for the investigation of person–situation–behavior interactions. Applied to the present study it becomes possible to classify the observed use made of problem solving strategies in terms of (a) the subjects using them, (b) the tasks in relation to which the behavior occurs, and (c) the strategies per se, both sequentially and simultaneously.

Sequential analysis is carried out by collapsing the data contained in the three–mode matrix in such a way as to form conventional two–mode matrices. Collapsing the data across tasks results in a subjects by strategies matrix, which allows the identification of factors in the domain of strategies when the intercorrelations between strategies are factored. By factoring intercorrelations between subjects, types of individuals could be identified. If the data are collapsed across persons, a strategies by tasks matrix results, and possible factors in the domain of tasks can be identified. A factor, in this case, would be defined as a cluster of tasks which resemble one another with respect to the kinds of strategies they elicit from subjects attempting to solve them.

As in principal components analysis the three–mode factor model aims to describe each mode in terms of a reduced number of dimensions or factors. In this regard, the three–mode model operates on the assumption that there is some "average" or "idealized" factor matrix (Tucker & Messick, 1963) which connects the strategy factors with the task factors. This matrix represents something like what would have been obtained by separate two–mode factor analyses for each task had these analyses been weighted together.

In the three–mode model this weighting is performed within the model in such a way that subjects and tasks influence the entries in the strategy mode through their respective matrices. Between subjects and between tasks differences are taken into consideration in the weighting of strategy scores. Where, as in the present study, different task situations are considered, the strategy use matrix is weighted differently for each task, depending on the entries in the tasks matrix. If, for example, there is no tasks strategies interaction the tasks matrix might contain only *one* factor, loading on all tasks, whereas the existence of a tasks–strategies interaction might be indicated by the identification of several tasks factors.

In addition to the identification of appropriately weighted factors in each dimension, Tucker's three–mode factor analysis performs a simultaneous analysis of all three modes of input data, and produces a three dimensional matrix which represents in a direct manner the interrelationship between the factors obtained in the various modes. In other words, a reduced three–mode matrix, referred to by Tucker as the "core" matrix, shows the relationships between the strategy factors, task factors, and person factors.

If person factors are found, the existence of an interaction between persons and tasks and/or problem solving strategies has been demonstrated. Each person factor can then be interpreted on the basis of the relationship between strategy factors and task factors it represents. In other words each person factor can be represented as a layer or slice of the three dimensional core matrix. Each such person slice is made up of "loadings" that describe the relationship between strategy factors and task factors for an "idealized" subject, i.e., a subject whose characteristics are representative of the particular person factor. It becomes possible, therefore, to indicate for each person factor the most characteristic set of strategies used for each set of tasks which forms a task factor and vice versa.

FACTOR ANALYSES FOR SEPARATE TASKS

Before carrying out the three–mode factor analyses, separate principal components analyses were performed, one for each task, using program PA2 from the *SPSS, Statistical Package for Social Sciences* (Nie, Hull, Jenkins, Steinbrenner & Bent, 1975) on a Cyber 7044 computer. In the diagonal of the correlation matrix this method employs communality estimates initially established by the squared multiple correlation between a given variable and the remaining variables in the matrix, and refined by an iterative procedure. The analyses were performed on both the proportion data and the raw data.

Table 10.1 provides a summary of the factor analyses and shows the number of strategy factors which were extracted for each task. Kaiser's criterion, suggested by Guttman and adapted by Kaiser (1963, 1964), which specifies that only factors having latent roots greater than one should be considered as common factors, was used as a basis for the determination of the number of factors to be extracted. Cattell (1966) has pointed out that Kaiser's criterion is likely to be most reliable when the number of variables lies between 20 and 50. He suggests that in analyses

TABLE 10.1
Summary of the Results of the Principal Components Analyses
Performed on Each Task

Task	Number of Factors Extracted		% Variance Accounted		% Variance Accounted First P.C.	
	Prop. Data	Raw Data	Prop. Data	Raw Data ·	Prop. Data	Raw Data
1 Binet	7	6	63.0	69.4	15.3	25.5
2 ∷∷	8	7	70.7	72.6	13.6	20.1
3 15 × 30	8	7	69.7	68.6	12.5	19.1
4 Pebbles	7	7	62.8	66.7	12.1	17.9
5 Platform	7	7	64.4	67.2	14.2	22.9
6 6m→4Δ	8	7	70.2	69.9	14.2	21.8
7 9m→1h	9	8	71.9	69.5	13.8	20.7
8 Poem/Statue	9	8	71.6	71.9	12.0	19.2
9 Praise/P.	9	9	68.0	74.3	10.2	15.5
10 Fly/Tree	9	8	72.2	70.5	13.2	20.2
11 Wood Alcohol	8	8	68.7	68.3	12.0	12.5
12 8TB/2	8	7	68.8	70.3	13.2	21.9
Mean	8.08	7.42	68.41	69.93	13.03	19.78
SD	0.76	0.76	3.34	2.11	1.30	3.26

where the number of variables is less than 20 there is a tendency for this criterion to result in the extraction of a conservative number of factors. This tendency to be conservative is regarded as desirable for the present study, which is exploratory only.

No significant differences were found between the proportion and raw data analyses in the numbers of significant factors extracted or in the percentages of variance accounted for by the first seven to eight factors. The first principal components identified in the raw data analyses appeared to account for a larger percentage of variance than the first principal components in the proportion data analyses. This difference was found not to be significant statistically ($\chi^2 = 1.09$, $df = 11$, $p > .05$). The significantly greater between strategies variances of the percentages accounted for by the first principal components ($F = 6.29$, $df = {}^{12}/_{12}$, $p < .01$) suggests that less informational overlap between the strategy variables was contained in the proportion data than in the raw data. More extreme scores would have occurred at both ends of the distribution in the raw scores analyses, a phenomenon which is attributable to the larger number of sources of variation contained in the raw data. This finding is as expected because, as was pointed out previously, the ipsatization of the data and the subsequent analyses on the basis of proportions had to result in a levelling of individual and task differences.

Table 10.2 shows the structures of the first principal components obtained for each of the 12 tasks, with the upper and lower sections of the table referring to the results of analyses of raw and proportion data respectively.

The similarity of the first principal components obtained for each task was investigated by computing Pearson's r for each possible pair of columns in Table 10.2. The fact that the observed strategy variables were expressed in the same metric across all 12 principal component analyses made this comparison meaningful. Homogeneity of the variances of the loadings obtained for each of the principal components was established, $F_{Max\ 12,17} = 2.07, p > .05$, and $F_{Max\ 12,17} = 1.92, p > .10$, for the raw and proportion data analyses respectively, using Hartley's test (Winer, 1971, p. 206).

Matrices showing the intercorrelations between tasks, representing the similarity between each pair of tasks on the basis of the size of the loadings of the 18 strategy variables on the first principal components, are presented for the raw and the proportion data on the right hand side of Table 10.2. The size of the correlation coefficients represents the degree of similarity between each pair of tasks in terms of the relative contributions made by each of the 18 strategy variables to the computation of the first principal components. In addition to this the between tasks correlation matrices provide an indication of the similarity of each task to all others tasks on the basis of the first principal components. For example, the first row of the between tasks correlation matrix contains the correlation coefficients between Task 1 [Binet] and the other 11 tasks. The underlined coefficients in Table 10.2 were those judged to be high enough to suggest similar factors among the various tasks. It was decided to regard a correlation of .70 as the minimum value required before suggesting similarity or congruence between tasks, because correlation coefficients of this size and larger would ensure that at least approximately 50% of the similarity between the tasks can be accounted for by similar patterns of the strategy variables investigated in this study.

The presentation of the results of the analyses of the raw data will precede that of the proportion data.

Raw Data [Focus on the characteristics of tasks.] Inspection of the between tasks correlation matrix based on the analysis of the raw data showed Tasks 2 [⋮⋮] and 6 [6m→ 4Δ] to be most similar. The correlation coefficient between these tasks was $r = .91$.

Tasks 10 [Fly/Tree] and 11 [Wood/Alc.], Tasks 2 [⋮⋮] and 7 [9m→1h], Tasks 5 [Platform] and 6 [6m→4Δ], and Tasks 7 [9m→1h] and 12 [8TB/2] were each correlated at a level of $r = .80$ or above. Other highly parallel factors can be determined from Table 10.2 in the same manner.

Strategy Variable	Task												$\bar{x}^1$	SD
	1	2	3	4	5	6	7	8	9	10	11	12		
	Raw Data													
1 First Reading	.26	.03	.05	.17	.19	-.03	.20	.13	-.05	-.02	-.17	.18	.12	.08
2 Re-read	.50	.25	.50	.38	.34	.42	.19	.17	.25	-.01	-.03	.12	.26	.16
3 Chunk/Summ.	.37	.45	.33	.40	.58	.69	.30	.42	.05	.21	-.02	.45	.36	.19
4 Ref. to text/check	.38	.36	.25	.51	.34	.28	.07	.18	.04	-.17	-.23	.07	.24	.14
5 Id. parts from input	.38	.43	-.19	.47	.36	.41	.14	-.07	-.01	-.07	.12	.32	.25	.16
6 Irrelevant behavior	.00	-.23	-.18	.22	-.08	-.04	-.24	.42	.17	.08	.29	.09	.17	.11
7 Plan/Hyp.	.85	.77	.26	.67	.52	.77	.85	.85	.58	.74	.65	.66	.68	.16
8 Trial + Error	.48	.56	.28	.23	.42	.45	.55	.23	.57	.64	.41	.65	.46	.14
9 Compare/Rel. Trials	.49	.39	.24	.03	.29	.29	.31	.23	.48	.22	.13	.21	.28	.13
10 Cont. activity	.43	.69	.29	.58	.36	.63	.73	.44	.57	.60	.45	.64	.53	.13
11 Calcul./Detail	.60	.33	.87	.19	.24	.26	.04	.04	.29	.19	.24	.05	.28	.23
12 Reason	.24	.26	.03	.34	.52	.36	.44	.36	.04	.17	.18	.35	.27	.14
13 Self related	.40	.34	.68	.50	.41	.31	.28	.70	.35	.73	.49	.57	.48	.15
14 Justification	.25	.52	.36	.58	.55	.51	.61	.46	.13	.60	.41	.55	.46	.14
15 Emotional	.61	.37	.58	.14	.09	.34	.24	.50	.35	.37	.24	.49	.36	.16
16 Judgm./Verif.	.75	.90	.75	.65	.74	.84	.79	.71	.67	.51	.14	.80	.69	.19
17 Pause	.35	-.00	.42	-.06	.08	.10	-.24	.11	-.24	-.06	-.08	.30	.17	.13
18 Memory	.36	.15	.25	.25	-.01	-.03	.22	.20	.49	.63	.42	.33	.28	.17
Eigenvalue	4.33	4.13	3.62	3.44	3.21	3.93	3.72	3.46	2.79	3.64	2.25	3.94		
PCT Variance	25.50	22.90	20.10	19.10	17.90	21.80	20.70	19.20	15.50	20.20	12.50	21.90		
$\bar{x}^1$	.43	.37	.32	.35	.33	.36	.30	.34	.26	.30	.20	.38		
SD	.20	.28	.29	.21	.22	.26	.31	.25	.26	.31	.24	.23		

Reference to the average correlation coefficients, i.e., the row means, calculated for each task on the basis of its correlations with the other 11 tasks indicates that Tasks 2 [∷] and 7 [9m→1h] were the tasks whose first principal components showed most relative similarity with those of the other tasks. Task 3 [15 × 30] showed the least similarity with the other tasks on the basis of the importance of the relative contributions of the 18 strategy variables to the first principal component factor. As was shown in Table 9.1, Task 3 [15 × 30] was the easiest task presented. Its solution required relatively little time and it could therefore be expected to be shown to be atypical in its strategy requirements.

Tasks 2 [∷], 6 [6m→4Δ], 7 [9m→1h], 5 [Platform], and 12 [8TB/2] showed considerable similarity in terms of the parallelism of their first principal components. All five tasks were difficult and their solutions required a certain amount of lateral thinking, in the De Bono sense.

The attempt to assess similarities or dissimilarities in the structure of the first principal components between the tasks by determining the degree of parallelism between the first principal components of each pair of tasks was supplemented by a second method of investigating possible similarities.

The second method employed was a graphic one. The contributions of each strategy variable to the first principal components of the 12 tasks

10.2
Resulting from Separate Analyses of the 12 Tasks

		2	3	4	5	6	7	8	9	10	11	12	$\bar{x}_r^I$	SD_r
				Between Tasks Correlations of First Principal Components										
1	Binet	.74	.60	.29	.42	.63	.55	.37	.61	.39	.25	.46	.48	.15
2	:::		.38	.68	.80	.91	.87	.49	.63	.56	.37	.75	.65	.19
3	15 x 30			.07	.25	.31	.19	.28	.36	.34	.11	.25	.29	.14
4	Pebbles				.70	.71	.67	.56	.34	.41	.35	.53	.48	.21
5	Platform					.86	.74	.44	.24	.31	.10	.59	.50	.26
6	6m→4Δ						.79	.55	.45	.42	.27	.71	.60	.22
7	9m→1h							.62	.67	.71	.52	.80	.65	.19
8	Poem/St.								.52	.69	.57	.70	.53	.13
9	Praise/P									.76	.66	.56	.53	.16
10	Fly/Tree										.88	.79	.57	.20
11	Wood/Alc.											.58	.42	.24
12	8TB/2												.61	.16

(Continued)

were compared on the basis of their deviations from the mean loading of the strategy computed across tasks. A zero abscissa was established by transforming the loadings for each strategy across tasks, i.e., rows into z-scores.

This method permits a direct comparison of the similarity of the first principal components across all tasks on the basis of the relative distances of the profiles from the average strategy loadings. For each strategy variable positive and negative deviations from the mean loadings are reflected above and below the abscissa respectively.

This type of representation of the relative divergencies from each strategy's mean loading indicates similarities between tasks in terms of relatively greater positive or negative deviations from each strategy's mean importance for certain groups of tasks.

Fig. 10.1 represents graphically, for each strategy variable, the deviation of its correlation with the first principal component for each separate task from its average correlation computed across tasks. For example, inspection of the profile of Strategy 1 (First reading), ST1 in Fig. 10.1, indicates clearly a tendency for tasks with brief instructions to show a pattern of relatively greater negative deviation, and for tasks whose stimulus passages required a larger amount of first reading relatively greater positive deviation. This indicates the relative similarity between

TABLE 10.2

Strategy Variable	1	2	3	4	5	6	Task 7	8	9	10	11	12	$\bar{x}$[1]	SD
							Proportion Data							
1 First Reading	-.54	.71	.36	.69	-.24	.69	.52	-.57	.39	-.52	.31	.33	.49	.16
2 Re-read	.13	.30	-.14	-.73	-.75	.30	.68	-.07	.02	-.10	-.00	.54	.31	.29
3 Chunk/Summ.	-.15	.05	-.04	-.15	.12	-.13	.00	-.08	.29	.02	.00	.09	.09	.08
4 Ref. to text/check	-.02	.18	-.18	-.27	-.42	.13	.33	-.21	.12	-.24	.85	.59	.30	.23
5 Id. parts from input	.15	-.15	.79	-.29	.07	.32	.08	-.08	-.04	-.03	.00	.06	.17	.22
6 Irrelevant behavior	.00	.35	.76	.28	-.02	.42	.21	.47	.15	-.00	-.13	.51	.28	.24
7 Plan/Hyp.	.63	-.70	-.12	-.11	.50	-.55	-.31	.54	.73	.70	-.32	-.52	.48	.22
8 Trial + Error	.21	.07	.10	-.04	.30	-.05	-.50	.23	-.08	.48	-.06	-.07	.18	.17
9 Compare/Rel. Trials	-.11	-.20	-.21	.06	-.01	.01	-.21	-.37	-.36	-.42	.01	-.09	.17	.15
10 Cont. activity	.20	.07	-.08	.60	.52	-.10	-.53	.39	.17	.64	-.24	-.53	.34	.22
11 Calcul./Detail	-.67	-.09	-.64	.12	-.02	.41	-.03	-.14	-.72	-.07	-.16	.20	.27	.26
12 Reason	.04	-.05	.24	-.05	.32	.10	.15	.40	.12	.21	.11	.23	.17	.11
13 Self related	.34	-.02	-.16	.29	.14	-.12	-.08	.15	-.08	.42	-.24	-.02	.17	.13
14 Justification	.14	-.05	-.08	.02	.16	-.31	-.29	.41	-.16	.19	-.05	-.16	.17	.12
15 Emotional	.56	-.20	-.03	-.13	-.29	.09	.22	.15	-.00	.06	.01	.06	.15	.16
16 Judgm./Verif.	.61	-.68	-.15	-.22	.58	-.68	-.45	.25	-.15	.07	.02	-.51	.36	.25
17 Pause	-.05	.08	-.09	-.06	-.27	.45	.43	-.06	.12	-.06	.79	.20	.22	.23
18 Memory	.19	.47	-.23	.30	.06	.27	-.21	-.02	.03	.33	-.17	-.03	.19	.14
Eigenvalue	2.60	2.44	2.25	2.18	2.55	2.56	2.48	2.16	1.83	2.38	2.05	2.38		
PCT Variance	15.30	13.60	12.50	12.10	14.20	14.20	13.80	12.00	10.20	13.20	12.00	13.20		
$\bar{x}$[1]	.26	.25	.24	.25	.27	.29	.29	.26	.21	.25	.19	.26		
SD	.23	.24	.24	.22	.22	.21	.19	.18	.22	.23	.25	.21		

[1] Absolute values of the loadings were used in the computation of mean loadings and standard deviations of loadings, because the interest was in the relative size of the computed loadings with regard to the signs of the loadings.

the first principal components of the tasks on the basis of the differential importance of Strategy 1 (First reading).

Strategy 2 (Rereading), ST2, showed greater positive deviations for tasks with relatively longer instructions, and for tasks which were perceived to be difficult or unclear initially and which therefore tended to be reread. Task 3 [15 × 30], an easy task with brief instructions, tended to be reread by highly anxious "number phobic" subjects. Tasks 7 to 12 showed relative deviations in the downward direction on this variable, suggesting less than average use of Strategy 2. While the solutions to these tasks were not obvious, the requirements of the tasks can be regarded as immediately clear after a first reading of the stimulus passage.

Strategy 11 (Calculation/Detail), ST11, showed a similarity between the first principal components of Tasks 1 [Binet], 2 [∷], and 3 [15 × 30], the tasks requiring mathematical calculation and work on task detail (e.g., Task 2, where the position of each line tended to be considered in sequence). The relatively similar, negatively divergent, pattern of the remaining tasks can be explained by the fact that the solutions to these tasks required a more abstract and holistic approach.

Other similar groups of tasks can be determined on the basis of the relative divergencies of the strategy variables from the across tasks means

(Continued)

| | | | Between Tasks Correlations of First Principal Components | | | | | | | | | | |
	2	3	4	5	6	7	8	9	10	11	12	x_r^1	SD_r
1 Binet	-.58	.04	-.31	.38	-.70	-.40	.64	.31	.62	-.29	-.55	.44	.20
2 !!!		.24	.38	-.55	.78	.52	-.45	.08	-.36	.27	.66	.44	.20
3 15 x 30			.09	.02	.30	.23	.13	.38	-.12	.02	.24	.16	.12
4 Pebbles				.33	.22	-.26	-.04	.06	.11	-.20	-.21	.20	.11
5 Platform					-.67	-.86	.60	.10	.65	-.52	-.82	.50	.27
6 6m→4Δ						-.57	-.12	-.56	.37	.76	.52	.23
7 9m→1h							-.49	.16	-.65	.57	.85	.52	.24
8 Poem/St.								.23	.80	-.47	-.45	.44	.23
9 Praise/P									.27	.09	-.08	.17	.11
10 Fly/Tree										-.57	-.63	.49	.23
11 Wood/Alc.											.52	.35	.19
12 8TB/2												.52	.26

contributions made by the strategy variables to the first principal components. However, the correlations between the first principal components were

from Fig. 10.1 in a similar manner. Further reference to relative similarities between tasks on the basis of specific strategy variables will be made in the comparison of the findings from the raw and proportion data later in this chapter.

Because the representation shown in Fig. 10.1 is based on z-score transformations of the data, not only the comparison of patterns displayed by specific strategy variables between raw and proportion data, but also a comparison of tasks across strategy variables becomes possible in the comparison of first principal components.

Clearly the graphic method provides a somewhat different picture of task similarities from the picture provided by the correlations. The reason for this difference derives from the fact that the two methods address different questions. The correlations provide information concerning the degree to which the structures of the principal components of two tasks parallel each other. The graphic method focuses on differences in the relative magnitude of the loadings of the individual strategies. The findings suggest that, although the general patterns of congruence between the first principal components of certain groups of tasks are similar, the relative magnitudes in which they occur differ.

The analyses of raw data emphasize certain performance differences more than others. For example, a number of trends were overshadowed

FIG. 10.1.   Divergencies of strategy correlations with the first principal components for each task from the mean strategy correlations.

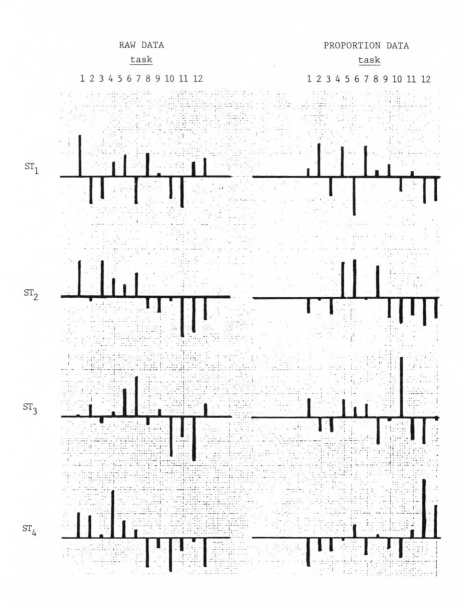

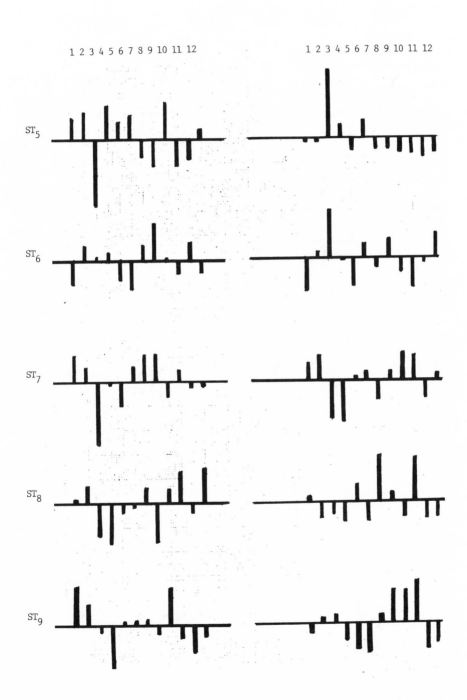

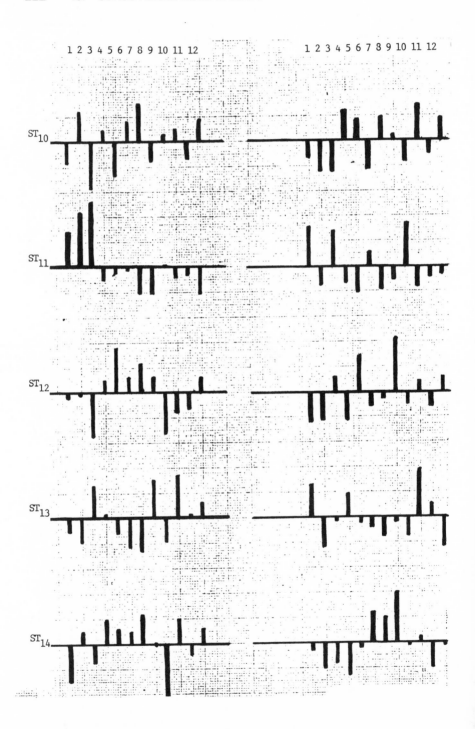

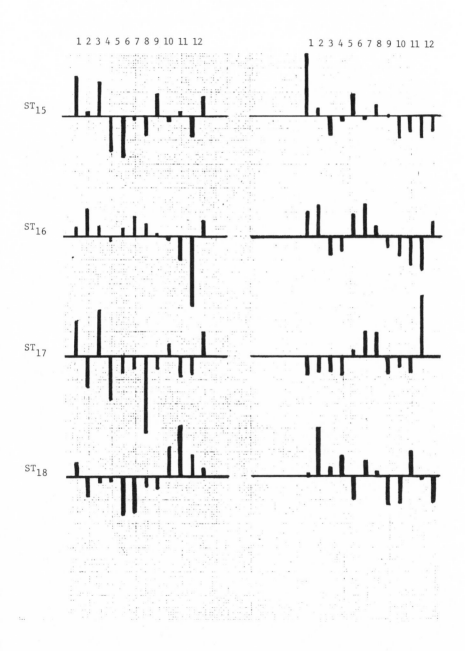

by the large number of Strategy 1 (First reading) responses. The use of raw data in the analysis results in the major focus being on the characteristics of the task and on differences in subject performance between tasks.

If the major interest concerns types and patterns of problem solving operations or strategies, which may or may not be investigated in relation to the characteristics of tasks or individual differences, the raw data have to be transformed into proportions prior to analysis.

Proportion Data   [Focus on the structure of performance.] The first principal components obtained in the task specific factor analyses based on the proportion data showed the largest degree of parallelism between the first principal components of the following tasks:

Task pair	r
T7[9m→1h] and T12[8TB/2]	.85
T8[Poem/St] and T10[Fly/Tree]	.80
T2[∶∶∶] and T6[6m→4Δ]	.78
T6[6m→4Δ] and T12[8TB/2]	.76

Task 5 [Platform] showed high negative correlations of $r = -.86$ and $r = -.82$ with Tasks 7 [9m→1h] and 12 [8TB/2] respectively. This suggests a strong inverse agreement in the relative proportionality between these factors.

Judging from the mean size of the correlation coefficients obtained by the pairwise comparisons of first principal components, the principal components of Tasks 6, 7, and 12 each appeared to be more parallel to those of the other 11 tasks than were the principal components of the remaining tasks.

As in the case of the raw data analyses Task 3 [15 × 30] shared the lowest mean correlation with the other 11 tasks. An explanation for this finding is provided, as in the case of the raw data, by the fact that Task 3 was the easiest task. However, in the case of the raw data analyses the brevity of this task made it atypical in its relative strategy requirements. Its relative dissimilarity to the other tasks in the analyses of the proportion data is more likely to have resulted from the fact that most subjects solved this task; that the tendency in this task was to use only two of the strategies, namely Strategies 1 (First reading), and 11 (Calculation/Detail); and that during the solving activity relatively large amounts of attention were given to solution irrelevant details (ST6).

The first principal components of Tasks 6 [6m→4Δ], 7 [9m→1h], and 12 [8TB/2] were most highly correlated. As can be ascertained by inspection of Figure 10.1, these three tasks were similar in that they elicited less self-related activity (ST13) and a considerably greater amount of critical appraisal, judgment, and verification (ST16) than the other tasks.

Oblique and orthogonal rotations were performed on the strategy factors with latent roots greater than one (Kaiser, 1963, 1964) obtained for each task on the bases of the raw and the proportion data. The factors were not found to be correlated in any of the tasks. Because of this, the two types of rotation produced virtually identical results. For the sake of simplicity, the orthogonal rotations will be discussed here. Most of the factors were found to be easily interpretable. Some similarities were detected in the rotated factors for the different tasks, but in general the combinations of variables producing the factors differed from task to task. The three most general rotated factors which were identified on the basis of the raw data analyses might be described as follows:

1. *Persistent, solution oriented, critical, task relevant reasoning.* An example of this type of factor was Varimax factor 1 identified in Task 1 [Binet], the highest loading strategy variables of which were as follows:

Strategy variable	Loading
10. Continued activity	.66
16. Judgment/Verification	.60
7. Plan/Hypothesis	.54
5. Identification of solution requirements	.52
11. Calculation/Detail	.50
8. Trial and Error	.43

Similar factors were identified in the varimax solutions of 8 of the 12 tasks (Task 1 factor 1, Task 2 factor 1, Task 3 factor 5 Task 4 factor 2, Task 5 factor 1, Task 6 factor 3, Task 7, factor 1, and Task 12 factor 1). Only the similarities tasks, Tasks 8 to 11 inclusive, did not contain a factor similar to this type. This type of factor shows an obvious tendency to load on complex operations.

2. *Stimulus passage or directions bound activity.* The structure of this type of factor is exemplified by factor 3 of Task 2 [∷], which had the following major loadings:

Strategy variable	Loading
2. Rereading	.57
5. Identification of imp. parts of solution from stimulus passage	.56
4. Reference to text	.48
11. Continued activity	.41

Similar factors were identified in Task 4 factor 5, Task 6 factor 1, Task 7 factor 5, Task 12 factor 3. This type of factor contains mainly heuristics.

3. Emotional, self-involved, defensive testing of idiosyncratic rather than stimulus passage or solution oriented hypotheses. An example for this type of factor is provided by factor 3 obtained in the factor analysis of Task 1 [Binet]. The highest loadings of this factor were as follows:

Strategy variable	Loading
15. Emotional behavior	.68
13. Self involved behavior	.58
14. Justification	.54
16. Judgment/Verification	.50
7. Plan/Hypothesis	.47

Other occurrences of factors similar to this were Task 2 factor 4, Task 6 factor 2, Task 8 factor 1, and Task 12 factor 1.

The rotated factors resulting from the analyses of the proportion data appeared to be more task specific. It was mentioned previously that in the proportion data differences between subjects and, to some extent, across tasks have been eliminated, which must be expected to result in less homogeneity of strategy use. The raw data provide information regarding the question of *what* subjects tend to do in the problem situation. The proportion data allow the investigation of *how* each task is dealt with. A leveling of differences in task lengths and other specific problem require- ments and differences in the speed with which individuals work on the problem have been eliminated. The factor analyses of the proportion data must therefore be expected to provide information concerning the differ- ences in the patterns of strategy use between tasks rather than informa- tion concerning similarities. It might be assumed therefore that once the differences in general task characteristics have been removed, it can no longer be expected that one or a small number of characteristic sets of problem solving behaviors are applicable to all or most tasks, but that the strategies become much more task dependent.

Another way of assessing the relative comparability, between rotated factors obtained in the task specific factor analysis might have been by correlating the factor scores computed on the basis of the varimax rotated factors between all tasks. For example, the first varimax rotated factor obtained in the factor analysis of Task 1 could have been correlated with every other varimax rotated first factor obtained in the factor analyses of the other 11 tasks, etc.

However, while the assessment of factor similarity across analyses by comparison of the first principal components could be regarded as provid- ing a reasonably valid description of the parallelism of these factors as determined by the relative amounts of contribution made by the strategy variables, the comparison of rotated factors across a variety of analyses must be expected to result in less valid findings. The solutions of the separately performed factor analyses may be quite incomparable because of differences in the rotations. It is not legitimate, therefore, to assume solely on the basis of the above described factor comparisons, that the strategies tend to be task dependent. Differences in rotation may have resulted in the incomparability of the solutions from the separate factor analyses computed for each task. For example, some of the factors which were compared across tasks accounted for varying amounts of common variance. Some factors accounted for large portions of common variance and others accounted for quite small amounts. Some of the latter factors may not have been retained for rotation in some tasks, and might therefore have caused noncomparable solutions. Also, the factor analyses performed independently for each task do not make allowance for the dependence between scores for the same subject.

A three–mode factor analysis in which variations in strategy variables, tasks, and subjects, can be investigated simultaneously, seemed a more appropriate method in the present study in which the same strategy variables and individuals were investigated in relation to a set of different tasks. The assumption that all possible combinations of the three modes occur (Tucker, 1966; Gorsuch, 1974) is met by the data. In other words all individuals have a score for every strategy variable for every task on which data were collected.

THREE–MODE FACTOR ANALYSIS

The Model

The operation of Tucker's three–mode factor analysis model can be explained as analogous to the principal component model of conventional two dimensional factor analysis. As in principal component analysis the three–mode factor model aims to describe each mode in terms of a reduced number of dimensions or factors. In this regard, the model operates on the assumption that there is some "average" factor matrix connecting the strategy variables with the strategy factors. This matrix is something like what would have been obtained by separate factor analyses for each task, had these analyses been weighted together. The method of weighting was explained at the beginning of this chapter.

The basic output from a three–mode factor analysis as applied to the data from the present study consisted of:

a. *a strategy factor matrix* $_k Q_k$ (with elements a_{im}), which describes the strategy variables in terms of strategy factors;

b. *a task factor matrix* $_jP_j$ (with elements b_{jp});
c. *a person factor matrix* $_i^M{}_i$ (with elements c_{kq}).
These three matrices are connected by means of
d. *a core matrix,* $_{pq}G_m$ (with elements g_{pq}) which indicates how the various kinds of factors are interrelated.

This core matrix can be conceptualized as containing the scores of each idealized subject for each idealized task for each idealized set of strategies.

As in conventional two–mode factor analysis, three–mode factor analysis allows for the rotation of the matrices of the model, so that different sets of matrices may relate in different ways to the same observed data.

Tucker's model can be summarized mathematically by the following equation:

$$X_{ijk} = \Sigma_m \, \Sigma_p \, \Sigma_q \, a_{im} \, b_{jp} \, c_{kq} \, g_{mpq} + y_{ijk} + e_{ijk},$$

where X_{ijk} is the score of subject i on task j for strategy variable k, and where the coefficients a_{im} describe the individual i in terms of the person factors m. The coefficients b_{jp} describe the tasks in terms of the task factors p, and the coefficients c_{kq} describe the strategies used in terms of the strategy factors q. The expression g_{mpq} is the entry in the three–mode or core matrix, which is regarded as a manifestation of the fundamental relationships of all relevant variables in relation to the phenomena under investigation because it relates the factors obtained in each of the three modes, m, p, and q to one another.

The expression $\Sigma_m \, \Sigma_p \, \Sigma_q \, a_{im} \, b_{jp} \, c_{kq} \, g_{mpq}$ represents the common variance of the observed scores on the combination variables, while y_{ijk} and e_{ijk} denote the unique variances and error respectively.

In the present study both oblique (BINORMAMIN) and orthogonal (Varimax) rotations were performed on the strategy, task, and person factor matrices. Compensational rotations were performed on the core matrix for both the oblique and the orthogonal procedures. As in the case of the task specific two–mode factor analysis, the results of the oblique and the orthogonal rotations in the three–mode analyses were close to identical, as the factors were found to be uncorrelated. The orthogonal solutions will be discussed for the sake of simplicity.

Method of Analysis

A computer program contained in the SOUPAC package (University of Illinois, 1975) was used to perform the three–mode factor analyses according to Tucker's method 1 (Tucker, 1966), which allowed analysis with unique variance for the combination variables.

Two three–mode factor analyses were performed, one on the raw scores representing strategy use, and one on the proportion scores.

Data input for a traditional factor analysis is usually in the form of a rectangular table or matrix. The observations entered into a three–mode factor analysis may be visualized as being presented in the form of a rectangular prism. In the present study the data for each subject (variable i) were presented separately in a table containing 18 columns for the 18 problem solving strategies (variable k) under investigation, and 12 rows for the 12 tasks (variable j) presented to each subject. The height of the prism is made up of 89 of these tables, one for each subject, imagined in layers or slices. Each of the three dimensions, subjects, tasks, and strategies of this prism would be referred to by Tucker (1963, 1964) as a "mode of classification," shortened to "mode," the latter term being preferred to the term "dimension" to avoid confusion which might result from using the term "dimension" for two different concepts. The term dimension thus retains its traditional use, i.e., for factors yielded by the analysis, while the term mode refers to combination variables which provide the input for factor analysis.

Each of the 18 strategy measures on each task was considered as one variable. This part of the data therefore consisted of 216 variables. The intercorrelations among these variables were interpreted as Tucker's matrix $_{(ik)}R_{(jk)}$ (Tucker, 1966) which is analogous to a multitrait–multimethod matrix proposed as a basis for valid analysis by Campbell and Fiske (1959), in this case a multistrategy–multitask intercorrelation matrix. This matrix then presents all of the intercorrelations resulting from the measurement of the 18 strategies used in each of the 12 tasks.

The subscript notation (jk) originates from Tucker (1966) and is used to label a set of combination variables. In the case of the present study each of these combination variables is made up of a combination of one of the 18 problem solving strategies (k) and a task (j).

Tucker's three–mode factor analysis model makes no assumptions in relation to the scaling of the input data. However, as the size of the factor loading produced by a variable is determined not only by the communality of the variable with the factor, but depends also on the scaling of the variable, the scaling of the elements of the input matrices is of considerable importance. What type of transformation is applied depends on the means and standard deviations of which variables are of interest, and which differences are not desirable.

In the first instance three–mode analyses were performed on the unstandardized raw and proportion data because it was assumed that differences in strategy use would reflect task and/or individual differences, and should therefore be retained. In both the proportion and raw data analyses, the first factors extracted in each of the three modes accounted for more than 99% of the variances of the respective modes. The plotting of successive latent roots, however, appeared suggestive of the possibility of a number of quite distinct factors in each of the modes. This trend showed strong agreement with the results which had been obtained previously when separate two–mode analyses were performed for each of the 12 tasks. The number of factors was determined by use of the following criteria: breaks in the plots of the eigenvalues, interpretability of the factors and for the strategy mode, the results from the preliminary two–mode analyses were taken into consideration.

Similarly large first factors have previously been obtained in three–mode factor analysis (Bartussek, 1973; Bernstein & Wicker, 1969). Bernstein and Wicker (1969), in a study of the concept of novelty, based on the ratings of a number of animal slides on a series of adjective scales, found the loadings on their first extraordinarily strong factor to correlate highly with mean ratings on each adjective scale. In the present study, too, the loadings on the first large factors for persons, tasks, and strategy variables correlated .80, .89, and .98 respectively with the mean variable values for the respective modes. This phenomenon can be explained as a direct result from the application of principal components procedures to matrices of cross products rather than to correlation matrices. In the factor analysis of matrices which are not correlation matrices or covariance matrices, the means of the variables are contained in the factor loadings.

For both proportion and raw data the first strategy factor is interpretable as a "first reading" factor, resulting from the fact that Strategy Variable 1 (First reading) was by far the most consistently and frequently used variable. Its resulting high mean values would, in turn, have produced very large cross products values, which may have somewhat flooded the picture and thus masked the contributions of other significant variables.

Because the aim of the present study was less to identify the strategy variable or variables which, in absolute terms, were used most frequently, than to identify possible strategy factors, i.e., to identify groups of variables which might occur together, a decision was made to rescale the raw input data for the three–mode analyses by standardizing the scores in the strategy mode (k) across subjects (i), and across tasks (j). Through this standardization, matrix $_kQ_k$ becomes a correlation matrix, but the other two matrices remain cross products matrices, a fact which has to be kept in mind later when attempts are made to interpret the resulting matrices of factor loadings. The standardization of column vector $_{ij}X_k$ results in the elimination of mean and standard deviation differences between the strategy variables (k), but retains differences in means and standard deviations in the task and subject combination variables.

Further justification for the above described type of standardization was provided by the consideration of a possibility that the unstandardized values of strategy use, although obtained on the basis of their occurrence in units of time—presumably a ratio scale—might have in fact provided a ranking only of individuals and tasks with respect to strategy use, because different meanings may be attached to the time units for different individuals, and to their work on different tasks. An interval scale—at least, is required if differences of strategy use in different tasks and across different individuals are to be compared. Standardization of the strategy mode variables *(k)* across the task *(j)* and subject *(i)* modes provides a type of definition of the k variables, according to which the units of this variable, strategy use, are equalized across subjects and tasks.

The results presented in the following pages are based on the application of Tucker's three–mode factor analysis to the raw data of the present study after standardizing the scores for the strategy mode *(k)* across the subject and task combination mode *(ij)*.

The results of the three–mode factor analysis which was performed on the proportion data will be presented after the results of the raw data analyses. Standardization of the proportion data was not regarded as legitimate because the patterns of strategy use between subjects and between different tasks had been made comparable as a result of the ipsatization of the scores.

THREE–MODE ANALYSIS OF RAW SCORES

Determining the Number of Factors

As was stated previously, Tucker's three–mode factor analysis involves finding the latent roots and latent vectors of three different matrices of cross products, one for each mode. The "scree test" (Cattell, 1966) was used to provide a criterion in the determination of the number of factors to be extracted in each mode. Kaiser's criterion, which was used to determine the number of factors to be extracted in the two–mode analyses, could not be utilized in the three–mode analysis, because of the size of the eigenvalues obtained in analyses based on matrices of cross products.

When the roots of the matrices were plotted in decreasing orders of magnitude, it was found that their size dropped sharply at the beginning and then decreased more slowly. The scree test involves the examination of the plotted latent roots for sharp breaks or bends. The determination of the number of factors to be rotated involves a decision as to at which point succeeding roots add so little to the proportion of variance already accounted for that their contribution can be regarded as non significant.

Table 10.3 presents the first 10 latent roots for each of the three modes.

TABLE 10.3

First Ten Latent Roots of the Cross Products Matrices[1]

(Raw Scores)

Root	Strategy mode (k)		Task mode (i)		Subject mode (i)	
	Eigenvalue	% Variance	Eigenvalue	% Variance	Eigenvalue	% Variance
1	5322.42	27.69	6804.97	35.40	5768.68	30.00
2	3238.97	16.85	2917.64	15.18	4549.79*	23.67
3	1663.12	8.65	1935.81	10.07	870.40	4.53
4	1413.03	7.35	1777.08*	9.24	701.44	3.65
5	1317.67*	6.85	1588.10	8.26	546.34	2.84
6	1005.58	5.23	975.14	5.07	507.46	2.64
7	958.44	4.99	810.13	4.21	413.58	2.15
8	876.52	4.56	655.05	3.41	386.36	2.01
9	784.72	4.08	631.10	3.28	360.11	1.87
10	724.19	3.77	501.67	2.61	342.86	1.78
Sum of N^2 Roots	19226	100%	19226	100%	19226	100%

[1]The starred values indicate the last latent roots judged to be significant for the particular cross products matrix.

[2]N represents the total number of roots extracted in the analysis, and equals 18 for the strategy mode, 12 for the task mode and 89 for the subject mode.

Considering the number of factors in the strategy mode first, the pattern of roots indicated a number of possible breaks. After some trial rotations with two, three, and five factors, a five factor solution was selected on the basis of interpretability as well as because the sixth and subsequent latent roots appeared to account for increasingly less significant amounts of variance.

In the task mode four factors were retained for rotation. The difference of 654.11 between the fourth and fifth roots is considerably larger than the difference between any pair of successive roots beyond this point. Further support for the retention of four task factors was gained by the finding that the rotation of axes with this number of factors yielded a more plausible solution, which was not improved by the addition of further factors. The four factor solution for the task mode was preferred to a highly plausible two factor solution because the latter was regarded as accounting for too small a proportion of the common variance between the tasks.

Two factors were retained in the subject mode because a clear break appeared to have occurred between the second and third latent roots, the difference of 381.44 between these roots being more than four times the size of the difference between the next larger pair of successive roots beyond this point.

Both oblique (BINORMAMIN) and orthogonal rotations (Varimax) of the axes were performed. The results of these methods of rotation were virtually identical, because the factors obtained in each of the three modes were uncorrelated. To simplify the presentation the results of the orthogonal rotation will be discussed here.

To summarize, the number of factors for retention was established as five for the strategy mode, four for the task mode, and two for the subject mode. The resulting strategy, task, and person factor matrices were rotated orthogonally (Varimax), and the core matrix was rotated in a compensatory way, as mentioned earlier.

Strategy Mode

The structure of factors resulting from the orthogonal solution of the strategy mode is shown in Table 10.4.

The five rotated factors can be described as follows:

Strategy factor 1 (KF1) represents a mechanical stimulus passage oriented approach, characterized by much rereading of the passage or instructions and by *attempts to memorize the task as presented*. The strategy variables with the highest loading on this factor are ST2 (Rereading) and ST18 (Memory); with a high negative loading on ST15 (Emo-

TABLE 10.4
Orthogonally Rotated Factor Matrix of the Strategy Mode (k)
(Raw Scores)

| Strategy variable | Factor | | | | |
ST	KF1	KF2	KF3	KF4	KF5
1. First reading	.02	.63	-.06	-.23	-.02
2. Rereading	.55	.21	.05	.11	.09
3. Chunk/Summarize	.00	.02	.13	.21	.41
4. Ref. to text/check	.03	-.06	-.08	.51	-.15
5. Id. parts from input	.08	.08	.01	.45	-.06
6. Irrelevant activity	.00	-.01	.05	.37	.07
7. Plan/Hypothesis	.16	.01	-.05	.27	.04
8. Trial + Error	-.15	-.05	-.03	.36	.06
9. Comp./Rel. Trials	.12	.41	.04	.04	-.02
10. Cont. activity	.07	.03	-.01	.01	.45
11. Calcul./Detail	.06	-.30	-.05	-.19	.45
12. Reason	.03	.19	.64	-.06	-.02
13. Self-related	-.10	.12	-.15	-.11	.46
14. Justification	-.06	-.13	.69	-.02	-.03
15. Emotional	-.61	.02	.16	.08	.14
16. Judgm./Verif.	-.08	-.27	.06	.13	.16
17. Pause	-.24	.28	-.05	.11	.24
18. Memory	.41	-.24	.15	.13	.25

tional). The lowest loadings were obtained by ST6 (Irrelevant activity) and ST3 (Chunk/Summarize stimulus passage).

ST4 (Ref. to text), which represents brief references to various points of the text, usually used for checking; ST12 (Reasoning); and ST15 and ST16, representing justification behavior and critical judgment, and verification of text or work on the task, also obtained particularly low loadings on this factor.

Strategy factor 2 (KF2) is described by variables characterizing the *critical analysis of input data,* i.e., the stimulus passage as a whole, with little attention to detail, specific calculations, etc. Variables referring to chunking, summarizing, or other study of detail in the text or solution activity showed the lowest loadings on this factor.

Strategy factor 3 (KF3) can be interpreted as a solution oriented *justification and reasoning factor.* ST14 (Justification) and ST12 (Reasoning) show the highest loadings on this factor. Reading and other references to the stimulus passage including ST5 (Identif. of solution or part of solution from text) have the lowest loadings on this factor. ST16 (Judgment/Verification) also produced a low loading of .05 on this factor.

Strategy factor 4 (KF4) represents *task relevant, solution oriented heuristics.* This factor is characterized by such strategies as ST8 (Trial and Error) and ST9 (Plan/Hypothesis) which occur in combination with frequent references to the stimulus passage. ST4 (Ref. to text) provides the highest loading on this factor.

Strategy factor 5 (KF5) characterizes *ego-involved persistent,* at times *laborious attempts* to reach a solution in a stepwise manner, *with a focus on detail rather than on the problem as a whole.* Attention is mainly on small parts or sections of the problem. Specific calculations and other manipulations of detail play an important role.

Two factors, i.e., KF1 and KF2, can be described as input or stimulus passage directed, while factors KF3 and KF5 might be regarded as solution directed. KF4 is a factor combining both stimulus passage and solution directed activity.

Task Mode

Table 10.5 shows the structure of the four task factors *(JF)* after orthogonal rotation of the axes in the task mode.

As can be seen from Table 10.5, with the exception of Task 12 [8TB/2], each task showed significant loading on one factor only. The loadings for

TABLE 10.5
Orthogonally Rotated Factor Matrix for the Task Mode (Raw Data)

Task	JF1	JF2	JF3	JF4
1. Binet	.11	.11	.13	.78
2. ∷∷	-.06	-.26	.61	.25
3. 15x30	-.07	.07	-.07	.29
4. Pebbles	.81	-.18	-.16	.13
5. Platform	.50	.05	.13	-.14
6. 6m→4△	-.04	-.03	.64	-.08
7. 9m→1h	.10	.10	.23	-.08
8. Poem/St.	.07	.56	.01	.19
9. Praise/P.	-.01	.40	-.00	.05
10. Fly/Tree	-.03	.39	-.01	.00
11. Wood/Alc.	-.04	.38	-.01	-.03
12. 8TB/2	.23	.33	.33	-.39

Task 12 were not among the highest in their contribution to any of the factors, but the task provided moderate loadings on each of the four factors.

It should be remembered here that, as noted previously, the factor loadings in the task and subject modes are not correlations with a factor, and must therefore be assessed in terms of their relative magnitude. The following grouping of the tasks was suggested by the factors on this basis.

Task factor 1 (JF1) was characterized by high loadings on Tasks 4 [Pebbles] and 5 [Platform], and a lesser, but relatively substantial loading on Task 12 [8TB/2]. This factor could perhaps be labelled a De Bono type *creativity tasks* factor.

Task factor 2 (JF2) was shown to be a *similarity items factor*. All similarities tasks, i.e., Tasks 8 to 11 inclusive, and Task 12 [8TB/2] had positive loadings of considerable size on this factor. Task 2 [: : :] had a relatively substantial negative loading on this task. What Task 12 [8TB/2] has in common with the similarities items is possibly its requirement of the logical exploration of the relationship between two parts. There is a need to discriminate between essential and superficial aspects of this relationship.

Task factor 3 (JF3) is a factor of *performance tasks*. The highest loading tasks were Tasks 6 [6m→4Δ], 2 [: : :], and 7 [9m→1h]. Task 12 [8TB/2] again showed a substantial positive loading.

Task factor 4 (JF4) is characterized by tasks requiring calculation in terms of the actual manipulation of numbers. The highest loadings on this factor, which might be labelled as a *mathematical tasks* factor, were obtained from Tasks 1 [Binet] and 3 [15 × 30], with Task 12 [8TB/2] showing a substantial but negative loading. Further discussion of the factors is deferred until the discussion of the core matrix and the general discussion presented in Chapter 13.

Subject Mode

The factor matrix for the subject mode is not reproduced here because of the space that would be required. The elements of this matrix are each subject's loading on the subject factors. As was stated previously, two subject factors were rotated.

In an endeavor to interpret these factors more clearly, the relationship of high[1] loadings on either of the person factors with a number of back-

---

1. Loadings which were larger than 0.1

TABLE 10.6
Achievement Levels Summed Across all 12 Tasks for Subjects
Loading Highly on Subject Factors 1 and 2 Respectively

| | Number of Tasks Achieved at Level | | |
Subject factor	A Correct or nearly correct	B Task discontinued	C Wrong
IF1	158 (33%)	109 (23%)	213 (44%)
IF2	164 (46%)	59 (16%)	137 (38%)

ground variables was investigated. The 40 subjects with the highest load-ing on Subject factor 1 were compared with the 30 individuals with the highest loading on Subject factor 2 on the background variables of sex, level of education, achievement, time taken on the tasks, and intelligence.

The first two of these variables showed no significant differences be-tween the two factors. The values of $\chi^2_{df1} = 0.50$ and $\chi^2_{df3} \times 0.69$ were obtained for sex and educational level respectively.

The comparison of overall achievement summed over the 12 tasks across the high loading subjects of each factor becomes possible on the basis of Table 10.6.

The difference in the pattern of overall achievements between the sub-jects characterizing either of the factors is obvious and highly significant ($\chi^2_{df2} = 14.65, p < .001$).

The comparison of achievement levels obtained by the high loading subjects on the two factors on each individual task resulted in significant differences for Task 1 [Binet], $\chi^2_{df2} = 11.30, p < .01$; Task 6 [6m→4Δ], $\chi^2_{df2} = 19.97, p < .001$; and Task 7 [9m→1h], $\chi^2_{df2} = 7.15, p < .05$. The differences obtained for the remaining tasks failed to reach the $p = .05$ level of significance, with the differences for Tasks 3 [15 × 30], 10 [Fly/Tree], and 12 [8TB/2] coming close to the specified level of significance.

Both the time taken for the 12 tasks and intelligence showed significant differences between Subject factor 1 and Subject factor 2 subjects. The mean time taken for the total exercise of working on the 12 given tasks for the 40 highest loading individuals on the first subjects factor was 347.80 three-second units ($SD = 85.90$). The corresponding mean time taken by the 30 highest loading individuals on the second factor was 647.90 three-second units ($SD = 114.19$). The difference between these group means is significant; $t = 12.06, df 68, p < .001$.

The difference in intelligence between the persons characterizing the first and second subject factors respectively was assessed by a compari-son of the mean BD scaled scores of the two groups. The difference between the mean BD score for the first subject factor of 9.75 ($SD = 2.61$)

and the corresponding score for the second subject factor of 11.83 (SD = 2.52) was found to be highly significant; t = 9.39, df 68, p < .001.

To summarize, it can be said that individuals characterized by the first "idealized" subject factor differed from those characterized by the second "idealized" subject factor in their levels of achievement, overall time taken for the tasks and intelligence. Subject factor 2 persons tended to be of higher intelligence, took more time over the total of the 12 tasks, and achieved a relatively larger number of correct or nearly correct solutions than Subject factor 1 persons. Subject factor 1 subjects showed a considerably stronger tendency to discontinue the task as shown in Table 10.6.

The Subject factors are further interpreted in the presentation of information as contained in the core matrix.

Rotated Core Matrix

The rotated core matrix, as explained previously, provides an indication of the structure of the relationship between the task factors and the strategy factors for each "idealized" subject. The "loadings" or weights of the core matrix contain some information as to why particular tasks (or strategy variables) clustered together to form a factor. By making it possible to investigate the interrelationships between these two sets of factors with respect to different types of problem solvers, a more complex analysis of the problem solving process becomes possible, at least theoretically.

Table 10.7 is designed to constitute the three dimensional core matrix. It consists of two 4 × 5 matrices, the elements (loadings) of which show the relationships between the task factors and the strategy factors for the members of each of the two subject factors. The matrix contained in the upper section of the table shows the interrelationship between task factors and strategy factors for the members of Subject factor 1, while the matrix presented in the lower section of the table represents the task–strategy relationship for the members of Subject factor 2.

The values in the core matrix must be interpreted in terms of relative magnitude. It should also be noted that no subject in the study corresponds exactly to either of the idealized individuals, but that the subjects approximate a particular idealized individual to the extent to which they load on either of the subject factors.

Table 10.7 makes it possible to indicate which types of strategies each idealized subject preferred for a particular type of task. For example, the first idealized individual would apply to tasks loading highly on the creativity task factor (JF1), mainly solution oriented, task relevant heuristics as represented by Strategy factor 4 (KF4), with perhaps a slight

TABLE 10.7
Rotated Core Matrix

| Subject factors | Task factors | Stimulus Pass. Oriented | | Solution Oriented | | Ego Involved |
| | | Strategy Factors | | | | |
		KF1	KF2	KF3	KF4	KF5
IF$_1$	JF$_1$ Creativity	4.14	- 1.16	- 6.76	19.58	- 4.92
	JF$_2$ Similarity	1.48	5.56	3.64	-17.59	-17.52
	JF$_3$ Performance	8.65	- 5.15	- 5.82	- 4.85	4.74
	JF$_4$ Mathematical	-1.53	-14.02	7.86	- 1.86	- 7.60
IF$_2$	JF$_1$ Creativity	-6.23	7.39	- 4.44	37.65	13.67
	JF$_2$ Similarity	-0.77	14.26	9.86	-18.08	-13.74
	JF$_3$ Performance	0.09	- 1.34	- 4.04	2.77	35.41
	JF$_4$ Mathematical	-2.78	-15.53	15.47	- 0.29	- 4.54

attempt to memorize the task requirements as presented, i.e., Strategy factor 1 (KF1). One might infer that this idealized individual would apply trial and error procedures (ST8) to the De Bono type creativity tasks characterized by JF1, and test hypotheses (ST7) in an appropriate manner (ST5), on the basis of frequent reference to the text of the stimulus passage (ST4), because these strategy variables have high loadings on one or both the strategy factors with the highest loadings on the creativity tasks factor (JF1) in the first row of Table 10.7. Similar analyses of the relations represented in the cells of the rotated core matrix can be carried out for all task factors for each of the idealized subjects. In this way it becomes possible to determine the types of strategies which tended to be used for particular types of tasks by subjects loading high on either of the two subject factors.

In addition to the above noted strong positive relationship between the De Bono type creativity tasks, characterized by Task factor JF1 and Strategy factor KF4, and a lesser relationship with KF1, this task factor showed a sizeable negative relationship with Strategy factors KF3 and KF5. Subject factor 1 subjects tended not to apply justification and other reasoning strategies to these De Bono type tasks, nor was there much evidence of ego-involved laborious persistence as characterized by KF5.

The latter findings are congruent with the previously discussed tendency of Subject factor 1 subjects to be of relatively lower intelligence, and to discontinue the task more readily.

The problem solving of the subjects approximating Subject factor 1 was further characterized by a relatively strong interrelationship between Strategy factor KF1 and the Performance tasks factor, JF3. This type of relationship was absent among Subject factor 2 subjects. This means that the attempts of Subject factor 1 subjects to deal with the rather difficult performance tasks tended to be stimulus passage bound, and showed less ego-involvement than the attempts of Subject factor 2 individuals. Persons of the latter type tended to deal with these performance tasks, JF3, mainly by applying KF5 type strategies of ego-involved, persistent, at times laborious, but certainly solution oriented methods.

With respect to the De Bono type tasks, JF1, the Subject factor 2 subjects' problem solving behavior was characterized by an even stronger relationship between Task factor JF1 and Strategy factor KF4 than had been found in the case of Subject factor 1 subjects. But Subject factor 2 subjects used the KF4 strategies in combination with KF5 strategies of again solution oriented ego-involved persistence, rather than in combination with KF1. Critical analysis of the input data, as characterized by KF2 also showed a positive interrelationship with the De Bono type creativity task performance for the individuals characterized by Subject factor 2.

The interrelationship between the Mathematical tasks factor, JF4 and the strategies factors showed relatively strong similarity between both subject factors. Justification and reasoning, KF3, and critical analysis of the stimulus passage, KF2, showed the highest positive and negative interrelationships respectively. This pattern would seem to be as expected for tasks with relatively straight–forward, easily interpretable instructions and reasonably obvious strategy requirements.

The performance patterns of both idealized individuals on the Similarities tasks, JF2, again differed in the strength of the interrelationship between JF2 and the strategies factors rather than in the direction of the relationship. Critical analysis of the stimulus passage, thus seeking the best possible understanding of the task requirements, i.e., KF2, and justification and reasoning, i.e., KF3, provided the most relevant strategies for both types of problem solvers.

Summarizing the results of the three–mode factor analysis of the raw data, four factors were found to describe the task mode, five factors characterized different dimensions in the strategy mode, and two factors represented different groups in the subject mode. The latter mode accounted for a relatively smaller amount of variance than had the factors identified in the other modes.

The factors in the task mode categorized the problems presented to the subjects in the present study into De Bono type Creativity tasks (JF1), Similarities tasks (JF2), Performance tasks (JF3), and Mathematical items (JF4). Of the factors obtained in the strategy mode two (KF1 and KF2) could be described as stimulus passage oriented, two factors (KF3 and KF5) were solution oriented and one factor (KF4) combined both types of strategy orientation in a positive manner.

It is of interest to note that the types of strategies used, i.e., the strategy factors, appeared not to discriminate between the two "idealized" subjects in relation to the Mathematical (JF4) and Similarities tasks (JF2). In their work on the De Bono type Creativity tasks (JF1) and on the Performance tasks (JF3) the solution oriented, task relevant heuristics (KF4) and ego involved persistent laboring (KF5) tended to be relied on for JF1 and JF3 respectively by all subjects. The *strength* of the interrelationships between the task and strategy factors differed for the two subject factors with respect to all task factors.

The strategy factors describing the second and subsequent most relied on sets of strategies tended to differ both in type and size. The latter tendency, while observable for all task factors, was found to be particularly pronounced in the case of the De Bono type Creativity tasks, characterized by Task factor JF1 and the Performance tasks making up Task factor JF3.

THREE–MODE ANALYSIS OF THE PROPORTION
DATA

Determining the Number of Factors

The number of factors to be extracted in each of the modes was determined by applying the same criteria which had been applied in the three–mode analysis of the raw data. Table 10.8 shows the first ten latent roots for the three modes respectively.

Inspection of roots presented in Table 10.8 suggests unidimensionality of each of the variable sets represented in the three modes. The first eigen-value obtained in each mode accounts for close to 100% of the "variances" of the respective modes. It must be remembered here that the importance of the latent roots is being judged not on the basis of correlations but on the basis of cross products. The concept of "percentage of variance" accounted for therefore lacks meaningfulness. As was pointed out previously, any assessment of relative importance of factors or variables has to be based on relative differences in the magnitude of values.

The identification of single dimensions in subject, task, and strategy modes respectively resulting from the application of three–mode factor analysis to the proportion data is not surprising. Expressing the strategy use for each subject as a proportion of the subject's total time used for each task separately was expected to result in a reduction of individual differences and in a reduction of differences between tasks.

As has been mentioned previously in factor analysis of matrices which are not correlation matrices or covariance matrices, and which have not been standardized in other ways, the means of the variables are contained in the factor loadings. This must be expected to result in the possibility of disproportionately high contributions of single variables with high mean values, rather than sets of important variables, in the determination of the structures of such factors.

Despite the plausibility of the finding of unidimensionality of subject, task, and strategy modes when proportion data are analyzed, the patterns of eigenvalues in Table 10.8 were scrutinized for possible breaks, which might suggest numbers of factors for experimental rotations in an exploratory fashion.

In the subject mode a further break between the second and third roots was regarded as a possible justification to rotate two subject factors. It was decided to rotate four factors each in the task and the strategy modes after exploratory rotations with three and two factors.

The decision to rotate two subject factors, four task factors, and four strategy factors was made partly on the basis of the suggestion of possible breaks in the plots of the latent roots, partly because this combination of rotated factors appeared readily interpretable, and partly on the basis of

TABLE 10.8
First Ten Latent Roots of the Cross Products Matrices[1]
(Proportion Data)

Root	Strategy mode (k)		Task mode (j)		Subject mode (i)	
	Eigenvalue	% Variance	Eigenvalue	% Variance	Eigenvalue	% Variance
1	1210214.45	99.981	1210140.49	99.975	1210121.82	99.973
2	84.32	0.007	133.12	0.011	196.89*	0.016
3	49.44	0.004	42.55	0.004	12.16	0.001
4	28.53*	0.002	39.19*	0.003	7.42	0.001
5	14.87	0.001	19.76	0.002	6.77	0.001
6	11.67	0.001	15.18	0.001	6.18	0.001
7	11.22	0.001	14.01	0.001	5.70	0.000
8	5.80	0.000	12.38	0.001	5.07	0.000
9	5.54	0.000	7.54	0.001	5.02	0.000
10	3.84	0.000	6.87	0.001	4.58	0.000
Sum of N^2 Roots	1210439		1210439		1210439	
		100		100		100

[1] The starred values indicate the last latent roots used in an exploratory rotation of the particular products matrix.
[2] N represents the total number of roots extracted in the analysis, and equals 18 for the strategy mode, 12 for the task mode and 89 for the subject mode.

the knowledge gained from prior task specific analyses of the proportion data and the three–mode analyses of the raw data.

The structures of the orthogonally rotated factors of the strategy and task modes are briefly summarized in the next sections.

Strategy Mode

One common and three unique factors were identified, the former being characterized by a number of solution directed heuristics. The number of factors rotated had little influence on the occurrence of unique factors. The combination and order, in terms of comparative magnitudes of the strategy variables loading on the common heuristics factor, naturally varied according to the number of factors extracted.

The four strategy factors might be described as follows:

Strategy factor 1 ($K_{Prop}1$), with a loading of 0.99 on the strategy variable ST11 (Code 219: Calculation/Detail) characterizes mathematical calculations in terms of the manipulation of actual numbers, and the focus of attention on part or details of the problem. This unique factor describes solution directed activity.

Strategy factor 2 ($K_{Prop}2$) contains most of the solution directed heuristics, excluding ST11, and shows a moderate loading on ST2 (Code 112: Rereading). The highest loadings were as follows:

	Strategy variable	Loading
St7	Plan/Hypothesis	.66
ST10	Continued activity	.51
ST16	Judgment/Verification	.31
ST8	Trial and error	.29
ST2	Rereading	.27

Strategy factor 3 ($K_{Prop}3$) had a loading of 0.98 on the strategy variable ST9 (Compare/Relate former trials) characterizing a solution directed type of activity in which the subject concentrated on keeping track of previous attempts and strategies applied in the problem solving.

Strategy factor 4 ($K_{Prop}4$) was a unique factor characterized by strategy variable ST1 (First reading), which obtained the highest loading in the analysis of all strategy mode variables.

In summary, one might note that three of the four factors were unique factors and that two of the unique factors and the common factor characterized solution oriented activity. Only one of the factors, $K_{Prop}1$, produced by the "First reading" strategy variable, ST1, could be regarded as stimulus passage oriented.

TABLE 10.9
Orthogonally Rotated Factor Matrix for the Task Mode
(Proportion Data)

Tasks		Factors			
		$J_{Prop}1$	$J_{Prop}2$	$J_{Prop}3$	$J_{Prop}4$
T1	[Binet]	.38	.08	.00	.00
T2	[∷]	.02	.51	-.05	-.00
T3	[15x30]	.49	-.12	.12	-.00
T4	[Pebbles]	-.01	.21	.49	.00
T5	[Platform]	-.02	.20	.67	-.00
T6	[6m→4△]	.02	.48	-.04	-.00
T7	[9m→1h]	.00	.49	.04	-.00
T8	[Poem/St]	.40	.01	.02	-.00
T9	[Praise/P]	.46	.04	-.08	.00
T10	[Fly/Tree]	-.00	.00	-.00	1.00
T11	[Wood/Alc.]	.49	-.01	-.05	.00
T12	[8TB/2]	.01	.45	.06	-.00

Task Mode

Table 10.9 shows the factor matrix resulting from the orthogonal rotation of four factors in the task mode.

Among the four rotated task factors one unique factor, $J_{Prop}4$, was obtained. Rotating two, three, or eight factors did not alter this part of the orthogonal solution. Task 10 [Fly/Tree] produced a unique factor in all these solutions.

Task factor 1,($J_{Prop}1$) was characterized by tasks with straightforward easily understood solution requirements. The rules for these problems were obvious, and the first reading of the task, i.e., strategy variable ST1, could be followed immediately by solution directed activity. The highest loading tasks on this factor were the similarities items, Tasks 8 to 11, Task 3 [15 × 30] and Task 1 [Binet].

Task factor 2,($J_{Prop}2$) might be described as a performance factor, in spite of the contribution made by Task 12 [8TB/2]. While in terms of first presentation, i.e., its stimulus passage, Task 12 may appear to differ considerably from the performance tasks, Tasks 2, 6, and 7, it is feasible to consider that the solution requirements, in terms of strategy use, of Task 12 may have been quite similar to those of the performance tasks. The instructions of Task 12 may have elicited visualization of the task, and imagery. The task in common with the other tasks loading highly on factor $J_{Prop}2$ certainly elicited a considerable amount of trial and error activity, ST8, hypothesis testing, ST7, and other solution directed heuristics.

Another possibility is that task factor $J_{Prop}2$ in fact characterized tasks which were difficult, and the stimulus passage of which did not reveal or lead to immediate plans of solution directed problem solving action. Some support for this interpretation may be gained by the fact that the two other difficult tasks, Tasks 4 [Pebbles] and 5 [Platform] showed, comparatively speaking, moderately high loadings on this factor.

Task factor 3,($J_{Prop}3$) was characterized by the high positive loadings of Task 4 [Pebbles], and Task 5 [Platform], the De Bono creativity tasks.

Task factor 4,($J_{Prop}4$) was, as previously noted, produced by Task 10 [Fly/Tree].

Subject Mode

It was decided to rotate factors for exploratory purposes. As in the case of the three–mode factor analysis of the raw data, the meaningfulness of the two subject factors was explored in relation to a number of external variables and criteria.

Because of the strength and general applicability of the first rotated subject factor, differences between subjects approximating either of the idealized subjects were made by comparing the subjects with comparatively high loadings on Subject factor 2 *($I_{Prop},2$)* with those subjects not loading highly on this factor. No subject was found to load highly on both factors.

No differences were found between the subjects regarded, as a result of this somewhat arbitrary procedure, as characterized by either of the subject factors with regard to educational level ($\chi^2 = 3.23$, $df = 3, p > .05$), sex ($\chi^2 = 3.25$, $df = 2, p > .05$), or overall level of achievement across the 12 tasks ($\chi^2 = 1.62$, $df = 3$, $p > .05$). Separate analyses performed for each task showed that the two sets of subjects produced on the basis of the two orthogonally rotated factors of the subject mode did not differ with regard to the proportion of their members solving or nearly solving (Achievement level A), deciding to discontinue (Achievement level B), or failing to solve the task (Achievement level C) in any of the tasks.

A significant difference was found, however, between the two groups characterized by the two factors in the subject mode, in the mean time[2] taken by subjects for the total exercise of solving the 12 tasks ($\bar{X}_{IF1} = 516.73, SD_{IF1} = 165.20; \bar{X}_{IF2} = 433.00, SD_{IF2} = 152.99; t_{IF1-IF2} = 2.48, df = 43, p < .02$).

No difference in intelligence ($t = 0.81$, $df = 43, p > .05$) was found

---

2. Mean times and standard deviations given in units of three-second intervals.

TABLE 10.10
Rotated Core Matrix (Proportion Data)

Subject factors	Task factors		K_{Prop}^{F1}	K_{Prop}^{F2}	Strategy Factors K_{Prop}^{F3}	K_{Prop}^{F4}
			Calc./Det.	Heuristics	Comp./Rel.	First reading
I_{Prop}^1	J_{Prop}^1	Easy Input	1.13	0.07	0.36	0.19
	J_{Prop}^2	Performance	0.04	0.73	0.12	0.36
	J_{Prop}^3	Creativity	-0.02	0.11	-0.01	1.01
	J_{Prop}^4	[Fly/Tree]	-0.02	-0.02	-0.02	1100.00
I_{Prop}^2	J_{Prop}^1	Easy Input	5.77	2.18	3.64	3.89
	J_{Prop}^2	Performance	-0.19	6.41	0.91	1.81
	J_{Prop}^3	Creativity	0.41	1.23	1.38	7.35
	J_{Prop}^4	[Fly/Tree]	1.74	0.68	2.55	1.76

between the two groups. The mean scaled scores obtained on the WAIS Block Design Test, which was used to estimate levels of intellectual functioning, were $\bar{X}_{BD} = 11.23$, $SD = 2.72$ and $\bar{X}_{BD} = 10.76$, $SD = 2.75$ for Subject factor 1 and Subject factor 2 subjects respectively.

The two factors of the subject mode will be discussed further in relation to the rotated Core Matrix in the next section.

Rotated Core Matrix

Table 10.10 provides an indication of the interrelationship of the strategy, task, and subject factors explored in the three–mode factor analysis of the proportion data.

The most striking item of information contained in Table 10.10 is the disproportionately high value in the cell relating Task factor $J_{Prop}4$ with Strategy factor $K_{Prop}4$ for Subject factor 1, i.e., $I_{Prop}1$.

In an attempt to interpret this finding the performances of Subject factor 1 and Subject factor 2 subjects on the important Task 10 [Fly/Tree] were compared in more detail.

Although, as previously noted, the mean times taken for the total of all 12 tasks differed significantly for the two groups of subjects, the difference in the mean times taken for Task 10 [Fly/Tree] showed no significant difference ($t = 0.45$, $df = 43$, $p > .05$). The mean times, expressed in three–second units, were $\bar{X}_1 = 18.30$, $SD = 15.47$, and $\bar{X}_2 = 16.82$, $SD = 15.72$ for Subject factor 1 and Subject factor 2 subjects respectively.

Membership of Subject factor group was found to be independent of the pattern of mean times taken by subjects of varying levels of achievement on Task 10 [Fly/Tree] ($\chi^2 = 1.21$, $df = 2$, $p > .05$). All subjects achieving solution of Task 10 took considerably less time than subjects who discontinued or produced a wrong solution.

No significant differences were found between the Subject factor groups in the proportions of time spent on strategy variables, ST1 (First reading) ($t = 0.07$, $df = 43$), or ST11 (Calculation/Detail) ($t = .66$, $df = 43$), but the mean proportions of time spent using strategy ST9 (Comp./Rel. trials) of $\bar{X}_1 = 21.46\%$, $SD = 16.47$ and $\bar{X}_2 = 29.93\%$, $SD = 18.87$ for Subject factor 1 and Subject factor 2 subjects respectively differed significantly ($t = 2.26$, $df = 43$, $p < .05$).

An interpretation of the latter finding might be that in their work on Task 10 Subject factor 1 subjects tended to either solve, give up, or produce a wrong answer on the basis of their first reading of the stimulus passage, while Subject factor 2 subjects showed some evidence of solution directed activity by externalization of ST9, i.e., considerable attempts to keep track of their own problem solving activity by frequent attempts to relate and review their various attempts and hypotheses and in this way monitor their own progress and save covering the same ground repeatedly.

It must be stressed again that the above presented material resulted from the exploratory rotation of factors, which, on the basis of the relative magnitude of their importance, should have been ignored. The rotations were performed solely in an attempt to search for possible tendencies.

On the basis of the three–mode analysis of the proportion data, three modes representing strategy variables, task types, and individual differences between subjects must each be regarded as unidimensional. This finding is as expected if one remembers that the procedure of analyzing the use made of the here investigated set of problem solving strategies on the basis of subject and task specific proportions resulted in the disregard of between tasks and between subjects differences. This resulted in the loss of the most relevant elements of information in the simultaneous analysis of the relationship between strategies, tasks, and subject variables in the problem solving process.

SUMMARY OF FINDINGS

The findings reported in the present chapter can be summarized as follows:

The *principal components analyses* which were performed separately for each task resulted, on the average, in seven to eight significant factors which met Kaiser's (1963, 1964) criterion of common factors. For most tasks, these factors included complex operations, heuristic and noncognitive factors. In each of the task specific analyses, the factors accounted for approximately 70% of the total variance. On the average, the first principal components in the raw score and in the proportion score analyses accounted for 20% and 13% of the variance respectively.

These findings support the impression gained from the findings reported in Chapter 9, that the overall pattern of strategy use is similar across tasks. It is recognized that the correlation coefficient does not define the values of two variables uniquely, and that the values on two variables could be altered in an infinite number of ways without any resulting change in the correlation between the variables. Any comparability identified between factors on this basis, therefore, refers only to the direction and the degree of the relationship between the factors, and not to specific values obtained for individual strategies. Because of this, a method was designed by which observed similarities between the first principal components of the processes operating during the work on different tasks can be interpreted in relation to the differential importance of specific strategy variables. Definite task groupings suggested themselves on this basis, e.g., groupings according to task difficulty (defined here in terms of the percentage of subjects failing to solve the task), amount of reading required by the stimulus passage, amount of mathematical calculation, etc.

Three similar rotated factors were found to occur with reasonable consistency across the 12 factor analyses. These could be described as a persistent, solution oriented, critical reasoning factor of mainly complex operations; a stimulus passage or directions bound factor basically characterized by heuristic activities; and an emotional, self-involved, defensive testing of idiosyncratic rather than stimulus passage or solution oriented hypotheses factor. The latter factor loads to a considerable degree on noncognitive variables.

The three–mode factor analysis by means of which the interaction of task characteristics and individual differences in influencing the structure of the problem solving process was investigated, resulted in five easily interpretable factors in the strategy mode. Three of these factors (KF1, KF3, and KF5) appeared to parallel the above noted three rotated factors which were identified most frequently in the task specific factor analyses. The additional strategy factors identified in the rotated three-mode factor analysis described the critical analysis of input data (i.e., KF2) and a factor characterized by a process which combined a number of solution directed heuristics with frequent references to the stimulus passage (i.e., KF4).

The four factors identified in the task mode of the three–mode factor analysis were described by creativity tasks, the similarity items, performance tasks, and tasks requiring the actual manipulation of numbers.

Two interpretable subject factors were identified on the basis of the three–mode analysis. It was possible to relate these factors to the operation of the contextual variables of achievement, speed, intelligence, and perseverance.

Rotation of the core matrix (which provides a representation of the structure of the relationship between the factors obtained in the three modes) made it possible to indicate the types of strategies which subjects, described by each of the subject factors, preferred for particular types of tasks. In this manner, the results of the three–mode factor analysis provide a considerably more comprehensive description of the problem solving process than has been available as a result of previous studies, which have tended to focus on only one aspect of the problem solving process at a time.

The results reported in this chapter identified a number of highly consistent structural components of the problem solving process which were replicated across tasks. These, and a number of more task specific factors, were replicated and became more interpretable in the results of a three-mode factor analysis. The latter methodology made it possible to show that subgroups of individuals can be characterized by the particular patterns of strategies they apply in their attempts to solve particular types of tasks.

11

The Utility of the Strategy Variables in the Identification of Individual and Group Differences

Individual differences in all areas of intellectual functioning have traditionally been determined and described in terms of measures based on the outcome of cognitive performance. This chapter reports on a number of investigations which sought to establish the usefulness of structural components of the process of problem solving itself as a means for the identification of individual differences in cognitive functioning.

More specifically, the set of questions addressed was whether preferred problem solving operations and strategies might provide an indication of individual or group differences in competence, speed of problem solving, level of education, and measured intelligence.

The results of analyses performed on data providing the information required to draw conclusions in relation to these questions are presented separately for the four areas mentioned above, and are summarized in the concluding section of this chapter.

DISCRIMINANT ANALYSIS

A series of discriminant analyses were performed on the amounts of use made of the 18 strategy variables by subjects who were grouped in turn according to competence, speed of problem solving, and level of education.

Discriminant analysis is a multivariate technique which may be interpreted "as a special type of factor analysis that extracts orthogonal factors of the measurement battery for the specific task of displaying and capitalizing upon differences between criterion groups" (Cooley &

Lohnes, 1971, p. 243). The analysis creates new variables, called *discriminant functions,* which maximally separate the respective groups of problem solvers. These especially created variables are linear combinations of the original variables, and can thus be represented in general form mathematically by the equation,

$$y = a_1 z_1 + a_2 z_2 + \ldots a_k z_k$$

where the z's are standardized values (z–scores) for k variables which have been chosen to enter into the analysis; in the present study the 18 strategy variables. One usually expects more than one discriminant function since, unless the variation between groups is on a continuum, *one* dimension may not adequately represent all of the information available in the data to separate the groups.

The loadings $a_1, \ldots, a_k$ can be interpreted as showing the relative importance of each variable in the particular discriminant function being examined. The number of variables needed, k, to optimally separate the groups, can usually be reduced to less than the original number of variables. This means that some of the variables will be found to contribute very little to the discriminant functions and can be omitted.

The maximum number of discriminant functions which can be derived in each analysis is restricted, however, to either one less than the number of groups $(g - 1)$, or equal to the number of variables entered into the analysis *(k)*, whichever is less (Cooley & Lohnes, 1971).

In the present study, the discriminant analyses were followed by classification analyses. The purpose of these analyses was to compare the utility of psychological assessment based on variables which are components of the performance process itself with traditional outcome based assessment. The classification analyses performed determined the percentage of subjects which would have gained membership of their groups obtained through traditional criteria solely on the basis of their scores on the discriminating process variables. Again, a separate analysis was performed for each task.

Classification functions are usually different from discriminant functions and are created in such a way as to maximize the probability of correctly classifying the individuals into appropriate groups according to the strategy patterns used in their problem solving.

The results of analyses based on the proportion data, in which for each strategy in turn the frequency scores for each subject and task were expressed as a proportion of each individual subject's total problem solving time for a given task, will be presented first.

The results of the discriminant and classification analyses of the raw data will be reported in less detail. The reason for this is that the proportion data were expected to provide a better basis in the search for possible general mechanisms underlying differences in problem solving behavior than the raw data. While ipsatization of the scores in this manner results in the masking of differential task difficulties and subject abilities, it allows for a comparison of relevant problem solving strategies across tasks and subjects by controlling possible interaction effects of task difficulty and subject ability. The performance of separate discriminant functions on ipsatized scores for each task thus provides multiple replications in this investigation of the discriminatory and predictive power of relevant strategy variables involved in problem solving in a variety of situations.

The results of the discriminant and classification function analyses for the previously mentioned grouping criteria will be presented in the following sequence: (1) competence, (2) speed of problem solving, (3) level of education, and (4) measured intelligence.

THE IDENTIFICATION AND CLASSIFICATION OF INDIVIDUAL DIFFERENCES ON THE BASIS OF THE PROBLEM SOLVING STRATEGIES USED BY SUBJECTS OF VARYING LEVELS OF COMPETENCE

Problem solving competence was, as previously noted, operationally defined in terms of the outcome or achievement of the problem solving activity for each of the 12 tasks, and measured by classifying the results of each subject's performance into one of the following predetermined, all inclusive, and mutually exclusive categories of problem solving competence:

- *competence level (A)—correct or nearly correct* solution,
- *competence level (B)*—the subject *gives up,* i.e., chooses to discontinue the task before a solution is reached, and
- *competence level (C)—wrong solution.*

The scores from each one of the 89 subjects in their attempts to solve 12 tasks were utilized in these analyses. A total of 1068 observations of problem solving competence were thus obtained and classified into the above three levels, as follows:

- 414 cases (39%) of correct or near correct solutions, i.e., group A
- 226 cases (21%) in which the subject abandoned the task before completing it, i.e., group B.
- 428 cases (40%) in which problem solving resulted in a wrong answer, i.e., group C.

TABLE 11.1
Summary of Discriminant and Classification Analyses According to Competence Levels

Task	N Signif. Functions	Eigenvalue	Canonical Correlation	% Trace	Wilks' Lambda	χ^2	df	p	% Correctly Classified
1 [Binet]	2	.93	.69	66.0	.35	83.21	34	.000	74.2
		.48	.57	34.0	.67	31.10	16	.013	
2 [:::]	2	1.08	.72	68.3	.32	89.24	36	.000	74.2
		.50	.58	31.7	.67	31.86	17	.016	
3 [15 × 30]	1	.66	.63	74.0	.49	56.22	36	.017	92.1
4 [Pebbles]	0	(.39	.52	58.7	.57	44.67	36	.152	68.5)
5 [Platform]	2	.72	.65	57.7	.38	75.98	36	.000	76.4
		.53	.59	42.3	.65	33.34	17	.010	
6 [6m→4△]	2	.73	.65	62.4	.40	71.56	36	.000	71.9
		.44	.55	37.6	.69	28.59	17	.038	
7 [9m→1h]	2	.77	.66	58.5	.37	78.81	36	.000	82.0
		.54	.59	41.5	.65	34.12	17	.008	
8 [Poem/St]	0	(.43	.55	78.1	.62	37.14	36	.416	79.8)
9 [Praise/P]	1	.74	.65	64.3	.41	70.40	36	.001	75.3
10 [Fly/Tree]	1	1.01	.71	83.6	.41	69.16	36	.001	78.7
11 [Wood/Alc.]	1	.67	.63	75.1	.49	56.10	34	.010	65.2
12 [8TB/2]	0	(.49	.57	70.9	.56	45.93	36	.124	78.7)

The research question investigated in this part of the study was: Does the pattern of problem solving strategies used distinguish clearly between the three predetermined categories of problem solving competence, i.e., (A) correct or nearly correct solution, (B) gives up, and (C) wrong solution.

Separate discriminant analyses were performed for each of the 12 tasks to:

1. identify which of the 18 strategy variables contributed to the separation of the three problem solving competence levels, and
2. examine the pattern of separation achieved by the discriminant functions; in other words to examine whether successful and unsuccessful solvers and those who decided to abandon the task prematurely, could in fact be separated according to the use they made of the 18 problem solving strategies.

Table 11.1 summarizes the results of the 12 discriminant analyses by showing all statistically significant ($p < .05$) discriminant functions. To indicate the relative importance of each function, eigenvalue, percentage of trace, and canonical correlations between the 18 strategy variables and the variables which define competence level group membership are given. The eigenvalue is a special measure computed in the process of deriving each discriminant function. In each discriminant analysis, the sum of eigenvalues is a measure of the total variance packed in the discriminating variables. The percentage of trace is a single eigenvalue expressed as a percentage of the sum of eigenvalues. Wilks' Lambda and its transformation into χ^2 to express statistical significance, and the percentage of subjects which would have gained membership of their original competence groups solely on the bases of their scores on the discriminating strategy variables, are also included in Table 11.1.

As can be seen in Table 11.1, five of the tasks yielded two significant discriminant functions each, four tasks showed a distinctive pattern of separation between the competence groups resulting from one significant discriminant function each, and three tasks failed to exhibit distinctive patterns of problem solving strategies between the sets of subjects grouped according to competence.

Reference to the last column of Table 11.1 shows that the percentage of cases which were correctly identified as to problem solving competence level ranged from 92% to 65% across the nine tasks which yielded at least one significant discriminant function. The mean percentage of cases correctly classified, i.e., the mean percentage of cases which would have gained membership of their original competence levels solely on the basis of their scores on the discriminating problem solving strategies was

76.67% (SD = 6.98%). Other classification results confirm that distinctive patterns of problem solving strategies characterized the three levels of problem solving competence.

The discriminant function analyses of the following tasks resulted in two significant discriminant functions:

Task 1. [Binet]
Task 2. [⁞ ⁞ ⁞]
Task 5. [Platform]
Task 6. [6m→4Δ]
Task 7. [9m→1h]

Each of the following tasks yielded one significant function:

Task 3. [15 × 30]
Task 9. [Praise/Punishment]
Task 10. [Fly/Tree]
Task 11. [Wood/Alcohol]

Tasks 4 [Pebbles], 8 [Poem/Statue], and 12 (8TB/2) did not produce any significant discriminant functions.

In order to investigate whether all 18 variables were needed for good discrimination, a stepwise discriminant analysis was performed. Only two instances of noncontribution of strategy variables were found across the nine tasks in which significant discriminant functions were obtained. Variable 6 (130: Irrelevant Beh.) did not contribute in the case of Task 1 [Binet] and Variable 5 (120: Ident./Parts) failed to discriminate in Task 11 [Wood/Alcohol].

The structures of the significant first and second discriminant functions are shown in Tables 11.2 and 11.3 respectively. The relative importance of the discriminant functions can be judged from the percentage of available discriminating variance accounted for by the function and from the size of the canonical correlation coefficient computed between the 18 strategy variables and the variables defining group membership. Both these indicators of the potency of the discriminant functions are given in Tables 11.2 and 11.3.

The average percentage of available discriminating variance which was accounted for by the first discriminant function across the nine tasks which yielded significant discriminant functions was 67.77%; the standard deviation among the percentages of discriminating variance accounted for was 8.48%.

The mean canonical correlation across the nine significant first discriminant functions was .64, and the standard deviation was 0.06, which shows a considerable measure of association between the discriminant

TABLE 11.2

Standardized Discriminant Function Coefficients for Significant
First Discriminant Functions for Competence Levels A, B and C

Strategy	Task											
	1[a]	2[a]	3	4[b]	5[a]	6[a]	7[a]	8[b]	9	10	11	12[b]
1	-.93	-.28	-.23	1.17	-.89	-.55	-.44	.14	-.58	-.06	-1.00	-.17
2	-.80	.14	-.26	-.89	.97	-1.02	-.11	-.35	.28	-.04	-.11	.33
3	-.69	-.33	-.31	-.06	-.26	-.54	-.14	.10	-.41	-.07	.09	.16
4	-.37	.12	.07	-.21	-.34	-1.38	-.05	-.07	-.26	-.12	-.30	-.10
5	-.06	-.39	.16	-.33	-.37	-.84	-.03	.13	-.08	.40	.30	.15
6	–	.27	-.19	.20	-.36	-.81	.46	-.62	.23	.00	.01	.15
7	-.96	-.19	.31	-.16	.13	-2.45	-.03	-.40	-.55	.84	.27	.50
8	-1.26	-.10	-.41	.09	.49	-3.19	.52	-.23	.06	.16	.27	-.23
9	-1.39	.06	.14	-.30	-.23	-.27	.19	-.45	-.78	.23	.22	-.03
10	-.44	.47	.03	-.22	-1.65	-1.65	-.81	-.08	-.48	.17	.08	-.11
11	-.90	-.01	.20	.07	-.11	-1.25	.02	-.69	-.44	.59	-.06	-.14
12	.05	.92	.48	-.52	-.20	.15	-.17	.41	-.90	-.34	.45	.21
13	.05	.22	.28	-.18	.42	.47	.11	-.21	-.26	.24	.29	.17
14	.75	-.02	-.44	.00	.60	.69	.30	-.37	-.22	.30	.13	-.10
15	.24	.21	.26	-.21	.00	-.91	.54	-.20	.25	.31	-.06	.47
16	.49	-.36	.83	-.25	.30	-1.32	.16	-.57	-.03	.68	.12	-.39
17	.58	-.12	-.25	-.66	.00	-.72	.11	-.16	-.25	-.16	.11	-.10
18	.57	.67	-.25	-.67	-.22	-.91	.10	.12	-.34	-.19	.27	.56
% available discrim. variance accounted for	66.0	68.3	74.0	58.7	57.7	62.4	58.5	78.1	64.3	83.6	75.1	70.9
Canonical correlation	.69	.72	.63	.52	.65	.65	.66	.55	.65	.71	.63	.57

[a] Two significant discriminant functions.
[b] No significant discriminant functions.

257

TABLE 11.3
Standardized Discriminant Function Coefficients for
Significant Second Discriminant Functions
for Competence Levels A, B and C

Strategy	Content	1	2	5	6	7
1	First read.	-2.44	- .86	-1.28	-.17	.03
2	Reread	-1.29	- .80	-1.09	.06	-.01
3	Chunk/Summ.	-1.41	- .76	- .79	-.20	-.45
4	Ref. Text	- .06	- .35	-1.09	.38	-.26
5	Ident./Parts	- .66	- .02	- .46	.66	-.40
6	Irrelevant	— —	- .83	- .18	-.33	.41
7	Plan/Hyp.	-1.18	- .65	- .40	.47	-.40
8	Trial & Error	- .82	-1.25	.01	.95	-.51
9	Comp./Rel.	-1.84	.07	- .58	-.25	.04
10	Cont. Activity	-2.09	-1.03	- .74	.26	-.53
11	Calc./Detail	-1.34	- .58	.13	.26	-.35
12	Reasoning	-2.09	.08	- .60	.52	-.43
13	Self Reliance	- .42	- .73	- .67	.11	.37
14	Justify	- .78	- .04	- .16	.39	.18
15	Emot.	- .71	- .04	.11	-.10	-.72
16	Judg./Verif.	-1.29	- .89	- .66	.30	-.51
17	Pause	- .50	.01	- .36	.25	-.33
18	Memory	- .49	.85	- .22	.57	.34
% available discrim. variance accounted for		34	31.7	42.3	37.6	41.5
Can. Correlation		.57	.58	.59	.55	.59

functions and the set of strategies which define the group memberships for the three levels of problem solving competence.

The average discriminant scores were found for each of the three problem solving competence levels. These means are given in Table 11.4.

Table 11.4 shows that the first discriminant function produced a large separation between successful and near successful solvers and the other two groups in Tasks 2 [⁞ ⁞], 7 [9m→1h], 9 [Praise/Punishment], 10 [Fly/Tree], 11 [Wood/Alcohol] and 12 [8TB/2].

For Tasks 1 [Binet] and 5 [Platform] the first discriminant functions produce the largest separation between individuals who abandon the task prematurely and the other two groups. In the case of Task 1, the second discriminant function separates the group of subjects who presented wrong solutions from the other two groups, while the second function of Task 5 separates successful solvers from the other two groups.

In the cases of Tasks 3 [15 × 30] and 6 [6m→4Δ], the first discriminant function produced the largest distance between the group presenting wrong solutions and the other two groups.

TABLE 11.4

Average Discriminant Scores (Centroids) for First and Subsequent
Significant Discriminant Functions for Competence

Group Code	Achievement Sample	Task											
		1	2	3	4	5	6	7	8	9	10	11	12
A	Solvers	.73	2.09	-.26	-.86	-.18	1.38	-1.56	.39	-.92	-.76	-1.26	-1.15
		(.64)	(-.44)			(-1.36)	(.39)	(-.31)					
B	Gives up	-2.48	-.39	-.75	.49	1.39	-.82	.71	-.96	1.10	.72	.88	1.12
		(.72)	(.76)			(.24)	(.66)	(-.82)					
C	Nonsolvers	-.03	-.61	2.38	.42	-.61	-.16	.25	-1.10	.63	1.42	.28	-.31
		(-.71)	(-.78)			(.43)	(-.76)	(-.79)					

Note: The values in brackets are the centroids for the significant second discriminant functions.

259

The absolute value of each of the loadings represents the relative contribution of its associated variable to the discriminant function. The sign merely indicates whether the contribution made by the variable is positive or negative.

A high positive loading of a strategy variable on the significant function means that the more use is made of the particular variable, the greater is the discriminating power of the variable. Conversely, a high negative loading on a variable which contributes highly to the discrimination between groups can be interpreted as indicating that the less use is made of such a strategy variable the higher is the variable's contribution to the separation between the three groups.

Strategy variable 1 (Code 111: First reading) showed high negative loadings for Tasks 1, 5, 6, 10, and 12, suggesting that the less time spent on this strategy the stronger was the contribution of this variable to the discrimination between the problem solving competence levels. Other stimulus passage related variables like strategy variables 2 (Code 112: Rereading) and 4 (Codes 114 and 116: References to text) showed high negative loadings on tasks with little text, again suggesting that the discriminatory power of these variables was greater the less attention was paid to the stimulus passage in these tasks. This finding was supported by the finding that subjects in group B, i.e., subjects who abandoned the task before completion tended to spend significantly less time using strategy variable 1 (Code 111: First reading) and other stimulus passage related variables, than did subjects in either of the remaining competence groups. As can be noted in Table 11.4, the first discriminant functions were found to produce the largest separation between group B and the other two groups in all tasks but Task 10. In a considerable number of tasks the second function also tended to isolate this group more than the others.

Although the relevance of strategy variables differed according to the type of task, the variables discriminating most highly between the three competence groups, with some consistency across tasks were: strategy variables 1 (Code 111: First reading) and 7 (Code 211: Plan/Hypothesis). Strategy 7 (Code 211: Plan/Hypothesis) had high negative loadings for Tasks 1, 6, and 9 and loaded positively in the case of Task 10, while strategy variable 8 (Code 211–16: Trial and Error) loaded highly but negatively in the case of Tasks 1 and 6. Strategy 10 (Code 215: Ongoing activity) showed high negative loadings on Tasks 5, 6, and 7.

While for most tasks a small number of strategy variables were found to discriminate highly between the competence groups, work on Tasks 1 [Binet] and 6 [6m→4Δ] resulted in highly discriminatory power of nearly all strategy variables.

Using the same 18 strategy variables as in the discriminant analyses, classification functions were computed for each task separately. In the first instance the responses from all 89 subjects were used in this computation. The same data were then used to identify most probable group membership in accordance with the classification functions. The results are shown in Table 11.5.

According to this table the number of students correctly classified, i.e., the number of students who would be classified into their original competence groups solely on the basis of their scores on the 18 strategy variables investigated here, for Task 1 are shown to be 28 + 6 + 32 = 66, which is 74.2% of the 89 subjects in the study. Of the 36 students who solved or nearly solved Task 1, none resembled the profile of those who gave up before completing the task, but eight resembled the profile of students who did not solve the task.

Further interpreting performance on Task 1, of the ten students who gave up, two performed like those who solved the problem satisfactorily, and the profile of two of the students was similar to that of those who failed to solve the problem. Of the 43 subjects who failed to solve the problem, nine performed like solvers and two resembled the group who gave up, but 32 of 43 subjects who failed to solve this task used a distinctive set of strategies typical of their competence group, their competence level therefore being predicted correctly.

Classifications according to the strategies used for the other 11 tasks can be interpreted from Table 11.5 in the same manner.

The percentage of correct classifications obtained in the above described analyses is high, which indicates that distinctive patterns of strategy use can discriminate between subjects of varying levels of problem solving competence.

Across the 12 tasks the average correct predictions on the basis of the discriminating strategy variables of actual group membership were as follows: actual group A membership, i.e., subjects who solved or nearly solved the task, was on the average predicted correctly for 73.07% of the cases ($SD = 17.56$). Actual membership of group B, i.e., subjects who gave up, was predicted correctly on the average of 57.68% of the time ($SD = 26.55$); and the average correct predictions of group C membership, i.e., wrong answer, was 73.51% ($SD = 13.78$).

The generally lower percentage of correct predictions and the larger standard deviation for group B is not unexpected and can be explained by the fact that a multitude of variables might be responsible for the fact that a subject discontinues the task before completion. The percentages of correct prediction except for Tasks 8 [Poem/Statue] and 10 [Fly/Tree] are, however, considerably higher than would be expected by chance.

TABLE 11.5

Predicted Group Membership for 89 Subjects According to Achievement

Task	Actual group	Predicted Group A N	A %	B N	B %	C N	C %	Total N	Percentage correctly classified
1 [Binet]	A	28	77.8	0	0	8	22.2	36	
	B	2	20.0	6	60.0	2	20.0	10	74.2
	C	9	20.9	2	4.7	32	74.4	43	
2 [::::]	A	12	70.6	4	5.3	1	2.9	17	
	B	2	23.5	31	81.6	5	29.4	38	74.2
	C	1	5.9	10	13.2	23	67.6	34	
3 [15x30]	A	77	97.5	1	1.3	1	1.3	79	
	B	0	0	1	100.0	0	0	1	92.1
	C	5	55.6	0	0	4	44.4	9	
4 [Pebbles]	A	17	56.7	0	0	13	43.4	30	
	B	1	6.7	8	53.3	6	40.0	15	68.5
	C	4	9.1	4	9.1	36	81.8	44	
5 [Platform]	A	9	47.4	1	5.3	9	47.4	19	
	B	1	4.3	19	82.6	3	13.0	23	76.4
	C	2	4.3	5	10.6	40	85.1	47	

(Continued)

TABLE 11.5 *(Continued)*

		n	%	n	%	n	%	n	%
6 [6m→4△]	A	16	72.7	2	9.1	4	18.2	22	71.9
	B	1	3.3	20	66.7	9	30.0	30	
	C	2	5.4	7	18.9	28	75.7	37	
7 [9m→1h]	A	16	80.0	1	5.0	3	15.0	20	82.0
	B	0	0	26	86.7	4	13.3	30	
	C	2	5.1	6	15.4	31	79.5	39	
8 [Poem/St]	A	61	93.8	2	3.1	2	3.1	65	79.8
	B	4	66.7	1	16.7	1	16.7	6	
	C	9	50.0	0	0	9	50.0	18	
9 [Praise/P]	A	34	85.0	1	2.5	5	12.5	40	75.3
	B	4	30.8	6	46.2	3	23.1	13	
	C	6	16.7	3	8.3	27	75.0	36	
10 [Fly/Tree]	A	52	94.5	0	0	3	5.5	55	78.7
	B	5	55.6	1	11.1	3	33.3	9	
	C	7	28.0	1	4.0	17	68.0	25	
11 [Wood/Alc.]	A	11	45.8	2	8.3	11	45.8	24	65.2
	B	0	0	7	35.0	13	65.0	20	
	C	3	6.7	2	4.4	40	88.9	45	
12 [8TB/2]	A	11	55.0	0	0	3	50.0	6	78.7
	B	0	0	12	52.2	11	47.8	23	
	C	2	3.3	3	5.0	55	91.7	60	

When only two of the competence levels are considered at a time, the percentage of cases which can be correctly classified increases, because with only two alternatives instead of three, the chances of misclassification are reduced.

The data obtained from the performances of each possible pair of competence groups were subjected to discriminant analyses. The percentages of correct classifications are given in Table 11.6.

The average percentage of correct classification across the tasks which had yielded significant discriminant functions were 92.5% ($SD = 2.5\%$), 88.6% ($SD = 3.2\%$), and 84.8% ($SD = 5.1\%$) for the comparisons of Groups A and B, B and C, and A and C respectively.

Inspection of Table 11.6 shows that the performance data on nine of the 12 tasks resulted in the significant discrimination between subjects contained in Groups A and C, i.e., solvers and nonsolvers, on the basis of their use of group distinctive problem solving strategies.

Five of the 12 tasks produced significant discriminant functions separating subjects who gave up from those who produced wrong solutions, and seven of the 12 tasks separated Groups A and B, i.e., solvers and those who gave up.

The performance data relating to Tasks 1 [Binet], 2 [: : :], 5 [Platform], 7 [9m→1h], and 9 [Praise/Punishment] yielded significant discriminant functions in all the pairwise comparisons. Inspection of the pattern of loadings on the discriminant functions in these tasks showed this pattern not to be easily summarizable. Different strategy variables appeared to be responsible for the discrimination between the competence levels, but there was some overlap, solution directed activity being more consistently and strongly involved than other strategies. A greater similarity was observed in the pattern of loadings on the discriminant functions obtained for different tasks separating each two competence levels than was found for the same task discriminating between different sets of competence groups.

This observation suggests that distinctive patterns of problem solving strategies can be identified in the performance of individuals of different levels of problem solving competence, and that these patterns show some degree of validity across tasks.

THE IDENTIFICATION AND CLASSIFICATION OF INDIVIDUAL DIFFERENCES IN STRATEGY USE IN RELATION TO SPEED OF PROBLEM SOLVING

Speed of problem solving was measured by counting the number of three-second response units used by each individual for each task. Subjects were then classified as fast or slow depending on whether their solution

TABLE 11.6
Percentage of Correct Classifications for Each Pair
of Competence Groups

Pair of Groups	Task	N	N Correctly Classified	Percent Correct	Average Percentage of Significant Discrims Classifying Correctly
A	1	46	44	95.7**	
	2	55	51	92.7**	
	3	80	79	98.7	
	4	45	39	86.7	
Versus	5	42	39	92.9**	92.5%
	6	52	46	88.5**	(SD = 2.5%)
	7	50	48	96.0**	
B	8	71	67	94.4	
	9	53	48	90.6*	
	10	64	57	89.1	
	11	44	40	90.9*	
	12	29	28	96.6	
B	1	53	49	92.5**	
	2	72	61	84.7*	
	3	10	10	100.0	
	4	59	46	78.0	
Versus	5	70	62	88.6**	88.6%
	6	67	53	79.1	(SD = 3.2%)
	7	69	59	85.5**	
C	8	24	24	100.0	
	9	49	45	91.8**	
	10	34	29	85.3	
	11	65	52	80.0	
	12	83	69	83.1	
A	1	79	63	79.7**	
	2	51	47	92.2**	
	3	88	82	93.2**	
	4	74	56	75.7	
Versus	5	66	56	84.8*	84.8%
	6	59	51	86.4**	(SD = 5.1%)
	7	59	53	89.8*	
C	8	83	70	84.3	
	9	76	63	82.9**	
	10	80	70	87.5**	
	11	69	52	75.4*	
	12	66	61	92.4	

*Discriminant Function significant at p ≤ .05 level.
**Discriminant Function significant at p ≤ .01 level.

time for a given task was equal or below, or above the group's median solution time for that task.

Newell and Simon (1972) have theorized that problem solving behavior is a function of the interaction between an organism, with certain constraints and abilities, and the task environment.

To achieve solution of a problem the individual selects and applies strategies. The outcome of the subject's problem solving efforts is determined, therefore, by the interaction which occurs between the strategy pattern and the essential characteristics of the task, within the boundaries set by the constraints and abilities of the individual and the external environment in which problem solving takes place.

Applying Newell and Simon's theoretical framework, hypotheses concerning a number of factors can be tested. Constraints and abilities might be measured as amount of time taken and result or outcome of problem solving activity (i.e., proficiency or competence to solve), and the task environment is provided by the particular problem. The design of the present study makes an investigation of the task environment possible by the comparison of problem solving patterns across different tasks, and it allows for an assessment of trends in the relationship between subject competence, strategies, and the influence of speed.

As was shown in Chapter 9, Table 9.12, the time taken for work on each problem tends to be related to the number of different strategies used, with more slowly working subjects using a significantly larger number of different strategies than faster working subjects. On the basis of variety of strategy use, however, problem solving competence was found to be independent of speed.

The more time taken for work on the problem, the greater is the opportunity for the application of a greater diversity of strategies. The fact that speed and diversity of strategies used are unrelated to competence suggests that the success or failure of the problem solving activity might be dependent on the appropriateness of the strategies used by the individual.

Discriminant analyses were performed, one for each task.

For each of the 12 tasks only one significant discriminant function was obtained. Table 11.7 provides a summary of the results of the discriminant analyses and their predictive strengths in terms of their eigenvalues and the canonical correlations between the 18 problem solving strategies assessed here, and the group membership variables.

The canonical correlations ranged from 0.84 to 0.61, the mean canonical correlation being 0.74 ($SD = 0.08$). The size of the canonical correlations shows a strong measure of association between the discriminant functions and the set of strategies which define the group membership for fast and slow subjects respectively. The centroids for each group, given in

TABLE 11.7
Summary of Discriminant and Classification Analyses for the Time-on-Task Variable

Task	N. Signif. Functions	Eigenvalue	Canonical Correlation	% Trace	Wilks' Lambda	χ^2	df	p	Centroids Fast	Slow	% Correctly Classified
1 [Binet]	1	1.48	.77	100	.40	72.06	17	.000	1.39	-1.04	93.3
2 [:::]	1	1.00	.71	100	.50	55.03	18	.000	.94	-1.05	86.5
3 [15 x 30]	1	1.78	.80	100	.36	80.85	18	.000	-1.17	1.49	91.0
4 [Pebbles]	1	2.42	.84	100	.29	97.15	18	.000	-1.56	1.52	92.1
5 [Platform]	1	1.91	.81	100	.34	84.36	18	.000	1.41	-1.32	93.3
6 [6m→4△]	1	.76	.66	100	.57	44.46	18	.000	-.87	.85	84.3
7 [9m→1h]	1	.98	.70	100	.51	53.98	18	.000	-1.01	.95	85.4
8 [Poem/St]	1	1.18	.74	100	.46	61.68	18	.000	-1.04	1.11	88.8
9 [Praise/P]	1	.65	.63	100	.61	39.62	18	.002	-.70	.90	83.1
10 [Fly/Tree]	1	1.23	.74	100	.45	63.52	18	.000	-1.16	1.04	87.6
11 [Wood/Alc.]	1	.59	.61	100	.63	36.99	17	.003	-.82	.70	84.3
12 [8TB/2]	1	2.10	.82	100	.32	83.30	18	.000	-1.48	1.38	94.4

TABLE 11.8
Standardized Discriminant Function Coefficients for the Time-On-Task Variable

Strategy	Task 1	2	3	4	5	6	7	8	9	10	11	12
1	1.85	1.08	-1.43	-2.61	.80	-1.27	-1.57	-1.28	-1.58	-.09	-1.82	-1.60
2	.25	-.13	- .11	- .94	-.97	.28	.57	.38	- .22	.38	- .13	.07
3	.67	-.01	- .16	- .74	-.45	.14	- .04	- .07	- .43	-.27	- .72	.01
4	.16	.00	.61	.15	-.24	- .24	- .31	- .78	- .87	.00	- .44	- .38
5	.01	.03	.15	.32	-.21	.61	- .17	- .18	.19	.06	—	- .29
6	—	.04	- .16	- .22	-.22	.23	- .06	.03	- .41	.38	- .20	.04
7	.36	-.22	.21	- .33	-.75	.61	.47	.21	- .90	.62	- .68	.08
8	.27	-.35	.19	.33	-.22	.27	.26	.13	.27	.25	- .52	.08
9	.53	-.19	.32	.49	-.10	.23	.14	- .66	-1.01	.66	-1.12	- .03
10	.63	-.19	.09	.41	-.66	- .03	- .45	.04	- .73	.56	- .43	- .33
11	1.19	.08	- .47	.14	-.34	- .11	- .08	.37	-1.21	.81	- .86	- .13
12	.49	.22	- .20	- .05	-.09	.19	.12	.05	- .65	.00	- .31	- .19
13	.23	-.13	.29	- .38	-.41	- .16	- .02	- .19	- .26	.17	- .43	- .24
14	.27	-.31	.01	.03	.08	- .09	- .28	- .26	- .25	.34	- .73	- .16
15	.48	.29	- .18	.06	.07	- .09	- .17	- .35	- .10	.24	- .40	- .00
16	.07	-.37	.18	- .54	-.43	.00	.29	.07	- .56	.40	.14	- .02
17	-.05	-.35	- .47	- .59	-.13	- .01	- .27	- .54	- .55	-.08	- .13	- .01
18	-.08	-.27	- .08	- .59	.11	.27	.16	- .38	- .21	.55	.16	.16
Canonical correlation	.77	.71	.80	.84	.81	.66	.70	.74	.63	.74	.61	.82

268

Table 11.7, produced a good separation between fast and slow subjects on all tasks.

Judging from the structure coefficients presented in Table 11.8 the functions based on the proportion data separating fast from slow subjects in all 12 tasks appear to load strongly on strategy variable 1 (Code 111: First reading) and two other stimulus passage directed behaviors, variables 2 (Code 112: Rereading) and 4 (Code 114–116: Reference to text/scan/check), as well as on variables 7 (Code 211: Plan/Hypothesis), 9 (Code 214–218: Review former trials), and 11 (Code 219: Calculation/Detail). The contents of these variables provide a logical indication for their relationship to problem solving speed.

Over all tasks strategy variable 1 (Code 111: First reading) shows the highest average correlation with the functions discriminating between subjects working with varying speed; significantly high structure coefficients were obtained in the following tasks:

| | Task | Structure coefficient | Mean percentage of time spent | |
			Fast group	Slow group
1	[Binet]	1.85	26.99	11.77
2	[⋮⋮]	1.08	9.30	2.55
5	[Platform]	0.80	27.93	13.84
3	[15 × 30]	−1.43	43.26	15.25
4	[Pebbles]	−2.61	51.17	29.78
6	[6m→4△]	−1.27	9.74	2.94
7	[9m→1h]	−1.57	15.12	5.16
8	[Poem/St.]	−1.28	23.50	5.54
9	[Praise/Pun.]	−1.58	19.34	5.93
11	[Wood/Alc.]	−1.82	22.93	5.23
12	[8TB/2]	−1.60	18.38	6.18

For Tasks 1, 2, and 5 where the strategy had a high positive loading on the discriminant function, the contribution of the variable to the discrimination between the slow and fast working groups was greater, the more use was made of the variable. For tasks which showed a high negative loading on the variable, the interpretation is that the less use made of the strategy, the higher is the variable's contribution to the discrimination between the fast and slow subjects.

It is of interest to note that for all tasks the mean percentage of time spent on strategy variable 1 was significantly larger for the fast group than for the slow group. This suggests that it may be the fact that sufficient time is spent on the most important or relevant variables that enables subjects to solve problems fast and efficiently. In Chapter 9, it was pointed out that solvers tended to spend significantly less time and apply fewer different strategies than nonsolvers.

In the previous section an attempt was made to explain differences between subjects of varying problem solving competence in relation to speed of problem solving. Speed of problem solving was found to be independent of competence level with respect to the average number of different strategies used. The results of the discriminant function analyses using the criterion of time for grouping, suggest that speed, rather than being a variable which determines the outcome of the problem solving and the strategy pattern used, is itself determined by the relevance of the strategies chosen by subjects. In other words, it is not the time taken or available to solve a problem which determines success, but it is the correct apportioning of time to relevant strategies which determines the speed with which a problem is solved.

It was reported in Chapter 9 that subjects who discontinued problem solving before reaching a solution, i.e., competence level B, spent significantly less time on strategy variable 1 (Code 111: First reading) and other stimulus passage directed activities than either the group of solvers or the group whose problem solving resulted in wrong solutions.

It was acknowledged previously that the strategy variables measured here can not be regarded as representative of single functions, but represent sets of variables or collective variables, of which only some components have been identified. The consistent finding that subjects who subsequently abandoned the task made less use of variable 1, for instance, may not have been due to the fact that these subjects read the stimulus passage faster, but may have resulted rather from the fact that other cognitive activity going on parallel to reading may not have operated in the case of these subjects. It is also possible that these subjects simply did not read the passage carefully enough. Both these problem solving behavior patterns could also be the result of low motivation for the given tasks on the part of the subjects concerned.

The second highest average loading on the discriminant functions was obtained for strategy variable 11 (Code 219: Calculation/Work on detail). The following tasks produced the most sizable structure coefficients:

	Task	Structure coefficient	Mean percentage of time spent	
			Fast group	Slow group
1	[Binet]	1.19	31.85	24.04
10	[Fly/Tree]	0.81	14.65	21.33
3	[15 × 30]	−0.47	40.25	44.11
8	[Poem/Statue]	−0.37	14.63	28.70
9	[Praise/Pun.]	−1.21	15.25	27.71
11	[Wood/Alcohol]	−0.86	8.53	12.50

Strategy variable 2 (Code 112: Rereading of stimulus passage) showed high negative correlations with the time discriminating function for the following tasks:

Task	Structure coefficient	Mean percentage of time spent	
		Fast group	Slow group
4 [Pebbles]	−0.94	8.05	18.69
5 [Platform]	−0.97	19.31	21.58
7 [9m→1h]	−0.57	15.12	5.16

suggesting that the less rereading and checking of the task instructions occurred the more this variable contributed to the discrimination between fast and slow subjects. In other words time spent reading and rereading the above problems was spent at the cost of solving the tasks reasonably quickly. A number of slow subjects used their time reading and rereading these tasks, instead of attempting to work towards solutions.

High negative loadings of variables 3 (Code 113–117: Chunk and summarize stimulus passage information) and 4 (Code 114–116: Reference to text/scan/check) for Tasks 4 [Pebbles], 5 [Platform], 9 [Praise/ Punishment], and 11 [Wood/Alcohol]; and for Tasks 8 [Poem/Statue], 9 [Praise/Punishment], and 11 [Wood/Alcohol] respectively, further support the suggestion that slow subjects failed to spend their time on using relevant solution oriented heuristics, and instead concentrated on details of the stimulus passage itself.

The searching for and specifying of hypotheses, Variable 7 (Code 211: Plan/Hypothesis) contributed significantly to the discrimination between fast and slow subjects for the following tasks:

Task	Structure coefficient	Mean percentage of time spent	
		Fast group	Slow group
1 [Binet]	0.36	8.00	14.12
6 [6m→4Δ]	0.61	14.45	20.69
10 [Fly/Tree]	0.62	3.41	12.29
4 [Pebbles]	−0.33	9.13	13.56
5 [Platform]	−0.75	9.24	14.05
7 [9m→1h]	−0.47	17.37	18.29
9 [Praise/Pun.]	−0.90	11.66	10.32
11 [Wood/Alcohol]	−0.68	8.53	12.50

Tasks which produced high negative structure coefficients on the discriminant function appear to be those which were more likely to have been perceived by subjects as puzzles or trick problems and may thus have elicited less deductive reasoning, and more, for instance, trial and error or stimulus directed activity, than the tasks with high positive structure coefficients.

Strategy variable 9 (Code 214 + 218: Compare and relate parts; review former trials and hypotheses) contributed significantly to the discrimination between fast and slow solvers, and produced high loadings for the similarities items, and Tasks 1 [Binet] and 4 [Pebbles]. Relevance of this variable can be logically justified in the similarities tasks, which require the subject to perceive the common elements of the terms he is asked to compare (Matarazzo, 1972). The stimulus passages of Tasks 1 and 4 provide a considerable amount of information and sequentially important directions. Again strategy variable 9 appears to provide a relevant tool.

It is of interest to note opposite signs for the sizable loadings of this variable for Tasks 1 [Binet], 3 [15 × 30], 4 [Pebbles], and 10 [Fly/Tree] as against the other similarities items: Tasks 8 [Poem/Statue], 9 [Praise/Punishment], and 12 [Wood/Alcohol]. This, in relation to the discrimination between fast and slow subjects, might suggest that time spent comparing and relating "concrete" features of concepts of the latter group type operates in a different way than it might in the case of mathematical and other abstract concepts.

On the basis of the same 18 strategy variables as used in the discriminant analyses, classification functions were computed for each task separately for fast and slow subjects. The results of the classification analyses are presented in Table 11.9. The percentages show the proportion of members of the fast and slow groups which would have gained membership of these groups solely on the basis of their use made of the 18 strategy variables investigated here.

The mean percentage of correct classifications of the subjects across all 12 tasks was 88.68% ($SD = 4.03\%$). Membership of the fast group was on the average predicted correctly 83.21% of the time ($SD = 6.81\%$), while the mean percentage of correctly classified cases for the slow group was 93.86% ($SD = 4.71\%$). The proportions of correct classifications obtained here are rather high, which suggests that distinctive patterns of strategy use can discriminate between subjects working at different speeds. It is necessary to keep in mind, however, that the chances of misclassification are considerably lessened in the case of only two categories for classification. The relatively higher percentages of correct classifications on the basis of speed can therefore not be directly compared with the classifications according to educational level and competence.

The results of the discriminant function and classification analyses of the raw data were similar, though not identical, to those based on the proportion of total problem solving time data. As in the case of the proportion data the raw data yielded one significant discriminant function for each task. The separation of the group centroids and their locations were similar indeed to those obtained from the analyses of the proportion data. The average percentage of correctly classified cases across all tasks on the basis of the raw scores on the 18 strategies was 93.73% ($SD = 3.07\%$), which is even higher than the percentage of correctly classified cases in the analyses of the proportion data.

TABLE 11.9
Predicted Group Membership for Subjects Classified
According to Speed of Work

| Task | Actual group | Predicted Group | | | | Total |
| | | Fast | | Slow | | Percent correctly classified |
		N	%	N	%	N	
1 [Binet]	Fast	35	92.1	3	7.9	38	93.3
	Slow	3	5.9	48	94.1	51	
2 [⠿]	Fast	38	80.9	9	19.1	47	86.5
	Slow	3	7.1	39	92.9	42	
3 [15×30]	Fast	48	96.0	2	4.0	50	91.0
	Slow	6	15.4	33	84.6	39	
4 [Pebbles]	Fast	37	84.1	7	15.9	44	92.1
	Slow	0	0	45	100.0	45	
5 [Platform]	Fast	38	88.4	5	11.6	43	93.3
	Slow	1	2.2	45	97.8	46	
6 [6m→4△]	Fast	33	75.0	11	25.0	44	84.3
	Slow	3	6.7	42	93.3	45	
7 [9m→1h]	Fast	34	79.1	9	20.9	43	85.4
	Slow	4	8.7	42	91.3	46	
8 [Poem/St]	Fast	37	80.4	9	19.6	46	88.8
	Slow	1	2.3	42	97.7	43	
9 [Praise/P]	Fast	40	80.0	10	20.0	50	83.1
	Slow	5	12.8	34	87.2	39	
10 [Fly/Tree]	Fast	34	81.0	8	19.0	42	87.6
	Slow	3	6.4	44	93.6	47	
11 [Wood/Alc.]	Fast	30	73.2	11	26.8	41	84.3
	Slow	3	6.3	45	93.8	48	
12 [8TB/2]	Fast	38	88.4	5	11.6	43	94.4
	Slow	0	0	46	100.0	46	

The patterns of loadings on the discriminant functions was also similar for proportion and raw data, with one major difference. The rank order of the strategy variables, on the basis of the size of the structure coefficients differs slightly. Variable 1 (Code 111: First reading) which produced the highest average structure coefficient across tasks in the proportion data did not load significantly on the discriminant functions in the raw data analyses. The actual time taken for the first reading of the passage can be expected to be determined to a considerable extent by stimulus passage length and difficulty rather than by subject or strategy characteristics. This would result in a levelling of differences between groups. In analyses of proportion data, however, individual differences in the use of this variable become apparent. The relationship between variables is more readily revealed here than in the raw data analyses which permit the masking of variable relationships by task and subject characteristics.

In the findings on the basis of the raw scores strategy variable 11 (Code 219: Calculation/Detail) becomes the most highly loading variable. This seems logical, as the speed with which calculations and similar work on detail are performed can be expected to make a more significant contribution to the discrimination between fast and slow problem solvers than the first reading of the passage.

THE IDENTIFICATION AND CLASSIFICATION OF INDIVIDUAL DIFFERENCES ON THE BASIS OF THE PROBLEM SOLVING STRATEGIES USED BY SUBJECTS OF VARYING LEVELS OF EDUCATION

The population of subjects who took part in the present study consisted of four separate a priori groups, first year university students majoring in psychology, second year teachers college students, Year 11 high school students, and Year 12 high school students.

Discriminant analyses were used to determine whether the problem solving strategy patterns of these groups represent different locations on a single continuum, or whether the performances of the different groups would suggest several distinct types of problem solving behavior. The problem under investigation was whether these groups could be distinguished from one another on the basis of distinctive patterns of strategy use in their problem solving. More specifically, it was hypothesized that, if the patterns of problem solving behaviors of the different groups could be considered to be on one continuum, discriminant analysis would yield only one significant function. Alternately, if the problem solving strategies investigated here did not discriminate between the a priori groups no significant discriminant function would be obtained. If more than one distinctive pattern of strategies used could be identified more than one significant discriminant function would be obtained.

The research questions to be answered were:

a. can discriminant analysis clearly distinguish between the problem solving behaviors of the four a priori groups;
b. can the pattern of separation of the four groups be interpreted on the basis of the discriminant functions; and
c. which of the 18 strategy variables examined in the present study contributed to separating the four groups.

As in the two previously reported sets of discriminant analyses, the problem solving behaviors of the total of 89 students belonging to four a priori groups was investigated in terms of the use the students made of the selected 18 strategy variables. The problem solving behavior of any one student could thus be represented as a profile of strategies used, which one might imagine as a point in an 18-dimensional space. Each axis of this space would consist of one of the strategy variables. The variables are orthogonal to one another.

If the a priori groups provide a meaningful separation of subjects in terms of the problem solving strategies investigated here, one would expect the subjects not to be scattered randomly over the 18-dimensional space, but to be located at different points of the multivariate space. "To the extent that individuals in each group are tightly clustered in a particular region of the k-space, and to the extent that there is little overlap between the regions occupied by different groups, discriminatory analysis can provide useful information" (Nunnally, 1978, p. 454).

Table 11.10 summarizes the results of the discriminant analyses of the proportion data by reporting the statistically significant functions for each of the 12 tasks in the same way as the results of the competence and time discriminant analyses were reported. The results of the classification analyses, i.e., the percentages of cases of the a priori groups which would have gained membership of their original groups on the basis of their loadings on the discriminatory strategy variables, are given in the last column of Table 11.10.

As can be seen from the table, for eight of the tasks one significant discriminant function was obtained. This function accounted on the average for 61.79% ($SD = 10.93\%$) of the total sums of variances packed in the discriminating variables.

Three tasks, Task 5 [Platform], Task 6 [6m→4Δ], and Task 9 [Praise/ Punishment] yielded two significant discriminant functions each. On the

TABLE 11.10

Summary of Discriminant and Classification Analyses for the A Priori Groups

Task	N Signif. Functions	Eigenvalue	Canonical Correlation	% Trace	Wilks' Lambda	χ^2	df	p	% Correctly Classified
1 [Binet]	1	1.02	.71	60.1	.28	100.54	51	.000	71.9
2 [::::]	1	1.27	.75	67.3	.26	106.07	54	.000	67.4
3 [15 x 30]	1	1.58	.78	73.6	.24	112.19	54	.000	67.4
4 [Pebbles]	1	.77	.66	62.2	.37	76.73	54	.023	62.9
5 [Platform]	2	1.19	.74	56.7	.22	118.95	54	.000	66.3
		.54	.59	26.0	.48	57.97	34	.006	
6 [6m→4△]	2	2.34	.84	73.7	.15	147.08	54	.000	75.3
		.59	.61	18.6	.51	53.08	34	.020	
7 [9m→1h]	0	.57	.60	55.4	.42	67.35	54	.105	58.4
8 [Poem/St]	1	.59	.61	45.0	.34	83.43	54	.006	66.3
9 [Praise/P]	2	1.03	.71	51.1	.23	116.27	54	.000	69.7
		.71	.64	35.0	.46	60.97	34	.003	
10 [Fly/Tree]	1	.81	.67	63.6	.37	78.08	54	.018	62.9
11 [Wood/Alc.]	1	.62	.62	47.5	.35	82.79	51	.003	61.8
		.48	.57	36.8	.56	45.14	32	.062	
12 [8TB/2]	1	2.25	.83	75.0	.17	137.10	54	.000	68.5

average these functions accounted for 87.03% (SD = 4.87%) of the total variances. The discriminant analysis performed on the data for Task 7 [9m→1h] did not produce any significant discriminant function.

In these analyses all the responses of all 89 subjects were used in deriving both the discriminant functions and the classification functions.

The structures of the first and the significant second discriminant functions obtained for each task are shown in Table 11.11.

Judging from the structure coefficients, the nature of the strategy variables and the tasks in the three cases in which two significant discriminant functions were obtained, these functions appear to be measuring

1. uncritical, somewhat emotional stimulus passage directed global approach. Attention to irrelevant aspects of the task.
2. critical, analytic approach with much consideration of detail, reasoning, checking, verifying, and justifying moves.

In the cases in which only one significant discriminant function was obtained the structure of this function appeared to vary according to the type of task. The most frequently occurring discriminating strategy variables were strategy variables 7 (Code 211: Plan/Hypothesis) and 12 (Code 220: Reasoning), followed by strategy variable 1 (Code 111: First reading). These discriminant functions are therefore similar to both the above described types of functions, and could be regarded as a combination of both.

The locations of the group centroids on the significant functions also help to describe the nature of the group differences. A centroid is an average discriminant score, that is, the point which represents the average profile of a group. It is "the point about which the points for individuals in a group balance in all directions" (Nunnally, 1978, p. 454). If groups are well discriminated by an analysis, the centroids are reasonably far apart, and the members of each group are found to hover around their appropriate centroid. The centroids are given in Table 11.12.

In the present study most tasks show the first discriminant function to produce a reasonably large separation between the Year 12 students and the other three groups.

The significant second discriminant functions tended to either separate all four groups from one another or separate tertiary students from high school students.

An exception occurred in Task 9 [Praise/Punishment], where the first discriminant function separated Year 11 students from the other three groups. A reason for this difference in the pattern of separation between groups may lie in the fact that this youngest and least mature group of students may have a greater ego-involvement in these concepts, and

TABLE 11.11
Standardized Discriminant Function Coefficients for First and Significant
Second Discriminant Functions for the A Priori Groups

Strategy	1st Discrim. Function Task												2nd Discrim. Function Task		
	1	2	3	4	5[b]	6[b]	7[a]	8	9[b]	10	11	12	5[b]	6[b]	10[b]
1	-1.35	.13	-1.21	-1.53	.91	.94	-.15	-.27	.44	.11	-.09	-.32	2.35	-.33	.26
2	-.78	.32	-.12	-1.53	2.24	.56	-1.28	.07	.28	-.16	-.04	.43	3.48	.35	-.02
3	-.90	.22	-.39	.65	.94	.53	-.46	-.36	-.13	.28	-.28	.04	1.65	-.20	-.54
4	-.48	-.07	-.20	.12	.60	1.13	-.38	.16	.78	-.15	-.05	.54	1.50	.91	-.39
5	.04	-.22	-1.08	.54	.78	.10	-.32	.10	.30	.34	—	-.45	1.03	.72	-.17
6	—	.29	.22	.42	.56	.70	-.42	.34	.61	-.33	.00	-.11	.92	.58	.10
7	-.74	.87	.63	.46	1.21	1.68	-.80	-1.07	.00	.89	.90	.61	1.72	.61	.15
8	-1.11	.63	.08	-.07	.27	1.79	-.85	-.35	-.18	.24	-.27	-.44	.74	1.13	.38
9	-1.48	-.18	-.01	.25	-.06	.40	-.27	-.14	.64	-.02	.18	.15	.62	.23	.30
10	-.68	.90	-.22	.63	1.55	1.65	-.72	.29	.47	-.07	.16	.75	2.32	.93	.61
11	-1.42	-.19	-.77	-.01	-.38	-.44	-.07	-.34	1.39	-.06	-.06	-.51	.19	.48	.26
12	-1.06	.02	1.04	-1.02	-.34	-.20	-.49	.35	.23	.11	.54	-.38	.50	-.02	.11
13	-.65	.59	-.39	.22	.75	.48	-.26	.23	.07	-.08	.05	.49	.87	-.15	.34
14	-.24	.27	-.35	.17	.68	.57	-.18	.18	-.15	.52	.12	.31	.91	-.17	.01
15	-.36	.58	-.07	.18	.67	.75	-.32	.44	.26	-.09	-.22	-.07	.49	.29	.07
16	-.11	.43	-.34	-.09	.22	.75	-.38	-.17	.81	-.22	-.36	.49	.49	-.06	.01
17	-.80	-.73	-.21	-.24	-.58	-1.78	-.86	-.10	.20	-.44	-.23	-.03	.65	-.07	-.42
18	-.17	.29	-.24	.75	.59	.70	-.04	.16	-.18	-.12	.17	-.02	.83	.14	-.15
% avail. discrim. variance accounted for	60.1	67.3	73.6	62.2	56.7	73.7	55.4	45.0	51.1	63.6	47.5	75.0	26.0	18.6	35.0
Canonical Correlation	.71	.75	.78	.66	.74	.84	.60	.61	.71	.67	.62	.83	.59	.61	.64

[a] Discrim. Function not significant at .05 level.
[b] First and second Discrim. Functions significant.

TABLE 11.12
Average Discriminant Scores (Centroids) for First and Subsequent
Significant Discriminant Functions for the A Priori Groups

Code	Sample							Task						
		1	2	3	4	5	6	7a	8	9	10	11	12
100	University	.91	.93	-.68	.16	-.64 (-1.13)	.32 (-.94)	.95	.15	-.63 (.99)	.61	.96	.87
200	Teachers' College	.68	.76	-.70	.95	.95 (-.14)	.61 (-.54)	.17	.26	-.35 (.46)	1.09	.62	1.09
500	Year 11	-.09	-.01	-.42	.15	.79 (.46)	1.00 (.87)	-.11	.53	1.30 (-.27)	-1.08	-.62	.26
600	Year 12	-1.92	-2.20	2.61	-1.70	-1.84 (.83)	-3.14 (.28)	-1.32	-1.57	-1.22 (-1.42)	-.10	-.88	-3.05

[a]Discriminant Function not significant at $p \leqslant .05$ level.
Note: The values in brackets are the centroids of the significant second discriminant functions.

TABLE 11.13
Predicted Group Memberships for 89 Subjects of the A Priori Groups

Task	Actual group		Predicted Group								Total	
			100		200		500		600			
			N	%	N	%	N	%	N	%	N	%
1	Uni.	100	15	68.2	3	13.6	4	18.2	0	0	22	71.9
	TC	200	3	15.0	14	70.0	3	15.0	0	0	20	
	Yr 11	500	3	9.7	3	9.7	24	77.4	1	3.2	31	
	Yr 12	600	0	0	2	12.5	3	18.8	11	68.8	16	
2		100	16	72.7	2	9.1	3	13.6	1	4.5	22	67.4
		200	3	15.0	12	60.0	5	25.0	0	0	20	
		500	3	9.7	6	19.4	22	71.0	0	0	31	
		600	0	0	0	0	6	37.5	10	62.5	16	
3		100	12	54.5	5	22.7	5	22.7	0	0	22	67.4
		200	6	30.0	13	65.0	1	5.0	0	0	20	
		500	4	12.9	3	9.7	24	77.4	0	0	31	
		600	1	6.3	2	12.5	2	12.5	11	68.8	16	
4		100	10	45.0	4	18.2	7	31.8	1	4.5	22	62.9
		200	4	20.0	12	60.0	3	15.0	1	5.0	20	
		500	3	9.7	3	9.7	24	77.4	1	3.2	31	
		600	2	12.5	0	0	4	25.0	10	62.5	16	

(Continued)

TABLE 11.13 (Continued)

5	100	15	68.2	2	9.1	3	13.6	2	9.1	22	66.3
	200	1	5.0	13	65.0	5	25.0	1	5.0	20	
	500	6	19.4	4	12.9	21	67.7	0	0	31	
	600	2	12.5	2	12.5	2	12.5	10	62.5	16	
6	100	16	72.7	2	9.1	4	18.2	0	0	22	75.3
	200	3	15.0	13	65.0	4	20.0	0	0	20	
	500	4	12.9	3	9.7	24	77.4	0	0	31	
	600	1	6.3	1	6.3	0	0	14	87.5	16	
7	100	12	54.5	3	13.6	6	27.3	1	4.5	22	58.4
	200	2	10.0	11	55.0	7	35.0	0	0	20	
	500	4	12.9	5	16.1	19	61.3	3	9.7	31	
	600	0	0	2	12.5	4	25.0	10	62.5	16	
8	100	14	63.6	2	9.1	4	18.2	2	9.1	22	66.3
	200	4	20.0	11	55.0	2	10.0	3	15.0	20	
	500	3	9.7	4	12.9	23	74.2	1	3.2	31	
	600	2	12.5	0	0	3	18.8	11	68.8	16	
9	100	12	54.5	5	22.7	3	13.6	2	9.1	22	69.7
	200	2	10.0	14	70.0	3	15.0	1	5.0	20	
	500	0	0	4	12.9	26	83.9	1	3.2	31	
	600	1	6.3	4	25.0	1	6.3	10	62.5	16	

(Continued)

281

TABLE 11.13 *(Continued)*
Predicted Group Memberships for 89 Subjects of the A Priori Groups

Task	Actual group	Predicted Group								Total	
		100		200		500		600			
		N	%	N	%	N	%	N	%	N	%
10	100	10	45.5	3	13.6	8	36.4	1	4.5	22	62.9
	200	4	20.0	13	65.0	2	10.0	1	5.0	20	
	500	1	3.2	1	3.2	26	83.9	3	9.7	31	
	600	3	18.8	1	6.3	5	31.3	7	43.8	16	
11	100	11	50.0	3	13.6	7	31.8	1	4.5	22	61.8
	200	3	15.0	11	55.0	5	25.0	1	5.0	20	
	500	1	3.2	2	6.5	27	81.1	1	3.2	31	
	600	0	0	3	18.8	7	43.8	6	37.5	16	
12	100	14	63.6	4	18.2	4	18.2	0	0	22	68.5
	200	6	30.0	12	60.0	2	10.0	0	0	20	
	500	9	29.0	0	0	22	71.0	0	0	31	
	600	0	0	1	6.3	2	12.5	13	81.3	16	

282

hence be more strongly influenced by personal attitude to and reasonably recent experience of praise and punishment, than the other groups. Inspection of the mean percentages provided some support for this type of reasoning. These showed that the Year 11 students tended to produce vastly fewer hypotheses in their work on this task than the other groups. Year 11 students showed greater emotional involvement and criticism of this task, and tended to talk about the concepts of praise and punishment as separate entities rather than attempting to find an answer to the problem "In what way are praise and punishment alike?"

Using the same 18 strategy variables as in the discriminant analysis, classification functions were computed for each task separately to identify the most probable group membership for each subject on the basis of the discriminating strategy variables. The results are shown in Table 11.13.

According to this table, the number of students correctly classified, i.e., the number of students who would be classified into their original a priori groups solely on the basis of their scores on the 18 strategy variables investigated here, for Task 1 are shown to be $15 + 14 + 24 + 11 = 64$, which is 71.9% of the 89 subjects in the study. Of the 22 University students, three were misclassified as belonging to the Teachers College group, four resembled the profile for the Year 11 students, and none resembled the Year 12 students.

Still interpreting performance on Task 1, of the 20 Teachers College students, three performed more like the University students and three more like the Year 11 students. Again there was no similarity with the performance pattern observed among the Year 12 group.

In the Year 11 group, three cases each were misclassified as University and Teachers' College students, and one case resembled the Year 12 students. The Year 12 group contained five cases which did not resemble the rest of the group. Three of these students resembled the Year 11 group and the pattern of strategy use of two students resembled that of the Teachers' College group.

The classification according to strategies used for the other 11 tasks can be interpreted from Table 11.14 in the same manner.

Across all the 12 tasks, an average of 66.54% of cases were classified correctly ($SD = 4.46\%$). For each a priori group the average percentages correctly classified across tasks were as follows:

University students	59.87%	($SD = 9.90\%$)
Teachers' College students	62.73%	($SD = 4.94\%$)
Year 11 students	76.58%	($SD = 5.02\%$)
Year 12 students	64.23%	($SD = 13.62\%$)

Task 7 was excluded in the above calculations because the analysis of performance data on this task had not resulted in a significant discriminant function.

TABLE 11.14
Percentage of Correct Classifications For Each Pair of
A Priori Groups

Pair of Groups	N	Task	Percent Correct	Average Percentage of Significant Discrims Classifying Correctly
University		1	81.0	
		2	95.2*	
		3	69.0	
		4	76.2	
	42	5	90.5*	93.63%
Versus		6	95.2*	(SD = 2.71)
		7	81.0	
		8	83.3	
		9	78.6	
Teachers'		10	78.6	
College		11	83.3	
		12	71.4	
University		1	77.4*	
		2	83.0*	
		3	77.4	
		4	79.2	
	53	5	84.9*	84.88%
Versus		6	84.9*	(SD = 4.57)
		7	73.6	
		8	81.1	
		9	88.7*	
		10	83.0	
Year 11		11	90.4*	
		12	81.1	
University		1	97.4*	
		2	94.7*	
		3	89.5*	
		4	86.8	
	38	5	86.8	92.97%
Versus		6	92.1*	(SD = 2.95)
		7	92.1*	
		8	89.5*	
		9	92.1*	
		10	84.2	
Year 12		11	91.9*	
		12	97.4*	

(Continued)

TABLE 11.14 *(Continued)*

Pair of Groups	N	Task	Percent Correct	Average Percentage of Significant Discrims Classifying Correctly
Teachers' College		1	86.3*	
		2	80.4*	
		3	82.4	
		4	82.4	
	51	5	82.4	88.30%
Versus		6	82.4	(SD = 4.48)
		7	76.5	
		8	86.3	
		9	92.2*	
		10	92.2*	
Year 11		11	88.5*	
		12	90.2*	
Year 11		1	91.5	
		2	89.4*	
		3	93.6*	
		4	91.5*	
	47	5	93.6*	90.0%
		6	99.9*	(SD = 5.90)
Versus		7	80.9*	
		8	87.2*	
		9	89.4*	
		10	83.0	
Year 12		11	80.9*	
		12	93.6*	
Teachers' College		1	97.2*	
		2	94.4*	
		3	94.4*	
		4	91.7*	
	36	5	91.7*	94.83%
		6	97.2*	(SD = 2.48)
Versus		7	91.7	
		8	86.1	
		9	91.7	
		10	88.9	
Year 12		11	81.1	
		12	97.2*	

*Discriminant Function significant ($p \leqslant .05$).

The results of comparisons of all possible pairs of a priori groups by performing discriminant and classification analyses for two groups at a time are presented in Table 11.14. The average percentages of correct classifications across tasks which yielded significant discriminant functions are presented in the last column of Table 11.14.

These percentages are very high because the chances of misclassification are considerably reduced when only two instead of four groups are compared at a time.

Inspection of Table 11.14 shows that only three tasks discriminated between university and Teachers College students, while the other groups were found to be separated by significant discriminant functions on a larger proportion of the tasks.

Tasks 2 and 6 were found to produce significant discrimination in all but two of the comparisons listed in Table 11.14. Inspection of the pattern of loadings on the significant discriminant function in relation to these tasks for each of the pairwise a priori group comparisons showed for both tasks a very similar structure of the discriminant functions separating the Teachers College students from both the high school groups and the separation of the two high school groups. The discriminant functions separating the University students from any of the other three groups, though equally significant, showed different structures from each other and from the above described patterns. Members of the University group may have been more likely to use more efficient, i.e., task relevant, problem solving strategies than members of the other groups.

The most noteworthy finding of this section, however, is that educational level, which, as shown in Chapter 9, failed to be a significant variable in relation to measures of the outcome of problem solving performance, is reflected in differences between the profiles of components of the process of the performance itself which are typical for groups at different levels of education. These results are discussed further later in this chapter and in Chapter 13.

THE IDENTIFICATION AND CLASSIFICATION OF INDIVIDUAL DIFFERENCES IN STRATEGY USE IN RELATION TO MEASURED INTELLIGENCE

An estimate of measured intelligence was obtained from performance on the WAIS Block Design Test (Wechsler, 1955). For the purposes of the present analysis, subjects whose BD scaled score was higher than the median score, calculated for the total group, were regarded as the "high" intelligence group, while subjects whose BD scaled score equalled or was lower than the median score for the total group were regarded as the "low" intelligence group. The high and low groups consisted of 39 and 50 subjects respectively.

Table 11.15 shows the results of the discriminant functions performed. Only two tasks, Task 5 [Platform] and Task 6 [6m→4Δ] yielded a significant discriminant function.

In view of the discussion presented in previous chapters this finding is not surprising. The results presented in Chapter 9 suggest a tendency for measured intelligence to influence the problem solving process in more difficult tasks only.

The fact that the discriminant analyses were performed on two rather coarse and arbitrarily derived levels of the variable of intelligence may have prevented the observation of phenomena of the type suggested on the basis of the overall analysis of variance reported in Chapter 9, where subjects of five intelligence levels were compared, and where a tendency was observed for subjects operating at the average level of intelligence to be less different from one another, when compared in relation to a number of contextual variables, than subjects at higher or lower levels of measured intelligence.

In addition to this, and as was noted earlier, the use of the Block Design test to provide an estimate of measured intelligence, although justifiable on the basis of the test's consistently high correlation with more comprehensive IQ measures (Matarazzo, 1972), provided a rather superficial assessment of measured intelligence. The latter variable was therefore regarded basically as a categorical variable.

SUMMARY OF FINDINGS

In this chapter, it was shown that differences between individuals and between groups in problem solving competence, speed of performance, educational attainment, and IQ category—which are usually measured by means of scores resulting from performance—are reflected in characteristics of the problem solving process itself, i.e., in the actual behaviors of subjects during their work on the task.

In fact, it was shown that an index of process similarity or dissimilarity (where process similarity is understood as the similarity of the profiles of process components, i.e., the problem solving behaviors and strategies constituting the process) may well constitute a superior, and is certainly a more sensitive, means of assessment of intellectual functioning than traditional outcome measures. For example, the levels of educational attainment of subjects in the present study did not evolve as a significant variable in the analysis of global scores of performance outcomes. In analyses based on process variables making up the performance itself, all

TABLE 11.15

Results of the Discriminant Function Analyses for High and Low Block Design Score Groups

Task	N Signif. Functions	Eigenvalue	Canonical Correlation	% Trace	Wilks' Lambda	χ^2	df	p	% Correctly Classified
1 [Binet]	0	.25	.45	100	.80	17.79	17	.40 NS	69.7
2 [⋮⋮]	0	.28	.46	100	.78	19.24	18	.38 NS	69.7
3 [15 × 30]	0	.29	.47	100	.77	20.14	18	.33 NS	67.4
4 [Pebbles]	0	.31	.49	100	.76	21.48	18	.26 NS	74.2
5 [Platform]	1	.75	.66	100	.57	44.28	18	.001	80.9
6 [6m→4△]	1	.63	.62	100	.61	38.52	18	.003	80.9
7 [9m→1h]	0	.36	.51	100	.74	24.06	18	.15 NS	74.2
8 [Poem/St]	0	.35	.51	100	.74	23.58	18	.17 NS	75.3
9 [Praise/P]	0	.26	.45	100	.80	18.06	18	.45 NS	66.3
10 [Fly/Tree]	0	.42	.54	100	.71	27.45	18	.07 NS	70.8
11 [Wood/Alc.]	0	.24	.44	100	.80	17.40	17	.43 NS	68.5
12 [8TB/2]	0	.28	.46	100	.78	19.20	18	.38 NS	70.8

four levels of educational attainment could be distinguished from one another.

The first significant discriminant function tended to show the average profile of the problem solving strategies applied by Year 12, i.e., final year high school students, to differ most from the profiles of the other three groups. An explanation of this finding might be provided by the fact that Year 12 students in Australia are preparing for a highly competitive public examination in each subject area. Entrance to tertiary studies and the opportunities for employment in certain branches of public life are contingent on the scores obtained in these examinations. The problem solving protocols from the Year 12 students were obtained approximately three months before the above described examination. It is possible that these students were responding to cognitive tasks in a different, perhaps more proficient, manner than they might have at another stage in their lives.

The significant second discriminant functions separated all four groups from one another, with a tendency to separate university students from the other groups. This finding is not unexpected, as university students are initially selected and continue their studies on the basis of their intellectual performance. The problem solving strategies used by them in tasks of the type investigated in the present study may well have been different from those which were found to be typical for subjects in the other groups.

In the investigation of the problem solving processes of various achievement groups, a rather complex but interpretable pattern evolved. In the case of easier tasks, one significant discriminant function was obtained. This finding, which was replicated in four tasks, means that differences and resemblances in the problem solving processes of solvers, nonsolvers, and those who gave up might be based on a single index of process similarity. The content of the particular discriminating dimension that was identified in relation to the easier tasks might be described as consisting of critical reasoning behaviors based on the stimulus passage, in other words, the choice of task appropriate problem solving behaviors.

In the more difficult tasks, two significant discriminant functions were obtained. This finding held for both verbal and performance tasks. The first discriminant functions consistently loaded most strongly on solution directed heuristics, in particular on lengthy trial and error activity. The second discriminant functions consisted of stimulus passage related heuristics, and tended to include relatively substantial loadings of judgment and verification behaviors.

Structurally, these second significant discriminant functions identified in more difficult tasks were similar to the single significant discriminant functions found in easier tasks. More detailed interpretation in the case of the more difficult tasks appeared to be somewhat limited. Inspection of the centroids (cf. Table 11.4) would suggest that the patterns according to which various combinations of the achievement groups resembled each other might be task dependent. For example, in relation to Task 2 [: : :], with respect to the first discriminant function, the problem solving processes of the group who gave up resembled those of the nonsolvers more than they resembled the processes of the solvers. However, in the same task, with respect to the second discriminant function, the problem solving processes of solvers and nonsolvers resembled one another more than either of them resembled the processes of those subjects who gave up. In the case of Task 5, [Platform], this pattern appeared to be reversed. Further research concerning the role of "Trial and Error" type behaviors is required to provide a better understanding of the here observed phenomena.

As is discussed further in Chapter 13, the results of the discriminant analyses computed for speed of problem solving performance support the findings discussed in Chapters 9 and 10. These findings suggest that time on task, rather than being a variable which determines the outcome of problem solving performance and the pattern of strategies used during the process of performance, is itself determined by the relevance of the subjects' problem solving behaviors and strategies in relation to the requirements of the task.

Speed of performance was investigated at two levels. Therefore, only one discriminant function was possible. The finding of significant discriminant functions in all 12 tasks suggests that performance differences with respect to speed of problem solving can be accounted for on the basis of resemblances and differences in the component variables making up the problem solving processes in fast and slow working subjects respectively.

Although the sizes of the loadings of some of the variables constituting the discriminating dimensions varied with respect to task types, the major loadings in all 12 tasks were provided by strategy variable 1 (Code 111: First reading). On the average (excepting Task 10 [Fly/Tree]), this loading was at least three times larger than the other loadings constituting the discriminant functions. This finding suggests that differences in the speed of problem solving are the result of what goes on at the time of the subject's initial contact with the task, irrespective of the length of the stimulus passage, the task instructions, or the task type. The specific mechanisms operating at this stage cannot be determined within the framework of the present study. Further research is required which might combine design features of the present study with experimental procedures. This approach could lead to information regarding the role of such variables as reading skill, speed of decoding and encoding, etc., and hypothesize other processes which might be taking place during the period of "First reading."

The number of significant discriminant functions, where not constrained by the number of a priori categories, appeared to be determined by the demand characteristics of the task. It makes sense that the type, complexity, length, etc., of the task would influence the type and number of response based criteria according to which the performance of individuals or groups might be described.

However, the percentage of "correct" classifications, i.e., the proportion expressed in percentage terms where the classification of subjects on the basis of process profiles agreed with the a priori grouping on the basis of outcomes of performance, was independent of task type and group of subjects. An exception to this occurred, obviously, in the classification analyses of problem solving achievement where achievement and task were logically related, i.e., achievement was judged in relation to tasks.

Within and across tasks, the agreement between the process based classifications and those based on outcome measures were high. In relation to problem solving achievement, 92.5% of cases ($SD = 2.5\%$) in the categorization of solvers (group A) versus those who gave up (group B), 84.8% ($SD = 5.1\%$) of solvers (group A), versus nonsolvers (group C), and 88.6% ($SD = 3.2\%$) of groups B versus C were correctly classified.

Achievement was the most objective of the a priori classification variables. It was easy to determine whether a subject had solved the task to criterion, had failed to do so, or had abandoned the task prematurely. As can be seen in the relevant tables of this chapter, the percentages of correct classifications in relation to speed of performance and educational level were relatively high also.

As noted at the beginning of this summary, the level of agreement between the classifications shows that process components of problem solving performance per se reflect and describe what has traditionally been "measured" on the basis of outcome variables.

Another interpretation of the present findings might be that traditional outcome based measures, because they appear to be definable in process terms, may well have a better validity for classification purposes than has been suggested in recent years.

The present study showed in at least one area, i.e., educational attainment, that process measures are more sensitive than outcome measures of problem solving. Because of inferences required in relation to most outcome measures, it is not possible to investigate whether nonagreement in classification based on such measures and process measures are the result of misclassifications resulting from one or the other methodology.

What is important, however, is that the results of the present study have shown that differences in a number of important and frequently assessed contextual variables, which have traditionally been inferred on the basis of performance outcomes, can be determined on the basis of and in terms of the actual operations and strategies problem solvers utilize during their work on the task.

The high agreement found in the classification analyses between categorizations on the basis of outcome variables and process profiles would suggest that, for most purposes, process profiles would provide not only a greater level of validity of measurement, as they can identify which problem solving behaviors caused the performance differences, but also that they are of greater diagnostic value for the design of intervention procedures which meet the assessed needs of individual subjects or particular groups in relation to specifiable intellectual and educational tasks.

Where the aim of psychological assessment is not primarily for purposes of classification and labelling, but "for indicating how intellectual performance can be improved" (Glaser, Pellegrino, & Lesgold, 1977, p. 508), profiles of the operational components of the cognitive performance itself carry considerably greater promise than traditional outcome measures.

12

Contingencies and Interdependencies of Sequential Problem Solving Behaviors

The investigations described in the preceding chapters led to the identification of important structural components of problem solving processes, which were identified on the basis of the total amounts of use made of various problem solving behaviors which were applied by individuals in their attempts to solve different types of tasks. The concern was to assess the importance of certain types of behaviors as functional elements of the performance.

It was shown that the problem solving strategies used by individuals and groups in their attempts to solve tasks might account for differences in the outcome of performance. Individual differences in the ability to solve problems, speed of task completion, measured IQ, and level of education were reflected in the strategies used.

While the findings relating to the structural components of the problem solving process identified in this study are important, it is obvious that they are a mere preliminary step. It is essential not to lose sight of the fact that a complex psychological process such as problem solving is not merely a concatenation of the components into which an investigator chose to decompose it for the sake of analysis, but that these structural components are likely to be highly interdependent.

THE DYNAMICS OF THE PROCESS

The term process is applied to dynamic phenomena and thus might not be representable in terms of static entities. Complex and far-reaching interdependencies of operations have to be expected, as problem solvers orchestrate operations available to them in their attempts to produce solutions.

This chapter reports on an initial and exploratory attempt to extend the study of structural components of performance to an investigation of the *dynamics* of the process. To do this, a number of analyses were conducted which preserve the time sequences in which the problem solving operations were performed. The aim of these analyses was to investigate whether characteristic behavioral sequences could be identified, and, given that characteristic patterns were to be found, whether such sequences might reveal individual and group differences.

The behaviors, categorized for each three-second unit, were summarized in the form of one–dependent transition matrices, i.e., matrices the elements of which are sequence pairs. The transition matrices obtained for different tasks and for different groups of subjects were then compared on the basis of a Markoff chain model of analysis (Kruskal & Tanur, 1978). This model assumes that the problem solving behaviors in subsequent units are dependent on preceding ones, i.e., that an individual's problem solving behavior in a three-second unit "U is dependent on the behavior which occurred in Unit "$U-1$".

Another assumption is that the further removed the units are in time, the lower is their dependency. The model is not restricted to first order dependencies, nor to the number of transition matrices which can be compared (Kemeny, Snell, & Thompson, 1966; Levine & Burke, 1972). The obtained matrices can be compared through the application of a χ^2 test with the appropriate degrees of freedom.

The transition matrices were too large to be included in this report. A brief description of the organization of the transition matrices may be useful at this point. The entries in all the transition matrices were row majored, which means, for example, that a strategy in category 2 (Code 112: Rereading) followed by the use of strategy 7 (Code 211: Plan/ Hypothesis) be represented in the cell corresponding to row 2 and column 7. For example, cell 2.7 has a frequency count of eight responses. This means that 4.3% of strategy 2 responses were followed by strategy 7 responses, that 1.5% of all strategy 7 responses were preceded by the use of strategy 2, and that 0.5% of all behavior transitions consisted of transitions from strategy 2 to strategy 7.
behavior transitions consisted of transitions from strategy 2 to strategy 7.

On the other hand, the use of a strategy judged to fall into category 7 (Code 211: Plan/Hypothesis) followed by the use of a behavior judged to fall into category 3 (Code 113 – 117: Chunk/Summarize text) would be represented as one of the 18 responses contained in cell 7,3. The entries in this cell show that 3.4% of all the strategies immediately following strategy 7 were of strategy 3 type, and that of all strategy 3 responses observed in Task 1, 9.4% were preceded by strategy 7. Other cells of the transition matrices can be interpreted in the same way.

For each of the 12 tasks three major types of comparisons of the transition matrices were made. First, the overall matrices were compared for groups of subjects of varying levels of achievement, speed of problem solving, and measured intelligence. Second, the patterns of transitional behaviors were compared along the time dimension for the total sample and the above mentioned criterion variables. These analyses included (a) comparisons of overall trends over different periods of time, during problem solving of the one-step behaviors following each other, and (b) the relative contributions made by specific behavior sequences to changes in the pattern of strategy use over time. The time segments investigated here were the beginning, middle, and end periods of the problem solving process. Third, the rate of shifts in problem solving behaviors and the relative amounts of repetitive behaviors were compared. The three sets of results obtained from the above specified comparisons of the transition matrices will be reported consecutively in the order in which they were presented in the immediately preceding paragraph.

OVERALL TRANSITION MATRIX COMPARISONS

The overall transition matrices of solvers and nonsolvers, fast and slow working subjects, and between two extreme levels of measured intelligence, were compared.

The specific research questions investigated in this section were (a) whether there are differences in the pattern of sequential problem solving behaviors for various levels of the above specified three contextual variables, when the groups are compared on their overall transition matrices, and (b) whether there are differences in the relative frequencies of transition behaviors between the above groups, when compared on each specific type of transition.

For the purpose of this analysis subjects whose problem solving resulted in acceptable or nearly acceptable solutions were regarded as solvers, while subjects who decided to discontinue the task before solution, and subjects whose work did not result in an acceptable solution were regarded as nonsolvers. Subjects who worked on the task less than the median amount of time were regarded as fast workers, while those who took the median length of time or longer were regarded as slow workers. Individuals whose WAIS Block Design scaled score was lower than nine were, for the purposes of the present comparison regarded to be of "low" measured intelligence, while individuals with scaled scores of 13 and above were regarded to be of "high" measured intelligence.

Separate transition matrices were prepared for each of the 12 tasks for solvers, nonsolvers, fast workers, slow workers, high IQ subjects, and low IQ subjects, i.e., 36 separate transition matrices were prepared. For each task three pairs of matrices were prepared, i.e., solvers versus non-solvers, fast versus slow workers, and high IQ versus low IQ subjects. In each case the statistical procedure compared an entire matrix with another, e.g., the matrix of transition behaviors or strategies for solvers was compared with the transition matrix for the nonsolvers for Task 1, then Task 2, and so on. The same procedure was applied to the matrices of fast and slow subjects, and to those of the high IQ and low IQ subjects.

(a) The Overall Pattern of Sequential Problem Solving Behaviors

Markoff chain comparisons of the matrices of the respective pairs of the above described transition matrices yielded significant χ^2 values for all pairs of transition matrices ($p \leq .01$) for the achievement and speed variables, and for seven out of the 12 tasks[1] for the intelligence variable, and showed, with reference to research question (a), that the here investigated contextual variables appeared to have influenced the pattern of sequential problem solving behaviors and strategies. The consistently significant differences of the pairs of transition matrices in the case of all 12 tasks suggest that different patterns of sequential components might distinguish the problem solving processes not only of solvers and nonsolvers, but that characteristics of the problem solving process itself might be found to account for differences in speed and levels of measured intelligence also. Although made on the basis of overall comparisons, the above suggestions are strengthened by the fact that the 12 tasks used in the present study were of quite different content and difficulty.

The most obvious overall difference between the pairs of transition matrices for the different criterion groups was that, with the exception of Tasks 3 [15 × 30] and 8 [Poem/Statue], nonsolvers produced many more transitions than solvers. Slow workers produced between twice and ten times as many transitions across the 12 tasks as did fast working subjects, while the high intelligence group produced considerably fewer transitions in the case of Tasks 1 [Binet] and 3 [15 × 30] than the low intelligence groups. In the case of Tasks 2 [⦂⦂⦂], 7 [9m→1h], 8 [Poem/Statue], 9 [Praise/Punishment], and 12 [8TB/2] this effect was reversed. These findings obviously converge with those relating to preferences and the variety of strategies used, presented in Chapter 9.

---

1. The transition matrices for subjects of the two extreme intelligence groups were found to differ significantly ($p < .001$) in the case of Tasks 1 [Binet], 2 [⦂⦂⦂], 3 [15 × 30], 7 [9m→1h], 8 [Poem/Statue], 9 [Praise/Pun.], and 12 [8 TB/2].

(b) *Comparison of Specific Behavior Sequence Frequencies*

Research question (b) was concerned with possible differences in the relative frequencies of specific transitions between subjects belonging to the above noted criterion groups, i.e., solvers versus nonsolvers, fast and slow workers, and subjects of high or low measured intelligence.

In order to investigate this matter and to assess the relative importance and contribution of each possible transition pair to the overall differences in the problem solving processes of subjects belonging to the various criterion groups, the sums of the columns of the transition matrices were compared for each behavior transition separately for each task. Of the 36 χ^2 tests performed, only one failed to reach significance at or beyond the level of $p = .05$. The performance on Task 10 [Fly/Tree] failed to reveal process differences which would discriminate the problem solving of high intelligence subjects from subjects with low measured intelligence. In the case of other tasks, the comparisons of the column totals of the transition matrices discriminated between high and low intelligence groups, between solvers and nonsolvers, and between fast and slow working subjects.

Tables 12.1 to 12.3 summarize the total frequencies of all possible transitions, i.e., the column totals of the previously discussed entire transition matrices, for solvers and nonsolvers, fast and slow workers, and high and low intelligence groups respectively. To facilitate comparisons, the frequencies of transitions are expressed as percentages of the total number of observed transitions in each task.

Tables 12.1 to 12.3 are interpreted as follows. For example, row 1 columns 5 and 6 of Table 12.3 indicate that high IQ subjects produced a considerably greater proportion of transitions to strategy 1 than did low IQ subjects in Task 3, i.e., 23.5% of the transition behaviors of the high IQ subjects in this task were to strategy 1, while only 6.3% of the low IQ subjects showed this pattern. In the same Table, it can be seen that in the case of Task 12, 11.8% of the problem solving strategies used by high IQ subjects were followed by strategy 16, while only 6.8% of the responses of the low IQ subjects were followed by a behavior categorized as strategy 16.

Inspection of Tables 12.1 to 12.3 shows some interesting consistencies. Transitions from other problem solving behaviors to behavior 7 (Code 211: Plan/Hypothesis) discriminated in the case of all three sets of criterion groups. A tendency can be observed in most tasks for nonsolvers, slow workers, and the high intelligence group to have moved to this behavior with greater relative frequency than solvers, fast workers, and low intelligence subjects respectively.

Table 12.2 suggests that fast workers spent in all 12 tasks a significantly

TABLE
Solvers (S) Versus Non-solvers (N): Total

Transition to strategy	T1S	T1N	T2S	T2N	T3S	T3N	T4S	T4N	T5S	T5N	T6S
1	10.0	10.9	2.1	2.3	12.5	5.6	38.8	31.7	15.9	15.9	2.6
2	3.8	6.0	2.4	3.2	0.8	0	16.3	17.6	19.8	21.8	3.5
3	5.1	5.4	1.9	2.4	5.0	2.0	5.0	7.8	8.3	5.5	3.3
4	0.9	2.1	0.8	2.0	1.0	0	2.7	3.1	7.3	5.1	4.3
5	1.4	1.2	1.2	1.9	0.4	0	4.9	5.1	4.1	3.6	2.0
6	0	0	0.1	0.3	0.1	0	0.6	1.1	0.2	0.8	0.3
7	15.4	14.4	16.6	22.9	7.4	8.7	9.8	14.0	8.7	15.0	18.3
8	2.9	5.2	20.4	20.6	1.9	2.0	0.3	0.4	0.7	0.7	14.5
9	8.7	13.8	0.8	0.7	0.8	0.5	0.2	0	1.2	0.1	0.2
10	8.2	5.6	23.8	16.3	1.0	1.5	6.7	6.6	10.1	11.0	20.4
11	29.8	21.7	1.8	1.1	48.3	46.4	0.2	0.2	0	0.5	0.9
12	2.3	0.5	2.7	0.5	1.9	5.6	1.9	1.1	3.3	1.0	2.4
13	2.0	0.7	3.3	1.6	6.1	9.2	1.8	1.9	6.5	6.7	2.4
14	0.7	1.4	1.5	1.8	3.1	0	3.0	3.3	4.0	3.2	3.8
15	1.2	3.3	1.0	2.2	3.2	5.6	1.0	1.2	0.3	1.5	1.1
16	5.1	4.9	13.2	16.5	4.0	10.2	3.6	4.0	6.6	6.4	16.3
17	2.5	2.5	2.7	2.1	1.5	2.0	2.7	0.7	2.2	0.8	1.4
18	0.1	0.4	3.4	1.9	1.0	0.5	0.4	0.2	0.8	0.4	2.3

TABLE
Fast (F) Versus Slow (S) Workers: Total

Transition to strategy	T1F	T1S	T2F	T2S	T3F	T3S	T4F	T4S	T5F	T5S	T6F
1	21.1	7.9	4.5	1.4	24.9	6.7	48.9	26.6	24.3	12.3	4.7
2	1.9	5.9	3.9	2.8	0	0.9	9.4	20.9	19.7	22.1	3.9
3	7.0	4.8	3.1	2.1	5.5	4.0	6.5	7.2	5.2	6.4	2.9
4	1.2	1.7	2.3	1.6	0	1.0	1.4	3.8	6.3	5.2	7.1
5	1.0	1.3	2.1	1.7	0	0.4	3.7	5.7	4.3	3.4	2.2
6	0	0	0.8	0	0	0.1	1.1	0.8	0.6	0.7	1.2
7	8.8	16.3	19.3	22.7	7.4	7.7	9.4	14.4	10.9	15.1	16.2
8	1.2	5.0	20.3	20.6	0	2.6	0.2	0.5	0.3	0.9	19.5
9	9.8	12.2	0.2	0.9	0	1.0	0	0.1	0.1	0.4	0.3
10	6.5	6.7	18.2	17.3	0	1.4	7.2	6.4	9.5	11.4	13.9
11	34.9	22.5	1.7	1.0	52.1	46.6	0.1	0.2	0	0.6	1.9
12	1.4	1.2	0.9	0.8	4.1	2.3	1.2	1.4	1.0	1.7	1.0
13	0.6	1.5	1.3	2.1	1.4	8.4	2.2	1.7	6.0	7.0	2.0
14	1.1	1.1	1.1	2.0	1.4	2.7	2.8	3.4	3.1	3.4	2.4
15	1.2	2.7	2.6	1.8	1.4	4.4	0.8	1.3	1.8	1.0	2.4
16	1.4	5.8	12.9	17.1	0.5	6.9	2.9	4.4	4.8	7.1	15.1
17	0.8	2.9	2.2	2.1	1.4	1.7	1.8	1.0	0.8	1.2	1.7
18	0.0	0.3	2.5	2.0	0	1.1	0.3	0.2	1.2	0.2	1.6

12.1
Percentages of Transitions (To Columns)

T6N	T7S	T7N	T8S	T8N	T9S	T9N	T10S	T10N	T11S	T11N	T12S	T12N
2.4	4.5	4.1	3.9	2.2	3.4	2.3	3.4	1.6	4.1	1.2	4.5	6.8
3.7	14.6	15.4	4.4	6.9	0.5	2.1	3.2	1.6	3.2	1.6	1.5	6.8
3.4	2.3	2.5	1.4	0.9	1.7	0.9	1.6	1.5	2.8	1.4	4.1	5.6
4.6	5.0	4.4	6.8	4.2	1.8	3.0	4.0	1.0	1.8	0.4	1.3	3.2
2.0	2.0	2.1	0.1	0	0.2	0	0	0.6	0	0.1	1.3	1.8
0.8	0	0.4	1.6	8.4	2.5	5.1	2.7	1.0	1.8	1.9	0	1.1
21.5	20.3	19.6	11.0	14.8	14.4	11.3	7.4	17.5	13.8	12.8	20.0	23.9
21.1	5.1	11.2	1.4	1.4	0.8	1.4	0.6	1.0	2.3	1.2	6.5	3.5
0.6	0.3	0.4	18.6	16.4	25.3	19.5	31.4	21.3	22.9	28.9	0	0.5
11.5	25.6	12.3	7.1	4.5	13.2	7.1	4.5	7.9	5.0	6.4	33.8	23.3
1.9	1.6	0.7	27.3	21.1	15.7	32.7	19.4	23.9	24.3	28.3	1.5	0.6
1.0	1.0	0.7	2.7	1.0	6.0	0.2	3.4	1.1	3.2	0.6	1.3	0.8
1.4	0.4	1.2	1.6	4.2	2.8	1.1	1.8	3.9	4.6	2.8	3.7	3.9
2.3	2.6	3.7	1.8	2.6	3.0	1.5	3.7	1.9	2.8	1.6	4.1	3.8
3.0	0.9	4.0	1.9	2.2	0.3	1.8	2.2	2.8	1.4	3.6	0.2	1.6
16.4	12.4	14.0	3.7	6.9	3.5	5.3	2.9	7.1	5.5	4.6	13.1	9.5
1.4	1.0	2.7	3.6	1.7	3.4	3.9	5.3	2.4	0.5	2.2	3.0	2.3
0.8	0.1	0.5	0.9	0.5	1.3	0.8	2.7	1.6	0	0.6	0	0.9

12.2
Percentages of Transitions (To Columns)

T6S	T7F	T7S	T8F	T8S	T9F	T9S	T10F	T10S	T11F	T11S	T12F	T12S
1.7	7.9	3.0	7.5	2.0	4.7	1.8	5.8	1.8	3.8	1.0	13.3	4.4
3.6	20.0	13.8	6.7	5.2	1.9	1.3	2.7	2.3	1.2	2.0	6.0	6.4
3.6	2.6	2.5	1.9	1.1	1.9	0.9	3.6	1.2	3.8	1.0	4.5	5.8
3.7	6.6	3.9	11.8	4.1	5.4	1.4	7.2	1.4	1.2	0.4	4.9	2.4
1.9	2.6	2.0	0.3	0	0	0.1	1.8	0.1	0	0.1	2.3	1.6
0.5	1.3	0.1	1.1	5.4	3.7	4.3	1.3	1.8	2.0	1.9	1.8	0.7
22.3	18.4	20.1	8.6	13.7	11.8	12.7	5.4	14.5	11.0	13.3	18.8	25.1
19.9	6.0	11.3	0.8	1.6	0.4	1.5	0	1.0	1.7	1.2	2.7	4.1
0.6	0	0.5	21.1	16.8	24.1	20.7	31.4	24.7	30.1	27.5	0.5	0.5
13.1	11.2	15.9	3.7	6.6	8.8	9.7	1.3	7.3	6.4	6.1	27.2	23.5
1.7	0.5	1.0	19.3	26.1	21.7	28.1	22.0	21.8	27.5	27.8	1.1	0.6
1.4	0.7	0.8	1.3	2.2	4.5	1.6	2.2	2.1	1.4	0.8	0.8	0.9
1.5	0.8	1.2	1.9	2.9	0.9	2.2	0.4	3.4	2.0	3.4	4.1	3.8
2.7	3.5	3.5	1.6	2.3	2.2	2.0	1.3	2.9	2.9	1.4	2.5	4.2
2.7	3.5	3.4	2.9	1.8	0.9	1.4	4.0	2.3	2.0	3.7	1.3	1.5
16.8	11.2	14.5	4.5	5.2	4.3	4.8	4.9	5.3	2.0	5.5	6.9	10.8
1.3	3.4	2.1	3.5	2.6	2.2	4.3	4.5	3.5	1.2	2.2	1.3	2.7
0.9	0	0.6	1.6	0.5	0.6	1.2	0	2.5	0	0.7	0	1.1

TABLE
High (BD>13) Versus Low (BD<9) IQ Subjects:

Transition to strategy	T1 >13	T1 <9	T2 >13	T2 <9	T3 >13	T3 <9	T4 >13	T4 <9	T5 >13	T5 <9	T6 >13	T6 <9
1	13.1	11.8	1.8	3.0	23.5	6.3	27.1	33.5	14.6	15.9	2.0	3.1
2	2.0	5.4	2.6	3.9	0	1.2	11.9	19.1	11.5	28.8	2.1	7.7
3	6.6	5.4	1.5	2.7	5.9	3.9	9.5	6.6	6.3	6.7	3.3	1.6
4	0.3	3.8	1.5	3.0	0	0	3.8	5.1	3.3	7.1	1.7	5.0
5	2.3	0	1.7	2.6	0	0	5.4	4.7	6.0	1.2	2.3	1.8
6	0	0	0.3	0.3	0	0	0.9	1.5	0	0.4	0	1.6
7	14.6	11.8	25.1	20.4	9.8	10.6	17.1	11.6	16.1	11.7	21.1	13.3
8	3.1	7.7	17.6	23.3	0	0.4	0.1	0.3	1.0	0.6	15.6	26.1
9	11.1	15.2	1.7	0.5	0	2.0	0	0	0.3	0.5	0	0.6
10	8.9	3.6	17.2	12.1	0	0	6.3	6.2	12.7	9.5	17.5	14.2
11	28.0	22.8	0.6	1.8	47.1	49.0	0	0.3	0	0.0	1.4	2.9
12	3.1	1.1	0.5	0.9	5.9	1.2	1.7	2.1	3.3	1.4	2.1	2.1
13	0.9	0.4	2.4	1.2	0	7.5	3.1	1.4	9.0	5.0	3.3	0.9
14	0.6	0.9	2.5	1.6	5.9	0	4.7	2.3	2.8	2.7	5.1	1.0
15	1.4	1.8	1.3	2.0	2.0	6.3	1.2	1.4	0.7	2.5	1.2	1.3
16	3.7	4.3	17.6	13.1	0	7.8	4.4	3.3	9.2	3.7	20.5	14.7
17	0.3	4.1	0.8	2.3	0	2.0	1.3	0.7	0.7	1.8	0.2	1.5
18	0	0	3.4	5.4	0	2.0	1.5	0	2.5	0.5	0.5	0.7

greater percentage of time than slow workers in their first reading of the stimulus passage. Slow workers tended to move to behavior 7 (Code 211: Plan/Hypothesis) and to behavior 16 (Code 400: Judgment/Verification) more frequently, and to behavior 11 (Code 219: Calculation/Detail) less frequently than fast workers.

Table 12.3 shows that the high intelligence group moved less frequently to behavior 2 (Code 112: Rereading) than did the low intelligence group. This tendency is observed in all tasks except Tasks 2 [: : :], 3 [15 × 30], 9 [Praise/Punishment], and 11 [Wood/Alcohol], and might suggest less concentration and a lower memory span for the low intelligence group. Consistently more transitions to behavior 7 (Code 211: Plan/Hypothesis) were observed for high intelligence subjects than for low intelligence subjects across all 12 tasks. Behavior 11 (Code 219: Calculation/Detail) and behavior 16 (Code 400: Judgment/Verification) also showed an overall tendency to discriminate between the two criterion groups.

Behavior 15 (Code 320: Emotional) occurred rarely and did not discriminate between any of the three sets of criterion groups. Other transitions appeared to be more task specific in their discriminatory power in relation to the criterion groups.

PATTERNS OF BEHAVIOR SEQUENCES

The results presented in this section focus on the pattern of problem solving behaviors along the time dimension rather than on the overall frequencies of specific behavior transitions. More specifically, the re-

12.3
Total Percentages of Transitions (To Columns)

T7 >13	T7 <9	T8 >13	T8 <9	T9 >13	T9 <9	T10 >13	T10 <9	T11 >13	T11 <9	T12 >13	T12 <9
3.0	6.4	1.9	3.0	1.6	3.3	1.6	2.8	0.5	1.9	5.2	10.2
9.0	15.7	3.2	6.5	2.3	1.9	1.6	4.4	2.1	0.8	4.1	8.0
3.0	1.8	1.3	1.5	0.3	2.3	1.6	1.7	1.0	2.7	6.2	4.1
2.8	6.2	5.7	6.1	0.6	6.0	2.7	3.9	0.5	0.8	2.8	5.7
1.3	2.1	0	0	0	0	0	2.2	0	0	3.1	1.8
0.1	1.5	14.8	0.8	9.1	1.9	2.2	0.6	3.6	0.4	0.1	3.5
20.9	22.4	21.3	11.4	21.7	6.5	10.3	3.3	24.0	7.2	23.7	20.7
17.5	8.5	2.2	2.3	1.0	1.4	0	0	2.6	0.4	3.4	4.5
0.4	0	9.4	19.0	17.2	24.2	30.8	32.0	28.1	34.2	0.1	0.8
15.5	13.9	6.2	3.8	11.3	3.7	3.8	0	6.3	3.0	24.9	23.6
0.3	0	13.2	33.5	15.5	31.2	28.1	31.5	16.1	35.7	0.3	1.2
0.8	0.5	3.0	1.5	2.9	0	3.8	0.6	2.6	0	1.7	0.8
0.6	0.5	0.8	1.5	1.9	0	1.1	2.2	4.2	1.5	4.2	2.9
4.1	3.3	2.4	1.1	2.9	1.4	2.2	2.2	2.6	1.1	4.8	2.5
1.9	3.1	1.6	0.4	0.6	1.9	0	0.6	1.0	2.3	1.0	1.4
17.9	11.8	7.5	4.2	6.1	8.4	6.5	8.8	4.2	4.9	11.8	6.8
0.8	2.3	5.1	1.1	2.3	6.0	1.1	3.3	0	3.0	2.8	1.4
0.3	0	0.3	2.3	2.6	0	2.7	0.0	0.5	0	0	0

search questions concerned ways in which problem solving processes differed throughout the time of problem solving for the respective pairs of criterion groups. Of particular interest were the behaviors succeeding each other in relation to questions such as: Did the problem solving processes of solvers and nonsolvers, fast and slow workers, and high and low intelligence groups, differ throughout the period of problem solving, or could characteristics of particular criterion groups be observed at different points or periods of problem solving time? Did preferences in problem solving behaviors change over time, or was the contribution of specific behaviors consistent and relatively constant over time?

The above specified research questions were investigated by means of the following three types of analyses:

a. An overall one-step sequence comparison of the distributions of the behaviors preceding each specific behavior.

b. An analysis of problem solving behavior sequences over time, i.e., the investigation of trends in the first, second, and third part of the problem solving activity.

c. A comparison of the relative contribution of specific problem solving behaviors to the variations of the problem solving process over time.

a. One-step Comparisons of the Distributions of Problem Solving Behaviors Preceding Each Behavior Type: The research question considered here might be stated as follows: "Is there a difference between the respec-

TABLE 12.4
Distribution of One-Step Behavior Sequences: Results of χ^2 Comparisons of Behavior Distributions — Tasks 1-6

Transition to Strategy	Task 1			Task 2			Task 3			Task 4			Task 5			Task 6		
	χ^2	df	p	χ^2	df	p	χ^2	df	p	χ^2	df	p	χ^2	df	p	χ^2	df	p
Solvers versus Nonsolvers																		
1	22.43	8	<.01				101.87	12	<.001	9.46	6	NS	15.00	3	<.01			
2	114.44	15	<.001	83.27	14	<.001				42.63	11	<.001	54.00	10	<.001	110.05	10	<.001
7				19.48	9	<.05				59.98	11	<.001	47.94	11	<.001	15.64	7	<.05
8	23.00	5	<.001	55.64	11	<.001												
9							141.77	12	<.001				83.38	7	<.001	37.17	9	<.001
10	72.81	11	<.001	54.68	14	<.001										97.75	11	<.001
11																		
16																		
Fast versus Slow																		
1	66.78	7	<.001				236.17	9	<.001	16.72	8	<.05	18.74	4	<.01			
2	85.84	14	<.001	41.05	14	<.001				40.56	10	<.001	35.70	11	<.001	42.11	11	<.001
7				33.42	15	<.001				29.02	11	<.01	112.89	11	<.001	35.39	13	<.001
8	44.34	9	<.001	59.42	10	<.001												
9							164.97	11	<.001				31.43	8	<.001	17.14	9	<.05
10	66.31	14	<.001	33.49	15	<.01										67.69	15	<.001
11																		
16																		
High IQ versus Low IQ																		
1	153.4	6	<.001				147.1	8	<.001	43.08	3	<.001	14.26	5	<.02			
2	83.29	10	<.001	182.24	14	<.001				50.53	8	<.001	87.57	9	<.01	119.91	11	<.001
7				88.32	9	<.001	97.75	6	<.001	33.64	12	<.001	41.78	11	<.001	56.61	10	<.001
8	87.96	8	<.001	11.44	7	NS												
9							171.81	6	<.001				57.29	8	<.001	18.84	7	<.02
10	198.98	11	<.001	40.15	11	<.001										83.54	13	<.02
11																		
16																		

tive criterion groups in the relative distribution of behaviors immediately preceding each particular problem solving behavior?"

To investigate this question, the frequencies of behaviors in each respective column of the pairs of the complete transition matrices, which accounted for at least 10% of the responses of either group, were compared by means of χ^2 tests. Within the columns only cells accounting for 5% or more of the respective transitions in either group were considered. This accounts for the variation in the degrees of freedom contained in Tables 12.4 and 12.5. Tables 12.4 and 12.5 show the results of χ^2 comparisons for Tasks 1 to 6 and Tasks 7 to 12 respectively for all three pairs of criterion groups.

The results shown in Tables 12.4 and 12.5 resulted from tests of the hypothesis that solvers and nonsolvers, fast and slow workers, and high intelligence and low intelligence subjects respectively, differ in the distribution of sequences of each particular behavior during problem solving. The behavior categories were column categories, which means that the cells compared contained one-step sequence behaviors to each column behavior category.

Inspection of the results in Tables 12.4 and 12.5 of solvers versus nonsolvers first, reveals significant differences across a number of tasks for behaviors 1 (Code 111: First reading), 2 (Code 112: Rereading), 7 (Code 211: Plan/Hypothesis), 8 (Code 212: Trial and Error), 10 (Code 215: Continued activity), 11 (Code 219: Calculation/Detail), and 16 (Code 400: Judgment/verification). These results suggest that solvers tended to proceed to these behaviors from different preceding behaviors more than did the nonsolvers. This interpretation gains some power as a result of certain consistencies of the findings across different tasks. On the other hand, these results suggest that a considerable amount of variance between tasks may be due to the requirements of specific tasks. Behaviors 7, 8, 9, and 11 were significant in the case of some tasks and not in others. Variable 11 (Code 219: Calculation/Detail) for instance produced highly significant differences between solvers and nonsolvers in the tasks requiring mathematical manipulation, i.e., Tasks 1 [Binet], 3 [15 × 30], 6 [6m→4Δ], and 11 [Wood/Alcohol], and showed nonsignificant results for most of the similarities tasks.

Behavior 16 (Code 400: Judgment/Verification) discriminated between solvers and nonsolvers in the three nonverbal tasks, Task 2 [∷∷], Task 6 [6m→4Δ], Task 7 [9m→1h], and in the two difficult verbal tasks, Task 11 [Wood/Alcohol] and Task 12 [8TB/2]. On the other hand, behavior 2 (Code 112: Rereading) discriminated particularly well in Tasks 4 [Pebbles], 5 [Platform], and 7 [9m→1h], which were characterized by long stimulus passages, and in the case of Task 7 by instructions which subjects found rather difficult to comprehend. In a similar manner transitions

TABLE 12.5
Distribution of One-Step Behavior Sequences: Results of χ^2 Comparisons of Behavior Distributions — Tasks 7-12

Transition to Strategy	Task 7 χ^2	df	p	Task 8 χ^2	df	p	Task 9 χ^2	df	p	Task 10 χ^2	df	p	Task 11 χ^2	df	p	Task 12 χ^2	df	p
Solvers versus Nonsolvers																		
1	52.74	10	<.001	29.08	7	<.001	0.52	2	NS	11.21	5	<.05	5.11	4	NS	18.41	6	<.01
2	8.11	5	NS	6.11	3	NS	2.91	2	NS	6.00	3	NS	9.59	3	<.05			
7	6.12	3	NS	1.46	3	NS	0.36	5	NS	43.70	6	<.001	41.83	5	<.001	3.12	6	NS
8				0.11	2	NS												
9	40.76	5	<.001				2.25	2	NS	0.12	2	NS	38.34	4	<.001	58.60	7	<.001
10																		
11																		
16	27.52	6	<.001															
Fast versus Slow																		
1	31.61	5	<.001	30.76	8	<.001	49.19	9	<.001	94.11	10	<.001	35.70	12	<.001	30.70	8	<.001
2	37.44	11	<.001	29.74	5	<.001	56.68	10	<.001	36.82	5	<.001	11.70	5	<.05	21.40	11	<.05
7	81.08	14	<.001	40.19	8	<.001	43.50	11	<.001	46.93	10	<.001	22.64	12	<.05	22.74	11	<.05
8	82.73	5	<.001							2.20	2	NS						
9	34.80	11	<.001	112.50	12	<.001	43.08	11	<.001				57.20	11	<.001	17.32	7	<.05
10				38.50	7	<.001												
16	97.69	11	<.001															
High IQ versus Low IQ																		
1	67.94	4	<.001				101.64	9	<.001	147.37	9	<.001				40.16	6	<.001
2	133.68	10	<.001	90.07	11	<.001	163.30	11	<.001				194.45	10	<.001	68.19	14	<.001
7	165.05	11	<.001	136.54	13	<.001	196.11	11	<.001	258.49	10	<.001	187.89	11	<.001	113.58	8	<.001
8							90.01	8	<.001									
9	90.57	8	<.001	144.64	9	<.001	25.68	5	<.001	83.37	5	<.001	254.7	10	<.001	53.17	10	<.001
16	101.21	11	<.001															

to other behavior categories can be related to specific task requirements not only in their discrimination between solvers and nonsolvers, but also on the basis of their provision of distinctions between fast and slow workers, and the characterization of the problem solving processes of high versus low intelligence subjects.

The problem solving processes of fast and slow workers differed in behavior 1 (Code 111: First reading) in all tasks but Task 2 [: : :], a performance task and the only stimulus passage which provided a graphic representation of task requirements. Behavior 7 (Code 211: Plan/ Hypothesis) discriminated between fast and slow workers in all tasks except Task 3 [15×30], a straightforward computational task not expected to require hypothesizing, and Tasks 2 [: : :] and 6 [6m→4Δ], which were performance tasks with clear requirement specifications. On the other hand, the three performance tasks, Tasks 2 [: : :], 6 [6m→4Δ], and 7 [9m→1h] provided a significant discrimination between fast and slow solvers on the basis of the transitions to behavior 8 (Code 212: Trial and Error).

Comparisons of the distributions of the one-step transition behaviors of the groups of subjects with high measured intelligence and low measured intelligence revealed an equally consistent pattern. Among the transition behaviors which discriminated significantly between the two groups were those to behavior category 7 (Code 211: Plan/Hypothesis) for all tasks with the exception of Task 10 [Fly/Tree], to behavior category 8 (Code 212: Trial and Error) for the performance tasks, Tasks 2 [: : :], and 6 [6m→4Δ], to behavior category 2 (Code 112: Rereading) for the tasks with lengthy or difficult to comprehend instructions, i.e., Tasks 4 [Pebbles], 5 [Platform], and 7 [9m→1h]; to behavior category 9 (Code 214 + 218: Compare/Relate + Review former trials) for the similarities items, i.e., Tasks 8 to 11 inclusive, and for Task 1. The antecedent behaviors immediately followed by behavior 16 (Code 400: Judgment/Verification) discriminated significantly between high and low IQ subjects in the case of the difficult tasks, 2 [: : :], 6 [6m→4Δ], 7 [9m→1h], and 12 [8TB/2], repeating the pattern observed in the discriminatory power of transitions to this behavior in relation to solvers and nonsolvers, and fast and slow workers.

To summarize, it can be said that inspection of Tables 12.4 and 12.5 shows a pattern of considerable consistency in the types of transitions which were found to discriminate significantly in the case of all three criterion groupings. The results of comparisons between solvers and nonsolvers differed somewhat from those of the other two criterion groups as a number of transition behaviors failed to discriminate significantly between solvers and nonsolvers. A reason for this may be that intragroup differences in the use of behaviors during the problem solving of these tasks were greater than intergroup differences. It is also possible that the general directions given to subjects at the commencement of the problem solving sessions, which stressed that the investigator's interest was *not* whether the subjects solved the tasks but in *how* they went about solving them, may have led some subjects not to solve tasks and may therefore have made a valid distinction between solvers and nonsolvers impossible. Despite these discrepancies the overall picture presented in Tables 12.4 and 12.5 suggests that differences in the sequential pattern of a number of transition behaviors discriminated between the criterion groups in all tasks. Differences between the respective criterion groups in the relative distribution of behaviors immediately preceding each particular problem solving behavior were thus demonstrated.

The finding that the distributions of the immediate antecedents of certain components of the problem solving process differ between subjects grouped according to the above contextual variables, which have traditionally been accepted as relevant to the problem solving process, provides strong support for a hypothesis that the problem solving processes of solvers, fast workers, and highly intelligent subjects differ from those of nonsolvers, slow workers, and less intelligent subjects. The knowledge that the distribution of behaviors preceding a specific type of behavior differs for particular criterion groups calls, as a logical next step, for a description of the nature of these differences.

During work on Task 1 [Binet] all responses of the group of solvers, fast workers, and high IQ subjects respectively, classified as behavior category 1, i.e., 100% of all behavior category 1 responses exhibited by these groups, were preceded by a behavior category 1 behavior. This makes sense, if one remembers that this behavior category represents the First reading of the stimulus passage. However, only 99.1% of the First reading behaviors of the nonsolvers and the slow workers, and only 98.5% of these behaviors among the low IQ subjects, were preceded by a First reading behavior. Responses preceding First reading observed among subjects in the latter groups included extraneous remarks, displays of emotion and "jumping to conclusions" regarding solutions before the First reading of the stimulus passage was completed.

In Task 1, 20.8% of all behavior category 17 (Code 500: Pause) responses displayed by nonsolvers, were preceded by a category 1 behavior (Code 111: First reading), while only 8.3% of all "Pauses" occurring during work on Task 1 by solvers followed immediately after "First reading" behavior.

The most conspicuous consistency, which was noted was that in all tasks listed, low IQ subjects followed the First reading of the task with behavior category 17 (Code 500: Pause) with considerably greater frequency than did high IQ subjects. This finding might suggest that the low IQ subjects may have found it more difficult to comprehend the stimulus passages or that they may have found it less easy to select initial solution strategies. Another possibility is that the low IQ subjects may have found it more difficult to concentrate on the task, and that the Pauses following First reading may have been filled with extraneous thought.

Inspection of the differences in the percentages of transition behaviors preceded by First reading for each behavior category for all three criterion groups revealed that the major relative differences between solvers and nonsolvers tended to occur in the stimulus passage directed behavior categories, i.e., categories 1 to 5, while the most conspicuous relative differences between fast and slow workers and between the two IQ groups tended to occur, apart from the Pause category, in the transitions from First reading to solution directed behavior categories, i.e., categories 7 to 12, or across all categories. An overall consistency was observed in the direction of the differences in the percentages of transitions from behavior category 7 (Code 211: Plan/Hypothesis) between solvers, fast workers, and the high IQ group on the one side, and between nonsolvers, slow workers, and the low IQ group on the other. The appropriateness of the transitions seemed to be task specific rather than general. Comparing the relative percentages, the transition from Plan/Hypothesis to behavior categories 10 (Code 215: Continuing activity) and 12 (Code 220: Reasoning) might be regarded as major contributors to the differences between the pairs of criterion groups. Again, the direction of the differences in percentage seemed to depend on the requirements of specific tasks.

The distribution of important behaviors immediately following behavior category 9 (Code 214 + 218: Compare/Relate + Review former trials) was also investigated. The transition to behavior category 17 (Code 500: Pause) was the only one which occurred for the low IQ group with consistently larger frequency than for the high IQ group. The difference between these two groups was however, less large than that observed in the case of the transitions from behavior category 1. The transitions from the solution directed behavior category 9 (Code 214 + 218: Compare/ Relate + Review former trials) to categories 8 (Code 212: Trial and Error), 12 (Code 220: Reasoning), 14 (Code 315: Justification), 16 (Code 400: Judgment/Verification), and where appropriate 18 (Code 600: Memory) contributed most significantly to the process differences between the criterion groups.

Transitions from Calculation/Detail to self-related, emotional, and justification behaviors, i.e., behavior categories 13 (Code 311–314; Self-related), 14 (Code 215: Justification), and 15 (Code 320: Emotional), and to behavior category 16 (Code 400: Judgment/Verification) may largely account for the differences in problem solving processes of the criterion groups. Behavior category 16 (Code 400: Judgment/Verification) followed Calculation/Detail significantly more frequently in the solvers' group than in the nonsolvers' group. Behavior categories 13, 14, and 15 succeeded Calculation/Detail considerably more frequently in the case of non-solvers, however. Slow workers and low IQ subjects, and in Tasks 3 and 11 also nonsolvers, showed a previously noted tendency to move to a Pause more frequently than their respective comparison groups. The directions of other behavior transitions seemed once again to be task specific.

What follows "Judgment/Verification" behavior depends on both the task and the characteristics of the subjects. The direction of the differences in the frequencies of transitions from this variable differed both across criterion groups and between tasks. The same is true for the influence of behavior category 2 (Code 112: Rereading), and for the transitions from behavior category 10 (Code 215: Continuing activity).

Behavior category 8 (Code 212: Trial and Error) affects subjects in the various criterion groups differentially. In all three tasks, solvers and fast workers showed a tendency to move from Trial and Error behavior to behavior category 9 (Code 214 + 218: Compare/Relate + Review former trials) with considerably greater frequency than did nonsolvers and slow workers. In contrast to this, the same trend was observed among low IQ subjects and not, as might be expected, in the high IQ group.

b. Comparison of Behavior Sequences over Time-Transition Trends in the First, Second, and Third Parts of the Problem Solving Activity: The following research question was investigated: "Are there differences in the overall patterns of transitions over time, in units of thirds of the total time taken to solve each problem, between solvers and nonsolvers, fast and slow workers, and high and low IQ groups?"

To gain some insight into the overall influence of time on problem solving behavior, the investigation of the above question was preceded by an investigation of overall trends in transition behaviors over time for the total sample. The total problem solving period for each subject on each task was divided into three equal sequences. The total matrices of transition behaviors during the three parts of the problem solving process can be compared by inspection of Table 12.6, which lists for each task separately the percentage of transitions to each of the 18 behavior categories during each of the three thirds of the problem solving process.

Inspection of the first five columns of Table 12.6 shows that transitions to stimulus passage oriented behaviors were more frequent in the beginning third of problem solving than during the latter parts of the process. A small but interesting deviation from this pattern is noted for Tasks 4 [Pebbles] and 5 [Platform], both creativity tasks with relatively difficult stimulus passages, where an equal or larger percentage of transitions to behaviors 2 (Code 112: Rereading), 3 (Code 113 − 117: Chunk/

Summarize), 4 (Code 114–116: Ref. to text, Scan, Check), and 5 (Code 120: Identification of problem or part from given information) occurred during the middle third of the problem solving process.

There is a trend for transitions to behavior 7 (Code 211: Plan/ Hypothesis) and 8 (Code 212: Trial and Error) to occur more frequently in the middle and last thirds of the process, with a tendency of the latter transition to occur relatively most frequently during the end third, perhaps after other strategies have failed. The same is true for transitions to behavior 10 (Code 215: Continuing activity) and 16 (Code 400: Judgment/ Verification). A general trend can be observed for transitions to solution oriented and judgmental behaviors to occur more frequently during the middle and last thirds of the process, generally with little difference in relative frequencies between the middle and last quarters. This latter trend could be regarded as not unexpected especially in the case of untimed tasks.

The transition behaviors of the respective pairs of criterion groups during the above specified three parts of the problem solving process were compared. The transitions to each of the 18 behavior categories of the solvers, fast workers, and high IQ subjects during the beginning third of the total problem solving period were compared with the transitions to these behavior categories of nonsolvers, slow subjects, and low IQ subjects for the identical proportion of total problem solving time by a 2×18 contingency table comparison for each task. In the same manner the patterns of transitions during the middle and end thirds were compared. The probability (p) values obtained in these comparisons by χ^2 tests with 17 degrees of freedom are presented in Table 12.7.

Although Table 12.7 contains a number of statistically significant ($p \leqslant$ .05) differences, particularly resulting from the comparisons of high IQ subjects with low IQ subjects, it was seen as more advisable, at this stage, not to emphasize these findings, but rather to restrict the discussion to a broader interpretation of a number of possible trends suggested by the table. A number of consistencies were revealed by the comparisons of problem solving transitions over time. Three patterns in particular seemed to suggest themselves, the type of pattern most likely being determined to a large degree by characteristics of the task itself.

Table 12.7 shows that, even in tasks where the transition differences between the comparison groups within the time periods studied failed to reach significance, divergencies between the groups under investigation varied in size.

One type of pattern (A) shows a consistent increase in the value of χ^2 between the beginning and end thirds of the process, which is reflected in the decrease in size of the p values presented in Table 12.7. This trend might be interpreted, for example, in the comparison of the processes of

TABLE 12.6
Percentages of Transitions to Each of 18 Behavior Categories During the Beginning, Middle and End Third of the Problem Solving Periods

Time Period	1	2	3	4	5	6	7	8	9	10	11	12	13	14	15	16	17	18
												Transition to Behavior						
1/3	31.3	6.9	7.7	3.3	2.0	0	9.5	0.7	8.0	3.9	17.4	0.7	0.7	0.5	1.9	2.9	2.6	0
2/3	0.3	5.7	5.9	1.2	1.2	0	18.6	4.9	17.5	6.2	26.1	1.2	1.4	0.7	2.4	4.1	2.5	0.2
3/3	0.1	2.8	2.4	0.2	0.7	0	16.3	7.2	10.1	9.7	31.6	1.7	1.6	2.0	3.1	7.5	2.4	0.6
1/3	6.7	5.3	4.4	3.9	2.5	0.1	21.5	22.0	0.2	10.8	1.2	0.8	1.6	0.9	1.5	11.7	2.4	2.4
2/3	0	2.3	1.8	0.9	1.6	0.1	23.1	20.5	0.8	19.8	1.0	0.6	2.5	1.2	1.3	19.3	1.5	1.4
3/3	0	1.6	0.9	0.5	1.3	0.5	21.1	19.3	1.2	21.7	1.3	1.2	1.4	3.0	3.1	16.9	2.4	2.5
1/3	31.6	1.3	7.6	1.6	1.0	0.3	11.8	0	0	1.3	19.1	2.0	9.5	2.3	4.3	1.0	4.3	1.0
2/3	1.6	0.7	4.6	0.3	0	0	8.9	2.6	1.0	2.0	53.8	4.9	7.9	2.0	3.6	4.6	0.7	1.0
3/3	1.3	0	1.8	0.3	0	0	3.5	3.3	1.0	0.3	66.8	2.3	2.8	3.0	3.0	9.5	0.3	1.0
1/3	80.4	8.1	3.3	2.1	1.6	0.1	1.2	0	0	0.2	0.1	0.2	0.5	0.9	0	0.5	0.2	0.3
2/3	18.5	24.5	11.0	3.6	7.1	0.7	15.1	0.4	0	5.6	0.3	1.5	1.1	2.2	1.0	5.2	2.0	0.4
3/3	2.5	19.8	6.7	3.2	6.3	1.9	22.0	0.7	0.1	14.1	0.1	2.3	4.0	6.4	2.2	6.1	1.5	0
1/3	46.5	26.5	4.7	6.8	1.7	0.1	3.3	0.2	0	0.8	0.1	0.4	4.8	0.5	0.6	1.3	1.3	0.5
2/3	0.9	25.6	8.7	7.0	4.9	0.8	17.7	0.6	0.2	9.5	0.2	1.7	9.8	2.6	1.7	5.9	1.2	0.8
3/3	0.3	12.6	4.7	2.8	4.4	1.1	20.4	1.4	0.7	21.9	0.8	2.2	5.5	6.9	1.5	11.7	0.7	0.3
1/3	7.0	6.6	5.1	9.5	2.9	0.5	17.1	18.7	0.1	9.5	2.4	1.1	0.8	2.0	1.8	11.8	1.9	1.1
2/3	0.1	2.7	3.6	2.0	2.2	0.5	24.4	22.9	0.4	13.1	1.6	0.9	1.7	1.9	2.1	17.7	1.1	1.0
3/3	0.3	1.6	1.5	2.1	0.9	1.1	21.6	17.8	1.0	17.2	1.2	1.8	2.3	3.8	3.8	19.5	1.3	1.2
1/3	12.4	25.1	2.5	8.7	2.5	0	15.7	5.7	0.2	9.7	0.4	0.2	0.2	1.8	1.9	8.8	3.5	0.6
2/3	0.2	12.5	3.3	3.2	1.9	0.2	22.9	11.2	0.2	17.5	1.9	0.6	1.2	3.6	3.9	13.8	1.2	0.6
3/3	0.1	8.4	1.9	1.7	2.2	0.8	20.5	13.0	0.5	16.9	0.5	1.4	1.7	4.9	4.5	18.4	2.3	0.2
1/3	9.3	11.6	1.7	10.8	0	3.9	15.2	0.2	13.6	3.0	18.5	0.8	1.5	0.5	2.2	3.4	3.0	0.8
2/3	0.3	3.5	1.7	4.0	0.2	4.0	12.4	1.7	17.3	5.2	29.5	2.7	4.5	2.5	1.5	5.0	3.0	0.8
3/3	0.3	1.4	0.6	2.9	0	4.9	10.1	2.6	21.8	9.3	26.5	2.4	2.4	3.1	2.3	6.1	2.4	0.9
1/3	7.9	2.7	1.9	6.5	0.2	3.5	8.8	0	22.5	5.6	25.1	2.1	1.9	1.2	0.2	6.0	2.7	1.3
2/3	0.2	1.0	1.3	1.1	0	6.9	16.4	1.7	16.8	12.0	28.1	1.7	2.3	2.9	0.2	3.2	4.0	0.2
3/3	0	0.8	0.5	0.2	0	2.2	13.0	1.7	24.9	11.0	24.9	3.5	1.3	2.5	2.8	4.5	4.5	1.8
1/3	6.8	3.6	3.8	4.7	0.2	1.1	12.4	0	23.7	1.9	20.5	2.8	3.6	1.5	2.6	4.1	3.6	3.2
2/3	0.2	2.3	0.4	2.1	0.6	2.1	12.6	1.0	25.4	7.8	25.4	2.1	2.1	4.6	1.5	6.5	2.1	1.3
3/3	0.4	1.1	0.7	0.5	0.4	2.1	12.7	1.2	29.2	8.6	19.6	1.6	2.7	1.8	3.7	5.3	4.6	3.7
1/3	4.4	3.7	3.5	1.2	0.2	2.9	12.7	0	29.3	4.0	21.8	1.0	4.0	1.3	3.1	2.9	2.9	1.2
2/3	0.4	1.1	1.0	0.4	0	1.5	15.1	1.1	26.1	6.9	33.5	1.1	3.4	1.5	1.7	4.0	0.6	0.4
3/3	0.3	0.5	0.5	0.3	0	1.1	11.1	2.6	28.2	7.4	28.5	1.0	1.6	2.4	4.8	6.6	2.3	0.6
1/3	19.7	9.8	9.8	4.3	1.9	0.5	19.1	1.2	0.3	15.5	0.5	0.9	4.1	3.1	0.8	5.1	2.5	0.9
2/3	0	5.9	4.5	3.5	1.9	1.5	27.6	4.5	1.1	25.1	0.7	0.3	3.3	4.4	0.9	12.0	2.0	0.8
3/3	0	3.5	2.4	1.2	1.5	0.9	24.0	5.6	0.1	32.4	0.7	1.3	4.4	3.9	2.6	12.3	2.6	0.6

310

TABLE 12.7

Probability Values (p) Obtained in the χ^2 Comparisons of Each Pair of Criterion Groups During the Beginning, Middle and End Third of Problem-Solving

Task	Competence				Time				IQ			
	1/3 p	2/3 p	3/3 p	Patt	1/3 p	2/3 p	3/3 p	Patt	1/3 p	2/3 p	3/3 p	Patt
1	.95	.92	.65	A	.02	.14	.24	B	.03	.99	.28	C
2	.54	.99	.79		.57	.99	.99	B	.72	.93	.93	B
3	.09	.77	.16	C	<.001	.18	.13		<.001	<.001	.01	
4	.99	.98	.91		.43	<.001	.99		.99	.73	.58	A
5	.99	.56	.86	A	.16	.88	.98	B	.04	.004	.96	
6	.99	.92	.72		.55	1.00	.99		.35	.12	.52	
7	.99	.99	.03	A	.04	.97	.95		.002	.97	.67	
8	.85	.45	.15	C	.01	.54	.75	B	.003	<.001	.003	
9	.29	.53	.13	C	.21	.97	.73		.003	<.001	.02	
10	.31	.59	.04	B	.02	.09	.04	C	<.001	.35	.68	B
11	.11	.26	.84	B	.78	.98	.66	C	.15	<.001	<.001	A
12	.61	.52	.95		.15	.95	.94		.22	.60	.88	B

solvers and nonsolvers in Task 8 [Poem/Statue] and in the high versus low IQ comparisons in Task 4 [Pebbles], as a suggestion that in the latter case high and low IQ subjects start off the solving process in similar ways, and that differences characterizing either group become more discernible as the problem solving process continues. This finding cannot be explained as a summation effect over the total period of problem solving time, as each third of the total period was investigated separately, and the numbers of transition behaviors in the cells which are compared here were equal.

Another type of pattern, pattern (B), seems to be the converse of pattern (A). Pattern (B) describes a consistently decreasing value of χ^2, hence an increase in the size of the probability value *(p),* which could be interpreted as an indication that after a different beginning, the problem solving behaviors of the comparison groups seem to become more similar. The problem solving process trends in Tasks 11 [Wood/Alcohol], 12 [8TB/2] of solvers versus nonsolvers, Tasks 5 [Platform] and 8 [Poem/Statue] for fast versus slow workers, and Tasks 10 [Fly/Tree] and 12 [8TB/2] are examples for pattern (B). In these tasks it was observed that the problem solving processes of the comparison groups differed at the beginning, and became more and more similar as problem solving proceeded.

Another pattern noted in Table 12.7 suggests that in some tasks the problem solving processes of the respective criterion groups were similar in the beginning and end thirds of the process, and that during the middle period of the total problem solving time, the comparison groups tended to differ most. The converse of this latter pattern was discernible also.

While the above presented broad description of trends does not provide a stringent test, the results of the present exploratory study would seem to have provided some evidence which would suggest that differences can be identified in the overall patterns of transitions over time for the criterion groups. More detailed analyses of the trends described in this section were performed in the investigation of research question 2(c).

c. *The Relative Contribution of Specific Behavior Transitions over Time*

The research question investigated here can be stated as follows: "Is there a difference in the relative contribution of each transition behavior to changes in the response patterns of the respective criterion groups over time?"

While research question 2(b) investigated the overall differences in the trends of transition behaviors over time, question (c) led to the investigation of which specific types of problem solving behavior change. In this way it became possible to determine whether the same transition behaviors contributed differentially over time, or whether different transitions tended to contribute to overall change during different stages of the problem solving process.

To investigate research question 2(c), the percentages of transitions to each of the 18 behavior categories out of the total number of transitions in the beginning, middle, and end third respectively, were tabulated for each task and for each criterion group. The frequency patterns of transitions were compared for each time period for each pair of criterion groups. Few of the χ^2 values reached significance at $p = .05$. The degree to which specific transition behaviors contributed to change in strategy use over time appeared to be task specific.

COMPARISON OF THE SHIFTS IN PROBLEM SOLVING BEHAVIORS AND THE RELATIVE AMOUNTS OF REPETITIVE BEHAVIORS

This section reports the results of investigations of possible differences between solvers and nonsolvers, fast and slow workers, and high and low IQ subjects respectively, in the relative amounts of time spent in repetitive behaviors.

The transition behaviors contained in the diagonal cells of the transition matrices were compared for solvers and nonsolvers, fast and slow workers, and high and low IQ subjects respectively by means of a χ^2 test for each task and pair of criterion groups.

Table 12.8 shows the percentages of behaviors accounted for in the diagonal cells, i.e., repetitive behaviors, for each task and criterion group.

Perusal of Table 12.8 shows that on the average, across all tasks, between 55 and 60% of all transition behaviors were accounted for in the diagonal cells in all three pairs of criterion groups. The fact that slightly less repetitive behavior was observed in Tasks 10 [Fly/Tree] and 11 [Wood/Alcohol] and on the average more than 55 to 60% of repetitive behavior occurred in Tasks 1 [Binet], 4 [Pebbles], and 5 [Platform] suggests that shorter tasks might elicit less repetitive behavior than longer tasks, and might, in fact, be accounted for by the longer stimulus passages of the latter tasks.

In a number of tasks the tendency can be observed that solvers, fast workers, and high IQ subjects spent a smaller proportion of their problem solving period engaged in repetitive behavior, than did nonsolvers, slow workers, and low IQ subjects respectively. Across all tasks these differences were not found to be significant.

The findings presented in Table 12.8, showing that on the average approximately 60% of all behavior transitions fall into the diagonal cells, suggest that for all subjects (irrespective of level of competence, speed of

TABLE 12.8
Comparative Percentages of Repetitive Behaviors Summarized
Across All Behavior Categories

Task	Competence		Time		Measured IQ	
	Solvers	Nonsolvers	Fast	Slow	High	Low
1	60.72	62.75	60.83	62.24	56.29	62.54
2	60.22	58.72	55.78	60.08	59.68	57.82
3	57.28	59.18	56.68	58.14	54.90	60.39
4	72.23	72.37	76.23	70.49	71.00	72.36
5	59.55	64.94	64.73	63.54	61.47	64.90
6	51.62	56.60	54.05	56.10	52.35	55.43
7	56.14	54.64	52.91	55.49	56.91	53.21
8	52.80	57.20	43.85	57.50	53.91	54.37
9	52.76	58.29	52.26	57.84	55.66	55.35
10	46.40	52.92	39.01	52.18	51.89	51.38
11	43.58	51.89	47.98	51.19	43.23	56.27
12	62.07	56.77	58.85	56.82	58.68	56.97
$\bar{x}$	56.28	58.86	55.26	58.47	56.33	58.42
SD	7.63	5.63	9.72	5.21	6.57	5.84
χ^2 $df11$	1.70		3.61		2.23	
p	$>.05$		$>.05$		$>.05$	

work, or level of measured intelligence) in whatever type of problem solving behavior they happen to be engaged, it is most likely that this type of behavior will be repeated in the subsequent three-second period. This finding, if replicated in other studies, can be expected to have important pedagogical implications.

The finding that sequential problem solving behaviors have such a high probability of being repetitive does not mean, however, that the probabilities of transitions to a different behavior would be the same for each behavior category. The latter subject will be discussed in a later section of this chapter.

While the summary of repetitive transitions presented in Table 12.8 and the above discussion might, at first glance, appear to suggest that there may be no difference in the amounts of repetitive behaviors displayed by the different groups, it must be noted that this observation relates to differences in the relative amounts of time spent in the repetition of specific behaviors, rather than to the number of transitions summed over all specific behavior categories.

The investigation of differences between the respective pairs of the criterion groups in the relative amounts of time spent in repetitive behaviors therefore again needs to consider the nature of the differences between the groups.

A first step in the attempt to reveal aspects of the nature of these differences was to briefly investigate the occurrences of repetitive behaviors at different temporal stages of the problem solving process, following the finding that there is such a high probability of sequential behaviors being repetitive across the problem solving process as a whole.

Tables 12.9, 12.10, and 12.11 show the comparative percentages of repetitive behaviors, summarized across all behavior categories during the beginning, middle, and end thirds of problem solving for solvers versus nonsolvers, fast versus slow workers, and high IQ versus low IQ subjects respectively.

Inspection of these tables shows that irrespective of the criterion by which the subjects were grouped, repetitive behaviors accounted on the average for between 52 and 60% of all behavior transitions across the 12 tasks. As noted in the discussion of Table 12.8, representing the comparative percentages of repetitive behaviors for the total problem solving period, shorter tasks appeared to elicit less repetitive behavior than longer tasks.

Solvers, fast workers, and high IQ subjects appeared to display less repetitive behavior during each of the three parts of the problem solving process than their counterparts, but apart from the performances of high

TABLE 12.9
Comparative Percentages of Repetitive Behaviors During the Beginning, Middle and End Thirds Summarized Across All Behavior Categories for Solvers and Nonsolvers

Task	Beginning Third Solvers	Nonsolvers	Middle Third Solvers	Nonsolvers	End Third Solvers	Nonsolvers
1	64.8	65.4	56.0	64.0	27.7	34.2
2	57.3	58.6	58.1	58.1	65.0	59.4
3	54.1	56.9	47.4	55.4	67.6	62.1
4	91.6	89.9	65.9	66.6	59.3	60.3
5	75.3	77.6	57.7	59.4	45.5	57.9
6	50.5	53.0	51.6	59.3	52.7	57.8
7	53.5	55.2	56.9	53.5	57.0	55.5
8	53.7	50.4	55.4	57.6	52.9	63.5
9	44.7	52.1	58.1	61.0	55.0	61.4
10	39.9	44.3	43.8	58.0	53.4	56.6
11	26.0	46.6	46.2	54.3	50.7	54.4
12	58.6	60.3	59.2	55.0	67.5	55.0
$\bar{x}$	55.8	59.2	54.7	58.5	54.5	56.5
SD	16.7	13.1	6.3	3.9	10.9	7.6
χ^2	5.82		3.18		5.31	
p	$df11$ >.05		>.05		>.05	

versus low IQ subjects and fast versus slow workers in the middle third, these differences were not significant statistically ($p > .05$).

These trends are again similar to those noted in the investigation of the total problem solving period as one unit.

The statistically significant differences which were observed in the middle period of problem solving activity between fast and slow workers, and between high and low IQ subjects seem to be due to differences in the variability of the proportions of repetitive behaviors within the relevant groups, as represented by the differences in the size of the standard deviations. The standard deviations for slow workers and low IQ subjects were considerably smaller ($SD_S = 3.4$; $SD_{LIQ} = 3.9$) than those of fast workers ($SD = 16.7$) and high IQ subjects ($SD = 13.4$). This means that fast workers and high IQ subjects varied the amounts of repetitive behaviors during the middle period of the problem solving process, possibly in keeping with the requirements of different tasks, while slow workers and low IQ subjects generally tended to display more repetitive sequences of behavior categories 1 (Code 111: First reading), 2 (Code 112: Rereading), 8 (Code 212: Trial and Error), and 11 (Code 219: Calculation/Detail), while high IQ subjects tended to be more repetitive in behaviors 7 (Code 211: Plan/Hypothesis), 10 (Code 215: Continuing activity), and 16 (Code 400: Judgment/Verification).

In all tasks, with the exception of Task 10 [Fly/Tree], in which the number of behavior transitions within the same behavior categories by high IQ subjects, did not differ significantly ($p > .05$) from that of the low IQ subjects, the time spent in repetitive behaviors by solvers, fast workers, and high IQ subjects differed significantly ($p \le .01$) from that of nonsolvers, slow workers, and low IQ subjects respectively. These findings suggest that there are differences between the respective pairs of criterion groups in the relative amounts of time spent in repetitive behaviors.

Perusal of Tables 12.9, 12.10, and 12.11 shows that differences in the pattern of repetitive behavior were to a large extent dependent on specific task requirements. It is obvious, however, that in many tasks solvers, fast workers, and high IQ subjects showed different patterns in the distribution of frequencies of repetitive behavior in stimulus passage oriented and solution oriented responses than their counterparts. Nonsolvers, slow workers, and low IQ subjects tended to have more repetitions of behavior 17 (Code 500: Pause) than solvers, fast workers, and high IQ subjects. This finding was noted earlier in this chapter, when the comparisons of the overall transition matrices were discussed.

The finding that the differences in amounts of repetitive behaviors between the pairs of the criterion groups, though significant, were not very large, may be explained by the fact that the sample in the present study was relatively homogeneous. Again it must be remembered that the pres-

TABLE 12.10

Comparative Percentages of Repetitive Behaviors During the Beginning,
Middle and End Thirds Summarized Across All Behavior Categories for
Fast and Slow Workers

Task	Beginning Third		Middle Third		End Third	
	Fast	Slow	Fast	Slow	Fast	Slow
1	72.9	63.2	58.9	61.2	49.0	62.0
2	59.5	58.0	70.9	60.4	56.2	61.6
3	68.5	50.8	32.8	54.2	58.5	69.0
4	97.5	87.3	74.1	63.0	57.2	61.5
5	82.9	75.2	59.5	58.8	52.0	57.1
6	55.5	51.4	93.7	59.1	53.2	57.7
7	56.1	54.4	53.5	54.4	49.0	57.8
8	39.2	53.0	41.6	60.1	49.7	59.3
9	42.9	52.1	58.5	60.4	53.8	61.4
10	32.7	44.3	39.1	54.1	40.3	58.2
11	33.7	46.6	49.8	54.0	58.0	52.4
12	61.1	60.1	58.6	53.9	56.3	56.1
$\bar{x}$	58.5	58.0	57.6	57.8	52.8	59.5
SD	19.9	12.3	16.7	3.4	5.2	4.1
χ^2 _df11_	11.22		21.06^1		3.98	
p	> .05		< .05		> .05	

[1] Critical values of χ^2 with 11 df are 19.68 and 24.72 at $a = .05$ and $a = .01$ respectively.

ent study is an exploratory one only. However, the differentiation between the criterion groups which was obtained in the present study
indicates that further replications of the study with more extreme groups
are warranted and might be expected to reveal larger differences.

SUMMARY

The aim in the present chapter was to attempt to investigate some of the
contingencies and interdependencies of problem solving behaviors as
they occur in sequence during the problem solving process. The analyses
which were performed were highly exploratory. They must therefore be
regarded as providing a beginning only in the investigation of the nature of
performance differences in problem solving on the basis of sequential
aspects of the process.

The results of the analyses described in this chapter further support the
findings presented in the preceding results chapters. Twelve tasks of varying content, length, and difficulty yielded data which identify processes
which account for differences in speed of work, and problem solving
achievement. Such process variables also account for differences in measured intelligence in seven of the tasks.

TABLE 12.11

Comparative Percentages of Repetitive Behaviors During the Beginning,
Middle and End Thirds Summarized Across All Behavior Categories for
High and Low IQ Subjects

Task	Beginning Third High	Low	Middle Third High	Low	End Third High	Low
1	65.2	72.1	54.8	59.9	56.1	54.8
2	60.0	60.4	57.5	57.3	61.1	55.5
3	72.3	54.1	11.2	55.4	55.6	70.7
4	87.3	93.4	62.6	60.3	63:0	63.0
5	70.8	82.3	56.3	64.5	56.8	48.2
6	48.2	53.1	54.4	60.4	53.4	56.9
7	53.9	55.2	56.1	50.5	59.7	53.5
8	48.0	48.3	55.2	63.7	57.3	51.9
9	50.0	47.9	58.8	59.0	56.3	56.9
10	44.5	36.0	54.1	58.9	52.5	58.3
11	34.6	48.3	48.5	59.6	42.3	60.2
12	59.0	64.5	58.3	53.8	58.3	51.8
$\bar{x}$	57.8	59.6	52.3	58.6	56.0	56.8
SD	14.4	16.2	13.4	3.9	5.3	5.9
χ^2 $df11$	7.41		28.71[1]		7.26	
p	>.05		<.05		>.05	

[1] Critical values of χ^2 with 11 df are 19.68 and 24.72 at $\alpha = .05$ and $\alpha = .01$ respectively.

Nonsolvers and slow workers produced considerably more behavior transitions than did solvers and fast workers. In the tasks in which significant differences between high and low IQ subjects were observed, the latter group produced considerably more transitions than the former. These findings parallel those discussed in Chapter 9.

The findings discussed in this chapter show that observed performance differences in problem solving can be accounted for not only in terms of certain structural components of the process, but that they may be accounted for also by the dynamics of the process, i.e., by the sequential patterns in which the structural components of the problem solving process occur. An interesting set of findings was presented by the observation that the component behaviors making up the problem solving processes, which were identified as discriminating between the processes of solvers and nonsolvers, fast and slow subjects, and high and low IQ subjects respectively, were preceded by different problem solving behaviors in the different criterion groups. The relative contribution of specific behavior sequences was found to be task dependent.

Another important finding was that, on the average, close to 60% of all transition behaviors were to behaviors of the same category, in other words, repetitive behaviors. In a number of tasks solvers, fast workers, and high IQ subjects were found to spend a smaller proportion of their problem solving time in repetitive behaviors than did nonsolvers, slow workers, and low IQ subjects respectively. However, in general— irrespective of level of competence, intelligence, or speed, and irrespective of the type of task and the particular problem solving behavior—the tendency was that it was most likely for a problem solving behavior to be repeated in the immediately following three-second unit. This finding, if it can be replicated, can be expected to have important educational implications.

The results of the exploratory analyses described in this chapter suggest the need for further studies of the nature of performance differences in process terms. The here presented speculative attempts to investigate differences in the sequential patterns of the behaviors and strategies making up the problem solving process need to be extended to the investigation of behavior sequences of varying lengths throughout the problem solving processes of subjects with varying characteristics.

The superficial investigation of the beginning, middle, and end thirds of the process constitute an initial attempt only. An obvious next step would be to try to identify and characterize certain blocks of operations which are qualitatively separated. Previous research and the initial findings in the present study suggest, for example, blocks relating to stimulus passage oriented behaviors, i.e., concerned with the processes of representation of the task, and solution oriented behaviors. Such blocks can be expected to occur separately or intertwined (Hayes & Simon, 1974). The role of relationships between heuristics and complex processes over time, and many other dimensions of the dynamics of the problem solving process are awaiting further investigation.

CONCLUSIONS

13 Conclusions and Implications

The content of this book has been presented in four parts. The first of these traces theoretical and methodological developments in the areas of intelligence and problem solving. Conceptual frameworks for the non-cumulative research literature in both domains are provided and ways in which research relating to individual differences in problem solving might contribute to the development of process related theories of intelligence are suggested. The second part of the book describes and discusses all aspects of the research methodology and organization of an empirical study of component processes of intellectual performance, and the development of a taxonomy of problem solving operations. A report on the reliability of the taxonomy and the chapters presenting the findings of the study based on converging methods of data analysis are contained in the third part.

In this final chapter, some conclusions and implications of the study are presented. After a restatement of the aim of the book, a general discussion of the design and methodology, and a summary of major findings, certain implications of the investigation for theory, research, and training are discussed.

THE AIM

The purpose of this book is to make a contribution to the understanding of problem solving and intelligence. All scientific endeavor combines two ingredients: theory and empirical evidence. One is unproductive without the other. Both are necessary for advances in knowledge and understanding.

This book is concerned with the existing body of theoretical knowledge as reflected in the extensive but fragmented literature, and with empirical evidence. In addition to this, it is concerned with alternatives in the means by which these ingredients can be combined, i.e., methodology.

The aim of the empirical study is to seek an explanation for generally observed, and accepted performance differences in the cognitive process itself; not in its outcomes, in correlates of performance, or in models of the nervous system.

The majority of previous research in both the areas of intelligence and problem solving has emphasized the products of problem solving. The nature of the processes that lead to the end product has been investigated less frequently.

The assessment, description, and evaluation of intellectual performance, competence, and educational achievement have traditionally been, and continue largely to be, based on outcome measures of processes, the contents of which are basically undefined. Psychological testing and the assessment of educational achievement have been based on the established psychometric tradition of determining individual differences. Psychometric approaches have essentially provided empirically based methods with few theoretical conceptions concerning the characteristics of either the subject matter tested or the psychological processes operating in the testees. Teachers as well as psychologists have, by virtue of whatever notion they might have about such concepts as intelligence, logical thinking, reasoning, cognitive skill and achievement, relied largely on experience and intuition in inferring the characteristics of human performance and capability on the basis of the results from psychometric tests.

It is undeniable that psychometrics has made a useful contribution to the development of scientific theory concerning human abilities, since the demonstration of individual differences in performance outcomes on a task is a necessary, though not sufficient, condition for the association between such abilities and test results.

In the physical sciences, it has always been acknowledged that the concrete definition of a concept becomes possible only if the concept is linked with a specific method of observation or measurement. Without this, the concept cannot contribute to the description or understanding of concrete physical phenomena. This postulation is not restricted to the investigation of physical phenomena but is of equal importance for the behavioral sciences, particularly for psychology and education. To suggest that certain competences or reasoning abilities have been developed in individuals while lacking methods for their identification, description, and analysis makes no sense. Therefore, the development of methods for the recognition, adequate operational definition, analysis, and eventual manipulation of skills and abilities constitutes an important challenge to those involved in psychological research.

While the attempted marriage between experimental psychology and psychometrics contributed a more theoretical orientation to the analysis of human abilities, the theorizing resulting from such research has been somewhat constrained on the one hand by the simplicity and lack of translatability of many laboratory type tasks, and on the other by the diversity and undefinability of ability factors identified in psychometric research. What tended to be ignored was that both the experimental investigation and the psychometric analysis of aspects of human intellectual functioning would require a more comprehensive investigation of systems of variables which can represent the major sources of variation affecting performance.

As was stated in Chapter 1, it was felt that an investigation concerned with the question of how people solve problems must be conducted within a framework which takes into consideration variables from at least three major domains, namely the psychological mechanisms that operate during the subject's attempt to solve the problem, individual differences, and characteristics of the task. Although the adequacy of the representation of variables from these domains might be questionable, and perhaps adequate representation is not possible at present, the research design of the empirical study reported in this book succeeded in providing a valid initial indication of the diversity and complexity of the variables which might interact in human problem solving, and of their relation to intelligence, speed, achievement and level of education.

The expectation was that a monitoring of problem solving behaviors and strategies used by subjects as they attempt to reach a solution to a given task may provide insights into the psychological mechanisms of the problem solving process, and that knowledge about problem solving processes gained in this manner could lead to instructional procedures which might result in the improvement of intellectual performance. This latter expectation is in keeping with developments during the past decade in theoretical and empirical research concerning the measurement of abilities and cognition, which emphasize the malleability and functional development of human behavior, including cognitive skills.

DESIGN AND METHODOLOGY

Four chapters of this book are devoted to introductions and discussions of significant methodological aspects of the empirical study of problem solving as a process. It is often noted that methodology is merely a tool of research. Broadly conceived, it is more than that. The methodology provides the basis on which the validity of the research findings can be evaluated. Methodology is thus a fundamental and crucial component of the research process.

Unfortunately, the involvement of particular component processes during cognitive performance cannot be demonstrated as readily as can the effect of operationally defined experimental manipulation. The processes constituting the performance itself tend not to be directly observable. The first task in the present study was thus to find a methodology which would make it possible to identify and monitor valid elements of the problem solving process.

A promising tactic appeared to be to generate data by means of the "thinking aloud" technique, and to analyze the complete problem solving protocols for each subject and task in terms of sequential three-second unit segments of the performance.

The "thinking aloud" protocols of 89 subjects, each of whom attempted to solve 12 different tasks, were analyzed with the aim of obtaining information regarding the problem solving process. The problem solving process was defined in terms of the interaction between three major sets of variables: the task, the subject, and the problem solving behaviors used by the subjects.

Preferred problem solving behaviors and behavior sequences were related to the criterion variables of competence, speed, IQ estimate, and level of schooling.

The representation of the problem solving process as an interaction of three sets of variables suggested itself on the basis of a thorough examination of the research literature, most of which, as shown in Chapters 2 and 3, appeared to have emphasized some or all of these dimensions of problem solving and intelligence, but investigated them separately. The method of data collection, protocol analysis, was derived from research within the framework of information processing, and was inspired particularly by the work of Newell and Simon (1972). The use of the three-second time segment as the unit of analysis was based on the results of educational research, particularly that of Flanders during the 1960s.

A way of testing the generality of the identified components of the problem solving process was to compare their applicability across a variety of different tasks. It was not assumed that the same set of operations or strategies would characterize performances on all tasks. Also, it was envisaged that individuals might show preferences for certain operations in particular tasks or more generally. The major benefit resulting from the use of a diversity of tasks was that it led to repeated observations of performance in different stimulus situations, and that it allowed the investigation of strategy–task relationships and subject–strategy–task interactions.

The subjects used in the present study were an unselected group of young adults at various levels of schooling. Another approach to the selection of subjects would have been to follow former information processing studies which analyzed the structure of problem solving performance by comparing the responses of experts and nonexperts. Although the latter research designs yielded valuable information about problem solving processes, they have significant limitations. First, one cannot assume that experts would necessarily perform with optimal efficiency. Also, if a better understanding of the process of problem solving is to lead to practical intervention, process-oriented training programs must do more than teach individuals to perform as experts do. For example, novices at a task or procedure must often be taught to use explicit procedural steps which experts perform almost automatically because their behavior repertoire contains strategy patterns resulting from long or frequent experience.

The group of 89 subjects who completed all 12 tasks in the present study was small enough to investigate thoroughly, yet large and diverse enough in problem solving competence, measured intelligence, and speed of problem solving to provide reasonable credibility as to the significance of the findings and the possibility of their more general applicability.

The methodology utilized provides a suitable means for the study of both the processes taking place during the performance of problem solving of particular individuals, and of the characteristics of groups. Thus, the study does not enter the realm of the old controversy concerning ideographic versus nomothetic research. Whether the immediate focus is on the cognitive performance of an individual or a group, this methodology allows the same rigor to be applied to data collection and analysis.

The subjects' "thinking aloud" protocols were analyzed in relation to the research questions raised in the study, and, more generally, to obtain information about the structure and the relationship between components of the problem solving process.

The information processing framework leads to a consideration of the problem solving process as an activity, a set of behaviors by means of which the subject comprehends and solves not only the overall problem posed to him or her, but also parts of the total problem or subproblems which impede the solution of the total problem. The appropriateness of the behaviors or strategies which the problem solver applies were expected to depend, to some degree, on the task, the problem solver's competence, speed of work, intelligence, and interactions between these. An understanding of the influence of such variables as intelligence, problem solving competence, and speed on the problem solving process seems crucial for the identification of sources of difficulties in problem solving, and for the development of procedures aimed at increasing problem solving efficiency.

To investigate what kinds of operations and strategies enable individuals to achieve high, fast, and efficient intellectual performance, the problem solving behaviors of solvers and nonsolvers, high and low IQ subjects, and fast and slow workers, were compared. Another factor of interest was the relationship of years of schooling to problem solving behaviors. The problem solving processes of subjects operating at different levels of education were compared.

Intelligence levels, obtained from performance on reputable IQ tests, have been assumed to affect all cognitive behavior; but little supporting research has been published in recent years. In fact, increasing doubts are expressed concerning the validity and reliability of psychometric tests, mainly because of the lack of research supporting the constructs postulated by them and the lack of research into the processes underlying performance on intelligence tests. Individual differences in such variables as speed of work and problem solving achievement have rarely, if ever, been related to components of the problem solving process itself.

A suitable taxonomy for the classification of problem solving strategies had to be developed. The initial plan had been to develop a taxonomy on the basis of the problem solving behaviors repeatedly investigated in the previous psychological literature. The results of a pilot study led to the recognition that a large number of the responses could not be directly translated into behaviors discussed in the research literature, while the latter contained many concepts which were not easily reconcilable with empirical data. It was decided, therefore, to produce a taxonomy on the basis of the empirical data.

This decision may prove advantageous for future research, as it allows for the inclusion of increasingly diverse and differentiated problem solving behaviors of particular individuals or groups, and is applicable to new types of tasks.

The choice of the 18 "summary" variables investigated thoroughly in the present study was guided by a desire initially to focus on characteristic descriptive variables, the utilization of which could be quantified in such a way that comparable quantities indicated comparable degrees of importance of the variables in relation to different tasks, and for different individuals. Although one can not be certain that this was achieved, it is highly probable that a reasonable approximation was made in the analyses of percentage data. Inter-rater agreement was extremely high, and there were strong consistencies as well as explainable differences between tasks.

From the point of view of the investigator, one of the major contributions of the present study may have been the design of a taxonomy of problem solving behaviors which provided a reliable means of presenting actual behaviors which were used by subjects in their attempts to solve a variety of different tasks. It was found that the problem solving behaviors of subjects could be classified on the basis of 18 categories. The taxonomy of problem solving behaviors, used in the present study, reveals information about the problem solving process because the use of these behaviors by subjects provides empirical evidence for the fact that the behaviors constitute components of the problem solving process.

One way to examine the contribution made by the approach utilized in the present study might be to consider the behavior categories contained in the present taxonomy in relation to categories utilized in previous process oriented research.

The taxonomy of problem solving behaviors developed in the present study provides the means for a more comprehensive analysis of the problem solving process than the reports of previous studies seem to reflect. The more comprehensive framework in which the present study was conducted and the utilization of multivariate statistical procedures allowed the examination of problem solving within the context of three key dimensions: the problem solver, the task, and the problem solving behavior. By investigating the problem solving process under varying combinations of variables from these dimensions, some of the effects of selected factors and their interaction could be shown. Although it was found that the basic problem solving processes were similar, the factors under investigation are shown to influence the subjects' preferences for strategies and the variety of strategies used.

As was pointed out in Chapters 2 and 3, previous research tended to focus on selected aspects of intelligence and problem solving in isolation. Intellectual performance is, however, a process in which at least task, subject, and behaviors interact, and the effects of these aspects have to be investigated in combination.

Many process studies which analyze the problem solving process were biased, for example, because they depended on introspection, i.e., they encouraged the subjects to discuss their responses and interpret the meaning of these responses. Other studies used retrospection, in which the subject reports behaviors after the task, or part of it has been completed, rather than while the behavior is occurring. Although the results of previous research concerned with the problem solving process have provided some insights into possible components of the process, their contribution to an understanding of the process as a whole has been limited because of their concentration on aspects of the total process. Researchers have not been able to build on each other's findings because different tasks tended to be used, and because most of the research did not result in the establishment of a more general theoretical model.

A comparison of the content of the taxonomy used in the present study with the behavior and stage concepts considered in previous research reveals that many of the latter variables are, in fact, subsumed under categories in the present taxonomy. The present taxonomy, however, goes beyond the results of previous individual studies, and was shown to account for all of the problem solving behaviors exhibited by the subjects in this study. The present taxonomy, therefore, provides a more comprehensive view of the problem solving process, and, equally importantly, the categories reflect the problem solvers' actual problem solving behaviors.

The major justification for the taxonomy used in the present study is its validity, which resulted from the endeavor to provide a detailed description of problem solvers' actual behaviors and from the fact that the categories were, therefore, developed from empirical data rather than obtained a priori from the research literature or other theoretical systems. The research was exploratory in nature, and the major purpose of the taxonomy was its utility as an initial tool, rather than its accuracy. The taxonomy provides a means for the description of the data collected in this study and is expected to provide a basis for further exploration of the problem solving process. Further empirical studies are required to determine whether different investigators would produce similar categories of problem solving behaviors.

Support for the taxonomy also stems from the similarity of a number of its categories with behavior descriptions found in the research literature. Comparisons were made in Chapter 7, where it was shown, for example, that the stages "preparation," "incubation," and "illumination" have recurred under various labels in the research literature of this century with reliable frequency (see Table 7.1 for examples). "Preparation" and "illumination" behaviors provide a considerable portion of the categories in the present taxonomy, particularly under the summary codes 110, 120 and 220, and 400 respectively. "Incubation" was not used as a category in the present study. The reason for this was that this concept, despite more recent empirical studies (e.g., Dreistadt, 1969; Murray & Denny, 1969; Olton & Johnson, 1976; Silveira, 1972), has not been operationally defined and is, as applied in the Gestalt literature, unlikely to refer to behavior identifiable under conditions set up by the present methodology. By not including the concept, the possibility of its relevance to the problem solving process is not denied. However, it is suggested that introspection or retrospection, rather than "thinking aloud," might be necessary components of a research methodology investigating this concept. As was noted previously, what is observed depends on the position of the observer. The aim in the present study is to investigate the problem solving process in terms of definable behaviors. The "thinking aloud" methodology was chosen as a vehicle for such observation. The choice of vehicle naturally restricts its utility for certain purposes.

In its conceptualization, design, and methodology, the present study built on previous research relating to both intelligence and problem solving. Intellectual performance as a process was investigated within a framework which combines psychometrics with a cognitive theoretical approach.

Newell and Simon's (1972) theoretical framework provided a means of conceptualizing the problem solving process in terms of a set of problem solving behaviors, the orchestration of which is dependent on the problem solver's proficiency, motivation, and task environment. This theoretical framework provided the basis for a more comprehensive approach to the investigation of problem solving than had been available previously.

A major benefit of the comprehensive information processing framework utilized in the present study was that it permitted the investigation of the influence of the interaction of major dimensions of the problem solving process on the problem solver as he or she adapts to the given task environment to accomplish a goal. Within this framework, it became possible for the present study to place a number of important aspects of problem solving into perspective. The problem solver could be observed to employ a behavior or a set of behaviors to meet his goal, and the problem solving behaviors employed during this process could be regarded as reflecting characteristics and constraints of the individual problem solver, his goals, and the task.

To summarize, several advantages of the present research design and methodology over previous approaches seem apparent. By conducting the study in a more comprehensive framework than was available in previous research, it became possible to analyze problem solving in terms of its major dimensions: the subject, the task, and the problem solving process. Previous research had, as was noted earlier, tended to examine these dimensions individually and in separation from one another. By analyzing problem solving in terms of the major sources of variation which influence it, more comprehensive information was obtained about the problem solving process itself, individual differences in the strategies used by subjects, and the behaviors applied by problem solvers when they deal with different types of tasks.

The application of the "thinking aloud" methodology and protocol analysis also provided an advantage over a number of previous studies, which employed introspection, forms of retrospection, "Tab Item" technique, and other more structured methods. As was noted earlier, protocol analysis, as employed in the present study, provided more immediate and reliable information about the problem solvers' behaviors. It preserved the sequence in which the behaviors occurred, and it provided as complete an account of the problem solving process as the subject was able to verbalize.

A major methodological contribution made by the present study might be to foster awareness of the potential of direct analysis of problem solving behaviors to uncover components of problem solving processes. It is suggested that the approach used here might be adapted and extended to other areas of cognitive behavior, for example, to the investigation of the reading, translation, and decision making processes.

MAJOR FINDINGS

The major finding of the present empirical study, which is replicated across subjects and across tasks, is that individual differences in problem solving competence, measured intelligence, speed of performance, and educational attainment—which are usually measured rather than defined on the basis of scores resulting from performance—are reflected in the process of performance itself, i.e., in the actual operations and strategies used by individuals during their work on the task.

In fact, it was shown that process based indices of intellectual functioning may well constitute a superior, and certainly a more sensitive means of assessment of intellectual functioning than traditional outcome measures. For example, levels of educational attainment (measured as years of schooling) of subjects in the study did not evolve as a significant variable in the analysis of global scores of performance outcomes, not even in the types or variety of operations utilized. Yet in the combinations of process variables making up the performance itself, distinct profiles of operations and strategies could be identified for each of the four levels of educational attainment.

The process differences which were identified relate both to certain structural components of the problem solving process, and to the sequential patterns in which certain structural components of the process occur. Other major process differences between subjects grouped on the basis of the above stated criteria relate to the variety of strategies used, and to the amounts of repetitive behaviors they applied in their attempts to solve the tasks. The relative contributions of specific sequences of behaviors appear to be dependent on the task. The discussion comes back to this point later in this chapter.

Although the results of the present study constitute a considerable extension of the understanding of the problem solving process, they contain no unreconcilable discrepancies with the findings of previous, even quite early, investigations of problem solving. Although the latter studies contributed important insights about the problem solving process, their focus on specific aspects of the phenomenon made it difficult to obtain from them a better understanding of the process as a whole. Because of this lack of comprehensiveness and integration, it is difficult, for instance, to decide whether a particular finding represented an effect of problem solving behavior, task characteristics, individual difference factors, or an interaction between any or all of these. The more comprehensive approach of the present study—which includes a taxonomy which is capable of accounting for all problem solving behaviors observed within the methodology chosen for the present study, various types of tasks, and a number of subject characteristics—might allow investigators to begin to formulate broader hypotheses about the problem solving process.

As was pointed out by Miller (1956) and reflected in information processing theories, the behavior repertoire of the problem solver is limited by general human constraints (e.g., short term memory and information transmission rate), and by constraints of his personal ability and experience. The problem solver's competence is reflected by the efficacy with which he or she interprets or anticipates solution requirements of the task and with which effective strategies to achieve a goal are planned and employed. The results of the present study indicate that all subjects planned strategies to solve the problems on the basis of the stimulus passage. It shows, thus, that subjects are able to adapt to the task environment. Newell and Simon postulated that problem solvers form and test hypotheses. Trends observed in the present study suggest that problem solvers form hypotheses, but that they appear to accept them unless they encounter difficulty. In other words, they may be applying their hypotheses in a trial and error fashion.

Newell and Simon's theory harmonizes with the results of the present study. Their theory of problem solving as an information processing system is general and attempts to encompass all problem solving behavior. It focuses on specific facets of the task in order to produce a plausible match, i.e., a computer program which provides an understanding of information processing during problem solving. Newell and Simon and their colleagues have not been concerned with the specification of major facets of the process itself, nor in individual differences. The present study goes further and attempts to present specific evidence as to how the behavior of the subject during problem solving is influenced by the task and various subject characteristics. Newell and Simon's theoretical framework contains the subject, the task, and behavior characteristics, but it does not specify interrelationships between the subject's behaviors and strategies, and such sets of variables as problem solving competence, speed, general intelligence, and the type of task. The present study provides more specific information about the problem solver's process of employing particular behaviors which may be appropriate to a given problem solving situation.

Psychologists and others concerned with the description and prediction of performance and level of ability rely upon the psychometric definition of task difficulty and on its concurrent or content validity to predict the difficulty level of tests. The examination of test items and other tasks in isolation cannot provide information as to the processes subjects, faced with them, will employ. In the present study 12 different tasks were used and the problem solving behaviors applied to them analyzed.

The problem solver's ability to adapt to the task environment, or conversely the influence of the task environment on the problem solving processes employed, was demonstrated as different strategy patterns were observed in relation to different types of tasks. Task similarities were reflected by the similarity of problem solving behaviors applied to them.

Information processing scientists concerned with the process of problem solving both in relation to puzzles (Newell & Simon, 1972) and in relation to real life problems, as discussed in Chapter 3, found that the effectiveness of problem solving performances is crucially dependent on the content and structure of the subject's knowledge about the particular task (Bhaskar & Simon, 1977; Brown & Burton, 1975; Chi, Feltovich, & Glaser, 1981; Chi, Glaser, & Rees, 1981; Greeno, 1978a,b; Reif & Heller, 1982). These and other studies found that the understanding and perception of task structure differed significantly between experts and nonexperts. The results of the present study are consistent with these findings as they showed that some subjects, for example, were better able than others to recognize subproblems, a recognition which was found to facilitate successful solutions. Some individuals solved problems more quickly and more efficiently than others. Solvers used fewer but more effective strategies than nonsolvers. Nonsolvers displayed more stimulus passage oriented behaviors than solvers. Solvers, high IQ subjects, and fast workers used problem solving behaviors which were more task relevant, i.e., efficient, than the strategies applied by nonsolvers, low IQ subjects, and slow workers.

The combination and interaction of simple heuristics and complex operations—direction-related, solution-related, trial and error, hypothesis testing, verification, and other activities—differed in relation to task characteristics, individual differences and in interactions between the latter two variables. Valuable insights were gained not only concerning the similarities and dissimilarities of the process profiles of solvers and nonsolvers, but also from the profiles of those subjects who chose to discontinue tasks prematurely.

Snow (1979) has suggested that individual differences in intelligence can be explained partly in terms of differences in the latencies of the execution of task components, as well as in terms of differences in the choices of components and in strategies used in their combination. Campione and Brown (1979), and Butterfield and Belmont (1977) corroborated this view with findings which suggest that mental retardation can be understood at least in part as a tendency of retarded individuals to select strategies which fail to match task requirements.

In the present study, speed of work was found to be related to estimates of measured intelligence only in the more difficult tasks, while a significant relationship between speed of work and achievement in problem solving was found in the case of easy tasks only.

In the case of more difficult tasks, more intelligent subjects worked faster, irrespective of the correctness of the solution. Solvers worked faster than nonsolvers. These findings support the high positive correlations between speed and the ability to solve complex tasks, which have been quoted in the research literature.

Carroll (1963), Bloom (1974), Glaser (1968) and others found that individuals vary widely in the amounts of time they require to achieve a particular task. It has generally been suggested that the provision of additional time will increase the probability of higher rates of achievement. The results of the present study provide an indication of the value and potential contribution which information processing analyses can make to the investigation of the relationship between time-on-task and achievement. Up to now time-on-task research has largely ignored the cognitive processes which take place during learning or problem solving.

The results of the current study would suggest that time-on-task, rather than being the variable which determines the outcome of problem solving, is itself determined by the appropriateness of the strategies utilized by the problem solver in relation to the requirements of the task.

The process analyses conducted in the present study go some way in providing evidence, previously lacking, for the logical explanation of the frequently replicated speed–success relationship. It was shown that time-on-task is, in fact, determined by the relevance of the problem solving strategies applied by the subject in relation to the requirements of the task. Fast working solvers used a significantly smaller variety of strategies than slow working solvers and nonsolvers. The task relevant and therefore efficient strategies were, in the present study, reflected in the first discriminant functions discussed in Chapter 11.

The principal component analyses which were performed for each task separately showed that approximately 70% of the variance in each of the 12 tasks was accounted for by similar patterns of overall strategy use. Three similar rotated factors were found to occur consistently: a critical reasoning factor, mainly composed of complex reasoning strategies, a stimulus passage or instruction-bound factor consisting largely of heuristic activities, and a factor which loaded to a considerable degree on noncognitive variables. The first two of these factors harmonize with dimensions postulated in recent hierarchical information processing theories, which differentiate explicitly or implicitly between cognitive processes according to the complexity of the operations constituting them. The distinctions of metacognitive and cognitive components of cognition (Brown, 1978; Sternberg, 1977b, 1980a), automated and control processes (Hunt, 1978; Schneider & Shiffrin, 1977), and the factors of heuristics and complex operations identified in the present study, though by no means identical, are sufficiently congruent to become a promising target for further research.

Although noncognitive and environmental sources of variation were ignored in the design of the present study, a third noncognitive factor occurred with some consistency in the process analyses. This provides a strong reminder that intellectual performance and achievement cannot be accounted for by the characteristics of the task requirements and those of cognitive performance alone, but that mediation and/or interference originating from noncognitive sources are always present.

The three–mode factor analysis, by means of which individual and group differences in problem solving strategies could be investigated with simultaneous regard to the characteristics of different tasks, replicated and extended the information concerning the structure of efficient intellectual performance. These analyses, described in Chapter 10, provide a methodology which can identify the sets of problem solving strategies which subjects, described by specific individual differences factors, prefer for different types of tasks with defined characteristics.

Classification analyses based on the results of multiple discriminant functions show high agreement between categorizations made on the basis of traditional outcome measures and those based on profiles of process components.

This set of findings might be interpreted to show that traditional outcome based measures, because they appear to be definable in process terms, may well have a higher validity for classification purposes than has been suggested in recent years. However, a better utilization of these findings would be to suggest that for most purposes process profiles would provide not only a higher level of theoretical explanation and greater validity of measurement—as they can identify which problem solving operations and strategies caused the performance differences—but also that they are of greater diagnostic value for the design of intervention procedures which meet the assessed needs of individuals or particular groups in relation to specifiable intellectual and educational tasks.

A truly process based theory of a complex cognitive activity such as problem solving must explain not only which process components are relevant, but also how the various components combine to produce performance. The structural components of the process, i.e., the operations and strategies used by individuals while engaged in problem solving, represent the building blocks only of the system of the problem solving process. The dynamic components, i.e., the rules on the basis of which the building blocks come together during the cognitive performance, constitute the system.

The discussion in this book has been restricted largely to the structural level. The concern has been with the identification and description of various important types of building blocks and their relationship to various outcomes of performance. Only in the last chapter of the previous section was an attempt made to extend this concern.

A highly superficial first attempt was made to investigate possible groupings of functional sequences which, linked together in appropriate ways, might lead to more successful and more efficient problem solving performance than less appropriate combinations of structural components.

Initial results provided support for the findings presented in previous chapters. Additional findings included the demonstration that, irrespective of level of competence, intelligence, or speed, and irrespective of task and the particular behavior, approximately 60% of all sequential problem solving behaviors were repetitive. However, solvers, fast workers, and high IQ subjects tended to spend a smaller proportion of their problem solving activity in repetitive behaviors than did nonsolvers, slow workers, and low IQ subjects.

Sequential operations of the beginning, middle, and end thirds of the problem solving process were found to differ structurally and quantitatively. Initial indications are that the differences in the outcome of performance, which, in this study, could be accounted for in terms of structural components of the performance itself, might be further defined on the basis of particular patterns of sequential operations.

IMPLICATIONS

Major general implications of the findings of the empirical study include that they may lead to the provision of a more valid basis for the analysis of individual differences in cognitive performance than are being offered by traditional procedures.

The monitoring of developmental changes in strategy use could enhance the study of cognitive growth and learning.

The representation of intellectual performance in terms of operationally defined, malleable problem solving behaviors constitutes a prerequisite for intervention procedures which are designed to enhance the individual's intellectual efficiency.

Implications for Theory

This book does not contain an explicit theory of intelligence. However, it provides strong support for an intelligence–problem solving performance linkage, and for the fundamental logic of process based assessment and description of general and specific intellectual abilities.

A major implication of the findings of the present investigation is its support for the theoretical position of regarding the problem solving process as a multidetermined but purposive process. The taxonomy which served as a means of describing the problem solving behaviors in the study was prepared from empirical observations. Its content and the observed pattern of preferences for problem solving behaviors of certain categories indicate that problem solvers worked on tasks which they were attempting to solve by purposefully selecting behaviors and strategies.

The frequency of use of behaviors such as Plan/Hypothesis (Code 211), Judgment/Verification (Code 400), and the checking back to the text behaviors (Codes 112–116) show that problem solvers, in fact, make predictions about the solution to a task on the basis of their knowledge and previous experience, as well as in relation to perceived task requirements.

The results of this investigation have shown that differential structural and dynamic patterns of problem solving strategies can be identified in the problem solving activity of subjects of varying competence and speed of performance. This suggests that, pending replication and further investigation of the present findings, it may become possible to predict performance outcomes and to describe problem solving processes operating for individuals, in particular task situations, on the basis of operationally defined and observable responses. The implications for diagnostic assessment, selection, and training to increase problem solving ability are obvious.

A further implication of the present findings is that tasks for which a generally agreed upon taxonomy is still lacking might be defined in terms of the behavior patterns which lead to solutions under specified conditions in specified populations. In practice, this may result in a procedure by which, instead of tasks or items being normed on the basis of the performance by a reference group, the identified behaviors elicited and displayed during the solution process will specify the tasks which may be most suitable for the assessment, selection, or training of subjects. In other words, tasks might be defined and categorized in terms of their demand characteristics for specified groups.

A basic understanding of the problem solving process can be gained when this process is considered as an interaction between variables from three major sources of influence. The ability of the individual to solve a problem efficiently is determined by his or her ability to apply adequate problem solving behaviors or strategies. The ability to apply strategies and the strategies themselves are influenced by the problem solver's general ability, motivation, and the task itself. The problem solving process does not occur in a vacuum. Because of this, it cannot be described in isolation but must be investigated on a theoretical basis which accounts for the major sources of influence on its content.

Of the major theoretical frameworks through which a summary of the relevant literature was presented in Chapters 2 and 3, only the information processing framework seeks to explain problem solving on the basis of the content of the problem solving process.

The results of the present empirical study can be regarded as consistent with much of Newell and Simon's (1972) theory. There is an important difference, however, between their and other information scientists' theoretical views and that of the present study. In previous information processing models, the subject's problem solving behaviors and strategies, even the constraints, provided the means to represent task requirements. The task was the central focus for such research. This explains also the influence of and the importance attributed to computers and computer programs in information processing and artificial intelligence type research. Problem solving computer programs went further than to "simulate" human behavior; many of them were aimed at solving problems in increasingly efficient ways.

Computer programs might provide a superior means to investigate *task requirements* than the observation of human behavior. In addition to other shortcomings of observational studies, a major problem in any attempt to study "objective" task requirements on the basis of the behaviors elicited by the task is to decide whose problem solving behavior "best" represents the demand characteristics of the task. Models originating from previous research in the information processing and artificial intelligence framework have tended to define the task in terms of its solution requirements as represented by the problem solving strategies applied by selected individuals.

In the present study the total focus was on the *problem solving process* itself. An attempt was made to investigate the structure and some of the dynamics of this process by taking as comprehensive a view as possible of the problem solving process and the major sources of variables influencing it.

The present study aims to *explain* problem solving as a process by representing it in terms of the interaction of the influences of its major sources of variance, while previous information processing models *used* the problem solving process to explain task demands and solution requirements.

With respect to the use made of the problem solving process as represented by observations made on or by individuals during their attempts to solve tasks, the information processing and the Gestalt approach have certain similarities. Both use material obtained from the problem solver to explain—in the case of the Gestalt model to infer—the characteristics of another major factor, which is part of the total problem solving situation. Strictly speaking, neither approach focuses on the problem solving process in its own right.

The protocol data obtained in this study support the notion that problem solvers, influenced by the constraints of the total system, deliberately apply strategies in their attempts to solve given tasks. The variety of strategies used, and the use made of a number of specific behaviors and behavior sequences, discriminated successfully between subjects of varying problem solving competence, general ability, speed, and educational achievement. As might have been expected, solvers used fewer different strategies than nonsolvers. Subjects who gave up before reaching a solution used a greater variety of strategies than both solvers and subjects who produced "wrong" solutions. This indicates that subjects who produced any solution at all were actively applying strategies they perceived to be appropriate, while subjects who gave up tried out many different strategies. On the other hand, a larger variety of different problem solving strategies was used by subjects of above average and high intelligence than by those whose estimated level of intellectual functioning was average or below average.

The findings of the present study strongly suggest that to a large degree the problem solving process remains similar regardless of the influences from the major sources of its variation investigated here. The subjects applied basically the same strategies regardless of their position on the factors influencing their problem solving behaviors. In other words, a similar strategy repertoire was observed in the problem solving processes of subjects of different competence, ability, and speed, and with respect to different types of tasks.

In their postulation of the problem solver as an active selector of behaviors, the present findings are supported by previous process oriented studies, which used the techniques of retrospection in combination with, or without, the requirement to justify the strategies selected. These studies, some of which were discussed in detail in previous chapters, provided evidence of the awareness of the subjects during the problem solving process and of their ability to select certain behaviors before others.

The theoretical view evolving from the present study is that an important prerequisite of effective intellectual functioning as manifested in the ability to solve problems is the acquisition of a repertoire of component operations which are combined in an integrated and mutually facilitating manner. The type and variety of available operations, and the appropriateness with which they are combined by the problem solver are dependent on the task, the problem solver's competence, intelligence, training, speed of work, and interaction between any or all of these.

Such a model of intellectual performance fits in with both the vast storage capacity of the central nervous system of man, and with the obvious limitation in processing capacity of the same system, when simultaneous processing of several complex tasks is required. It allows for the possibility of the development of automatic, more complex processing components on the basis of optimal combinations and interactions of simpler component processes and sequences. It must be part of the intellectual growth towards increasing ability and sophistication in problem solving, for the intelligent individual to develop a variety of such automatic processes, which, with practice, will provide the means for the simultaneous processing required for the solution of complex tasks in all spheres.

The research reported in this book was restricted to the investigation of simpler components of such complex processes, because the identification and description of these is a necessary prerequisite if we are to make progress towards an understanding at a level of greater complexity.

It is one thing to describe the general characteristics of component processes in isolation; it is quite another to recognize these same characteristics when they are part of an interactive system. The converse is true also. Because the components of a process are interdependent, individual differences observed on isolated variables can not be taken at face value. An observed difference between particular subjects or groups on one or more components of the problem solving process in isolation does not suffice to demonstrate that outcome differences actually arise from that particular component. Only the painstaking building up of mutually validating components of evidence can lead to strong theory.

Further developments are required in the "thinking aloud" technique. Most obvious is the need to devise a means for the registering of parallel behavior processes. The present research design did not allow for the monitoring of simultaneously operating processes. For example, it is possible that fast solvers were able to commence solution strategies during their "First reading" of the stimulus passage. The research literature provides considerable support for the suggestion that fast readers are able to extract more information from a short presentation of text, than slow readers (e.g. Huey 1908/1968; Jackson & McClelland, 1979), and that the processing of information during reading can occur simultaneously and interactively with other cognitive processing (Estes, 1975; Frederiksen, 1982; Rumelhart, 1977).

The research conducted in the present investigation builds on previous research concerned with the problem solving process, but aims to extend previous methods so that a more comprehensive picture can be presented. The pursuit of this aim made it necessary for the observer to stand back further. The view broadened, but a considerable amount of detail (observable in studies focusing on narrower aspects of the process) became blurred and was lost. An initial glimpse, rather than a definitive view of the problem solving process is provided.

Beyond contributing a set of identifiable components of the problem solving process, the present study might be regarded as having achieved the important general purpose of demonstrating that frequently observed, and generally accepted performance differences in problem solving can be accounted for in terms of the process itself, and that fundamental components of the problem solving process can be studied systematically. This demonstration should encourage other research workers to continue the investigation of vital components of this process.

The relevance of the findings of the present empirical study of problem solving to the conceptualization of intelligence is threefold:

First, the identification of component processes of intellectual performance such as problem solving, which manifest themselves in the performance of some individuals and not in others, makes a considerable contribution to the psychology of individual differences relating to such tasks. This contribution is enhanced if it can be shown that the processing components are wholly or in part responsible for observed differences in the outcome of the intellectual performance.

Second, this research can contribute to the development of an empirically based theory of intelligence, which takes into simultaneous account psychological processes, task characteristics, and individual differences.

Third, on the basis of identified process characteristics of the cognitive performance, a truly diagnostic model of intelligence may be created. Such a model should, at least theoretically, allow for training and intervention procedures which meet the specific need of individuals, such needs having been described in terms of malleable components of the problem solving performance itself.

Implications for Research

The fact that both qualitative and quantitative differences in strategy use could be identified in this relatively simple research design suggests that the contribution of information processing variables to individual differences in cognitive performance in more complex settings may be a substantial one.

The exploratory study reported here constitutes an initial attempt to represent the problem solving process in terms of the interaction of variables from the major sources influencing it. Further research of the problem solving process based on this type of model or on equally or more comprehensive ones is required.

Although major aspects of the problem solving process were identified and many interesting observations were made concerning the behaviors and strategies subjects employed during the problem solving process, many major issues were not explored in detail.

An important task for further research is to validate the findings of the present study with varying samples of subjects. Specifically the application of three–mode factor analyses for groups of subjects with varying specified characteristics would be useful.

At the present time, most experienced teachers subscribe to the view that teaching should be adapted to the needs of individual students. Yet the literature has tended to discuss the characteristics of problem solving and learning as if the variables involved would operate quite similarly with respect to all students. Strategies have tended to be discussed in relation to teaching and task presentation rather than in relation to learning and problem solving performance. The individual needs of students have been defined most frequently in terms of vaguely defined intellectual strengths and weaknesses, or in terms of differences in learning style. Little, if any consideration has been given to the need to impart to students the type of knowledge which will allow them to match strategies to the requirements of particular tasks.

Cross-cultural research has established that individuals reared in widely disparate cultures will develop different abilities, prefer different activities, and may be reinforced for different skills. The question of whether the component processes of intellectual performance, as reflected in preferred problem solving strategies of groups from nonwestern cultures are similar to those regarded as efficient in western cultures must be investigated before the component processes identified in the present study can be recommended in cross-cultural research.

As was noted previously, the same process components may be operating in different outcomes. Different components might lead to similar outcomes. Any one of a number of different process components could logically be responsible for a particular outcome. One of the next steps in this research should be the formulation and testing of hypotheses based on the findings of the present study. If a process based hypothesis leads to the prediction of a particular outcome, and that outcome does not result, the process explanation reflected by the hypothesis can be ruled out. A series of such studies may thus lead to sound theories concerning the process components which account for the largest body of observations, while ruling out rival theories.

One reason why it has been difficult to examine the components of cognitive performance is that there is rarely a clear notion of what component behaviors might be available for the performance of a particular task. Once strategies—the use or non-use of which shows compelling individual or group differences—have been identified further questions concerning the degree to which they might be transferred, manipulated and trained can be investigated.

The effects of the task need to be investigated further. Apart from the similarities items from WAIS, the tasks used in this study were not chosen with a view to resemblances. Because of this, subjects tended to work on only one sample of a particular type of task. A requirement to solve several similar tasks would increase the validity with which the influence of task characteristics on the problem solving process can be described.

Another promising approach might be to apply the methodology presented here in an investigation of problem solving in relation to one task which is presented at varying levels of complexity. Another strategy might be to utilize various levels of cues or stimulus conditions designed to induce problem solvers to utilize hypothesized strategy patterns. Broader sequences of component operations need to be investigated in relation to specified types of tasks.

Motivation and interests of the problem solver, and environmental variables, have not been explored in the present study. Investigations of major concern would include research relating to such issues as the influence of motivational and interest variables on the problem solving process, and their interaction with task and environmental characteristics.

Many of the specific problem solving behaviors and sequences identified in the protocols should be investigated more intensively. Other questions awaiting further investigation include the following: Why are less competent, less intelligent, and more slowly working subjects more repetitive in their application of problem solving behaviors and strategies than more competent, more intelligent, and fast working subjects respectively? What leads an individual to choose certain behaviors in preference to others, and what are the causes for the reluctance on the part of some subjects to use certain strategies?

An initial, speculative attempt to investigate such questions was made by analyzing the temporal relationship of sequential units of the process. To gain a better understanding of why individuals apply some and not other strategies while working on particular tasks, these analyses need to be extended. The one–dependent Markoff chain model needs to be supplemented by analyses of strings of problem solving behaviors of varying lengths. Also, as suggested by Sternberg and his coworkers, speculative descriptive research of cognitive processes needs to be followed up by studies which combine observational and experimental techniques (Sternberg, 1977a, 1977b; Sternberg & Ketron, 1982; Sternberg & Rifkin, 1979; Sternberg & Weil, 1980).

A number of hypotheses suggest themselves on the basis of findings concerned with the interaction of the components of the problem solving process investigated here. The most obvious question in this domain is probably: "Can less competent or slow workers become more efficient in their problem solving by learning the problem solving strategies used by more able or fast problem solvers?"

Implications for Training

The fundamental improvement of the processes of learning and instruction is the major concern at this current stage of educational theory and practice.

Prerequisites for producing in students reasoning skills and problem solving abilities which can lead to high cognitive competence are the development of techniques for an adequate description and analysis of reasoning processes, the possibility of exercising some control over their appropriate utilization, and the means for determining the extent to which these skills and abilities have been developed in or mastered by students.

In any situation in which the aim is to develop in individuals reasoning skills and strategies which are required for some type of problem solving, the need arises for having an adequate system of parameters, i.e., a set of operationally defined concepts, for the description and monitoring of the processes in question. The availability of these parameters is essential also for the diagnosis and systematic description of the instructional needs of the learners. Competence based instruction, appropriate remedial intervention, and therapy are impossible if one confines oneself to approximate, insufficiently defined "labels" of intellectual processes, which are expected to be facilitated during the course of particular instructional procedures or programs. No learning method or instructional program will lead to success if there is uncertainty concerning the parameters which must be developed and manipulated in the formation of the competence in question. The present research has gone some way towards the specification of important parameters.

The analysis of the problem solving process which was conducted in this study identified a number of important problem solving behaviors and strategies, and strategy sequences used by subjects in their endeavors to solve certain tasks. The behaviors which constitute the problem solving process and information concerning some of the ways in which they are influenced by components of the problem solving situation as a whole have implications not only for assessment and intervention procedures but also for the teaching of problem solving skills.

Implications for the teaching of problem solving strategies result from the comparison of the problem solving processes of solvers and those of nonsolvers, high and low IQ subjects, and individuals operating at various speeds. Because comparison groups (e.g., solvers, nonsolvers, and those who gave up) were found to employ basically the same problem solving strategies, but with different frequency and in different sequential patterns, it would seem to be useful to investigate the effects of teaching less proficient problem solvers to employ strategies according to the patterns observed during the problem solving of the more efficient problem solvers. For example, the more competent problem solvers used more solution oriented behaviors, and applied a larger number of hypotheses and judgment–verification responses than the less competent subjects. Less competent subjects could be taught to increase their use of such strategies. The results of the present study do not permit the conclusion that the problem solving strategies and behavior patterns of more efficient problem solvers caused them to perform better, faster, etc., but they suggest that it might be useful to determine whether the application of identical strategies would be of assistance to less efficient or slower subjects.

Finally, an implication originating from the methodology of the present study might be that the subjects' awareness of aspects of their problem solving behaviors and strategies might be utilized in diagnosis. The "thinking aloud" methodology revealed the ability of problem solvers to externalize at least some of their problem solving behaviors. Discussions with subjects in brief post experimental interviews showed that the problem solvers were able to discuss some of their problem solving behaviors, and seemed to enjoy doing so.

Soviet educationists (e.g., Gol'dberg, 1972; Kilpatrick, 1978; Krutetskii, 1976; Menchinskaya, 1969; and others) have recommended the use of this type of direct communication between teacher and student as an effective method of teaching. Few teaching methods and styles employed in schools in Western countries emphasize the potential benefits of this type of approach. It may be possible to utilize the "thinking aloud" technique in combination with discussions with subjects as a means of diagnosing problem solving difficulties and to assess the efficacy of training aimed to improve the individual's problem solving skill.

EPILOGUE

The present study may have raised more questions than it has attempted to answer. This might be regarded as proper in a domain in which to date little cumulative research has taken place. As was pointed out in the introductory chapters of this book, the literature contains large numbers of reports of research on isolated tasks, often on oddity problems. Many aspects of the problem solving process have been analyzed and the diversity of findings transmit a confused picture to those who want to know *how* people solve problems, and to the educator who wishes to teach his students to solve problems more successfully and efficiently.

The intention in the present study was to obtain a broader view of the problem solving process, and to develop a system which would permit the representation of actual problem solving processes by means of observable behaviors in a form which would relate the psychological processes, task characteristics, and individual differences.

The payoff may have been moderate in relation to the energy expended, but the research has resulted in a taxonomy which seems both stable and useful, and the application of which in the present study has yielded some interesting findings and promising leads for further investigations. The fact that the taxonomy based behavior descriptions provided a means for the representation of performance differences in process terms is encouraging.

As has been stressed at various points in this volume, the present study was an exploratory one only, and is expected to lead to more extensive research. The implications of the effects of the here only superficially investigated components of the problem solving process need to be explored more intensively; also their application to other problems and to defined groups of subjects. Only in this way will the utility of the taxonomy of problem solving behaviors and the approach to the study of the problem solving process suggested here be determined.

Much is yet to be learned about the processes of problem solving. The psychological mechanisms are not easily accessible. Because of this, no single methodology can be expected to provide a complete explanation of the phenomena of interest. In the above reported study, an attempt was made to probe the problem solving process from a number of directions and to examine the data by utilizing converging methods of statistical analysis.

A major goal of the present investigation will have been met if the study serves to encourage other investigators to undertake equally or more comprehensive studies of *how* people solve problems, to the point of providing an explanation of the problem solving process which is sufficient to lead to the valid and reliable evaluation of ability and performance, and to effective training in this central activity of human life.

The test of the real value of any psychological investigation relates to the extent to which it increases our understanding of human functioning. The study of how people solve problems; the type, number, and variety of operations and strategies they apply during this process; how characteristics of the task influence strategy choice, and how persons and groups of persons differ with respect to processing profiles, should meet the requirements of this test.

REFERENCES

Aiken, L. R. Ability and creativity in mathematics. *Review of Educational Research,* 1973, *43,* 405–432.

Allen, J. P., & Van Buren, P. *Chomsky: Selected readings.* London: Oxford University Press, 1971.

Allen, M. J., & Yen, M. *Introduction to measurement theory.* Belmont, California: Wadsworth, 1979.

Allison, R. *Learning parameters and human abilities* (Technical Report). Princeton, N.J.: Educational Testing Service, 1960.

Allport, D. A. The state of cognitive psychology: A critical notice of W. G. Chase (Ed.), "Visual information processing." *Quarterly Journal of Experimental Psychology,* 1975, *27,* 141–152.

Allport, G. W. *The use of personal documents in psychological science.* New York: Social Science Research Council, 1942.

Altman, J. Aspects of the criterion problem in small groups research: II. The analysis of group tasks. *Acta Psychologica,* 1966, *25,* 199–221.

American Psychological Association & National Council on Measurement in Education-*Standards for educational and psychological tests.* Washington, D.C.: American Psychological Association, 1974.

Ames, W. S. *A study of the process by which readers determine word meaning through the use of verbal context.* Unpublished Doctoral Dissertation. University of Missouri, 1965.

Amidon, J. E., & Flanders, N. A. *The role of the teacher in the classroom.* Minneapolis: Association for Productive Teaching, 1967.

Anastasi, A. Individual differences. In D. L. Sills (Ed.), *Encyclopaedia of the social sciences* (Vol. 7). New York: The Macmillan Co. & The Free Press, 1968.

Anastasi, A. *Psychological testing* (4th ed.). New York: Macmillan, 1976.

Anderson, B. F. *Cognitive psychology: The study of knowing, learning and thinking.* New York: Academic Press, 1975.

Anderson, J. R. *Language, memory and thought.* Hillsdale, N.J.: Lawrence Erlbaum Associates, 1976.

Arbib, M. A. *Algebraic theory of machines, languages and semigroups.* New York: Academic Press, 1969.

Armer, P. Attitudes toward intelligent machines. In E. A. Feigenbaum & J. Feldman (Eds.), *Computers and thought.* New York: McGraw Hill, 1963.

Asch, S. E. Effects of group pressure upon modification and distortion of judgments. In E. E. Maccoby, T. M. Newcomb & E. L. Hartley, *Readings in social psychology* (3rd ed.). New York: Holt, Rinehart & Winston, 1958.

Ashton, M. R. *Heuristic methods in problem solving in ninth grade algebra.* Unpublished Doctoral Dissertation. Stanford University, 1962.

Atkinson, R. C., & Shiffrin, R. M. Human memory: A proposed system and its control processes. In K. W. Spence & J. T. Spence, *The psychology of learning and motivation: advances in research and theory* (Vol. 2). New York: Academic Press, 1968.

Bain, A. *Mental science, a compendium of psychology and the history of philosophy.* New York: Appleton, 1870.

Bain, A. *The senses and the intellect.* London: Parker, 1855.

Bainbridge, L. Analysis of verbal protocols from a process control task. In E. Edwards & F. P. Lees (Eds.), *The human operator in process control.* London: Taylor & Francis Ltd., 1974.

Bainbridge, L., Beishon, J., Hemming, J. H., & Splaine, M. A. A study of real-time human decision-making using a plant simulator. In E. Edwards & F. P. Lees (Eds.), *The human operator in process control.* London: Taylor & Francis Ltd., 1974.

Bakan, D. A reconsideration of the problem of introspection. *Psychological Bulletin*, 1954, *51*, 105–118.

Bannerji, R. B. *Theory of problem solving*. New York: Elsevier, 1969.

Barron, F., & Harrington, D. M. Creativity, intelligence and personality. *Annual Review of Psychology*, 1981, *32*, 439–477.

Bartlett, F. *Thinking: An experimental and social study*. London: Allen & Unwin, 1958.

Bartussek, D. Zur Interpretation der Kernmatrix in der dreimodalen Faktorenanalyse von R. L. Tucker. *Psychologische Beiträge*, 1973, *15*, 169–184.

Battig, W. F. Some factors affecting performance in a word formation problem. *Journal of Experimental Psychology*, 1957, *55*, 96–103.

Benjafield, J. Evidence that "thinking aloud" constitutes an externalization of inner speech. *Psychonomic Science*, 1969, *15*, 83–84.

Benjafield, J. Evidence for a two-process theory of problem solving. *Psychonomic Science*, 1971, *23*, 397–399.

Bennedetti, D. T. A situational determiner of the Einstellungseffekt. *Journal of General Psychology*, 1956, *54*, 271–278.

Berlyne, D. E. *Structure and direction in thinking*. New York: Wiley, 1965.

Berner, E. S., Hamilton, L. A., & Best, W. R. A new approach to evaluating problem solving in medical students. *Journal of Medical Education*, 1974, *49*, 666–672.

Bernstein, A. L., & Wicker, F. W. A three–mode factor analysis of the concept of novelty. *Psychonomic Science*, 1969, *14*, 291–292.

Bhaskar, R., & Simon, H. A. Problem solving in semantically rich domains: An example from engineering thermodynamics. *Cognitive Science*, 1977, *1*, 193–215.

Bindra, D., & Scheier, I. H. The relation between psychometric and experimental research in psychology. *American Psychologist*, 1954, *9*, 69–71.

Binet, A. *L'étude expérimentale de l'intelligence*. Paris: Schleicher, 1903.

Binet, A., & Simon, T. Méthodes nouvelles pour le diagnostique du niveau intellectuel des anormaux. *Année Psychologique*, 1905, *11*, 191–244.

Block, N. J., & Dworkin, G. (Eds.). *The IQ controversy*. New York: Pantheon, 1976.

Bloom, B. S. *Taxonomy of educational objectives*. New York: Longman Green, 1956.

Bloom, B. S. Time and learning. *American Psychologist*, 1974, *29*, 682–688.

Bloom, B. S. *Stability and change in human characteristics*. New York: Wiley, 1964.

Bloom, B. S. Mastery learning and its implications for curriculum development. In E. W. Eisner (Ed.), *Confronting curriculum reform*. Boston: Little Brown, 1970.

Bloom, B. S., & Broder, L. Problem solving processes of college students. *Supplement to Education Monographs*, 73. Chicago: University of Chicago Press, 1950.

Boring, E. G. Intelligence as the tests test it. *The New Republic*, 1923, *34*, 35–36.

Boring, E. G. *A history of experimental psychology* (2nd ed.). New York: Appleton-Century-Crofts, 1950/1957.

Boring, E. G. A history of introspection. *Psychological Bulletin*, 1953, *50*, 169–189.

Bouchard, T. J. Current conceptions of intelligence and their implications for assessment. In P. McReynolds (Ed.), *Advances in psychological assessment*. Palo Alto, California: Science and Behavior Books, Inc., 1968.

Bourne, L. E. *Human conceptual behavior*. Boston: Allyn & Bacon, 1966.

Bourne, L. E., & Dominowski, R. L. Thinking. *Annual Review of Psychology*, 1972, *23*, 105–131.

Bourne, L. E. Jr., Ekstrand, B. R., & Dominowski, R. L. *The psychology of thinking*. Englewood Cliffs, N.J.: Prentice Hall, 1971.

Bower, G., & Trabasso, T. Concept identification. In R. C. Atkinson (Ed.), *Studies in mathematical psychology*. Stanford: Stanford University Press, 1964.

Braithwaite, R. B. *Scientific explanation: A study of the function of theory, probability and law in science*. Cambridge: Cambridge University Press, 1953.

Brée, D. S. The distribution of problem solving times: An examination of the stages model. *British Journal of Mathematical and Statistical Psychology.* 1975, *28,* 177–200. (a)

Brée, D. S. Understanding of structured problem solutions. *Instructional Science,* 1975, *3,* 327–350. (b)

Broadbent, D. E. *Perception and communication.* New York: Pergamon Press, 1958.

Broadbent, D. E. *Behaviour.* London: Methuen, 1964.

Brooks, R. *A model of human cognitive behavior in writing code for computer programs.* Unpublished Doctoral Dissertation. Carnegie Mellon University, 1975.

Brown, A. L. Knowing when, where and how to remember: A problem in metacognition. In R. Glaser (Ed.), *Advances in instructional psychology* (Vol. 1.). Hillsdale, N.J.: Lawrence Erlbaum Associates, 1978.

Brown, A. L., & French, L. A. The zone of potential development: Implications for intelligent testing in the year 2000. *Intelligence,* 1979, *3,* 255–273.

Brown, J. S., & Burton, R. R. Multiple representations of knowledge for tutorial reasoning. In D. G. Bobrow & A. Collins (Eds.), *Representation and understanding.* New York: Academic Press, 1975.

Bruner, J. S., Goodnow, J. J., & Austin, G. A. *A study of thinking.* New York: Wiley, 1956.

Brunk, L., Collister, E. G., Swift, C., & Stayton, S. A correlational study of two reasoning problems. *Journal of Experimental Psychology,* 1958, *55,* 236–241.

Brunswik, E. *Perception and representative design of psychological experimentation.* Berkeley, Calif.: University of California Press, 1956.

Bundy, A. Will it reach the top? Predictions in the mechanics world. *Artificial Intelligence,* 1978, *10,* 129–146.

Burack, B. The nature and efficacy of methods of attack on reasoning problems. *Psychological Monographs,* 1950, *63,* (Whole No. 313).

Burke, R. J., & Maier, N. R. F. Attempts to predict success on an insight problem. *Psychological Reports,* 1965, *17,* 303–310.

Burt, C. The concept of consciousness. *British Journal of Psychology,* 1962, *53,* 229–242.

Burt, C. Brain and consciousness. *British Journal of Psychology,* 1968, *59,* 55–69.

Buswell, G. T. Patterns of thinking in problem solving. *University of California Publications in Education,* 1956, *12,* 63–148.

Butcher, H. J. *Human intelligence: Its nature and assessment.* London: Methuen & Co. Ltd., 1968.

Butterfield, E. G., & Belmont, J. M. Assessing and improving the cognition of mentally retarded people. In I. Bialer & M. Sternlicht (Eds.), *Psychology of mental retardation: issues and approaches.* New York: Psychological Dimensions, 1977.

Byers, J. L., & Davidson, R. E. The role of hypothesizing in the facilitation of concept attainment. *Journal of Verbal Learning & Verbal Behavior,* 1967, *6,* 595–600.

Byrne, R. Planning meals: Problem-solving on a real data-base. *Cognition,* 1977, *5,* 287–332.

Campbell, D. T., & Fiske, D. W. Convergent and discriminant validation of the multitrait multimethod matrix. *Psychological Bulletin,* 1959, *56,* 81–105.

Campione, J. C., & Brown, A. L. Toward a theory of intelligence: Contributions from research with retarded children. In R. J. Sternberg & D. K. Detterman (Eds.), *Human intelligence.* Norwood, N.J.: Ablex, 1979.

Carlson, J. S., & Wiedl, K. H. Toward a differential testing approach: Testing the limits employing the Raven Matrices. *Intelligence,* 1979, *3,* 323–344.

Carroll, J. B. A model of school learning. *Teachers College Record,* 1963, *64,* 723–733.

Carroll, J. B. Stalking the wayward factors: Review of J. P. Guilford and R. Hoepfner. *Contemporary Psychology,* 1972, *17,* 321–324.

Carroll, J. B. *Psychometric tests as cognitive tasks: A new structure of intellect.* Princeton, N.J.: Educational Testing Service, 1974.

Carroll, J. B. Psychometric tests as cognitive tasks: A new 'structure of intellect.' In L. B. Resnick (Ed.), *The nature of intelligence.* New York: Wiley, 1976.

Carroll, J. B. How shall we study individual differences in cognitive abilities?—methodological and theoretical perspectives. *Intelligence,* 1978, *2,* 87–115.

Carroll, J. B. *Individual difference relations in psychometric and experimental cognitive tasks.* (Report No. 163). Psychometrics Laboratory. Chapel Hill: University of North Carolina, April, 1980. (a)

Carroll, J. B. Remarks on Sternberg's "Factor theories of intelligence are alright almost." *Educational Researcher,* 1980, *9,* 14–18. (b)

Carroll, J. B., & Maxwell, S. E. Individual differences in cognitive abilities. *Annual Review of Psychology,* 1979, *30,* 603–640.

Castellan, N. J., Pisoni, D. B., & Potts, G. R. *Cognitive theory* (Vol. 2). Hillsdale, N.J.: Lawrence Erlbaum Associates. 1977.

Cattell, J. McK. Mental tests and measurements. *Mind,* 1890, *15,* 373–380. Reprinted in W. Dennis (Ed.), *Readings in the history of psychology.* New York: Appleton-Century-Crofts, 1948.

Cattell, R. B. *Description and measurement of personality.* London: Harrap, 1946.

Cattell, R. B. *Personality and motivation structure and measurement.* New York: World, 1957.

Cattell, R. B. Theory of fluid and crystalized intelligence: A critical experiment. *Journal of Educational Psychology,* 1963, *54,* 1–22.

Cattell, R. B. *Handbook of multivariate experimental psychology.* Chicago: Rand McNally, 1966.

Cattell, R. B. *Abilities: Their structure, growth and action.* Boston: Houghton Mifflin, 1971.

Chaplin, J. P. *Dictionary of psychology.* New York: Dell Publishing Co., 1968.

Chase, W. G. Elementary information processes. In W. K. Estes (Ed.), *Handbook of learning and cognitive processes* (vol. 5). Hillsdale, N.J.: Lawrence Erlbaum Associates, 1978.

Chase, W. G., & Simon, W. A. The mind's eye in chess. In W. G. Chase (Ed.), *Visual information processing.* New York: Academic Press, 1973.

Cherry, C. *On human communication, a review, a survey, and a criticism.* New York: Wiley, 1957.

Chi, M. T. H., Feltovich, P. J., & Glaser, R. Categorization and representation of physics problems by experts and novices. *Cognitive Science,* 1981, *5,* 121–152.

Chi, M T. H., Glaser, R., & Rees, E. Expertise in problem solving. In R. J. Sternberg (Ed.), *Advances in the psychology of human intelligence.* Hillsdale, N.J.: Lawrence Erlbaum Associates, 1981.

Chiang, A., & Atkinson, R. C. Individual differences and interrelationships among a select set of cognitive skills. *Memory and Cognition,* 1976, *4,* 661–672.

Chomsky, N. Three models for the description of language. *IRE Transactions on Information Theory,* 1956, IT-2(3), 113–124.

Chomsky, N. Verbal behavior (a review of Skinner's book). *Language,* 1959, *35,* 26–58.

Chomsky, N. *Aspects of the theory of syntax.* Cambridge, Mass.: MIT Press, 1965.

Chomsky, N. The general properties of language. In C. H. Millikan & F. L. Darley (Eds.), *Brain mechanisms underlying speech and language.* New York: Grune & Stratton, 1967.

Claparède, E. Genèse de l'hypothèse. *Archives de Psychologie,* 1934, *24,* 1–155.

Clarkson, G. P. E. *Portfolio selection: A simulation of trust investment.* Englewood Cliffs, N.J.: Prentice Hall, 1962.

Cobb, H. V., & Brenneise, S. H. Solutions of the Maier string problem as a function of the method of problem presentation. *Proceedings of the South Dakota Academy of Sciences,* 1952, *31,* 138–142.

Cofer, C. N. (Ed.). *Verbal behavior and learning.* New York: McGraw Hill, 1961.

Cohen, G. *The psychology of cognition*. London: Academic Press, 1977

Cohen, J. A. The factorial structure of the WISC at ages 7–6, 10–6, and 13–6. *Journal of Consulting Psychology*, 1959, *23*, 285–299.

Cohen, J. A. A coefficient of agreement for nominal scales. *Educational and Psychological Measurement*, 1960, *20*, 37–46.

Cohen, J. A. Weighted Kappa: Nominal scale agreement with provision for scaled disagreement or partial credit. *Psychological Bulletin*, 1968, *70*, 213–220.

Cole, N. S. *Bias in selection*. (Research Report 51). Iowa City: American College Testing Service, 1972.

Cooley, W. W., & Lohnes, P. R. *Multivariate data analysis*. New York: Wiley, 1971.

Cronbach, L. J. The logic of experiments on discovery. In L. E. Shulman & E. R. Keeslar (Eds.), *Learning by discovery: A critical approach*. Chicago: Rand McNally Co., 1957. (a)

Cronbach, L. J. The two disciplines of scientific psychology. *American Psychologist*, 1957, *12*, 671–684. (b)

Cronbach, L. J. *Essentials of psychological testing* (3rd ed.). New York: Harper & Row, 1970.

Cronbach, L. J. Beyond the two disciplines of scientific psychology. *American Psychologist*, 1975, *30*, 116–128.

Cronbach, L. J., & Snow, R. E. *Aptitudes and instructional methods: A handbook of research on interactions*. New York: Prentice Hall, 1977.

Cross, K. P., & Gaier, E. L. Technique in problem-solving as a predictor of educational attainment. *Journal of Educational Psychology*, 1955, *46*, 193–206.

Crutchfield, R. S., & Covington, M. V. Programmed instruction and creativity. *Programmed Instruction*, 1965, *4*, 1–2.

Curtis, M. E., & Glaser, R. Changing conceptions of intelligence. *Review of Research in Education*, 1981, *9*, 111–148.

Dansereau, D. P., & Gregg, L. W. An information processing analysis of mental multiplication. *Psychonomic Science*, 1966, *6*, 71–72.

Darlington, R. B. Another look at cultural fairness. *Journal of Educational Measurement*, 1971, *8*, 71–82.

Das, J. P., Kirby, J., & Jarman, R. F. Simultaneous and successive synthesis: An alternative model for cognitive abilities. *Psychological Bulletin*, 1975, *82*, 87–103.

Davis, F. B. Research in comprehension in reading. *Reading Research Quarterly*, 1968, *3*, 499–545.

Davis, G. A. Current status of research and theory in human problem solving. *Psychological Bulletin*, 1966, *66*, 36–54.

Davis, G. A. *Laboratory studies of creative thinking techniques: The checklist and morphological synthesis methods* (Report No. TR 94). Madison: Wisconsin University, 1969.

Davis, G. A. *Psychology of problem solving*. New York: Basic Books, 1973.

Davis, G. A., & Manske, M. E. Effects of prior serial learning of solution words upon anagram problem solving: II. A serial position effect. *Journal of Experimental Psychology*, 1968, *77*, 101–104.

Davis, H. J. Verbalization, experimenter presence and problem solving. *Journal of Personality and Social Psychology*, 1968, *8*, 299–302.

Davis, J. H. *Models for the classification of problems and the prediction of group problem solving from individual results*. Unpublished Doctoral Dissertation. Michigan State University, 1961.

Day, R. H. *Human perception*. Sydney: Wiley, 1969.

De Bono, E. *The use of lateral thinking*. London: Jonathan Cape, 1967.

De Groot, A. *Thought and choice in chess*. The Hague: Mouton, 1965.

De Groot, A. Perception and memory versus thought. Some old ideas and recent findings. In B. Kleinmuntz (Ed.), *Problem solving: Research and theory.* New York: Wiley, 1966.

De Kleer, J. Multiple representation of knowledge in a mechanics problem solver. *Proceedings of the 5th Joint International Conference on Artificial Intelligence.* Cambridge, Mass.: MIT Press, 1977.

Dewey, J. *How we think.* New York: Holt, Rinehart, & Winston, 1910.

Dewey, J. *How we think: A restatement of the relation of reflective thinking to the education process.* Boston: Heath & Co., 1933.

Dewey, J. *Logic: The theory of inquiry.* New York: Holt, 1938.

Dienes, Z. P., & Jeeves, M. A. *Thinking in structures.* London: Hutchinson, 1965.

Dockrell, W. B. *The Toronto symposium on intelligence: 1969.* London: Methuen & Co., 1970.

Dodwell, P. C. *Visual pattern recognition.* New York: Holt, Rinehart & Winston, 1970.

Dominowski, R. L. How do people discover concepts? In R. L. Solso (Ed.), *Theories of cognitive psychology: The Loyola Symposium.* Hillsdale, N.J.: Lawrence Erlbaum Associates, 1974.

Donders, F. C. On the speed of mental processes. *Acta Psychologica,* 1969, *30,* 412–431. (Translated from the original by W. G. Koster from *Onderzoekingen gedaan in het Physiologisch Laboratorium der Utrechtsche Hoogeschool,* 1868–69. Tweede reek II, 92–120.

Dörner, D. Illegal thinking. In A. Elithorn & D. Jones (Eds.), *Artificial and human thinking.* Amsterdam: Elsevier Scientific Publishing Co., 1973.

Dreistadt, R. The use of analogies and incubation in obtaining insights in creative problem solving. *Journal of Psychology,* 1969, *71,* 159–175.

Dulany, D. E. Jr. Awareness, rules and propositional control: A confrontation with S–R behavior theory. In T. R. Dixon, & D. L. Horton (Eds.), *Verbal behavior and general behavior theory.* Englewood Cliffs, N.J.: Prentice Hall, 1968.

Duncan, C. P. Recent research on human problem solving. *Psychological Bulletin,* 1959, *56,* 397–429.

Duncan, C. P. Induction of a principle. *Quarterly Journal of Experimental Psychology,* 1964, *16,* 373–377.

Duncan, O. D., Featherman, D. L. & Duncan, B. *Socioeconomic background and occupational achievement: extensions of a basic model.* (Final Report, Project NO. 5-0074 [EO–191]). United States Department of Health, Education and Welfare, Office of Education, Bureau of Research, May 1968.

Duncker, K. On problem solving. *Psychological Monographs,* 1945, *58* (Whole No. 270).

Dunham, J. L., Guilford, J. P., & Hoepfner, R. Multivariate approaches to discovering the intellectual components of concept learning. *Psychological Review,* 1968, *75,* 206–211.

Dunnette, M. D. *Handbook of industrial and organizational psychology.* Chicago: Rand McNally, 1976.

Durkin, H. E. Trial–and–error, gradual analysis and sudden reorganization, an experimental study of problem solving. *Archives of Psychology,* 1937, *30* (Whole No. 210).

Eckart, C., & Young, G. The approximation of one matrix by another of lower rank. *Psychometrika,* 1936, *1,* 211–218.

Edwards, W. Bayesian and regression models in human information processing—a myopic perspective. *Organizational Behavior and Human Performance,* 1971, *6,* 639–648.

Egan, D. E. Testing based on understanding: Implications from studies of spatial ability. *Intelligence,* 1979, *3,* 1–15.

Eidhoven, J. E., & Vinacke, W. E. Creative process in painting. *Journal of General Psychology,* 1952, *67,* 139–164.

Elam, S. *Education and the structure of knowledge.* Chicago: Rand McNally, 1964.

Elstein, A. S., Shulman, L. S., & Sprafka, S. A. *Medical problem solving: An analysis of clinical reasoning.* Cambridge, Mass.: Harvard University Press, 1978.

Emmer, E. Direct observation of classroom behavior. In N. Flanders, & G. Nuthall (Eds.), The classroom behavior of teachers. *International Review of Education,* 1972, *18,* 508–528.

English, H. B., & English, A.C. *A comprehensive dictionary of psychological and psychoanalytical terms.* New York: Longmans, Green & Co., 1958.

Ennis, R. H. A concept of critical thinking: A proposed basis for research in the teaching and evaluation of critical thinking ability. In B. P. Komisar & C. J. B. MacMillan (Eds.), *Psychological concepts in education.* Chicago: Rand McNally, 1967.

Ennis, R. H. *Cornell Critical Thinking Test, Level X.* Urbana, Ill.: Critical Thinking Project, 1971.

Erickson, J. R., & Jones, M. R. Thinking. *Annual Review of Psychology,* 1978, *29,* 61–90.

Ericsson, K. A. Instruction to verbalize as a means to study problem solving processes with the 8 puzzle—a preliminary survey. *Reports from the University of Stockholm,* Department of Psychology, No. 458, Nov., 1975.

Ericcson, K. A., & Simon, H. A. Verbals reports as data. *Psychological Review,* 1980, 87, 215–252.

Erickson, S. C. Studies in the abstraction process. *Psychological Monographs,* 1962, *76* (Whole No. 537).

Ernst, G. W., & Newell, A. *GPS: a case study in generality and problem solving.* New York: Academic Press, 1969.

Estes, W. K. Learning theory and intelligence. *American Psychologist,* 1974, *29,* 740–749.

Estes, W. K. Intelligence and cognitive psychology. In L. B. Resnick (Ed.), *The nature of intelligence.* Hillsdale, N.J.: Lawrence Erlbaum Associates, 1976.

Estes, W.K. The information processing approach to cognition: a confluence of metaphors and methods. In W. K. Estes, *Handbook of learning and cognitive processes* (Vol. 5). Hillsdale, N.J.: Lawrence Erlbaum Associates, 1978.

Estes, W. K. The locus of inferential and perceptual processes in letter identification. *Journal of Experimental Psychology: General,* 1975, *104,* 122–145.

Evans, J. St. B. T. A critical note on Quinton and Fellow's observation of reasoning strategies. *British Journal of Psychology,* 1976, *67,* 517–518.

Evans, J. St B. T. & Wason, P. C. Rationalization in a reasoning task. *British Journal of Psychology,* 1976, *67,* 479–486.

Eysenck, H. J. Intelligence assessment: A theoretical and experimental approach. *British Journal of Educational Psychology,* 1967, *37,* 81–98.

Fechner, G. T. *Elemente der Psychophysik.* Leipzig: Breitkopf und Härtel, 1860.

Fechner, G. T. *In Sachen der Psychophysik.* Leipzig: Breitkopf und Härtel, 1877.

Feigenbaum, E. A. An experimental course in simulation of cognitive processes. *Behavioral Science,* 1962, *7,* 244–245.

Feigenbaum, E. A. The art of artificial intelligence: Themes and case studies of knowledge engineering. *Proceedings of the 5th Joint International Conference on Artificial Intelligence.* Cambridge, Mass.: MIT Press, 1977.

Feigenbaum, E. A., & Feldman, J. (Eds). *Computers and thought.* New York: McGraw Hill, 1963.

Ferguson, G. A. On transfer and human ability. *Canadian Journal of Psychology,* 1956, *10,* 121–130.

Ferguson, G. A. Human abilities. *Annual Review of Psychology,* 1965, *16,* 39–62.

Festinger, L. *A theory of cognitive dissonance.* Stanford, Calif.: Stanford University Press, 1957.

Fincher, J. *Human intelligence.* New York: Putnam, 1976.

Fine, B. *The stranglehold of the IQ*. Garden City: Doubleday, 1975.

Fischer, C. T. Intelligence defined as effectiveness of approaches. *Journal of Consulting and Clinical Psychology*, 1969, *33*, 668–674.

Fischer, G. H. *Einführung in die Theorie psychologischer Tests*. Bern: Hans Huber, 1974.

Flanders, N. A. *Teacher influence, pupil attitudes, and achievement*. Cooperative Research Monograph Series, 1965.

Flanders, N. A. Estimating reliability. In E. J. Amidon & J. B. Hough (Eds.), *Interaction analysis: Theory, research and application*. Reading, Mass.: Addison Wesley, 1967.

Fleishman, E. A. Toward a taxonomy of human performance. *American Psychologist*, 1975, *30*, 1127–1149.

Fleishman, E. A. Systems for describing human tasks. *American Psychologist*, 1982, *37*, 821–834.

Fleishman, E. A., & Bartlett, C. J. Human abilities. *Annual Review of Psychology*, 1969, *20*, 349–380.

Flügel, J. C. *A hundred years of psychology*. London: Gerald Duckworth, 1933.

Forehand, G. A. Constructs and strategies for problem solving research. In B. Kleinmuntz, *Problem solving: Research, methods and theory*. New York: Wiley, 1966.

Fowler, H. W., & Fowler, F. G. *The concise Oxford dictionary of current English* (6th ed.). Edited by J. B. Sykes. Oxford: At the Clarendon Press, 1978.

Frederiksen, J. R. A componential theory of reading skills and their interactions. In Sternberg, R. J. (Ed.), *Advances in the psychology of human intelligence*. Hillsdale, N.J.: Lawrence Erlbaum Associates, 1982.

French, J. W., Ekstrom, R. B., & Price, L. A. *Kit of reference tests for cognitive factors*. Princeton, N.J.: Educational Testing Service, 1963.

Frick, F. C. Information theory. In S. Koch (Ed.), *Psychology: A study of a science* (Vol. 2). New York: McGraw Hill, 1959.

Gagné, R. M. *Human tasks and the classification of behavior*. Paper delivered at 10th Annual Seminar on Psychology in Management, Purdue University, 1962.

Gagné, R. M. Problem solving. In A. W. Melton (Ed.), *Categories of human learning*. New York: Academic Press, 1964.

Gagné, R. M. *The conditions of learning*. New York: Holt, Rinehart, & Winston, 1965.

Gagné, R. M. Human problem solving: Internal and external events. In B. Kleinmuntz (Ed.), *Problem solving: research, method, and theory*. New York: Wiley, 1966.

Gagné, R. M. *The conditions of learning* (3rd ed.). New York: Holt, Rinehart & Winston, 1977.

Gagné, R. M., & Smith, E. C. A study of the effects of verbalization on problem solving. *Journal of Experimental Psychology*, 1962, *63*, 12–18.

Gall, F. J., & Spurzheim, G. *Recherches sur le système nerveux*. 1809. Paris: Schoell, 1809.

Galton, F. *Hereditary genius*. New York: The Macmillan Co., 1871.

Galton, F. *Natural inheritance*. New York: The Macmillan Co., 1889.

Gelman, R. & Gallistel, C. R. *The child's understanding of number*. Cambridge, Mass.: Harvard University Press, 1978.

Garfield, E. Essays of an information scientist (Vol. 1, 1962–1973). Philadelphia, Pa.: Institute for Scientific Information Press, 1977. (a)

Garfield, E. *Essays of an information scientist* (Vol. 2, 1974–1976). Philadelphia, Pa.: Institute for Scientific Information Press, 1977. (b)

Garrett, C. S. *Modification of the Scott coefficient as observer agreement estimate for marginal form observation scale data*. (Occasional Paper 6). Bloomington: Center for Innovation in Teaching the Handicapped. Indiana University, 1972.

Geach, B. The problem solving technique: As taught to psychiatric students. *Perspective in Psychiatric Care*, 1974, *12*, 9–12.

Gelernter, H. Realization of a geometry-theorem proving machine. In E. A. Feigenbaum & J. Feldman (Eds.), *Computers and thought*. New York: McGraw Hill, 1963.

Gerwin, D. Information processing data inferences and scientific generalization. *Behavioral Science*, 1974, *80*, 126–138.

Ghiselin, B. (Ed.). *The creative process*. Berkeley: University of California Press, 1952.

Gibb, E. G. Children's thinking in the process of subtraction. *Journal of Experimental Education*, 1956, *25*, 71–80.

Gibson, E. J. *Principles of perceptual learning and development*. New York: Appleton-Century-Crofts, 1969.

Glaser, R. Adapting the elementary school curriculum to individual performance. In *Proceedings of the 1967 Invitational Conference on Testing Problems*. Princeton, N.J.: Educational Testing Service, 1968.

Glaser, R., & Bond, L. (Eds.). Testing: Concepts, policy, practise and research. *American Psychologist*, 1981, *36*, Special issue. Number 10.

Glaser, R., Damrin, D. E., & Gardner, F. M. The Tab Item: a technique for the measurement of proficiency in diagnostic problem solving tasks. *Educational and Psychological Measurement*, 1954, *14*, 283–293.

Glaser, R., Pellegrino, J. W., & Lesgold, A. M. Some directions for a cognitive psychology. In A. M. Lesgold, J. W. Pellegrino, S. D. Fokkema & R. Glaser (Eds.), *Cognitive psychology and instruction*. New York: Plenum Press, 1977.

Gobits, R. *The measurement of insight*. Unpublished paper presented at the 2nd International Symposium on Educational Testing, Montreux, June 29–July 3, 1975.

Goddard, H. H. *The Kallikak family*. New York: Macmillan, 1912.

Goldberg, R. A., Schwartz, S., & Stewart, M. Individual differences in cognitive processes. *Journal of Educational Psychology*, 1977. *69*, 9–14.

Gol'dberg, Y. I. Methods used by the teacher in problem–solving instruction. In *Soviet Studies in the Psychology of Learning and Teaching Mathematics*, 1972, *6*, 125–131. (School Mathematics Study Group, Stanford University).

Goldstein, K. *The organism: A holistic approach to biology derived from pathological data*. Boston: Beacon Press, 1963.

Goor, A. *Problem solving processes of creative and non-creative students*. (Unpublished Doctoral Dissertation). University of North Carolina, 1974.

Gorsuch, R. L. *Factor analysis*. Philadelphia: W. B. Saunders, 1974.

Gould, J. D. Some psychological evidence of how people debug computer programs. *International Journal of Man Machine Studies*, 1975, *7*, 151–182.

Green, B. F. Intelligence and computer simulation. *Transactions of the New York Academy of Science*, 1964, Series 2, *27*, 55–63.

Green, B. F. Current trends in problem solving. In B. Kleinmuntz (Ed.), *Problem solving: Research, method and theory*. New York: Wiley, 1966.

Green, B. F. A primer of testing. *American Psychologist*, 1981, *36*, 1001–1010.

Greeno, J. G. The structure of memory and the process of solving problems. In R. Solso (Ed.), *Contemporary issues in cognitive psychology: The Loyola Symposium*. Washington: Winston, 1973.

Greeno, J. G. Indefinite goals in well structured problems. *Psychological Review*, 1976, *83*, 479–491.

Greeno, J. G. Process of understanding in problem solving. In N. J. Castellan, D. B. Pisoni, & G. R. Potts (Eds.), *Cognitive theory* (Vol. 2). Hillsdale, N.J.: Lawrence Erlbaum Associates, 1977.

Greeno, J. G. A study of problem solving. In R. Glaser (Ed.), *Advances in instructional psychology* (Vol. 1). Hillsdale, N.J.: Lawrence Erlbaum Associates, 1978 (a).

Greeno, J. G. Understanding and procedural knowledge in mathematics instruction. *Educational Psychologist*, 1978, *12*, 262–283. (b).

Greeno, J. G., & Bjork, R. A. Mathematical learning theory and the new "mental forestry." *Annual Review of Psychology*, 1973, *24*, 81–116.

Gregg, L. W. *Knowledge and cognition*. Hillsdale, New Jersey: Lawrence Erlbaum Associates, 1974.

Gregg, L. W., & Simon, H. A. Process models and stochastic theories of simple concept formation. *Journal of Mathematical Psychology*, 1967, *4*, 246–276.

Guilford, J. P. Three faces of intellect. *American Psychologist*, 1959, *14*, 469–479.

Guilford, J. P. Factorial angles to psychology. *Psychological Review*, 1961, *68*, 1–20.

Guilford, J. P. *The nature of human intelligence*. New York: McGraw Hill, 1967.

Guilford, J. P., & Fruchter, B. *Fundamental statistics in psychology and education* (6th ed.). New York: McGraw Hill, 1978.

Guilford, J. P., & Hoepfner, R. *The analysis of intelligence*. New York: McGraw Hill, 1971.

Hackman, R. J. Tasks and task performance in research on stress. In J. E. McGrath (Ed.), *Social and psychological factors in stress*. New York: Holt, Rinehart, & Winston, Inc., 1970.

Hadamard, J. *An essay on the psychology of invention in the mathematics field*. Princeton, N.J.: Princeton University Press, 1945.

Hafner, J. Influence of verbalization on problem solving. *Psychological Reports*, 1957, *3*, 360.

Hare, A. P. *Handbook of small group research*. New York: Free Press, 1962.

Harris, C. W. On factors and factor scores. *Psychometrika*, 1967, *32*, 363–379.

Hayes, J. R. On the function of visual imagery in elementary mathematics. In W. G. Chase (Ed.), *Visual information processing*. New York: Academic Press, 1973.

Hayes, J. R., & Flower, L. Uncovering cognitive processes in writing: An introduction to protocol analysis. Paper presented at the annual meeting of the *American Educational Research Association*, Los Angeles, CA., April, 1981.

Hayes, J. R., & Simon, H. A. Understanding complex instructions. In L. W. Gregg (Ed.), *Psychology of problem solving*. New York: Basic Books, 1974.

Haygood, R. C., & Bourne, L. E. Jr. Attribute and rule learning. *Psychological Review*, 1965, *72*, 175–195.

Hebb, D. O. The American revolution. *American Psychologist*, 1960, *15*, 735–745.

Heider, F. *The psychology of interpersonal relations*. New York: Wiley, 1958.

Helmholtz, H. von. *Handbuch der physiologischen Optik*. Braunschweig: Vieweg, 1856.

Helmholtz, H. von. *Vorträge und Reden* (5th ed.). Braunschweig: Vieweg, 1894.

Hendrix, G. A new clue to transfer of training. *Elementary School Journal*. 1947, *48*, 197–203.

Hilgard, E. R. Consciousness in contemporary psychology. *Annual Review of Psychology*, 1980, *31*, 1–26.

Hogarth, R. M. Process tracing in clinical judgment. *Behavioral Science*, 1974, *19*, 298–313.

Horn, J. L. Organization of abilities and the development of intelligence. *Psychological Review*, 1968, *75*, 242–259.

Horn, J. L. Human abilities: a review of research and theory in the early 1970s. *Annual Review of Psychology*, 1976, *27*, 437–485.

Horn, J. L. Trends in the measurement of intelligence. *Intelligence*, 1979, *3*, 229–240.

Horn, J. L., & Cattell, R. B. Refinement and test of the theory of fluid and crystallized intelligence. *Journal of Educational Psychology*, 1966, *57*, 253–270.

Houston, J. P. *Fundamentals of learning*. New York: Academic Press, 1976.

Houts, P. L. (Ed.) *The myth of measurability*. New York: Hart, 1977.

Huesmann, L. R., & Cheng, C. M. A theory for the induction of mathematical functions. *Psychological Review*, 1973, *80*, 126–138.

Huey, E. B. *The psychology and pedagogy of reading*. Cambridge, Mass.: MIT Press, 1968. (originally published New York: Macmillan, 1908)

Hull, C. L. The concept of the habit-family hierarchy and maze learning. *Psychological Review*, 1934, *41*, 33–52, 134–152.

Hull, C. L. *A behavior system*. New Haven, Conn.: Yale University Press, 1952.

Humphrey, G. *Thinking*. London: Methuen, 1951.

Humphreys, L. G. Statistical definitions of test validity for minority groups. *Journal of Applied Psychology*, 1973, *58*, 1–4.

Humphreys, L. G. The construct of general intelligence. *Intelligence*, 1979, *3*, 105–120.

Hunt, E. B. *Concept learning: An information processing problem*. New York: Wiley, 1962.

Hunt, E. B. Computer simulation: Artificial intelligence studies and their relevance to psychology. *Annual Review of Psychology*, 1968, *19*, 135–168.

Hunt, E. B. *What kind of computer is man?* (Technical Report No. 70-1-01). Department of Psychology, University of Washington, 1970.

Hunt, E. B. *What kind of computer is man? Cognitive Psychology*, 1971, *2*, 57–98.

Hunt, E. B. *Varieties of cognitive power. In L. B. Resnick (Ed.), The nature of intelligence*. Hillsdale, N.J.: Lawrence Erlbaum Associates, 1976.

Hunt, E. B. Mechanics of verbal abilities. *Psychological Review*, 1978, *85*, 109–130.

Hunt, E. B., Frost, N., & Lunneborg, C. Individual differences in cognition. In G. Bower (Ed.), *The psychology of learning and motivation: advances in research and theory* (Vol. 7). New York: Academic Press, 1973.

Hunt, E. B., Lunneborg, C., & Lewis, J. What does it mean to be high verbal? *Cognitive Psychology*, 1975, *7*, 194–227.

Hunt, E. B., Marin, J., & Stone, P. J. *Experiments in induction*. New York: Academic Press, 1966.

Hunt, J. McV. *Intelligence and experience*. New York: Ronald Press, 1961.

Hunter, J. E. Mental calculation. In P. C. Wason & P. N. Johnson-Laird (Eds.), *Thinking and reasoning*. Baltimore: Penguin, 1968.

Hutchinson, E. D. *How to think creatively*. New York: Abingdon Cokesbury, 1949.

Huttenlocher, J. Constructing spatial images: A strategy in reasoning. *Psychological Review*, 1968, *75*, 550–660.

Huttenlocher, J. Language and intelligence. In L. B. Resnick (Ed.), *The nature of intelligence*. Hillsdale, N.J.: Lawrence Erlbaum Associates, 1976.

Jackson, G. Another psychological view from the association of black psychologists. *American Psychologist*, 1975, *30*, 89–93.

Jackson, M. D. & McClelland, J. L. Processing determinants of reading speed. *Journal of Experimental Psychology: General*, 1979, *108*, 151–181.

Jacobson, V. *A linguistic feature analysis of verbal protocols associated with pupil responses to standardized measures of reading responses*. Unpublished Doctoral Dissertation. University of Minnesota, 1973.

James, W. *The principles of psychology* (Vols. 1 & 2). London: Macmillan, 1890.

Jarman, R. F., & Das, J. P. Simultaneous and successive syntheses and intelligence. *Intelligence*, 1977, *1*, 151–169.

Jeffries, R., Polson, P. G., Razran, L., & Atwood, M. E. A process model for missionaries-cannibals and other river-crossing problems. *Cognitive Psychology*, 1977, *9*, 412–440.

Jensen, A. R. How much can we boost IQ and scholastic achievement? *Harvard Educational Review*, 1969, *39*, 1–123.

Jensen, A. R. *Educability and group differences*. New York: Harper & Row, 1973. (a)

Jensen, A. R. *Genetics and education*. New York: Harper & Row, 1973. (b)

Jensen, A. R. *Bias in mental testing*. New York: Free Press, 1980.

Jensen, A. R. g: Outmoded theory or unconquered frontier? *Creative Science and Technology*, 1979, *2*, 16–29.

Jensen, A. R., & Munro, E. Reaction time, movement time and intelligence. *Intelligence*, 1979, *3*, 121–126.

Johnson, D. M. *The psychology of human judgment*. New York: Harper & Row, 1955.

Johnson, D. M. *Systematic introduction to the psychology of thinking*. New York: Harper & Row, 1972.

Johnson, E. S. An information-processing model of one kind of problem solving. *Psychological Monographs: General & Applied*, 1964, *78* (Whole No. 581).

Kagan, J. Reflection-impulsivity: The generality and dynamics of conceptual tempo. *Journal of Abnormal Psychology*, 1966, *71*, 17–24.

Kaiser, H. F. Image analysis. In C. W. Harris (Ed.), *Problems in measuring change*. Madison: University of Wisconsin Press, 1963.

Kaiser, H. F. *Psychometric approaches to factor analysis*. Paper presented at the Invitational Conference on Testing Problems, Educational Testing Service, Princeton, N.J., October 31, 1964.

Kaiser, H. F., & Caffrey, J. Alpha factor analysis. *Psychometrika*, 1965, *30*, 1–14.

Kamin, L. J. *The science and politics of IQ*. Hillsdale, N.J.: Lawrence Erlbaum Associates, 1974.

Karrier, C. Ideology and evaluation. In M. Apple et al. (Eds.), *Educational evaluation: Analysis and responsibility*. Berkeley: McCutchan, 1973.

Katona, G. *Organizing and memorizing*. New York: Columbia University Press, 1940.

Kaufman, A. S. Factor analysis of the WISC-R at eleven age levels between 6½ and 16½ years. *Journal of Consulting and Clinical Psychology*, 1975, *43*, 135–147.

Kaufman, A. S. *Intelligent testing with the WISC-R*. New York: Wiley, 1979. (a)

Kaufman, A. S. The role of speed on WISC-R performance across the age range. *Journal of Consulting and Clinical Psychology*, 1979, *47*, 595–597. (b)

Kearny, G. E., & McElwain, D. W. *Aboriginal cognition*. New Jersey: Humanities Press, 1976.

Keating, D. P., & Bobbitt, B. L. Individual and developmental differences in cognitive processing components of mental ability. *Child Development*, 1978, *49*, 155–167.

Keating, D. P., Keniston, A. H., Manis, F. R., & Bobbitt, B. L. Development of the search parameter. *Child Development*, 1980, *51*, 39–44.

Kemeny, G. J., Snell, J. L., & Thompson, G. L. *Introduction to finite mathematics*. Englewood Cliffs, N.J.: Prentice Hall, 1966.

Kendler, H. H., & Kendler, T. S. Problems in problem solving research. In *Current trends in psychological theory: a bicentennial program*. Pittsburgh: University of Pittsburgh Press, 1961.

Kendler, H. H., & Kendler, T. S. Vertical and horizontal processes in problem solving. *Psychological Review*, 1962, *69*, 1–16.

Kieras, D. E., & Greeno, J. G. Effects of meaningfulness on judgments of computability. *Memory and Cognition*, 1975, *3*, 349–355.

Kilpatrick, J. *Analyzing the solution of word problems in mathematics: an exploratory study*. Unpublished Doctoral Dissertation. Stanford University, 1967.

Kilpatrick, J. Research on problem solving in mathematics. *School Science and Mathematics*, 1978, *3*, 189–192.

Kish, L. Some statistical problems in research design. *American Sociological Review*, 1959, *24*, 328–338.

Klein, D. B. *A history of scientific psychology*. London: Routledge & Kegan Paul, 1970.

Kleinmuntz, B. (Ed.). *Problem solving: Research, method and theory*. New York: Wiley, 1966.

Kleinmuntz, B. (Ed.). *Formal representation of human judgment*. New York: Wiley, 1968.

Klinger, E. *Structure and functions of fantasy*. New York: Wiley, 1971.

Koch, S. *Psychology, a study of a science* (Vol. 2). New York: McGraw Hill, 1959.

Koffka, K. *Principles of Gestalt psychology.* New York: Harcourt, Brace & World, 1935.

Köhler, W. *Intelligenzprüfungen an Menschenaffen.* Berlin: Springer, 1917.

Köhler, W. *The mentality of apes.* (Translated by E. Winter). New York: Harcourt, Brace & World, 1925.

Köhler, W. *The mentality of apes.* London: Routledge, 1927.

Kohs, F. C. Block Design test. *Journal of Experimental Psychology,* 1920, *3,* 357–376.

Kohs, F. C. *Intelligence measurement.* London: Macmillan, 1923.

Kotovsky, K., & Simon, H. A. Empirical tests of a theory of human acquisition of concepts for sequential patterns. *Cognitive Psychology,* 1973, *4,* 399–424.

Krech, D. Dynamic systems, psychological fields and hypothetical constructs. *Psychological Review,* 1950, *57,* 283–290.

Kruskal, W. H., & Tanur, J. *International encyclopaedia of statistics* (2 Vols.). New York: Free Press, 1978.

Krutetskii, V. A. *The psychology of mathematical abilities in school children.* Chicago: University of Chicago Press, 1976.

Kuehn, A. A., & Hamburger, H. J. A. A heuristic program for locating warehouses. *Management Science,* 1963, *9,* 643–666.

Kuhn, T. S. *The structure of scientific revolutions.* Chicago: University of Chicago Press, 1962.

Lachman, R., Lachman, J. L., & Butterfield, E. C. *Cognitive psychology and information processing. An introduction.* Hillsdale, N.J.: Lawrence Erlbaum Associates 1979.

Larkin, J. H., McDermott, J., Simon, D. P., & Simon, H. A. Expert and novice performance in solving physics problems. *Science,* 1980, *208,* 1335–1342.

Larkin, J. H., & Reif, F. Understanding and teaching problem solving in physics. *European Journal of Science Education,* 1979, *1,* 191–203.

Lazerte, M. E. *The development of problem solving ability in arithmetic: A summary of investigations.* Toronto: Clark Irwin, 1933.

Levine, G., & Burke, C. J. *Mathematical model techniques for learning theories.* New York: Academic Press, 1972.

Levine, M. Human discrimination learning: The subset-sampling. *Psychological Bulletin,* 1970, *74,* 397–404.

Levy, L. H. *Conceptions of personality: Theory and Research.* New York: Random House, 1970.

Lewin, K. The conceptual representation and the measurement of psychological forces. *Contemporary Psychological Theory,* 1938, *2,* 3–32.

Light, R. J. Measures of response agreement for qualitative data: Some generalizations and alternatives. *Psychological Bulletin,* 1971, *76,* 365–377.

Loehlin, J. C., Lindzey, G., & Spuhler, J. *Race differences in intelligence.* San Francisco: Freeman, 1975.

Longstreth, L. E. Level I–Level II abilities as they affect performance of three races in the college classroom. *Journal of Educational Psychology,* 1978, *70,* 289–297.

Lord, F. M., & Novick, M. *The statistical theory of mental test scores.* Reading, Mass.: Addison Wesley, 1968.

Lorge, I., Fox, D., Davitz, J., & Brenner, M. A survey of studies contrasting the quality of group performance and individual performance. *Psychological Bulletin,* 1958, *55,* 337–372.

Lorge, I., & Solomon, H. Two models of group behavior in the solution of Eureka-type problems. *Psychometrika,* 1955, *20,* 139–148.

Luchins, A. S. Mechanization in problem solving: the effect of Einstellung. *Psychological Monographs,* 1942, *54* (Whole No. 248).

Luchins, A. S., & Luchins, E. H. *Wertheimer's seminars revisited. Problem solving and thinking* (3 Vols.). Albany, N.Y.: Faculty Student Association, State University of New York at Albany, Inc., 1970.

Lüer, G. The development of strategies of solution in problem solving. In A. Elithorn & D. Jones (Eds.), *Artificial and human thinking*. Amsterdam: Elsevier Scientific Publishing Co., 1973.

Lunneborg, C. E. *Individual differences in memory and information processing*. Seattle: University of Washington, Educational Assessment Center, 1974.

Lunneborg, C. E. Choice reaction time: what role in ability measurement? *Applied Psychological Measurement*, 1977, *1*, 309–330.

Luria, A. R. *The role of speech in the regulation of normal and abnormal behavior*. New York: Liveright, 1961.

Maccoby, E. E., & Jacklin, C. N. (Eds.). *The psychology of sex differences*. Stanford, Ca.: Stanford University Press, 1974.

MacCorquodale, K., & Meehl, P. E. On a distinction between hypothetical constructs and intervening variables. *Psychological Review*, 1948, *55*, 95–107.

Mace, C. A. Causal explanations in psychology. In C. Banks & P. L. Broadhurst (Eds.), STEPHANOS: *Studies in psychology: Essays presented to Sir Cyril Burt*. London: University of London Press, 1965.

Maier, N. R. F. Reasoning in humans. I. On direction. *Journal of Comparative Psychology*, 1930, *10*, 115–143.

Maier, N. R. F. Reasoning and learning. *Psychological Review*, 1931, *38*, 332–346. (a)

Maier, N. R. F. Reasoning in humans: II. The solution of a problem and its appearance in consciousness. *Journal of Comparative Psychology*, 1931, *12*, 181–194. (b)

Maier, N. R. F. The behavior mechanisms concerned with problem solving. *Psychological Review*, 1940, *47*, 43–58.

Maier, N. R. F. *Problem solving and creativity in individuals and groups*. Belmont, Ca.: Brooks/Cole Publishing Co., Wadsworth Publishing Co., 1970.

Maltzman, I. Effects of task instruction on solution of different classes of anagrams. *Journal of Experimental Psychology*, 1953, *45*, 351–354.

Maltzman, I. Thinking: From a behavioristic point of view. *Psychological Review*, 1955, *62*, 275–286.

Mandler, J. M., & Mandler, G. *Thinking: From association to Gestalt*. New York: Wiley, 1964.

Marks, M. R. Problem solving as a function of the situation. *Journal of Experimental Psychology*, 1951, *47*, 74–80.

Marx, M. H. The general nature of theory construction. In M. H. Marx (Ed.), *Psychological theory*. New York: Macmillan, 1951.

Maslow, A. H. *Motivation and personality*. New York: Harper & Row, 1954.

Maslow, A. H. *Toward a psychology of being* (Rev. ed.). Princeton, N.J.: Van Nostrand, 1968.

Matarazzo, J. D. *Wechsler's measurement and appraisal of adult intelligence*. Baltimore: William & Wilkins, 1972.

Mawardi, B. H. Thought sequences in creative problem solving. *American Psychologist*, 1960, *15*, 429.

Maxwell, A. E. *Analyzing qualitative data*. London: Chapman & Hall, 1975.

May, R. *Psychology and the human dilemma*. Princeton, N.J.: Van Nostrand, 1967.

Mayer, R. E. Different problem-solving competencies established in learning computer programming with and without meaningful models. *Journal of Educational Psychology*, 1975, *67*, 725–734.

Mayer, R. E. Comprehension as affected by structure of problem representation. *Memory and Cognition*, 1976, *4*, 249–255.

Mayer, R. E., & Greeno, J. G. Effects of meaningfulness and organization on problem solving and compatibility judgments. *Memory and Cognition,* 1975, *3,* 356–362.

Mayzner, M. S., & Tresselt, M. E. Verbal concept attainment: a function of the number and strength of positive instances presented. *Journal of Psychology,* 1962, *53,* 469–474.

McCormick, E. J. *Job dimensions: Their nature and possible uses.* Paper presented at APA Convention, Chicago, 1965.

McDermott, J. Some strengths of production system architectures. In J. M. Scandura & C. J. Brainerd (Eds.), *Structural/process models of complex human behavior.* Alphen aan den Rijn: Sijthoff & Noordhoff, 1978.

McGrath, J. E., & Altman, I. *Small group research: A synthesis and critique of the field.* New York: Holt, Rinehart, & Winston, 1966.

McGuire, C. H., & Babbott, D. *Simulation technique in the measurement of problem solving skills: A technology or conceptual breakthrough.* Paper read at American Educational Research Association National Council for Measurement in Education, Chicago, February, 1965.

McKellar, P. The method of introspection. In J. Scher (Ed.), *Theories of the mind.* New York: Free Press of Glencoe, 1962.

McNemar, Q. *Psychological statistics* (3rd ed.). New York: Wiley, 1962.

Medley, D. M., & Mitzel, H. E. Application of analyses of variance to the estimation of the reliability of observations of teachers' classroom behavior. *Journal of Experimental Education,* 1958, *27,* 23–35.

Medley, D. M., & Mitzel, H. E. Measuring classroom behavior by systematic observation. In N. L. Gage (Ed.), *Handbook of research on teaching.* Chicago, Ill.: Rand McNally, 1963.

Mednick, S. A. The associative basis of the creative process. *Psychological Review,* 1962, *69,* 220–232.

Melton, A. W. (Ed.). *Categories of human learning.* New York: Academic Press, 1964.

Menchinskaya, N. A. Intellectual activity in solving arithmetic problems. In *Soviet studies in the psychology of learning and teaching mathematics,* 1963, *3,* 7–53. (School Mathematics Study Group, Stanford University).

Mervis, C. B., & Rosch, E. Categorization of natural objects. *Annual Review of Psychology,* 1981, *32,* 89–115.

Merz, F. Der Einfluss des Verbalisierens auf die Leistung bei Intelligenzaufgaben. *Zeitschrift für experimentelle und angewandte Psychologie,* 1969, *16,* 114–137.

Messick, S. Beyond structure: In search of functional methods of psychological process. *Psychometrika,* 1972, *37,* 357–375.

Messick, S. Multivariate models of cognition and personality: The need for both process and structure in psychological theory and measurement. In J. Royce (Ed.), *Multivariate analysis and psychological theory.* New York: Academic Press, 1973.

Miller, G. A. The magical number seven, plus or minus two. *Psychological Review,* 1956, *63,* 81–97.

Miller, G. A., Galanter, E., & Pribram, K. *Plans and the structure of behavior.* New York: Holt, 1960.

Miller, L. A. Programming by non-programmers. *International Journal of Man Machine Studies,* 1974, *6,* 237–260.

Miller, R. B. *Task taxonomy: Science or technology.* New York: Poughkeepsie, IBM, 1966.

Minsky, M. Steps towards artificial intelligence. In E. A. Feigenbaum & J. Feldman (Eds.), *Computers and thought.* New York: McGraw Hill, 1963.

Minsky, M. *Semantic information processing.* Cambridge, Mass.: MIT Press, 1968.

Morgan, C. L. *An introduction to comparative psychology.* London: Scott, 1894.

Müller, J. *Handbuch der Physiologie des Menschen.* Coblentz: Hölscher, 1838.

Murray, H. C., & Denny, J. P. Interaction of ability level and interpolated activity (opportunity for incubation) in human problem solving. *Psychological Reports,* 1969, *24,* 271–276.

Myers, R. E., & Torrance, E. P. *Invitations to thinking and doing.* Boston: Ginn, 1964.

Necker, L. A. Observations on some remarkable phenomenon seen in Switzerland, and an optical phenomenon which occurs on viewing. *Philosophical Magazine,* 1832, *1,* 329–337.

Neimark, E. D., & Santa, J. L. Thinking and concept attainment. *Annual Review of Psychology,* 1975, *26,* 173–205.

Neisser, U. The multiplicity of thought. *British Journal of Psychology,* 1963, *54,* 1–14.

Neisser, U. *Cognitive psychology.* New York: Appleton Century Crofts, 1967.

Neumann, J. von. *The computer and the brain.* New Haven: Yale University Press, 1958.

Newell, A. Production systems: Models of control structures. In W. G. Chase (Ed.), *Visual information processing.* New York: Academic Press, 1973.(a)

Newell, A. You can't play 20 questions with nature and win. In W. G. Chase (Ed.), *Visual information processing.* New York: Academic Press, 1973.(b)

Newell, A., Shaw, J. C., & Simon, H. A. Chess playing programs and the problem of complexity. *IBM Journal of Research and Development,* 1958, *2,* 320–335.(a)

Newell, A., Shaw, J. C., & Simon, H. A. Elements of a theory of human problem solving. *Psychological Review,* 1958, *65,* 151–166.(b)

Newell, A., Shaw, J. C., & Simon, H. A. The processes of creative thinking. In H. E. Gruber, G. Terrell & M. Wertheimer (Eds.), *Contemporary approaches to creative thinking.* New York: Atherton Press, 1962.

Newell, A., Shaw, J. C., & Simon, H. A. Empirical explorations with the logic theory machine. In E. A. Feigenbaum & J. Feldman (Eds.), *Computers and thought.* New York: McGraw Hill, 1963.

Newell, A., & Simon, H. A. *Human problem solving.* Englewood Cliffs, N.J.: Prentice Hall, 1972.

Nie, N. H., Hull, C. H., Jenkins, J. G., Steinbrenner, K., & Bent, D. H. SPSS: *Statistical Package for the Social Sciences* (2nd ed.). New York: McGraw Hill, 1975.

Nilsson, N. *Problem solving methods in artificial intelligence.* New York: McGraw Hill, 1971.

Nisbett, R. E., & Wilson, T. D. Telling more than we can know: Verbal reports on mental processes. *Psychological Review,* 1977, *84,* 231–259.

Nunnally, J. C. *Psychometric theory.* New York: McGraw Hill, 1978.

Ogbu, J. *Minority education and caste.* New York: Academic Press, 1978.

Olshavsky, J. E. Reading as problem solving, an investigation of strategies. *Reading Research Quarterly,* 1976–77, *4,* 654–674.

Olton, R. M., & Johnson, D. M. Mechanisms in incubation in creative problem solving. *American Journal of Psychology,* 1976, *89,* 617–630.

O'Neil, W. M. Hypothetical terms and relations in psychological theorizing. *British Journal of Psychology,* 1953, *44,* 211–220.

Osborn, A. F. *Applied imagination* (3rd ed.). New York: Scribener, 1963.

Osgood, C. E. The similarity paradox in human learning: A resolution. *Psychological Review,* 1949, *56,* 132–143.

Osgood, C. E. *Method and theory in experimental psychology.* New York: Oxford University Press, 1953.

Paige, J. M., & Simon, H. A. Cognitive processes in solving algebra word problems. In B. Kleinmuntz (Ed.), *Problem solving: Research, method and theory.* New York: Wiley, 1966.

Patrick, C. Creative thought in artists. *Journal of Psychology,* 1937, *4,* 35–73.

Patrick, C. Scientific thought. *Journal of Psychology*, 1938, *5*, 55–83.

Patrick, C. Whole and part relationships in creative thought. *American Journal of Psychology*, 1941, *54*, 128–131.

Payne, J. W. *A process tracing study of risky decision making.* (Complex Information Processing Working Paper No. 274). Pittsburgh: Carnegie Mellon University, 1975.

Pearson, E. S., & Hartley, H. O. *Biometrika tables for statisticians* (2nd ed.). New York: Cambridge Press, 1958.

Pellegrino, J. W., & Glaser, R. Cognitive correlates and components in the analysis of individual difference. *Intelligence*, 179, *3*, 187–214.

Pellegrino, J. W., & Glaser, R. Components of inductive reasoning. In R. E. Snow, P. A. Federico & W. E. Montague, *Aptitude, learning and instruction* (Vol. 1). Hillsdale, N.J.: Lawrence Erlbaum Associates, 1980.

Perfetti, C. A. Language comprehension and the deverbalization of intelligence. In L. B. Resnick (Ed.), *The nature of intelligence*. Hillsdale, N.J.: Lawrence Erlbaum Associates, 1976.

Perls, F. S. *Gestalt therapy verbatim*. London: Bantam Books, 1972.

Petersen, A. C. Personal communication reported by J. A. Sherman, *Sex related cognitive differences*. Springfield, Ill.: Charles C Thomas, 1978.

Piaget, J. *The origins of intelligence in children*. London: Routledge & Kegan Paul, 1953.

Piaget, J. *Six psychological studies*. London: University of London Press Ltd., 1968.

Polanyi, M. *Personal knowledge: Towards a post-critical philosophy*. London: Routledge & Kegan Paul, 1958.

Polya, G. *How to solve it*. Princeton, N.J.: Princeton University Press, 1945.

Polya, G. *Mathematics and plausible reasoning* (2 Vols.). Princeton, N.J.: Princeton University Press, 1954.

Polya, G. *How to solve it* (2nd ed.). New York: Doubleday, 1957.

Popham, W. J., & Sirotnik, K. K. *Educational statistics: use and interpretation* (2nd ed.). New York: Harper & Row, 1973.

Posner, M. I., & McLeod, P. Information processing models: in search of elementary operations. *Annual Review of Psychology*, 1982, *33*, 477–514.

Quealy, R. J. Senior high school students use contextual aids in reading. *Reading Research Quarterly*, 1969, *4*, 512–533.

Quételet, L. A. J. *Sur l'homme*. Paris: Bachelier. 1835.

Quinton, G., & Fellows, B. J. "Perceptual" strategies in the solving of 3–term series problems. *British Journal of Psychology*, 1975, *66*, 69–78.

Raaheim, K. The concept of the deviant situation. *Psychological Reports*, 1963, *13*, 174.

Raaheim, K. *Problem solving and intelligence*. Oslo/Bergen/Tromso: Universitetsforlaget, 1974.

Radford, J. Reflections on introspection. *American Psychologist*, 1974, *29*, 245–250.

Radford, J., & Burton, A. *Thinking: Its nature and development*. New York: Wiley, 1974.

Rasch, G. *Probabilistic models for some intelligence and attainment tests* (Rev. ed.). Chicago: University of Chicago Press, 1980.

Rasch, G. *Probabilistic models for some intelligence and attainment tasks*. Copenhagen: Danish Institute for Educational Research, 1960.

Rasmussen, J., & Jensen, A. Mental procedures in real-life tasks: A case study of electronic trouble shooting. *Ergonomics*, 1974, *17*, 293–307.

Ray, W. S. Complex tasks for use in human problem solving research. *Psychological Bulletin*, 1955, *52*, 134–149.

Reed, S. K. Facilitation of problem solving. In N. J. Castellan, D. B. Pisoni & G. R. Potts (Eds.), *Cognitive theory* (Vol. 2). Hillsdale, N.J.: Lawrence Erlbaum Associates, 1977.

Reed, S. K., Ernst, G. W., & Bannerji, R. The role of analogy in transfer between similar problem states. *Cognitive Psychology*, 1974, *6*, 436–450.

Reif, F., & Heller, J. I. Knowledge structure and problem solving in physics. *Educational Psychologist*, 1982, *17*, 102–127.

Reitman, J. S. Skilled perception in GO; deducing memory structures from inter-response times. *Cognitive Psychology*, 1976, *8*, 336–356.

Reitman, W. R. *Cognition and thought*. New York: Wiley, 1965.

Resnick, L. B. *The nature of intelligence*. Hillsdale, N. J.: Lawrence Erlbaum Associates, 1976.

Resnick, L. B. Instructional psychology. *Annual Review of Psychology*, 1981, *32*, 659–705.

Resnick, L. B., & Ford, W. W. *The psychology of mathematics for instruction*. Hillsdale, N.J.: Lawrence Erlbaum Associates, 1981.

Revlis, R. Two models of syllogistic reasoning: Feature selection and conversion. *Journal of Verbal Learning and Verbal Behavior*, 1975, *14*, 180–195.

Rimoldi, H. J. A. A technique for the study of problem solving. *Educational and Psychological Measurement*, 1955, *15*, 450–461.

Rimoldi, H. J. A., Devanne, J., & Haley, J. Characterization of processes. *Educational and Psychological Measurement*, 1961, *21*, 383–392.

Rimoldi, H. J. A., Fogliatto, H. M., Erdmann, J. B. & Donnelly, M. B. *Problem solving in high school and college students*. Chicago: Loyola University Psychometric Laboratory, Publication No. 42, 1964.

Robinson, H. M. Visual and auditory modalities related to methods for beginning reading. *Reading Research Quarterly*, 1972, *8*, 7–39.

Rodgers, C. R. *Counseling and psychotherapy*. Boston: Houghton Mifflin, 1942.

Rosch, E., & Lloyd, B. B. (Eds.) *Cognition and categorization*. Hillsdale, N.J.: Lawrence Erlbaum Associates, 1978.

Rosenshine, B. *Teaching behaviours and student achievement*. Slough: National Foundation for Educational Research, 1971.

Rossman, J. *The psychology of the inventor*. Washington: Inventor's Publishing Co., 1931.

Roth, B. *The effects of overt verbalization on problem solving*. Unpublished Doctoral Dissertation. New York University, 1966.

Ruger, H. A. The psychology of efficiency. *Archives of Psychology*, 1910, *2*, (Whole number 15).

Rumelhart, D. E. Toward an interactive model of reading. In Dornic, S. (Ed.), *Attention and performance VI*. Hillsdale, N.J.: Lawrence Erlbaum Associates, 1977.

Rumelhart, D. E., & Abrahamson, A. A. A model for analogical reasoning. *Cognitive Psychology*, 1973, *5*, 1–28.

Rumelhart, D. E., & Norman, D. A. The computer implementation. In D. A. Norman & D. E. Rumelhart (Eds.), *Explorations in cognition*. San Francisco: W. H. Freeman, 1975.

Sackman, H. Experimental analysis of computer problem solving. *Human Factors*, 1970, *12*, 187–201.

Sanders, N. M. *Classroom questions: What kinds?* New York: Harper & Row, 1966.

Sattler, J. M. *Assessment of children's intelligence*. Philadelphia: W. B. Saunders, 1974.

Saugstad, P. An analysis of Maier's pendulum problem. *Journal of Experimental Psychology*, 1957, *54*, 168–179.

Saugstad, P. Availability of functions. A discussion of some theoretical aspects. *Acta Psychologica*, 1958, *13*, 384–400.

Saugstad, P., & Raaheim, K. Problem solving, past experience and availability of functions. *British Journal of Psychology*, 1960, *51*, 97–104.

Scandura, J. M. On higher order rules in problem solving. *Journal of Educational Psychology*, 1973, *10*, 159–160.

Scandura, J. M. *Problem solving: A structural/process approach with instructional implications*. New York: Academic Press, 1977.

Scandura, J. M., & Brainerd, C. J. *Structural/process models of complex human behavior.* NATO Advanced Study Institutes Series. Alphen aan den Rijn: Sijthoff & Noordhoff, 1978.

Scarr–Salapatec, S. Race, social class and IQ. *Science,* 1971, *174,* 1285–1295.

Schachtel, E. G. *Metamorphosis: On the development of affect, perception, attention and memory.* New York: Basic Books, 1959.

Scheerer, M. Problem solving. *Scientific American,* 1963, *208,* 118–128.

Scheffler, I. *Science and subjectivity.* Indianapolis: Bobbs-Merrill, 1967.

Schmidt, F. L., & Hunter, J. E. Racial and ethnic bias in psychological tests. *American Psychologist,* 1974, *29,* 1–8.

Schneider, W., & Shiffrin, R. M. Controlled and automated human information processing. I. Detection search and attention. *Psychological Review,* 1977, *84,* 1–66.

Scott, W. A. Reliability of content analysis: The case of nominal scale coding. *Public Opinion Quarterly,* 1955, *19,* 321–325.

Scott, W. S. Reaction times of young intellectual deviates. *Archives of Psychology,* 1940, *256,* 7–64.

Selz, O. *Über die Gesetze des geordneten Denkverlaufs.* Stuttgart: Spemann, 1913.

Selz, O. *Zur Psychologie des produktiven Denkens und des Irrtums.* Bonn: Cohen, 1922.

Shannon, C. E. The mathematical theory of communication. In C. E. Shannon & W. Weaver, *The mathematical theory of communication.* Urbana: University of Illinois Press, 1948.

Sharp, S. E. Individual psychology: A study of psychological method. *American Journal of Psychology,* 1898–1899, *10,* 329–390.

Shiffrin, R. M., & Schneider, W. Controlled and automated human information processing: II. Perceptual, learning, automatic attending and general theory. *Psychological Review,* 1977, *84,* 127–190.

Sidman, M. A note on functional relations obtained from group data. *Psychological Bulletin,* 1952, *49,* 268.

Siegel, S. *Nonparametric statistics for the behavioral sciences.* New York: McGraw-Hill, 1956.

Silveira, J. M. *Incubation: The effect of interruption timing and length on problem solution and quality of problem processing.* Unpublished Doctoral Dissertation. University of Oregon, 1972.

Silverstein, A. B. The appraisal of the stability of WAIS, WISC and WIPPSI short forms. *Journal of Consulting and Clinical Psychology,* 1970, *34,* 12–14.

Silverstein, A. B. A short-short form of the WISC-R for screening purposes. *Psychological Reports,* 1974, *35,* 817–818.

Silverstein, A. B. Two and four-subtest short forms of the Wechsler Adult Intelligence Scale—Revised. *Journal of Consulting and Clinical Psychology,* 1982, *50,* 415–418.

Simon, D. P., & Simon, H. A. Individual differences in solving physics problems. In R. D. Siegler (Ed.), *Children's thinking: What develops?* Hillsdale, N.J.: Lawrence Erlbaum Associates, 1978.

Simon, H. A. *The sciences of the artificial.* Cambridge, Mass.: MIT Press, 1969.

Simon, H. A. Complexity and the representation of patterned sequences of symbols. *Psychological Review,* 1972, *79,* 369–382.

Simon, H. A. The functional equivalence of problem solving skills. *Cognitive Psychology,* 1975, *7,* 268–288.

Simon, H. A. Identifying basic abilities underlying intelligent performance on complex tasks. In L. B. Resnick (Ed.), *The nature of intelligence.* Hillsdale, N.J.: Lawrence Erlbaum Associates, 1976.

Simon, H. A. Information processing models of cognition. *Annual Review of Psychology,* 1979, *30,* 363–396.

Simon, H. A., & Kotovsky, K. Human acquisition of concepts for sequential patterns. *Psychological Review*, 1963, *70*, 534–546.

Simon, H. A., & Newell, A. Heuristic problem solving: The next advance in operations research. *Operations Research*, 1958, *6*, 1–10.

Simon, H. A., & Reed, S. K. Modeling strategy shifts in a problem solving task. *Cognitive Psychology*, 1976, *8*, 86–97.

Skemp, R. R. *The psychology of learning mathematics*. Baltimore: Penguin Books, 1971.

Skinner, B. F. *The behavior of organisms*. New York: Appleton-Century-Crofts, 1938.

Skinner, B. F. *Science and human behavior*. New York: Macmillan, 1953.

Skinner, B. F. *Verbal behavior*. New York: Appleton Century Crofts, 1957.

Skinner, B. F. Teaching machines. *Science*, 1958, *128*, 969–977.

Skinner, B. F. An operant analysis of problem solving. In B. Kleinmuntz (Ed.), *Problem solving: Research, method and theory*. New York: Wiley, 1966.

Skinner, B. F. *About behaviorism*. New York: Alfred A. Knopf, 1974.

Smetana, F. O. Mapping individual logical processes. *Educational and Psychological Measurement*, 1975, *35*, 679–682.

Smith, B. O. The improvement of critical thinking. *Progressive Education*, 1953, *30*, 129–134.

Smith, H. K. *The responses of good and poor readers when asked to read for different purposes*. Unpublished Doctoral Dissertation. University of Chicago, 1964.

Smith, J. P. The effect of general versus specific heuristics in mathematical problem solving tasks. *Dissertation Abstracts International*, 1973, *34*, 5A, p. 2400.

Smith, R. D. Heuristic simulation of psychological decision processes. *Journal of Applied Research*, 1968, *52*, 325–330.

Snow, R. E. Theory and method for research on aptitude processes. In R. J. Sternberg & D. K. Detterman (Eds.), *Human intelligence: Perspectives on its theory and measurement*. Norwood, N.J.: Ablex, 1979.

Snow, R. E. Aptitude processes. In R. E. Snow, P. A. Frederico & W. E. Montague (Eds.), *Aptitude, learning and instruction* (Vol. 1). Hillsdale, N.J.: Lawrence Erlbaum Associates 1980.

Spearman, C. "General intelligence" objectively determined and measured. *American Journal of Psychology*, 1904, *15*, 201–293.

Spearman, C. *The nature of "intelligence" and the principles of cognition*. New York: The Macmillan Co., 1923.

Spearman, C. *The abilities of man*. New York: The Macmillan Co., 1927.

Speedie, S. M., Treffinger, D. T., & Houtz, J. C. Classification and evaluation of problem solving tasks. *Contemporary Educational Psychology*, 1976, *1*, 52–75.

Spence, K. W., & Spence, J. T. (Eds). *The psychology of learning and motivation: Advances in research and theory*. (Vol. 2) New York: Academic Press, 1968.

Spiegel, M. R., & Bryant, N. D. Is speed of processing information related to intelligence and achievement? *Journal of Educational Psychology*, 1978, *70*, 904–910.

Spiker, C., & McCandless, B. R. The concept of intelligence and the philosophy of science. *Psychological Review*, 1954, *61*, 255–266.

Squire, J. R. *The responses of adolescents while reading four short stories*. Urbana, Ill.: National Council of Teachers of English, 1964.

Staats, A. W. *Learning, language and cognition*. London: Holt, Rinehart, & Winston, 1968.

Staats, A. W., & Staats, C. K. *Complex human behavior*. New York: Holt, Rinehart, & Winston, 1963.

Stafford, R. E. *An investigation of similarities in parent-child test scores for evidence of hereditary components*. Unpublished Doctoral Dissertation. Princeton University, 1972.

Stallman, R. M., & Sussman, G. J. *Forward reasoning and dependency-directed backtrack-*

ing in a system for computer aided circuit analysis. MIT Artificial Intelligence Laboratory, Memo No. 380, September, 1976.

Stanley, J. C. *Improving experimental design and analysis.* Chicago: Rand McNally, 1968.

Steiner, I. D. Models for inferring relationships between group size and potential group productivity. *Behavioral Science,* 1966, *11,* 273–283.

Stephenson, W. Perspectives in psychology: XXVI. Consciousness out—subjectivity in. *Psychological Record,* 1968, *18,* 499–501.

Stern, W. L. Über die psychologischen Methoden der Intelligenzprüfung. Berlin: *V. Kongress der experimentellen Psychologie,* 1912, *16,* 1–109.

Sternberg, R. J. *The componential analysis of human abilities: intelligence, information processing and analogical reasoning* (2 Vols.). Unpublished Doctoral Dissertation. Stanford University, 1975.

Sternberg, R. J. Component processes in analogical reasoning. *Psychological Review,* 1977, *84,* 353–378 (a).

Sternberg, R. J. *Intelligence, information processing and analogical reasoning: The componential analysis of human abilities.* Hillsdale, N.J.: Lawrence Erlbaum Associates, 1977. (b)

Sternberg, R. J. *Contrasting conceptions of intelligence and their educational implications* (Technical Report No. 14). Yale University, New Haven, Conn. Department of Psychology, 1978.

Sternberg, R. J. Intelligence research at the interface between differential and cognitive psychology. In R. J. Sternberg & D. K. Detterman (Eds.), *Human intelligence: Perspectives on its theory and measurement.* Norwood, N.J.: Ablex Publishing Corporation, 1979. (a)

Sternberg, R. J. The nature of mental abilities. *American Psychologist,* 1979, *34,* 214–230. (b)

Sternberg, R. J. Sketch of a componential subtheory of human intelligence. *The Behavioral and Brain Sciences,* 1980, *3,* 573–614. (a)

Sternberg, R. J. Factor theories of intelligence are alright almost. *Educational Researcher,* 1980, *9,* 6–13, 18. (b)

Sternberg, R. J. The evolution of theories of intelligence. *Intelligence,* 1981, *5,* 209–230. (a)

Sternberg, R. J. Intelligence and nonentrenchment. *Journal of Educational Psychology,* 1981, *73,* 1–16. (b)

Sternberg, R. J. Nothing fails like success: The search for an intelligent paradigm for studying intelligence. *Journal of Educational Psychology,* 1981, *73,* 142–155. (c)

Sternberg, R. J., Conway, B. E., Ketron, J. L., & Bernstein, M. People's conceptions of intelligence. *Journal of Personality and Social Psychology,* 1981, *41,* 37–55.

Sternberg, R. J., & Detterman, D. K. (Eds). *Human intelligence: Perspectives on its theory and measurement.* Norwood, N.J.: Ablex, 1979.

Sternberg, R. J., & Ketron, J. L. Selection and implementation of strategies in reasoning by analogy. *Journal of Educational Psychology,* 1982, *74,* 399–413.

Sternberg, R. J., & Rifkin, B. The development of analogical reasoning processes. *Journal of Experimental Child Psychology,* 1979, *27,* 195–232.

Sternberg, R. J., & Weil, E. M. An aptitude–strategy interaction in linear syllogistic reasoning. *Journal of Educational Psychology,* 1980, *72,* 226–239.

Stevenson, H. W. The taxonomy of tasks. In W. Hartup & J. de Witt (Eds.), *Determinants of behavioral development.* New York: Academic Press, 1972.

Stevenson, H. W., & Odom, R. D. The relation of anxiety to children's performance on learning and problem solving tasks. *Child Development,* 1965, *36,* 1003–1012.

Stinessen, L. Effect of different training on solution of Katona's match-stick problems. *Scandinavian Journal of Psychology,* 1973, *14,* 106–110.

Stinessen, L. Verbalization of discovered principles for solving match-stick problems. *Scandinavian Journal of Psychology*, 1974, *15*, 203–206.

Sussman, G. J. *Some aspects of medical diagnosis*. MIT Artificial Intelligence Laboratory Working Paper No. 56, December 1973.

Sussman, G. J., & Brown, A. L. *Localization of failures in radio circuits: A study in causal and teleological reasoning*. MIT Artificial Intelligence Laboratory, Memo 319, December 1974.

Szekeley, L. Productive processes in learning and thinking. *Acta Psychologica*, 1950, *7*, 388–407.

Taylor, D. W. Thinking and creativity. *Annals of the New York Academy of Science*, 1960, *91*, 108–127.

Taylor, D. W. Thinking. In M. H. Marx (Ed.), *Theories in contemporary psychology*. New York: Macmillan, 1967.

Taylor, I. A. A transactional approach to creativity and its applications to education. *Journal of Creative Behavior*, 1971, *5*, 190–197.

Terman, L. M. *The measurement of intelligence*. Boston: Houghton Mifflin, 1916.

Terman, L. M., & Merrill, M. A. *Stanford-Binet Intelligence Scale. Manual*. 3rd Revision, Form L–M. London: Harrap, 1961.

Thomas, J. C. An analysis of behavior in the Hobbits-Orcs problem. University of Michigan: Human Performance Center, *Technical Report No. 31*, August, 1971.

Thomas, J. C. Jr. An analysis of behavior in the Hobbits-Orcs problem. *Cognitive Psychology*, 1974, *6*, 257–269.

Thomson, G. H. General versus group factors in mental activities. *Psychological Review*, 1920, *27*, 173–190.

Thomson, G. H. *The factorial analysis of human ability*. London: University of London Press, 1939/1951 (5th ed.).

Thorndike, E. L. Animal intelligence: An experimental study of the associative processes in animals. *Psychological Monographs, Review Supplements*, 1898, *6* (Whole No. 8).

Thorndike, E. L. Units and scales for measuring educational products. *Proceedings*, Conference on Educational Measurements. 1914. (Cited by J. Loevinger, The meaning and measurement of ego development. *American Psychologist*, 1966, *21*, 195–206 [page 202]).

Thorndike, E. L. Reading as reasoning: A study of mistakes in paragraph reading. *Journal of Educational Psychology*, 1917, *8*, 323–332.

Thorndike, E. L. *The measurement of intelligence*. New York: Teachers' College, Columbia University, 1925.

Thorndike, E. L. *The psychology of arithmetic*. New York: Macmillan, 1927.

Thorndike, R. L. Concepts of culture-fairness. *Journal of Educational Measurement*, 1971, *8*, 63–70.

Thorndike, R. L. *Applied psychometrics*. Boston, Mass.: Houghton Mifflin, 1982.

Thorndike, R. L., & Hagen, E. P. *Measurement and evaluation in psychology and education* (3rd ed.). New York: Wiley, 1969.

Thurstone, L. L. *Multiple-factor analysis: A development and expansion of "The vectors of mind."* Chicago: University of Chicago Press, 1947.

Thurstone, L. L. [Autobiographical chapter]. In C. Murchison (Ed.), *A history of psychology in autobiography* (Vol. 4). Worcester, Mass.: Clark University Press, 1952.

Tucker, L. R. The extension of factor analysis to 3 dimensional matrices. In N. Frederickson & H. Gullikson (Eds.), *Contributions to mathematical psychology*. New York: Holt, Rinehart & Winston, 1964.

Tucker, L. R. Some mathematical notes on three–mode factor analysis. *Psychometrika*, 1966, *31*, 279–311.

Tucker, L. R., & Messick, S. An individual differences model for multidimensional scaling. *Psychometrika*, 1963, *28*, 333–367.

Tuddenham, R. D. The nature and measurement of intelligence. In L. Postman (Ed.), *Psychology in the making: Histories of selected research problems.* New York: Knopf, 1962.

Tyler, L. E. *The psychology of human differences* (3rd ed.). New York: Appleton-Century-Crofts, 1965.

Tyler, L. E. Human abilities. *Annual Review of Psychology*, 1972, *23*, 177–206.

Uhr, L. *Pattern recognition.* New York: Wiley, 1966.

Underwood, B. J. *Psychological research.* New York: Appleton-Century-Crofts, 1957.

University of Illinois. *SOUPAC Statistical Systems Program Descriptions.* Urbana-Champaign: University of Illinois Computing Services Office, 1975.

Van de Geer, J. P., & Jaspars, J. Cognitive functions. *Annual Review of Psychology*, 1966, *17*, 145–176.

Vernon, P. E. *Intelligence: Heredity and environment.* San Francisco: Freeman, 1979.

Vernon, P. E. *The abilities and achievements of orientals in North America.* New York: Academic Press, 1982.

Vernon, M. D. *Perception through experience.* London: Methuen, 1970.

Vernon, M. D. *The psychology of perception* (2nd ed.). Harmondsworth, Middx: Penguin, 1971.

Vernon, P. E. *The structure of human abilities.* London: Methuen, 1950.

Vygotsky, L. S. *Thought and language.* Cambridge, Mass.: MIT Press, 1962.

Waber, D. P. *Sex differences in cognition: A function of maturation rates? Science*, 1976, *192*, 572–574.

Wallas, G. *The art of thought.* London: Jonathan Cape, 1926.

Wallbrown, F., Blaha, J., Wallbrown, J., & Engin, A. The hierarchical factor structure of the Wechsler Intelligence Scale for Children—Revised. *Journal of Psychology*, 1975, *89*, 223–235.

Warren, N. (Ed.). *Studies in cross-cultural psychology.* London: Academic Press, 1980.

Wason, P. C. On the failure to eliminate hypotheses in a conceptual task. *Quarterly Journal of Experimental Psychology*, 1960, *12*, 129–140.

Wason, P. C., & Johnson–Laird, P. N. *Psychology of reasoning: Structure and content.* London: B. T. Batsford, Ltd., 1972.

Watson, J. B. Psychology as the behaviorist views it. *Psychological Review*, 1913, *20*, 158–177.

Watson, J. B. *Behaviorism.* Chicago: University of Chicago Press, 1924.

Watson, J. B. *Behaviorism.* New York: Kegan Paul, Trench, Trubner & Co. Ltd., 1930.

Wechsler, D. *The measurement of adult intelligence.* Baltimore: Williams and Wilkins, 1939.

Wechsler, D. *Wechsler Intelligence Scale for Children* (WISC). New York: The Psychological Corporation, 1949.

Wechsler, D. *Wechsler Adult Intelligence Scale.* New York: The Psychological Corporation, 1955.

Wechsler, D. *The measurement and appraisal of adult intelligence* (4th ed.). Baltimore: The Williams Wilkins Co., 1958.

Wechsler, D. *Wechsler Preschool and Primary Scale of Intelligence.* New York: The Psychological Corporation, 1967.

Wechsler, D. *Wechsler Intelligence Scale for Children–Revised.* New York: The Psychological Corporation, 1974.

Weisberg, R., & Suls, J. M. An information processing model of Duncker's candle problem. *Cognitive Psychology*, 1973, *4*, 255–276.

Weiss, C. H. *Validity of interview responses on welfare mothers.* New York: Bureau of Applied Social Research, 1968.

Weiss, D. J., & Davison, M. L. Test theory and methods. *Annual Review of Psychology,* 1981, *32,* 629–658.

Weizenbaum, J. *Computer power and human reason.* San Francisco: W. H. Freeman & Co., 1976.

Wertheimer, M. Untersuchungen zur Lehre von der Gestalt. *Psychologische Forschung,* 1923, *4,* 301–351.

Wertheimer, M. *Productive thinking.* New York: Harper & Row, 1945, 1959.

Wesman, A. G. Intelligent testing. *American Psychologist,* 1968, *23,* 267–274.

West, D. J. *A hundred years of psychology.* By J. C. Flügel, revised by D. J. West. London: Methuen, 1964.

Whitely, S. E. Solving verbal analogies: Some cognitive components of intelligence test items. *Journal of Educational Psychology,* 1976, *68,* 234–242.

Whitely, S. E. Information-processing on intelligence test items: Some response components. *Applied Psychological Measurement,* 1977, *1,* 465–476.

Whitely, S. E. Measuring aptitude processes with multi-component latent trait models. *Journal of Educational Measurement,* 1981, *18,* 67–84.

Wickelgren, W. A. *How to solve problems. Elements of a theory of problems and problem solving.* San Francisco: Freeman & Co., 1974.

Wiener, N. *Cybernetics: or, control and communication in the animal and the machine.* Cambridge, Mass.: MIT Press, 1948.

Wilson, E. O. *Sociobiology: The new synthesis.* Chicago: University of Chicago Press, 1975.

Winer, B. W. *Statistical principles in experimental design* (2nd ed.). New York: McGraw Hill, 1971.

Wissler, C. The correlation of mental and physical traits. *Psychological Monographs,* 1901, *3,* 1–62.

Wittrock, M. C. The learning by discovery hypothesis. In L. S. Shulman & E. R. Kreisler (Eds.), *Learning by discovery.* Chicago: Rand McNally, 1966.

Woodworth, R. S., & Schlosberg, H. *Experimental psychology* (Rev. ed.). London: Methuen, 1954.

Wright, B., & Stone, M. H. *Best test design: Rasch measurement.* Chicago: Mesa Press, 1979.

Wundt, W. *Grundzüge der physiologischen Psychologie.* Leipzig: Breitkopf und Härtel, 1873.

Wundt, W. *Einleitung in die Psychologie.* Cited in J. C. Flügel, *A hundred years of psychology.* London: Duckworth, 1933.

Wundt, W. *An introduction to psychology.* London: Allen & Unwin, 1924.

Yoakum, C. S., & Yerkes, R. M. *Army mental tests.* New York: Holt, Rinehart & Winston, 1920.

Young, J. W. *Technique for producing ideas.* Chicago: Advanced Publications, 1940.

Yourdan, E., & Constantine, L. L. *Structured design.* New York: Yourdan, 1975.

Zeigarnik, B., & Lewin, K. (Eds). Über das Behalten von erledigten und unerledigten Handlungen. *Psychologische Forschung,* 1927, *9,* 1–85.

Appendix A
Listing of Tasks

TABLE A1
Verbatim Listing of the Tasks in Order of Presentation

Task Abbreviation	Content
1 [Binet]	I planted a tree that was 8 inches tall. At the end of the first year it was 12 inches tall; at the end of the second year it was 18 inches tall; and at the end of the third year it was 27 inches tall. How tall was it at the end of the fourth year?
2 [∴∴]	Without raising the pencil from the paper, draw 4 straight lines, which will include all 9 dots:

·   ·   ·

·   ·   ·

·   ·   ·

| 3 [15 × 30] | Multiply in your head 15 × 30. While you do it, tell me how you do it. |
| 4 [Pebbles] | The Pebbles |

Many years ago when a person who owed money could be thrown into jail, a merchant in London had the misfortune to owe a huge sum to a money–lender. The money–lender who was old and ugly fancied the merchant's beautiful teen–aged daughter. He proposed that they let Providence settle the debt, and told them that he would put a black pebble and a white pebble into a money–bag and then let the girl pick out one of the pebbles.

1 If she chooses the black pebble she would become his wife and her father's debt would be cancelled.

2 If she chooses the white pebble she would stay with her father but the debt would still be cancelled.

(Continued)

TABLE A1
(Continued)

Task Abbreviation	Content
	3 But if she refused to take a pebble, her father would be thrown into jail.
	Reluctantly the father agreed. They were standing on a pebble–strewn path as they talked, and the money–lender stooped down to pick up the two pebbles. As he picked up the pebbles, the girl, sharp–eyed with fright, noticed that he picked up two black pebbles and put them into the money–bag.
	The girl did something which solved the problem to her and her father's complete satisfaction. What did she do?
5 [Platform]	The Platform
	Imagine 4 regular kitchen knives, all equal in size, and 4 equal sized bottles which are arranged in the form of a square. Each side of the square is slightly longer than the length of one of the knives.
	With these 4 knives you are required to build a platform on the top of the bottles which will be stable and strong enough to support a 5th bottle. No knife can touch the ground, and the 4 bottles have to stay arranged as they are.
6 [6m → 4Δ]	From 6 kitchen matches build 4 equal and equilateral triangles. (matches supplied)
7 [9m → 1h]	Hold these 9 matches in the air with one hand, while your hand is actually holding only *one* match. (matches supplied)
8 [Poem/St]	In what way are poem and statue alike?
9 [Praise/P]	In what way are praise and punishment alike?
10 [Fly/Tree]	In what way are fly and tree alike?
11 [Wood/Alc]	In what way are wood and alcohol alike?
12 [8TB/2]	A man has 8 tennis balls. He knows that one of them is lighter than the rest. He is allowed to use a set of scales *twice only*. How can he isolate the lighter ball?

Appendix B
The Complete Taxonomy of Problem Solving Behaviors

TABLE B.1
Complete Taxonomy of Problem Solving Behaviors

	Response Category	*Code*	
D:	Directions/Instruction/Stimulus Passage related activity	100	
D_{Hypothesis}:	Survey of given information	110	
	1. First reading		111
	2. Re-reading/Repetition of instructions		112
	3. Chunking. Task–segmentation		113
	4. Reference to text, scanning, checking parts		114
	5. Questions to E (clarification only)		115
	6. Rehearse and absorb		116
	7. Summarize/pick out main points/rephrase text		117
D_C:	Identification of problem or its parts from given information	120	
	1. Recognition that problem exists		121
	2. Identification of boundaries/constraints		122
	3. Definition of problem or parts thereof		123
Negative*:		130	
	1. Direct attention to perceptually salient but irrelevant input data		131
	2. Failure to consider all important information provided		132
	3. Does not have sufficient vocabulary/does not understand		133
S:	Solution related activity	200	
S_{Hypothesis}:	Heuristics (Repertoire skills)	210	
	1. Search for plan/hypothesis		211
	2. Trial and error		212
	3. Start procedure again. Return to former hypothesis without changing it or adding to it		213

(Continued)

TABLE B.1
(Continued)

		Response Category	*Code*
	4.	Compare and relate. Look for common features among parts	214
	5.	Working on previously stated hypothesis. Continuing activity	215
	6.	Random application of general or previously learned rule (*not* 222) Plan false step/solution (knowing it is false)	216
	7.	Modification (always preceded by J400)	217
	8.	Survey/summarize what has been done/review former trials	218
	9.	Calculation/working out detail	219
S$_C$:		Reasoning	220
	1.	Recognition of important aspects or requirements of solution	221
	2.	Application of relevant rule. Identification of specific (additional?) problems to be overcome before proceeding to solution	222
	3.	Elimination [what aim/solution is *not*]	223
	4.	"Is there a trick involved?"	224
	5.	Reasonable approximation of a possible solution	225
	6.	Statement of rule/generalization	226
	7.	Solution	227
Negative:			
		Misunderstood task. Perceptual error.	230
PERS:	Self related activity		300
PERS$_{Hypothesis}$:	Idiosyncratic operations		310
	1.	Prediction of solution/part solution (intuitive otherwise 221)	311
	2.	Imagery (report of visualization of problem situation)	312
	3.	Introspection (self analysis, explanation of activity)	313
	4.	Retrospection (post hoc interpretation of problem solving activity)	314
	5.	Justification	315
PERS$_C$:	Emotional reactions		320
	1.	Comment on difficulty/ease of task/activity/self criticism	321
	2.	Frustration (expression of negative feeling about task or solving activity, mental block, swearing, etc.)	322

(Continued)

TABLE B.1
(Continued)

		Response Category		*Code*
		3. Lack of motivation (attempt or expressed desire to avoid/postpone solving—giving up)		323
		4. Expressed feeling of accomplishment, pleasure, relief, excitement		324
J:	Critical Evaluation/Judgment		400	
	$J_{Hypothesis}$:	Verification/critical assessment	410	
		1. Assessment of adequacy, suitability, etc., of progress/solution/or any part of the process of PS		411
		2. Recalculation, etc.		412
	J_C:	Judgment/evaluation	420	
		1. Self correction (*not* self criticism of $PERS_C$ 321) related to previous step, strategy, etc.		421
		2. Reservation *re* solution. Recognition of wrong move/failure		422
		3. Estimation of outcome of strategy hypothesis. Questioning of consequences of step/action/solution		423
P:	Pause		500	
	$P_{Hypothesis}$:	Activity filled pause, e.g., Irrelevant comment (*not* 300). Suggest break, stalling for time, etc.	510	
	P_C:	Unfilled pause	520	
		1. Silence		521
		2. *E* prodding after period of silence		522
		3. Fill-in on part of *S*, e.g., "Well, . . . , I mean . . . , Let's see . . . ," etc.		523
M:	Memory related activity		600	
	$M_{Hypothesis}$:	Attempts to utilize memory	610	
		1. Attempts to remember-recall previous experience		611
		2. Attempt to associate, compare, relate to previous experience or experience outside task		612
	M_C:	"Insight"	620	
		1. Sudden illumination		621
		2. Sudden association		622
		3. Memory flash		623

(Continued)

TABLE B.1
(Continued)

		Response Category	Code
C:		Changing the conditions of the problem	700
	$C_{Hypothesis}$:	Request for access to/or use of external aids/ tools, e.g., drawing of diagram/sketch of situation including conditions, e.g., drawing dots	710
	C_C:	Attempts to change the conditions of the problem	720
		1. Suggestion of hypothesis or solution which violates the conditions of the problem, e.g., "Can the rules be changed?"	721
		2. Expansion, i.e., arriving at and answer or operation by using the information from the stimulus passage and/or directions in such a manner that the original meaning is expanded, lengthened or otherwise altered	722

*category added to taxonomy after the pilot study.

Author Index

378

Subject Index